D1260071

*Neo-Confucian Orthodoxy
and the Learning of the Mind-and-Heart*

NEO-CONFUCIAN STUDIES
sponsored by
*The Regional Seminar in Neo-Confucian Studies,
Columbia University*

上古聖神繼天立極而道
統之傳有自来矣其見於
経則允執厥中者堯之所
以授舜也人心惟危道心
惟微惟精惟一允執厥中
者舜之所以授禹也

Neo-Confucian Orthodoxy and the Learning of the Mind-and-Heart

Wm. Theodore de Bary

COLUMBIA UNIVERSITY PRESS *New York, 1981*

Clothbound editions of Columbia University Press Books are
Smyth-sewn and printed on permanent and durable acid-free
paper.

Library of Congress Cataloging in Publication Data

De Bary, William Theodore, 1918–
   Neo-Confucian orthodoxy and the learning of the
mind-and-heart.

   (Neo-Confucian studies)
   Includes bibliographical references and index.
   1. Neo-Confucianism. 2. Neo-Confucianism—Japan.
3. Philosophy, Chinese. 4. China—Religion. I. Title.
II. Series.
B127.N4D4   181'.09512   81-3809
ISBN 0-231-05228-6   AACR2

Columbia University Press
New York   Guildford, Surrey

Printed in the United States of America

To Thomas Berry

Neo-Confucian Studies

Contents

Preface   ix

Part I: The Rise of Neo-Confucian Orthodoxy in Yüan
     China   1

Part II: The Neo-Confucian Learning of the Mind-and-
     Heart   67

Part III: Neo-Confucian Orthodoxies and the Learning
     of the Mind-and-Heart in Early Tokugawa
     Japan   187

Notes   217

Glossary of Names, Terms, and Titles Cited in the
     Text   247

Glossary of Chinese and Japanese Works Cited in the
     Notes   252

Index   261

Preface

Until recently it was the modern custom in China to blame Confucius or Confucianism for much that had gone wrong in the past. As late as the 1960s and '70s Confucius was portrayed, in the bizarre spectacle of the Cultural Revolution, as still a ubiquitous and malign presence on the contemporary scene. Made a scapegoat for many of the continuing ills of the Revolution, he also became a prime target for concerted ideological attack. In this role he served, as he had in the earlier revolutionary seizures which convulsed China for half a century, as a symbol of the new generation's contempt for the old order and their determination to be rid of all its traces. Yet in the end the goal of total liberation from the past has proved to be elusive. Even with the frenetic effort of the Great Leap Forward and the forced marches of the Red Guards, no way has been found for the Revolution to jump out of its Chinese skin. To face the past and come to terms with it now seems more in order than striving mightily but vainly to abolish it.

In the meantime, a somewhat different light has been cast on China's Confucian culture by the experience of the rest of East Asia. Japan, Korea, and Taiwan are also what might be called "post-Confucian" societies, in the sense that they shared in the Neo-Confucian culture of the premodern period, and—though less violently than on the mainland of China—they too have experienced some of the modernist reaction against it. Nevertheless, the dramatic successes of these countries in rapid modernization, by contrast to the slow pace of development elsewhere in Asia, Africa, and South America, and all the more notably in the absence of great natural resources other than their human endowment, has drawn new attention to a factor long overlooked in the common background of the peoples of East

Asia: a long-shared process of intellectual and moral preparation through Neo-Confucianism. Whereas previously the Neo-Confucian influence had been seen as inimical to modernization (and it was unquestionably averse to certain aspects of westernization), the idea that the peoples of China, Japan, Korea, Taiwan, Hongkong, and Singapore have benefited from the love of learning, commitment to education, social discipline, and personal cultivation fostered by Neo-Confucianism can now be entertained.

When these peoples had been adjudged by Westerners to be inferior, backward, and resistant to change, it was understandable that the "blame" for this should have been assigned to Neo-Confucianism as representing the dominant culture of premodern East Asia. Moreover, since it had stood par excellence as the distinguishing mark and common ideology of the educated elite in these several societies, it was natural that Neo-Confucianism should have become identified with established authority. Its involvement with the ruling class and association with state power gave it all the aura and prestige of an official doctrine. From this, in the eyes of many, it assumed the proportions of a formidable orthodoxy, stifling dissent and repressing all original or progressive thought.

Today as the peoples of post-Confucian East Asia impress us with their special aptitude for learning and their proficiency in the use of modern skills, and as we ourselves tend less to equate modernization simply with westernization, the time may have come to reassess Neo-Confucianism more as a positive educational force in the premodern era than as a negative, restraining orthodoxy. Yet it is still the latter image which one encounters in texts widely used today—an orthodoxy that represented "the unchanging core of Chinese thought," a system of "authority and obedience," and a metaphysics "accepted without question," so that "once established as an orthodoxy, [it] proved to be an intellectual strait-jacket reinforcing the growing rigidity of Chinese society."[1]

One reason for the persistence of this view is the paucity of attention paid to the actual content of early Neo-Confucian teaching and the remarkable way in which it came to be established as "or-

---

[1] J. K. Fairbank, E. Reischauer, and A. Craig, *East Asia: Tradition and Transformation* (New York: Houghton Mifflin, 1973), pp. 147, 150–51.

thodox." Simplistic views have gained ready acceptance when even cursory study of the historical record would have revealed many varieties, both philosophical and institutional, of Neo-Confucian orthodoxy. Without overstressing the complexities of the matter, one may easily distinguish the sense of orthodoxy adhered to in Neo-Confucian schools, in themselves many and diverse, from the forms of orthodoxy established by the different dynasties and regimes of East Asia in conformity with their own institutional patterns.

If these orthodoxies had anything in common, it was by inheritance from the teachings propagated soon after the death of the great Neo-Confucian master, Chu Hsi (1130–1200). Early formulations of his ideas have been little studied by modern scholars, however, and his followers have been dismissed as adding nothing new to them. This is explainable only in terms of the prevalent fallacy that ideas gain no new significance from being repeated. In point of historical fact, even secondhand ideas can have a powerful impact when introduced into new situations, as was the case at the court of Khubilai, where Neo-Confucian doctrines had decisive consequences for the way in which human affairs were to be conducted. Oblivious to this, historians of Chinese thought and philosophy have largely ignored the work of the so-called Chu Hsi school during the two centuries after his death: the transmission of his ideas, one is led to believe, occurred by some process of hypnotic transference or worshipful, ritual repetition. Yet no such simple assumption will explain how Chu's teachings, proscribed by the state at the time of his death, could have turned the tables and become so widely accepted within the ensuing century.

In the absence of closer study, misinterpretations and misconnections have gone unchecked. The impression has been widely conveyed that Neo-Confucianism owed its entrenchment as an orthodoxy to some kind of narcissistic reversion of the Chinese to a self-absorption with their traditional values, or to an isolationist withdrawal of the Chinese into the shell of an ethnocentric world-view. From this it was an easy step to conclude that Neo-Confucianism's installation as the official orthodoxy of the Ming dynasty went hand in hand with its expulsion of the Mongols, its seclusionist policy in foreign affairs, and its consequent loss of touch with the progress of world civilization. Neo-Confucianism then came to be seen as the quintessential expression of an attitude that rejected all foreign influence and smugly reasserted the superiority of things Chinese.

So plausible was this view, considering Neo-Confucianism's undoubted reaffirmation of certain basic Chinese values, that for those whose studies were already narrowly preoccupied with China, it was easy to overlook some rather obvious facts of Neo-Confucian history. One is that this teaching first became established in the curriculum of the official schools and civil service examinations under a foreign dynasty, that of the Mongols, whose culture could hardly have been more in contrast to the Chinese and whose power rested on maintaining a regime of conquest with a clear cultural identity. What interest could they have had in reasserting Chinese culture simply for its own sake, or in accepting as the official ideology a teaching which would blur their identity and subvert their own special prerogatives and control? But further, having overcome the natural resistance of the Mongols to anything purely conservative of Chinese values or defensive of Chinese interests, the Neo-Confucians went on to convert Central Asians in the service of the Mongols, as well as Koreans, Japanese, Vietnamese, and later Manchus, to the new teaching. How could this have been accomplished if the appeal of Neo-Confucianism had been primarily ethnocentric, rather than universalistic?

In this connection another common assumption has been that it was the Neo-Confucian natural-law philosophy, based on the central concept of ordered principle or reason (*li*), which had a universal value for authoritarian regimes of whatever national origin. Such a highly structured world-view, emphasizing a strict hierarchy of values and well-defined code of social morality, was ideal for the defense of the status quo and maintenance of entrenched power regardless of cultural differences. In effect, it consecrated the existing order and reinforced all forms of repression.

But with this view there have likewise been difficulties. Chu Hsi had insisted on the transcendence of principle precisely to deny its use to the established order. For him principle provided the basis for a continuing critique of human conduct and political institutions, which at their historical best in the Han, T'ang, and Sung dynasties

had never fully embodied it. Thus within the tradition the prime
values of Neo-Confucianism were as often invoked to support demands for change and reform as to justify the existing order. Certainly this was the case in the crucial developments surrounding the
"triumph" of Neo-Confucian reformers at the Yüan (Mongol) court.

A further difficulty with the view of the philosophy of principle as a closed authority system is the strong emphasis in Neo-Confucianism on the active role of the creative mind, responsive to
human needs, and in the frequency with which the early teaching
was identified with this Learning of the Mind-and-Heart (*hsin-hsüeh*)
rather than with principle understood as a given structure of laws.
Moreover, the prominence given to the active conscience and hu-
manitarian impulse has other implications for commonly held views
regarding the relationship of Neo-Confucianism and Buddhism. On
the one hand, Neo-Confucianism has been seen as a strong antifor-
eign reaction to the influence of Buddhism from India. On the other
hand, almost any reference to the mind, intuition, or enlightenment
in Neo-Confucianism has readily been taken as showing the influence of Buddhism. Each of these views contains something of a half-
truth, but half of just what, and how it is to be located in the teaching
and practice of the Chu Hsi schools, are questions which have
awaited clarification.

Study of the early Ch'eng-Chu Learning of the Mind-and-
Heart should go a long way toward resolving these questions; hence
the focus of this book. Such resolutions lie partly in the domain of
institutions and partly in the realm of ideas. Thus the first study
presented here focuses on the institutional background and political
involvements of Neo-Confucianism, especially in the Yüan period,
while the second explores further the ideas of this intellectual and
educational movement as they developed in the thirteenth and fourteenth centuries and in the works of certain major figures. The two
are largely parallel in time and complementary; in the actual historical development these two strands are interwoven and cannot be
neatly separated out. Consequently, there is in these essays a certain
amount of overlapping and cross-reference from one to the other.

The period covered by the first two essays, from the late Sung
to the early Ming, may seem like a passing moment, a brief transi-

tional phase, in the long history of Chinese thought. Largely overlooked though they have been, these two-hundred-odd years cover a wide span of Confucian scholarly activity, and this book must be understood to deal with very broad trends, as well as, in a highly selective way, with key figures in their development. The final section of this book brings together portions of earlier explorations of mine in the field of Neo-Confucian orthodoxy and what I now call the Learning of the Mind-and-Heart *(hsin-hsüeh)*. For the most part they pertain to a later period (the seventeenth century), and in particular to the development of this learning and orthodoxy in Japan, but they also relate to issues in Ming thought raised in Part II.

Taking a long view of Neo-Confucianism implies a broader conception of it than has been customary, one which recognizes that the life of Neo-Confucianism was not confined to China. This "orthodoxy" has been subject to social and cultural variation outside its homeland, though the latter is the usual focus of studies which have treated it as a Chinese, rather than as an East Asian, phenomenon.

The broader standpoint taken here, however, is new only in the sense that it includes the perspectives gained from outside vantage points. In its essence the problem of an inclusive definition of Neo-Confucianism is as old as the seventeenth century at least, when Huang Tsung-hsi (1610–1695) made the first comprehensive attempt to represent the tradition, or the "Way" as transmitted to his generation, and argued in the preface to his *Case Studies of Ming Confucians (Ming-ju hsüeh-an)* for a broad conception of the "Way" coming down from the Sung which allowed for many individual contributions to its rich and varied growth. Essentially the same standpoint is adopted here, but in a wider context.

"Neo-Confucianism" itself is a term coined by early Western observers who noticed new developments in Sung Confucian thought which were not simply reducible to their classical antecedents. The term remains useful inasmuch as it points to basic factors of both continuity and change in the tradition. Rather than specifying any one aspect of the new development as crucial, it allows for the possibility that several new trends combined to generate this most creative movement in the later history of Chinese thought.

In time this neoclassical movement itself became a tradition spoken of as the "learning of the Way" *(tao-hsüeh)* or the "orthodox tradition" *(tao-t'ung)* or by other designations to be discussed below. Given the inevitable changes in language, meaning, and the structure of experience that separate one age from another, there is always a question as to what tradition actually represents. Here it means simply the body of continuing discourse about central and perennial questions of life as defined within a culture, which presupposes one's understanding of the terms of the discourse that has preceded it. In other words, one cannot comprehend what is going on unless one has access to the past record which establishes the context of the discussion. Normally, it was through education that one gained such access in the past, and it is through the study of the traditional curriculum, or alternatives to it, that we today may understand on what basis the discourse has been conducted from generation to generation. Against this, then, we can measure the significance of discontinuities that arise in the process, including the extent of conceptual change.

Within the tradition one of the more common terms for Neo-Confucianism was *hsing-li hsüeh*, the "study [or learning] of human nature and principle." This specified that the understanding of human nature was a central focus of discussion. A variant was the term *li-hsüeh*, the study or the learning of principle, which was understood to mean the principles in things generally, though the ideal, integrating principle of human nature was central to it.

Another common term for Neo-Confucianism was *hsin-hsüeh*, the "Learning of the Mind-and-Heart," the main subject of this book. In more recent times this term has been applied to an outgrowth of Neo-Confucianism identified with Wang Yang-ming (1472–1529) and his putative predecessor Lu Hsiang-shan (1139–1193). Originally, however, it was applied to Neo-Confucianism as a whole, and expressed the idea that this "learning" offered an alternative to the Buddhist view of the mind, as well as a method of mental cultivation consistent with the Confucian view that value distinctions were intrinsic to the natural order in both the mind and things.

Another common designation for Neo-Confucianism was *sheng-hsüeh*, the "learning of the sages" or the "learning of sagehood." Originally this expressed a strong belief in the possibility of anyone's attaining sagehood through self-cultivation, but in the form of the *sheng-wang chih tao*, "the Way of the sage-kings," it also set forth an ideal of the human community ruled by the wisdom of sages and governed through sagely institutions.

Another important tendency in Neo-Confucianism emphasized the reality of the dynamic physical element in the universe and things, "ether" or "material force" *(ch'i)*. There was, traditionally, no term such as *ch'i hsüeh* applied to Neo-Confucianism as a whole, but modern scholars have referred to this major evolute from Neo-Confucian thought as the "philosophy of *ch'i*," and Huang Tsung-hsi himself was a representative of this widespread tendency in China, which had its counterparts elsewhere in the Neo-Confucian world.

Finally we return to the term *tao-hsüeh*, "learning of the Way," which made the claim that the Ch'eng-Chu school of Neo-Confucianism spoke for the Way as a whole, and did so with what one would have to call a sense of religious certitude. (This claim was viewed skeptically by those who applied the term *tao-hsüeh* to it ironically.) The initial dynamism of the movement, described in this book, derived from that school's powerful sense of mission in the world.

Huang Tsung-hsi, as I have said, was heir to all this and affirmed all these tendencies equally as fundamental aspects of the Way which he attempted to interpret and perpetuate in the seventeenth century. We need not perhaps adopt him as a model, but it would be unwise not to take at least as broad a view of things as he did. Therefore in what follows the term "Neo-Confucianism" is generally meant to embrace all these tendencies, while "Neo-Confucian orthodoxy" is used to designate the Ch'eng-Chu teaching in one or more of its forms claiming descent from Chu Hsi. The Learning of the Mind-and-Heart discussed herein was originally the heart of this orthodoxy. In the Ming this central ground was largely captured by the Wang Yang-ming school, but down into the nineteenth century, Ch'eng-Chu schools in China, Korea, and Japan, according to their own understanding of the matter, continued to claim it for their own.

Acknowledgments

Most of the research for these studies was conducted at Kyoto University in the fall and winter of 1979 and much of the writing was done at the Villa Serbelloni, the research and conference center of the Rockefeller Foundation at Bellagio, Italy in July 1980. It would be hard to conceive of a combination more conducive to scholarly work. For the hospitality of Kyoto University I have to thank Professors Yoshikawa Kōjirō, Kaizuka Shigeki, Kawakatsu Yoshio, and the Director of the Institute of Humanistic Sciences, Dr. Kawano Kenji. For stimulating scholarly discussions of the matters treated here I am grateful especially to Professor Shimada Kenji, to Professor Emeritus Okada Takehiko and Professor Araki Kengo at Kyushu University, and to Professor Ch'ien Mu of the College of Chinese Culture, Taipei. In addition I have benefited greatly from the suggestions of Professors Wing-tsit Chan, Hok-lam Chan, Herbert Franke, Irene Bloom, Conrad Schirokauer, and the members of the Regional Seminar in Neo-Confucianism at Columbia University. Most of the original source material was found in the collections of the Institute at Kyoto, of the Naikaku bunko, Seikadō, and Sonkeikaku in Tokyo, the Hōsa bunko in Nagoya, and the Palace Museum and National Central Library, Taipei. For their assistance in these connections I express my deep appreciation to Professors Takeuchi Yoshinori, Sakai Tadao, and Fumoto Yasutaka, and to Director Chiang Fu-tsung of the Palace Museum and Wang Chen-ku of the National Central Library, Taipei.

I have been most fortunate to have Professor Okada offer his calligraphic services for the inscription on the frontispiece of a passage from Chu Hsi's preface to his commentary on the Mean (*Chung-yung chang-chü*), a passage also prominently quoted by Chen Te-hsiu in his *Extended Meaning of the Great Learning*, ch. 2. Irene Bloom and Wing-tsit Chan have added further to the great debt I already owe them by the extraordinary help they have given in reading proofs. Finally, I should mention, even though I could never count or adequately acknowledge, the many ways in which this work has been aided by the stimulating comments and moral support of my wife, Fanny Brett de Bary.

A direct stimulus to the pursuit of these researches was my participation in the Conference on Yüan Thought held at Issaquah, Washington in January of 1978 under the chairmanship of Professor Hok-lam Chan. For the impetus it gave to this intellectual adventure on the part of an interloper in Yüan studies, I thank Professor Chan and the Committee on the Study of Chinese Civilization of the American Council of Learned Societies, which sponsored the conference. Several of the papers from that conference are cited herein, and will soon be published under the title *Yüan Thought: Essays on Chinese Thought and Religion under the Mongols.*

Part I: THE RISE OF NEO-CONFUCIAN ORTHODOXY IN YÜAN CHINA

Because Chu Hsi became such a dominant figure in East Asian thought, and because his Neo-Confucian teaching stood for so long as the established orthodoxy, it has been natural to think of it as officially accepted almost from the beginning and difficult to imagine a time when it was not. Yet its rise under Mongol rule actually represents one of the most significant innovations in Chinese history and one of the most consequential for the formulation of this teaching in later times.

Five years before his death in A.D. 1200, Chu Hsi was officially condemned as a heretic and propagator of false teachings. For several decades thereafter the official status of his teachings remained unsettled, though true believers never doubted his eventual vindication. Even when he was rehabilitated in the 1230s by the Sung court, it was in a manner that did little credit to either Chu or the court—a series of face-saving maneuvers and empty honors that accomplished little.[1] After making ritual obeisance to the memory of Chu Hsi and other Neo-Confucian patriarchs at the temple of Confucius, and passing out gifts and promotions to members of the educational establishment, the Emperor Li-tsung (r. 1225–1264) went back to the business of enjoying himself in his palace and letting the dynasty run off to its doom.[2] Nothing significant was done to institutionalize Chu's teaching in the one form essential to the implementation of state orthodoxy: prescribing it for the civil service examinations, which tended also to determine the school curriculum.[3] But in the deteriorating condition of the Sung dynasty, even this would have been a meaningless gesture.

Orthodoxy, when one thinks about it, has many stately mansions and even some humble abodes. Confucianism had no church to define its creed or contest the authority of the state. As an alternative locus of authority, however, it did have schools, and in the face of official disfavor or in the absence of more than token support from the state, it was the schools (especially the private academies or *shu-yüan*) which carried the burden of transmitting the orthodox tradition.[4] Scholars and teachers were prepared to act independently, ready to assume the initiative and responsibility themselves for transmitting the "learning of the Way" *(tao-hsüeh)*, and it was their growing success with this that made their support of the state, not the state's support of them, the real issue behind the court's belated tributes to Chu Hsi in the late Sung.

In the longer run, the teaching could be considered fully established in the traditional Chinese sense only if the values espoused by the teachers and schools were also sanctioned by the ruler in his selection of scholars who would assist in the governing of the empire. Thus the scholar and the ruler, the school and the state examination system, represented the two poles of orthodoxy for most Neo-Confucians. Recognizing, however, the priority of the former as the effective agents of transmission, we must look first to the motives and models which guided these scholars in their struggle to perpetuate the Way. Without question the principal mode in which it was conceived was the *tao-t'ung,* the "repossessing of the Way" or the "orthodox tradition."

The Orthodox Way: Endangered and Embattled

Among Neo-Confucians the classic champion of orthodoxy is Han Yü (768–824), whose essay "An Inquiry into the Way" *(Yüan tao)* is famous for its polemic against Buddhism and Taoism. Besides reasserting the basic ethical doctrines and public philosophy of Confucianism, Han Yü expounds on the indispensable contributions of the sage-kings to civilization and the incompatibility of their humane way of life with the asocial Way of Buddhism and Taoism. We need not dwell here on all of the significances of this text for later

Neo-Confucians, but we should note the manner in which the orthodox succession is described:

> To love universally is called humanity *(jen)*; to apply this in a
> proper manner is called righteousness *(i)*. The operation of these is
> the Way, and its inner power is that it is self-sufficient, requiring
> nothing from outside itself. . . . After the decline of the Chou and
> the death of Confucius, from the time of Ch'in's book-burnings, the
> Taoism of the Han and the Buddhism of the Wei, Chin, Liang, and
> Sui, when men spoke of the Way and power, of humanity and righ-
> teousness, they were approaching them either as followers of Yang
> Chu and Mo Tzu, of Lao Tzu, or of Buddha. Being followers of these
> doctrines, they naturally rejected Confucianism. Acknowledging
> these men as their masters, they made of Confucius an outcast, ad-
> hering to new teachings and vilifying the old. Alas, though men of
> later ages long to know of humanity and righteousness, the Way and
> its inner power, from whom may they hear them? . . .
>
> What is this Way? It is what I call the Way, not what the
> Buddhists and Taoists call the Way. Yao taught it to Shun, Shun to
> Yü, Yü to T'ang, and T'ang to kings Wen and Wu and the Duke of
> Chou. These men taught it to Confucius and Confucius to Mencius,
> but when Mencius died it was no longer handed down. . . .
>
> What should be done now? I say that unless Taoism and Bud-
> dhism are suppressed, the Way will not prevail; unless these men
> are stopped, the Way will not be practiced. . . .[5]

The point to be observed here, but one which often goes unnoticed in the midst of Han Yü's passionate reaffirmation of the
ancient Way, is that Confucius is described as an outcast in his own
time, and that the transmission of his Way is said to have been
broken off after Mencius. There was in fact no handing on or succession for over a thousand years until Han Yü took it upon himself to
rescue the Way from oblivion.

Later, in the Sung, Ch'eng I (1033–1107) again propounds the
orthodox "succession" in a memorial tribute to his older brother
Ch'eng Hao (1032–1085), and the same striking discontinuity is apparent:

> After the demise of the Duke of Chou, the Way of the sages
> was not carried on, and after the death of Mencius the teaching of
> the sages was not transmitted. When the Way was not carried on

there was no good government for a hundred generations, and when the teaching was not transmitted, there were no true scholars for a thousand years. Even without good government, scholars could explain the way of good government for the edification of men and transmission to later generations, but without true [Confucian] scholars the world fell into darkness and people lost their way, human desires ran amok, and heavenly principles were extinguished. The Master [Ch'eng Hao] was born 1,400 years after Mencius and was able to recover the teachings that survived in the classics, resolving to enlighten the people with this Way. . . .[6]

The same theme recurs in Ch'eng I's account of his brother's conduct of life:

In his pursuit of learning, when he was fifteen or sixteen, the Master heard Chou Mao-shu of Ju-nan [Chou Tun-i] discuss the Way. He gave up forthwith the endeavor to prepare for civil service examinations and enthusiastically made up his mind to seek the Way. As he did not know the essentials, he drifted among the different schools and went in and out of the Taoist and Buddhist schools for almost ten years. Then he returned to seek the Way in the Six Classics, and found it there. . . . He said that, after Mencius, the Learning of the Sage was no longer transmitted, and he took it as his own responsibility to restore the cultural tradition. . . . Since the Way has not been illuminated, perverse and strange doctrines have arisen in rivalry, have thrown mud at the eyes and ears of the people, and have submerged the world in dirt. Even people of great ability and bright intelligence have been tarnished by what they see and hear. . . . All this forms clusters of overgrowth and weeds in the correct path and an obstruction to the gate of the Sage. We must clear them away before people can enter the Way.[7]

In these passages what is emphasized is not the effective imparting of the Way through some unbroken apostolic or patriarchal succession, but first, its being cut off for so long; second, its rediscovery by an inspired individual; and third, the heroic dedication and effort required to defend it in a decadent age against insidious enemies. There is not the slightest claim of direct inheritance or authoritative succession. Instead, the very tenuousness of the tradition is stressed as if to enhance the crucial significance of its rediscovery.

It is this same tenuous and endangered character of the Way

to which Chu Hsi also draws attention in the preface to his Commentary on the *Mean (Chung-yung):*

Why was the *Mean* written? Master Tzu-ssu wrote it because he was worried lest the transmission of the Learning of the Way *(Tao-hsüeh)* be lost. When the divine sages of highest antiquity had succeeded to the work of Heaven and established the Supreme Norm, the transmission of the orthodox tradition *(tao-t'ung)* had its inception. As may be discovered from the classics, "Hold fast the Mean"[1] is what Yao transmitted to Shun.[8] That "the mind of man is insecure" and "the mind of the Way is barely perceptible," that one should "have utmost refinement and singleness of mind" and should "hold fast the Mean"[9] is what Shun transmitted to Yü. Yao's one utterance is complete and perfect in itself, but Shun added three more in order to show that Yao's one utterance could only be carried out in this way. . . .

Subsequently sage upon sage succeeded one another: T'ang the Completer, Wen and Wu as rulers, Kao Yao, I Yin, Fu Yüeh, the Duke of Chou and Duke Shao as ministers, received and passed on this orthodox tradition. As for our master Confucius, though he did not attain a position of authority, nevertheless his resuming the tradition of the past sages and imparting it to later scholars was a contribution even more worthy than that of Yao and Shun. Still, in his own time those who recognized him were only [his disciples] Yen Hui and Tseng Ts'an, who grasped and passed on his essential meaning. Then in the next generation after Tseng, with Confucius' grandson Tzu-ssu [reputed author of the *Mean*], it was far removed in time from the sages and heterodoxies had already arisen. . . .

Thereafter the transmission was resumed by Mencius, who was able to interpret and clarify the meaning of this text [the *Mean*] and succeed to the tradition of the early sages; but upon his demise the transmission was finally lost. . . . Fortunately, however, this text was not lost, and when the Masters Ch'eng, two brothers, appeared [in the Sung] they had something to study in order to pick up the threads of what had not been transmitted for a thousand years, and something to rely on in exposing the speciousness of the seeming truths of Buddhism and Taoism. Though the contribution of Tzu-ssu was great, had it not been for the Ch'engs we would not have grasped his meaning from his words alone. But alas, their explanations also became lost. . . .[10]

Chu goes on to explain with what difficulty he pieced together and pondered for himself the essential message of the *Mean* from the fragmentary material available to him. He reiterates not only the theme of the precariousness of the Way as transmitted by human hands, but also the successive struggles of inspired individuals in recovering its true meaning. Thus, "repossessing the Way," *tao-t'ung,* almost literally has the sense of "linking or stitching the Way together."

The Struggle to Repossess the Way

Although the essential truth was already contained in germ in the one utterance of Yao, says Chu, it took the active struggle, profound penetration, and unflagging commitment of lonely and misunderstood scholars to carry on that Way. If one compares Chu's frank acknowledgment of Confucius' low status and lack of recognition in his own time with the exaltation of Confucius in the Han dynasty,[11] one can grasp the significance of the humanizing tendency in the Sung school, which evokes the triumph of the human spirit over adversity instead of conjuring up a supernatural aura or relying on authority to compel assent. The appeal here is not to well-established tradition, but to the example of the indomitable individual overcoming the confusions of the day and rescuing an all-too-fragile tradition from near destruction.

For this "contribution" Confucius is accorded an even greater measure of credit than the sages, and when we note that Tzu-ssu and the Ch'eng brothers are also cited for their "contributions" (with Chu Hsi clearly in the process of making his), we can see how a "tradition" is being constructed, and with it a new mythology of the heroic scholar repossessing it.

As classic examples the Neo-Confucians had, in addition to the "noble man" *(chün-tzu)* of Confucius and Mencius, the heroic ideal of the "great man" *(ta-chang-fu)* whom Mencius described:

He who dwells in the wide house of the world, stands in the correct station of the world, and walks in the great path of the world; he who, when successful, practices virtue along with the people, and when disappointed, still practices it alone; he who is above the power of riches and honors to corrupt, of poverty and mean condi-

tion to turn away from principle, and of power and force to bend—
he may be called a great man. [3B:2]

This kind of heroism celebrates the eventual triumph of reason, restraint, and fidelity to virtue over the forces of violence and
the life of self-indulgence.[12] All this is embedded in the heroic ideal
of the Sung school, but it is intensified by the direct involvement of
its members in titanic political struggles and cultural conflicts such
as Mencius had not personally known.

In this period the scholar-official class had risen to new
heights of influence and responsibility for the conduct of affairs.
They now faced, as Chu warned, a profound inner crisis in relation
to the survival of both the dynasty and Confucian culture. Chu, as
the spokesman for the ideals of the educated elite in this age, puts
before them a model commensurate with the challenge.

Ch'eng I's tributes to his brother spoke of him as "making up
his mind to seek the Way," taking "it as his own responsibility to
restore the cultural tradition," and personally, "resolving to enlighten the people with this Way" after it had gone untransmitted
for 1,400 years. Ch'eng does not stop to mention Han Yü in this
context, or Chou Tun-i (1017–1073), from whom he had said only a
few lines earlier that his brother had "heard the Way." This would
only have cluttered up the story, and perhaps have detracted from
the image of Ch'eng Hao as the lone rediscoverer of the long-lost
Way. The truth being conveyed here is not historical or genealogical,
but dramatic and mythological. What Ch'eng seeks to portray, without much concern for literal details, is a role of almost epic proportions, expressive of the true vocation of the Confucian scholar-official who has risen to unparalleled responsibility for the political and
cultural leadership of the nation. In articulating this role, he high-
lights the active repossession of Confucian values and is not content
with mere passive acceptance of the tradition or custodial care of it.

Professor Wing-tsit Chan, in an important recent article on
Chu Hsi's "completion of the Neo-Confucian synthesis," cites Chu's
inclusion of Chou Tun-i in the line of Neo-Confucian succession
because of the latter's contribution to Chu's philosophy of principle.[13] Undoubtedly Chu and others took liberties in making creative

use of the succession scheme for their own purposes, depending upon the suasive purpose uppermost in their minds at a given time. Perhaps the most common theme running through Chu's several invocations of the "orthodox tradition" is that of the individual "finding the Way for himself" *(tzu-te),* as Mencius had expressed it, and "taking personal responsibility for the Way" *(tzu-jen yü tao).* [14] But in his preface to his Commentary on the *Mean* the most striking adaptation of "tradition" to Chu's philosophy of principle appears in a passage in which he cites the distinction between the human mind *(jen-hsin)* and the moral mind *(tao-hsin)* referred to in the *Book of Documents* or *History*, and discussed by the Ch'eng brothers. That distinction is identified as the essence of the orthodox tradition.

The difference between the human mind and the moral mind depends on whether it [the thought] arises from the selfishness that is identified with the physical form or originates from the correctness of the innate moral imperative, in accordance with which consciousnesses differ. The former may be precarious and insecure, the latter so subtle and elusive as to be barely perceptible. All men have this physical form and even the most intelligent invariably possess the "human mind," while even the most stupid also possess the "moral nature." These two are mixed in the heart and if we do not know how to control them, the insecurity will become even more insecure, the barely perceptible [Way] will become even less perceptible, and the impartiality of Heaven's principle [in the moral nature] will have no way of overcoming the selfishness of human desires. [15]

This formulation, juxtaposing human desires and the moral nature, had profound implications for the later development of Neo-Confucian thought that need not be elaborated here. But two immediate points of significance must be noted. One is that the full dimensions of the human struggle are clearly delineated: the encounter within man between his worst self and his true nature, between the instability and waywardness of the human mind, which account for the precariousness in the passing on of the orthodox tradition, and the inherent goodness and perfectibility of human nature, which correspond to the enduring rightness of the Way. The other implication is that this encounter centers on the mind and the individual's exercise of moral will. Again and again we will find Chu Hsi's successors stressing the same point: the need for the individual to make a decision for the Way, to take the responsibility upon himself and make an irrevocable commitment to advance that Way.

T'ang Chün-i has characterized Neo-Confucianism as a "revival of the Confucian faith in man" (here the essential goodness of man's moral nature), and as an "acceptance of the need to face all the negative factors [in man's nature] and to find a way of . . . realizing the positive ideal."[16] As set forth by Ch'eng I and Chu Hsi, the story of the orthodox tradition *(tao-t'ung)* is the epic struggle to achieve this ideal, and its heroes are the protagonists of the Way who engage in this encounter with the evil in human nature and society.

The Prophetic and the Scholastic in the School of the Way

"Prophetic" I use here to indicate an extraordinary access to and revelation of truth not vouchsafed to everyone, which by some process of inner inspiration or solitary perception affords an insight beyond what is received in scripture, and by appeal to some higher order of truth gives new meaning, significance, and urgency to certain cultural values or scriptural texts. Confucian tradition does not customarily speak of such a revelation as "supernatural," but it has an unpredictable, wondrous quality manifesting the divine creativity of Heaven. By contrast I use "scholastic" to represent an appeal to received authority by continuous transmission, with stress on external or public acceptance of it as the basis of its validity.

The following account of the Way by Chen Te-hsiu (1178–1235), a leader of the School of the Way just after Chu Hsi's death, illustrates the point:

The great source of the Way lies in Heaven; its application lies in the world beneath; its transmission lies with the sages. This is why Tzu-ssu in the [opening chapter of the] *Mean* distinguished between the nature, the Way, and the teaching. The nature is what all men, wise and foolish, possess in common; the Way is what past and present alike share in; and the clarifying of the Way and setting forth of the teaching to enlighten us men is a task to which no one but a sage is equal. Thus from the time of Yao and Shun to Confucius five hundred years elapsed before the latter sage appeared. After the death of Confucius, Tseng Tzu, Tzu-ssu, and Mencius recapitulated and extrapolated from these preceding developments. Hence in a period of over one hundred years there were one sage and three worthies to carry on the teaching in turn before the work of [the sage-kings] Yao, Shun, Yü, T'ang, Wen, Wu, and the Duke of Chou in inaugurating the constants of Heaven and establishing order among men became fully clarified. How else could this have come about except that Heaven had created such sages and worthies!

After the Warring States and the Ch'in dynasty, the teaching and practice of the Way were disrupted and dispersed, and there was no way to unify them. Tung Chung-shu [c. 179–104 B.C.] and Han Yü carried on through the Han and T'ang, but they were not always able to penetrate to the true source of the substance and function of the Way; so they could do no more than perpetuate the Way in their own time and could not undertake the full responsibility for transmitting the Way to later ages.

With Heaven's inaugurating of the sagely rule [of the Sung], letters and government flourished together in peace, and from the T'ien-hsi and Ming-tao eras [1017–1033] to the age of revival [the Southern Sung], great scholars appeared to proclaim this Way and take personal responsibility for it. Thus the Way of Confucius was rediscovered by Master Chou [Tun-i], the Way of Master Chou was further clarified by the two Ch'eng brothers, and the Way of the Ch'engs was brilliantly expounded by Master Chu. In his view the transmissions from Tseng Tzu, Tzu-ssu, and Mencius fitted together like the pieces of a tally. Man could not have achieved this without the aid of Heaven. Likewise with the learning of the Four Masters, how could they have offered such novel views and put forward new interpretations, such as their predecessors had not been able to arrive at, were it not simply due to Heaven?[17]

Thus Chen saw a kind of extraordinary inspiration or creativity at work which enabled specially endowed individuals to come to new understandings or make new discoveries, rather than depend on received opinion, and to impart them to others at a critical stage which called for the revitalization of tradition and reform of society.

Not all writers have the same purpose in expounding the "orthodox tradition." The theme of heroic rediscovery of the Way remains an option, but in the case of Chu Hsi's disciple Huang Kan (1152–1221), a different concern comes to the fore. His responsibility as Chu's immediate successor was to preserve the full legacy and essential spirit of his master. This was not a matter of rediscovery but of fidelity to the total vision elaborated by Chu—how to transmit his teachings and writings faithfully and convey the full magnitude of his synthesis. At this point for the first time direct inheritance becomes a factor in the perpetuation of the Way, that is, the actual carrying on of a school from one generation to another. Huang Kan then becomes a principal vehicle not only for the preservation of the Way but for the perpetuation of the *School* of the Way *(Tao-hsüeh)* and its transmission into the Yüan period. Accordingly, he offers a view of the orthodox tradition as a more coherent body of thought in his "Summary of the Transmission of the Orthodox Tradition of the Sages and Worthies." [18]

Huang begins with an account of the generation of man and things from the Supreme Ultimate, through the interaction of yin and yang and the Five Agents. After duly reciting the now familiar injunctions of Yao and Shun, he proceeds to offer a considerably expanded list of teachers in the line of succession, each identified by some maxim or catchword. Gone is Ch'eng I's and Chu Hsi's pointed emphasis on the wide gaps in transmission, the recovery of the long-lost teaching, the unprecedented contributions of solitary individuals in rescuing the Way from oblivion. This is not because Huang would suppress these aspects, since in any case Chu's account of them in the preface to the *Mean* remained required reading for all in the school, but because he wishes here to create an impression of continuity and coherence, of a collective and cumulative revelation.

Huang says in summary:

The sages and worthies passed it on from one to another, setting forth the teaching over the ages like the signs of Heaven [which the sages observe], incandescent and unchanging. Though different in the details [which each brought out], the more each contributed to the discussion the greater the clarity. This is what the scholar should follow and preserve; to deviate from it is to err. [19]

Like Ch'eng I, Chu Hsi had spoken with the prophetic voice of one personally inspired to proclaim the truth, an exhorter and admonisher, or with the "noble voice" of the epic in recounting the deeds of great men. Huang Kan's voice is that of the scholastic, ordering and systematizing the true teaching in the process of conserving it. He speaks for the academy, symbolically as Hsün Tzu had done among the ancients, literally as the prescriber of the curriculum that would be followed by the academies which carried this message into the Yüan and Ming.

But as Huang puts forward this codification for the Ch'eng-Chu school, being a teacher, like Chu himself, he senses a need to provide a definite focus for the learning process. Thus he concludes:

Therefore one should grasp its essence and make it manifest. With "abiding in reverent seriousness" as the fundamental basis, with the "fathoming of principle" as the means of extending knowledge, with the "overcoming of self" in order to extinguish selfishness, and with "preserving sincerity" in order to achieve practical realization—with these four things preserved in the mind-and-heart (hsin), one need have nothing beyond them of the transmission of the Way as taught by the sages and worthies.[20]

Every effort to assert an orthodoxy necessarily implies an interpretation, and this is no less true of Huang's summary. Despite his aim to be comprehensive, his selection of what is most essential in the tradition places strong emphasis on moral and spiritual self-cultivation as compared to philosophical speculation and scholarly inquiry. This emphasis serves as the key to his choices in the overall inventory of the Way, which stresses the same aspects among the teachings of the classical and Sung masters. Indeed, it becomes a virtual catechism of Neo-Confucian doctrine on self-cultivation, mind-control, self-conquest, ritual observance, reverence and righteousness, etc. Symptomatic of the trend is Huang's identification of Chou Tun-i with the sincerity of the sage and the restraining of desires, rather than with Chou's metaphysical formula of the ultimate reality, "Infinite and yet the Supreme Norm" (wu-chi erh t'ai-chi).[21] Symptomatic too is the lack of any explicit reference to such basic concepts as principle (li) and material force or "ether" (ch'i).

Herein we may detect the direction the School of the Way will take as it leaves the hands of Chu Hsi's designated successor and passes on down to the Neo-Confucian schools of the late Sung, Yüan, and early Ming. Both versions of the Way, prophetic and scholastic, appear in characterizations of the orthodox tradition by later writers, as for instance in the accounts of the roles of Chen Te-hsiu, Hsü Heng (1209–1281), Wu Ch'eng (1249–1333), and Wang Yang-ming (1472–1529),[22] where the prophetic and inspirational element dominates, in the more systematic versions noted by Professor Chan in relation to Hsü Ch'ien (1270–1337) and Chao Fu (c. 1206–c. 1299), and in subsequent criticisms of the School of the Way on both scores, i.e., for claiming some special revelation, as well as some special custody, of the Way.[23] That it was conceived as a creative process is shown in Wang Po's (1197–1274) linking of the *tao-t'ung* of the sages to the ordination *(tao-t'ung)* of Heaven-and-earth.[24]

Latent also within the tradition are the twin roles of the Confucian as reformer and as thinker, as doer/discoverer and as preserver. He speaks at times with the stern voice of the prophet and at others with the quiet, reflective tones of the scholar and philosopher.[25] There are few Neo-Confucians in the Yüan who do not combine these two roles in some degree. Often the prophetic calling expresses itself in political activism, but it may also be revealed in a critique of such actions on the basis of commitment to higher ideals. The scholarly vocation may also manifest itself in arguing the case for reform, invoking the lessons of the past, or alternatively in questioning the value of particular efforts in the larger perspective of history and philosophical reflection. Both roles joined in the propagating of orthodoxy through the collective effort of the school. What kept the scholastic movement from declining into mere pedantry, however, was no doubt the dynamism of the inspirational message. Its effect in stirring up individual consciences and disciplining individual wills may be seen in the accounts of Yüan academies by Yü Chi (1272–1348), Ou–yang Hsüan (1283–1357), and Hsiung Ho (1253–1312).[26]

The High Seriousness and "Paranoid Style" of the School of the Way

In Huang's catechism of the Way of the sages, he lists reverence or seriousness *(ching)* and righteousness or duty *(i)* each four times among the twelve teachings transmitted by the orthodox tradition. He also cites "abiding in reverence" *(chü-ching)* as the basis of all self-cultivation. The concept of *ching* has rich associations in the Neo-Confucian mind. It invokes the ancient religious attitude of the Confucians—an awe and fear of Heaven, a respect for human life, the underlying spirit of ritual order and filial piety. The Sung masters further expanded its meaning to comprehend the entire created order and the inherent creativity of the Way. For them this reverential response to life provided the motivation for all human action, and differentiated the Confucian Way from Buddhism and Taoism, which questioned the primacy of human value orientations.

In the Neo-Confucian context it is also appropriate to render the term *ching* as "seriousness," in the moral and intellectual sense, because of the importance attached by the Ch'engs and Chu Hsi to giving this universal value a specific focus or point of application, in line with the Neo-Confucian stress on practical realization *(shih-hsien)*, practical experience *(shih-chien)*, and practical studies *(shih-hsüeh)*. The object of reverence was not understood in the theistic or devotional sense as an object of worship, but as a definite form of action to which the attitude of seriousness and respect attaches. *Ching* in this sense meant collecting the mind and directing it toward one thing. Often this "one thing" represented the unity of all things in principle. A close analogue to Buddhist concentration is apparent, but in contrast to the undifferentiated wisdom and compassion of Mahayana Buddhism, predicated on the view of Emptiness, the Neo-Confucians insisted on the realism of their teaching as formulated in the doctrine of the unity of principle and the diversity of its particularizations *(li-i fen-shu)*. In this sense seriousness meant taking seriously a specific set of obligations or duties as represented by *i*, righteousness or duty, and as formulated in the concrete norms of ritual conduct and personal relationships. Thus the Neo-Confucian commitment to the Way carried with it a sense of deep responsibility for one's obligations in life, a feeling that one's life could not be lived frivolously or thoughtlessly but should always link self-respect and self-improvement to respect for others and advancement of all in the Way.

Among the Neo-Confucians we shall be discussing, this sense of seriousness applied with special force to public service. In his relationship to the ruler, the scholar-official was obliged to take most seriously the need for government to serve the general welfare *(kung)* rather than private or selfish interests *(ssu)*, and to examine the sincerity and rectitude of his own motives to insure that they could stand scrutiny in the light of day. Undoubtedly this put a heavy burden on the individual conscience, and could well induce hyper-seriousness in the overzealous. The Ch'engs and Chu, however, did not believe that such reverent seriousness need lead to scrupulosity. A stiff, constrained, or joyless attitude would indicate something forced and unnatural in one's self-cultivation; proper nurturing of the mind would balance the sense of urgent concern for others with a heightened awareness of one's natural powers. Properly disciplined and developed, these two aspects would follow the Mean easily, without any need to strain oneself or manipulate things.[27]

Others, however, saw the matter differently. Neo-Confucian conscientiousness was a reproach to them, the sense of special dedication to high ideals a form of pretentious pomposity. They saw the members of School of the Way as taking themselves *too* seriously. Khubilai, among others, seems to have had this feeling.[28] In fact such reactions dated back to the times of Ch'eng I and Chu Hsi themselves. Their commitment to high principles, not to be compromised for convenience's sake, may have inspired their own followers but set them apart from the common run. In scholarly matters Chu Hsi was often notably generous toward his critics and philosophical opponents, but in politics it was not so easy. Here much was immediately at stake for Chu Hsi, depending upon whether he and the emperor were in agreement on basic principles; if not, he would have to disassociate himself from the government. Those who took the shorter view found Chu's unwillingness to compromise haughty and unbending. Mutual defensiveness led to recriminations, factional strife to actual persecution—the banning of books, the driving of people from the government, official degradation, exile.

Ch'eng I, like his older brother, was a victim of intense persecution and died almost a martyr.[29] Chu's sense of a special mission to uphold the Way was confirmed by his own experience of defamation and persecution for allegedly spreading "false learning" *(wei-hsüeh)*.[30] For his part Chu could be magnanimous toward Wang An-shih (1021–1086), because at least this reform-minded statesman was serious, but he reserved special indignation for Su Tung-p'o (1036–1101), leader of the Szechwan faction in the Ch'eng brothers' time, whose frivolous *wu-wei* attitude toward life, literature, Buddhism, and Taoism seemed positively corrupt to Chu.[31]

In this embattled condition the School of the Way, in its struggle for survival, readily acquired a kind of "paranoid style," if I may borrow a term that Richard Hofstadter applies to the American political scene.[32] As the saying goes, "Just because I'm paranoid doesn't mean they aren't out to get me." Their enemies *were* out to get them, as Professor Liu and others have shown,[33] and the experience of genuine persecution left its mark on the Ch'eng-Chu followers, reinforcing the paranoid style to which their view of the Way's endangered state easily led them.

To give just one illustration of how the motif of heroic struggle under persecution reappeared in the Yüan, we may cite the case of Wang I (1303–1354), a private tutor and grass-roots volunteer who was to suffer a martyr's death in the cause of local reform. According to John Dardess, Wang "likened his cause to the righteous causes once championed by the Sung Confucian heroes, Ssu-ma Kuang [1019–1086] and Chu Hsi: both were set upon by evil-minded detractors, who accused them of villainous cliquism and heterodoxy, but history had in the long-run vindicated them."[34]

The wounds of partisan struggle, however, proved far from mortal to the School of the Way, as it not only recovered from them but, strengthened by the ordeal, emerged from the stigma of heresy to become the new orthodoxy. When Chen Te-hsiu led the school's resurgence in the late Sung, his achievement was described in the now familiar heroic vein in the School of the Way to which he himself had contributed.[35]

After setting forth the successive losses and recoveries of the Way over the ages, Chen told how Tung Chung-shu in the Han and Han Yü in the T'ang, "though meritorious in their defense of the Way for a time, were unable to pass on the responsibility for transmitting it for all time to come. Then when it came to the great Confucian scholars of our Sung dynasty, they succeeded to it and came forward to take the responsibility themselves for championing 'this culture' [as Confucius described his own mission]." This thought being father to the deed, Chen's biography in the *Sung History,* quoting Chen's colleague Wei Liao-weng (1178–1237), describes how, under persecution by the dominant leader at court, Han T'o-chou (1151–1202), the works of the great Sung thinkers had been suppressed and the Way had almost died out when Chen finally appeared at the eleventh hour and "singlehandedly took upon himself the responsibility for 'this culture' [*tzu-jen ssu-wen*], propounding and disseminating it, so that, with the proscription lifted, the true learning could be manifested clearly throughout the land. . . ."[36]

Thus the School of the Way, though in some ways an elitist movement, had to struggle against the establishment to survive, and exhibited much of the zeal and dynamism of a religion of the oppressed. One does not need to suppose, in order to explain their conduct, that its followers suffered from any great fantasies. Messianism and martyrdom came naturally to these high-minded believers, whose sense of dedication always demanded much sacrifice.

In his discussion of the intense seriousness and rigorism of the School of the Way, Shimada Kenji notes that the school had a reputation for going to silly extremes, for being just a little "nutty."[37] To illustrate this he cites the last prime minister of the Sung, Lu Hsiu-fu (1238–1279), fleeing in a boat with the child emperor in his care. In these final days before they made the ultimate sacrifice by drowning at sea, Lu lectured the young pretender on the basic principles of the *Great Learning,* explaining how peace and order in the world depended on the ruler's example of self-cultivation and exhorting the lad to live up to this ideal.[38]

As political advice this sounds utterly impractical, but the time had already passed for practical politics. Instead Lu bespoke the kind of religious acceptance cultivated by the Neo-Confucians, who invoked Confucius' saying, "Hearing the Way in the morning, one can die content in the evening" (*Analects* 4:8).[39] Paradoxically it may have been just this nutty, unyielding idealism which enabled the Neo-Confucians to survive the Mongol conquest and far outlive their conquerors.

The Neo-Confucians as a Disadvantaged Minority

In the early years of the Mongol conquest the Neo-Confucians found themselves a displaced minority, unlikely candidates
for power or position. Those who had been last-ditch defenders of
the Sung were shown no mercy by the barbarian; the Mongols
slaughtered or enslaved them with few compunctions. As gentle,
nonviolent Buddhists their khans stood about on a par with the
Ashikaga shoguns of Japan, who built serene Zen temples on the
wreckage of countless, war-ravaged human lives. Moreover, the
avowed hostility of the Ch'engs and Chu Hsi not only to Buddhism
but to foreign rule did not endear them to such a conqueror.

In the social scale of the early Yüan period many Confucian
literati saw themselves as placing near the bottom, with only beggars
beneath them.[40] Their former elite role as high officials had been
taken over by Mongols and Central Asians. The Chinese employed
in great numbers as subofficials were bureaucratic and clerical technicians, not classically trained Confucians. Practicing professionals
themselves, they generally resented the latter as incompetent ped-
ants. This relegated Confucians to the status of religionists, toler-
ated but less useful than medical doctors, craftsmen, hunters, and
peasants, and yet also unable to compete with Taoists and Buddhists
as liturgists or purveyors of mystery and magic to the masses.[41] In
these circumstances, functionally speaking, the high vocation to
which Neo-Confucians had thought themselves called in the Sung
was fundamentally questioned.

The possibility of some improvement in this situation arose
when Yeh-lü Ch'u-ts'ai (1190–1244) persuaded the Mongol ruler
Ögödei (r. 1229–1241) to make some adjustment to Chinese ways
and institute civil service examinations in 1237.[42] These were held
only once, however, and served to confirm a pattern which offered
Neo-Confucians little prospect of success in the future. In form these
examinations reproduced the system of the Chin dynasty in North
China, which in turn perpetuated the old Sung-style examinations.
Those recruited among the 3,040 successful candidates represented a

type of literary scholarship likewise antedating, and generally at odds with, the new School of the Way.

Indeed, at this time the Mongol territories in the North remained almost untouched by the Neo-Confucian movement in the South, though the writings of the Sung masters were not unknown there. The indigenous Chinese culture which survived in the North from the Chin dynasty was strongly literary and aesthetic in flavor; it idolized the brilliant and versatile poet Su Tung-p'o, ideological archenemy of the School of the Way.[43] Under the protection of local Chinese leaders, who were given much autonomy by the Mongols, especially in the Tung-p'ing region of the Northeast, Chinese scholarship of a type quite at variance with Chu Hsi's experienced a notable renascence. Its schools produced a generation of gifted scholars able to take advantage of the examinations held in 1237, but they fitted into a class of hereditary Confucian households, conforming to the hereditary pattern of the Mongols themselves, who served either Mongol military government or regional leaders of a traditional warlord type. Thus even though the indispensability of scholar-officials to Chinese bureaucratic administration was amply demonstrated, it in no way implied the inevitable resurgence of Neo-Confucianism as such. On the contrary, it meant that a Chinese establishment and Chinese culture had already entrenched themselves in the service of the Mongols and their local satraps quite without the benefit of the School of the Way.[44] Such a circumstance belies any assumption that the persistence of Chinese institutions and culture alone would insure the eventual triumph of Neo-Confucianism.

Under the Chin a kind of "iron curtain," as Professor Yoshikawa describes it, had impeded but not entirely prevented the spread of Chu Hsi's ideas and works to the North. Despite the flourishing nature of Chinese culture under the sinicized Jurchen, the honors paid to the shrine of Confucius by the Chin emperors, and even the awareness by some scholars of Chu Hsi's growing reputation in the South, the only significant discussion of Ch'eng-Chu philosophy came in the form of an attack by Li Ch'un-fu (1185–1231), who vigorously defended Buddhism and Taoism from Ch'eng-Chu criticisms.[45]

This being the state of affairs when the Mongols took over,

one can say that the Neo-Confucians remained largely unrepresented in the Confucian culture which had become established in the North. If the depressed and repressed bourgeoisie of traditional China represented, in Max Weber's words, a "pariah capitalism,"[46] the School of the Way in the early Yüan, so far removed from anything resembling an establishment, might be called a "pariah orthodoxy."

The Neo-Confucian Mission to Mongol China

How quickly much of this was to change under Khubilai! First as a young Mongol viceroy and then as heir apparent, Khubilai early learned the inherent limitations of tribal rule and the potential uses of Confucian scholars for Chinese-type administration. In the years preceding his assumption of the throne, and especially at his military encampment at Chin-lien ch'uan (near modern Chang-chia k'ou or Kalgan), Khubilai gathered around himself an able company of educated Chinese to plan the regularization and centralization of his rule.[47] At first a small "brain trust," this group was later expanded by the recruitment of at least a dozen Chinese with strong intellectual qualifications as well as leadership abilities, and had a significant influence upon the domestication of Mongol rule.[48] Typical of the group was Liu Ping-chung (1216–1274), a Ch'an Buddhist monk doubling as a Confucian official, whose bold planning and shrewd eye for talent, like Khubilai's, led to an extensive search for scholars and in the process to the unpremeditated introduction of Neo-Confucianism to the capital.[44] These activities are described by Professor Chan in his recent article, "Chu Hsi and Yüan Neo-Confucianism."[50]

Here I wish to draw particular attention to the almost contagious way in which Neo-Confucianism spread once it had broken through the North-South barrier. The initiative for this breakthrough came from Yao Shu (1203–1280), a Confucian scholar-official who failed to convince Khubilai that "the empire can be unified without killing a single person"[51] (that is, by Confucian methods), but did persuade him to spare Confucian captives in conquered territories and employ them in his administration.

On one such campaign Yao Shu prevailed upon the captive Neo-Confucian scholar Chao Fu to come to Peking and teach. Chao, on the verge of suicide after the loss of his family in the Mongol occupation of Te-an (Hupei), yielded to Yao's appeal that he should overcome his personal tragedy and not die a useless death, but should live on to transmit the teaching of the sages to the North.[52] It is the judgment of the *Yüan History*, echoed by subsequent historians, that "the North's coming to know the Ch'eng-Chu teaching all derived from the work of Chao Fu."[53] In its literal sense that may not be quite true, especially in regard to previous knowledge of Northern Sung developments, but it no doubt reflects accurately the catalytic effect of Chao Fu's teaching.

Professor Chan's description of this crucial event as a happy "accident of history" conveys its portentous significance for later times, but we should observe that it depended upon a high degree of receptivity among an able group of Confucian-trained scholars, and in both Yao's and Chao's cases, on their personal dedication to the Way and their ability to endure through devastating misfortunes, including, for Chao, the earlier persecution of the School of the Way by Han T'o-chou, and for Yao, similar painful losses and displacement by war.

The eagerness with which Chao's teaching was received in the North reflects, on the one hand, the relatively high level of Confucian culture maintained there, with a corresponding ability to understand and appreciate what Chao had to offer; and on the other hand, a certain hunger resulting from the Northerners' enforced deprivation of new developments in Sung philosophy up to this time. Yamada Keiji, a Japanese historian of Chinese scientific thought, describes North China's avidity for the new philosophy as being "like a desert soaking up water."[54] Yao Shu himself enthusiastically adopted the Ch'eng-Chu teaching, and followed it up by building an Academy of the Supreme Ultimate *(T'ai-chi shu-yüan)* in Peking with a collection of eight thousand volumes. He also printed and disseminated many Neo-Confucian texts, and erected a shrine to the Sung masters in his own village.[55]

Yao's colleague Tou Mo (1196–1280), another close confidant of Khubilai, came into possession of Chu Hsi's commentaries on the

Four Books through the good offices of Yao Shu, and responded to them as to a life-transforming revelation, saying that "all he had learned up to that time was worthless and his real education began with this."[56] When he lectured to the emperor on the basic principles of this teaching, he said, "Among the starting points for study of the Way of man none is greater than these texts. Without them one cannot become a man and take one's stand in the world."[57]

Yang Kung-i (d. 1294), who was to become a principal collaborator in producing the new Yüan calendar, also obtained through Yao Shu Chu's commentaries on the Four Books, the *Reflections on Things at Hand (Chin-ssu lu)*, and the *Elementary Learning (Hsiao-hsüeh)*, basic texts of the School of the Way. Their impact on him is described in terms of his "taking personal responsibility for this Way, making a complete change in his habits of life, and resolving no longer to engage in his former frivolous pursuits."[58] He declared, "The constants of human relations and daily living, the wondrous subtleties of Heaven's Way and human nature are all gathered together in these books. Now those who wish to enter upon a life of virtue have a gateway to it. Those who wish to advance in the Way have a path to follow."[59]

Liu Yin (1249–1293) is another scholar of the day for whom the new teaching, received through Yao Shu at Su-men, came as a revelation. Though his commitment to the Way, unlike that of so many of his contemporaries, was to take the form of principled abstention from politics rather than active engagement in government, the profound effect on Liu of this exposure to Ch'eng-Chu teaching is no less evident.[60]

Perhaps the most notable convert at this time was Hsü Heng, due to become the intellectual leader of the School of the Way, a mentor of Khubilai, and the successor to Chao Fu as the preeminent teacher of the time.[61] Hsü's thirst for something more than humdrum book learning had been revealed in his youth when he asked his teacher in his country village, "What is the use of studying books?" To which the teacher responded, "To take the examinations and advance to the official ranks." The young Hsü replied, "Is that all?"[62]

Indeed, Hsü's deeply questioning attitude became too much for his teacher, who despaired of satisfying his desire to understand the meaning of everything. But it was much later in life, after Hsü himself had become a mature scholar, that he first came into contact with Tou Mo, learned something of the Ch'eng-Chu teachings, and "took up the teaching of the Way as his personal responsibility (*i tao-hsüeh tzu jen*)."[63] When finally he met Chao Fu, Hsü was an established teacher himself and no impressionable youth, but he was so moved by Chu Hsi's commentaries on the Four Books, the *Elementary Learning*, and other Ch'eng-Chu school texts that he copied them by hand and took them back to his students, saying:

What I taught you before was all mixed up. Only now have I learned the proper way in which education should proceed. Henceforth anyone who wishes to study with me must discard the notes and commentaries which we have been using and change to the method of the *Elementary Learning*, starting with [such ordinary household tasks as] sprinkling and sweeping, everyday human dealings, and the fulfillment of simple virtue as the basis of one's education. Anyone who does not wish to do this should look for another teacher.

They are all said to have taken this to heart, burned the copybooks they had been using, and both young and old followed the example set by Hsü himself in performing the humble duties enjoined by the *Elementary Learning*.[64]

   This has the ring of a genuine religious conversion—not the kind of ecstatic experience which must often be suspect, but a reconciliation of the believer to the realities and tasks of everyday life. Up to this time Hsü had had the reputation of being something of an authority on the recondite and mysterious *Book of Changes*. Now when people asked his guidance in interpreting this obscure text, he told them they would be better off studying the *Elementary Learning*.[65]

   Several sources recounting Hsü's experiences at this time describe them in terms of his finding the Way for himself (*tzu-te*) or finding himself in deep accord with the new teachings. When Tou Mo was called to court, leaving Hsü to ponder things for himself, he was said to have become confirmed in his determination to accept the propagation of the Way as his own responsibility (*jen-tao*). Chu Hsi had said: "The Way is the necessary principle of all things. If one has heard the Way, he can live in accord with it and die content without any regrets."[66] Commenting on this same passage in the *Analects* about "hearing the Way in the morning and dying content in the evening," Hsü said simply, "This is the Way of the sage."[67]

The Neo-Confucian Program for Khubilai

Such experiences were not uncommon among the growing number of Neo-Confucian adherents in North China. What renders these cases of special importance is that they represent a group of leaders able to affect the future course of Khubilai's policies, the character of Mongol rule in China, and the legacy of the age to other times and peoples. Sun K'o-k'uan, a leading modern Chinese historian of the period, describes the quickening effect of this activist movement at court as seeking to "save the day" or "rescue the times" (*chiu-shih*) by engaging in studies and activities of "practical use in governing the world" (*ching-shih chih-yung*).[68] One of Hsü Heng's definitions of the Way was "the study of the affairs of the country."[69]

Since there were other idealistic values in Neo-Confucianism which justified noncooperation with the Mongols (e.g., upholding the purity of the Way) or even dictated resistance to them, it is significant that this group saw the sufferings of the people as "unbearable" to men of humane conscience and felt obliged to seize whatever opportunities presented themselves to educate the conqueror and mitigate the initial harshness of Mongol rule. As Ch'eng I had said earlier, "When sages and worthies know that the Way is being destroyed in the world, can they remain seated, watching the chaos, and refuse to save the world?"[70] Whether this humane impulse should manifest itself in participation or protest was a judgmental question, of course, but if we are to understand how Neo-Confucianism became involved with the state, it is from the experiences and attitudes of those who opted for participation that we must hope to learn.

Members of this group submitted several lengthy memorials to Khubilai, both in the planning stages of his early administration and as his policies for the consolidation of Mongol rule were being carried out. A good example of the advice given him is found in Hsü Heng's Five Point Memorial of 1266 (see pp. 36–38). To the proposals made by Hsü at this time and the support he was able to gain for them from Mongol and Chinese leaders, Sun K'o-k'uan and Yao Ts'ung-wu attribute a large measure of credit for the constructive enactments of Khubilai's reign.[71]

Another example is found in the memorial of 1260 by Hao Ching (1223–1275), a convert to the School of the Way from the ranks of those brought up under the influence of the poet and critic Yüan Hao-wen (1190–1257) and the surviving literary culture of the Chin. Hao Ching reviewed the rise and fall of past dynasties and rulers in terms of their success or failure in the employment of essential Han institutions.[72] Sun believes that Hao's recommendations for the unification of China under sinified administration were largely followed by Khubilai.[73]

Common to these proposals is an emphasis on the need for basic laws and institutions. In the larger Confucian sense these represent a kind of constitutional government, combining regular and systematic administration with strong education in public morality, especially through a proper school system. To some degree this attitude reflects a belief that certain institutions were essential to the embodiment of Neo-Confucian principles, but these reformers do not slight the need for institutions of a type which often had a non-Confucian provenance, that is, for which Legalists were the original spokesmen. They recognize the magnitude and complexity of administration in an empire grown far larger and more intractable than the states of Confucius' and Mencius' time, and they do not rely solely on moral exhortation. On the other hand, things could not be left as they were. There was an urgent need, after the long lapse of many institutions or the corruption of others, actively to redevelop them. Thus, instead of simply accepting the status quo, as many powerful elements at court would have preferred, the Neo-Confucians were proponents of change.

The advice given in these memorials to Khubilai is both general and specific. It shows the historian's familiarity with institutions of the past, as well as actual experience with the lives and problems of the common people and the need to adapt traditional institutions to the circumstances of Yüan rule. Hsü Heng's proposals for the reform and strengthening of agriculture are a case in point,[74] for Hsü considered himself a peasant, not a scholar-official set apart from the common people. A certain awareness of the facts of life is shown in his view that Confucian scholars should have a dependable livelihood of their own—preferably agriculture or commerce—rather than be dependent on the largesse of the ruler or the outcome of a competitive struggle for political office.[75]

Nor was Hsü's attention limited to the most immediate problems of the day. He and others of the group discussed a wide range of political, social, and intellectual issues, including medicine, pharmacopoeia, military affairs, penal matters, economics and finance, irrigation, water control, calendrical science, and the nonorthodox schools of philosophy.[76] Hsü is credited with being the moving force behind the effort at court to reform the calendar, and took part, along with his colleagues and protégés, Wang Hsün (1235–1281) and Yang Kung-i, in the development of the new Shou-shih calendar of 1280.[77]

Yao Shu's memorials to the throne show, if anything, an even more comprehensive and detailed approach than Hsü's to current problems. He deals with many concrete matters of administrative procedure and efficiency, official salaries, legal codes, courier services, the school system, taxation and corvée labor, military organization and military farms, the operation of the Grand Canal, the "ever-normal" granaries, price controls, standards of weights and measures, transportation, poor-relief and care of the aged, etc. Altogether he made thirty specific recommendations in his first series of submissions, followed by others dealing with problems in military defense, education, centralization and rationalization of administration, etc. Not lacking, of course, was a heavy component of advice with regard to the conduct of Confucian rituals for the edification of the people in all aspects of life.[78]

How fully these proposals were implemented, and how close Khubilai came to fulfilling the hopes of his advisers, is a large question, but the substantial outcome of these efforts is indicated by Hok-lam Chan's assertion that "within the next decade (i.e., 1260–1270) a thorough reorganization took place. This included an extensive sinicization of the bureaucracy and the restoration of traditional rites, music and other ceremonial features."[79]

Germane to our own inquiry, however, is another question: how much of this advice to the ruler, and how much of the program for Yüan China, is actually "Neo-Confucian" in any sense that bears on the rise of the School of the Way as an emerging orthodoxy? What of its content actually reflects the distinctive character of Ch'eng-Chu teachings, and how much is simply conventional Confucian political lore subscribed to by members of many schools or none? Surely a large proportion of the remedies proposed in the memorials above are of the time-tested Han Chinese variety, which had the support of others not identified with the School of the Way. For instance, a recent study by Herbert Franke has dealt with the political thought of Wang Yün (1227–1304),[80] a leading representative of the class of subofficials from the so-called Tung-p'ing group, not ordinarily classed with the orthodox school, and there is a large degree of consensus across party lines on the type of conventional political wisdom he offered the court. Indeed, one could argue that the distinguishing feature of Khubilai's regime was its pragmatism in building a political consensus, not its commitment to the School of the Way.

One possible response to this question would be to say that Neo-Confucianism necessarily contains much of preexisting tradition, and it is less the specific content that is new (since in any case the problems and options did not change too greatly from age to age) than it is the reformulation of a total vision of things that inspires the Neo-Confucian reformers, galvanizes their energies, and enables them to take the lead where new initiatives are required to overcome past inertia or present indifference. This is true, and not unimportant, but it will not meet the question satisfactorily if what we need to know is how the Ch'eng-Chu school interacted with the political process in the Yüan to create a new state orthodoxy.

Orthodoxy as the "Learning of the Emperors"

To get at the question in this form we must step back in time to consider the development of the Neo-Confucian Way as it was formulated in relation to rulership. In Ch'eng I's account of the orthodox tradition as championed by his brother, we may recall that he made a distinction between the way of sage rulership, which had lapsed, and the Way as taught by Confucius and Mencius, who were not themselves in a position to carry out their teachings. This for Confucians was an unnatural separation that could not be accepted willingly. Hence, alongside the "orthodox tradition" as taught by scholar-teachers to the world at large, there was an ancillary tradition of advice to the sovereign offered by scholar-ministers and directed at the reigning emperor's practice of the Way.

This ancillary tradition, less well known than the orthodox one but developed parallel with it, was expressed in different forms. As the "Teaching" or "Learning of the Sage-Emperors and Kings" (*ti-wang chih hsüeh*), it was meant to perpetuate the Way of government (*chih-tao*) practiced and transmitted in ancient times. For later rulers it was a reminder of the model they should emulate. When, for instance, Ch'eng Hao spoke to the Emperor Shen-tsung (1068–1085) on the Way of government and the emperor expressed discomfort at the idea—"That's something for a Yao or a Shun; how could I hope to do it!"—Ch'eng Hao knit his brows and replied, "For Your Majesty to talk like that does not bode well for the country."[81] The emperor, in a position of supreme power, had no moral right to disclaim the responsibility that attached to such power. Khubilai's Neo-Confucian ministers made the same claim upon him.

In terms of the minister's role as adviser to the ruler, there was a corresponding responsibility to speak out with the utmost candor, upholding the practical validity of the Way regardless of the consequences to him personally. This too asserted a high standard, and challenged the conventional understanding of the role of the minister as the humble slave of the emperor, utterly subservient to him.[82] Ch'eng I, reasserting the stance of Mencius, insisted that the relation between ruler and minister was primarily a moral one and obliged the minister to depart from the service of a ruler with whom he had fundamental differences in principle: "Unless the ruler honors virtue and delights in moral principles, . . . it is not worth while having anything to do with him" (*Mencius* 2B:2).[83]

In Chu Hsi's *Reflections on Things at Hand (Chin-ssu lu)* Ch'eng I is quoted as saying, "When a scholar is in a high position, his duty is to save his ruler from making mistakes and not to follow him in wrongdoing." [84] And "When one has resolved that if he 'can hear the Way in the morning, he will die content in the evening,' he will not be content for even a single day with what should not be agreed to." [85] Here the burden of action on behalf of the Way, which is usually expressed in terms of some specific human obligation, falls heavily on the relationship between minister and ruler, and the "Learning of the Emperors" *(ti-hsüeh)* has the sense of what the emperor should learn, or in other words, what the minister is obliged to impart to the ruler.

This function of lecturing to the emperor on the relationship of the Way to contemporary problems became institutionalized in the form of lectures on the classics from scholars and ministers who spoke from what was called the "classics mat" *(ching-yen)*. The lectureship goes back to the Han period, and the "classics mat," which represented symbolically a kind of sanctuary from which the minister was encouraged to speak out as the ruler's mentor, dates from the T'ang. Depending upon circumstances and the inclination of the reigning emperor, the institution lapsed or was revived from time to time. In the Sung, owing to the high distinction of the scholars and statesmen who served in this capacity, it became a prestigious position and retained that reputation down through subsequent dynasties. It also became a key practice of Neo-Confucian orthodoxy at the Korean Court of the Yi Dynasty. [86]

The greatest days of the lectureship and the "classics mat" in the Sung coincided with the evolution of the "orthodox tradition" into what became known as the School of the Way. Many of the same leading personages contributed to both it and the tradition of the classics mat or the Learning of the Emperors. Continuity of style and theme, as well as the importance of precedent in maintaining the independence of the position, produced a genre of literature recording utterances from the classics mat or the content of instruction given the emperor. [87]

In the eleventh century Fan Tsu-yü (1041–1098) compiled a work in eight fascicles *(chüan)* consisting of the advice and instruction which he gave to the Emperor Che-tsung in the early Yüan-yu period (1086–1093) and entitled *Ti-hsüeh* (Learning [or Teaching] of the Emperor[s]). This work deals in part with the tradition of counseling the emperor, giving examples from the classics and from earlier dynasties, and in substantial part also with the successive reigns of the Sung down to the Hsi-ning period of Emperor Shen-tsung (1068–1077). Fan Tsu-yü, a one-time associate of Wang An-shih and collaborator of Ssu-ma Kuang who eventually was sent into exile and entered into the martyrology of Neo-Confucianism,[88] was the author also of the *Mirror of the T'ang (T'ang chien)*, a manual of political advice based on events of the T'ang period, which became a standard textbook in the Neo-Confucian academies of the late Sung, Yüan, and Ming. Of the *Ti-hsüeh* the Catalogue of the Imperial Manuscript Library says that it deals with the emperor's obligation to advance his own learning and with the need for him to "rectify his own mind and engage in self-cultivation." Fan, it says, was devoted to this work of instruction, and was known for his directness of speech, clarity of expression, command of historical precedent, and detailed knowledge of relevant documents.[89] What is most noteworthy of it as a model for this genre of political advice is its combination of principle and practice, self-cultivation and scholarship.

A fuller discussion of the nature and contents of the work is reserved for the next essay, but it is worth noting here that Fan Tsu-yü anticipates, in the *Ti-hsüeh* and in his lectures and memorials to the throne, the importance which Chu Hsi and his successors in the late Sung and Yüan would attach to the method of self-cultivation in the *Great Learning*. "Order and disorder in the world all depend on the heart-and-mind of the ruler. If his heart-and-mind are correct, then the myriad affairs of the court will not be incorrect."[90]

A much shorter work, called "An Essay on the Learning of the Emperors" *(Ti-hsüeh lun)* by Ch'en Ch'ang-fang (1108–1148) speaks of a teaching/learning of the emperors and kings that passed down from Yao and Shun to Confucius and Mencius. The last two, however, were in no position to carry it out, and no later ruler had seriously attempted to do so. Nevertheless, the essential message survived the Ch'in's burning of the books in the third century B.C., principally in the text of the *Great Learning*, supplemented by the *Mean.* Its content is identified both as "the learning of the sage-emperors and kings *(ti-wang chih hsüeh-wen)*" and "the ruler's method of the mind" *(jen-chu hsin-fa)*. No other knowledge, no other capability, is so important for the ruler as being able to examine his own motives and conduct to insure that he is not misled into making errors of catastrophic consequence for the people. Quoting the *Great Learning,* Ch'en says:

> What is called "cultivation of the person" lies in "rectifying one's mind." If the person is moved by passion, he will not achieve correctness; if he is moved by fear, he will not achieve correctness; if he is moved by fondness for something, he will not achieve correctness; if he is moved by sorrow and distress, he will not achieve correctness.

Therefore, says Ch'en, "the ruler must rid himself of these four things and keep close watch over the substance of his mind."[91]

The Mind of the Ruler and the Hearts of the People

This same note is struck by Fan Ch'un-jen (1027–1101), son of the high-minded statesman and Neo-Confucian hero, Fan Chung-yen (989–1052), in his lectures from the classics mat:

> The basis of the state lies in the ruler, and the basis of rulership lies in the mind-and-heart. The learning of the ruler should be directed at rectifying his mind-and-heart, making his intentions sincere, taking humaneness as the basic substance, and not letting heterodox and superficial notions gain entry. Only thus will the issuing of orders and promulgation of decrees serve the welfare of the state and dynasty.[92]

A succession of leading scholar-statesmen in the Neo-Confucian pantheon, from the Ch'eng brothers and Ssu-ma Kuang down to Chu Hsi, contributed to the articulation of this line of instruction at court, originally quite independent of the School of the Way, and insured its close linkage to the developing "orthodox tradition." Ch'eng Hao stressed the "art of governing the mind-and-heart" *(chih-hsin chih shu)* on the part of the ruler as the basis for the Way of government. "To rule with a sincere heart-and-mind is to be a true king. . . . Your Majesty has the natural endowment of Yao and Shun and the position of Yao and Shun, but only if he takes it as his personal responsibility *(tzu-jen)* to have the mind of Yao and Shun can he fulfill their Way."[93]

Ch'eng I, who shared the duties of the classics mat with Fan Tsu-yü, author of the *Learning of the Emperors,* also pressed relentlessly for the ruler to take responsibility for his own actions.[94] In a memorial to the throne he further stressed the importance of the ruler's having a mind of his own, making a definite commitment to advance the Way, and taking responsibility for it.

Committing oneself means to be perfectly sincere and single-minded, to take up the Way as one's own responsibility *(i-tao tzu-jen),* to take the teachings of the sages as trustworthy, to believe that the governance of the kings can be carried out, to avoid following rigidly the advice of those nearby[95] or being swayed by public clamor, but to be determined to bring about a world order like that of the Three Dynasties [of old].[96]

Ch'eng I did not want to "pressure" the emperor, manipulate him, or use him. For the emperor to accept his own responsibility meant developing his own sense of self-respect—a penetrating observation to make of one who was outwardly the object of such fulsome respect and obedience from all others. But it was only a reflection of Ch'eng I's own strong sense of self-respect, which is shown in the episode involving the nonpayment of his stipend as lecturer from the classics mat. The convention at court was that the lecturer should submit an application for his salary to the Board of Revenue. This Ch'eng I would not do, even though he had to borrow money to live on. When asked about this, he replied that to apply for his salary as if for a favor was demeaning, and especially so for the lecturer from the classics mat. "The trouble is that today scholars and officials are accustomed to begging. They beg at every turn."[97] An abridged version of this incident is given in the *Reflections on Things at Hand,* a text well-known to Hsü Heng, and it may have influenced his views on the need for the scholar-official to have an independent livelihood.[98]

Chu Hsi, who adjudged Fan Tsu-yü's exposition of the "Way

of governing" to represent the "highest excellence," [99] emulated him in his own lectures from the classics mat and in his memorials. These latter cover a range of political issues, but their unifying theme recapitulates and brings together the developing concepts of both the orthodox tradition and the Learning of the Emperors. This is especially evident in Chu's sealed memorial of 1162. [100] Here Chu expresses a sense of responsibility to set before the emperor the Way of the emperors and kings as passed down from Yao and Shun. His account of it anticipates much that appears later in his preface to the *Mean*—the precariousness and fallibility of the human mind and the consequent need for study and self-examination on the part of the ruler. "Everything depends on what the ruler studies, and correctness or incorrectness here depends on his square-inch [of mind-and-heart]." [101] The order or disorder of the world hangs in the balance, just as the *Book of Changes* speaks of an infinitesimal deflection of the mind leading in the end to an infinite error. [102]

> Thus the extension of knowledge and investigation of things is like Yao and Shun's "refinement" and "singlemindedness"; to rectify the mind and make the will sincere is like Yao and Shun's "holding fast the Mean." What the ancient sages passed on by word of mouth and transmitted from mind to mind was just this and nothing more. . . .
>
> Coming down to Confucius, in getting the surviving teachings together he accomplished much, but despite his readiness to serve, he gained no position from which he might give all mankind the benefit of the Way, and so he retired and wrote the teachings down in the Six Classics in order to put them before rulers of succeeding generations. In them he stated the priorities of root and branch, beginning and end, what precedes and what follows, [explaining them] both in explicit detail and with great clarity. What we now see as the *Great Learning* in the *Record of Rites* [compiled] by Mr. Tai [in the Han dynasty] is just this. [103]

Chu urges the emperor not simply to rely on what he is told by Chu and others, but through objective study, subjective confirmation, and discussion with others, to find out for himself and in himself (*tzu-te*) the truth of the Way. [104] Thereafter he must develop long-range policies that go beyond the immediate reform of the administration and resistance to the barbarian. But above all, by his own constant self-examination the emperor must see to it that he rules in the interests of all *(kung)* and not out of selfish interest *(ssu)*. "There is no reason why Your Majesty, doing this, cannot uphold the shining teachings of the sage-emperors *(ti-hsüeh)* and follow in the footsteps of Yao and Yü."[105]

In his sealed memorial of 1188 Chu presents six matters requiring urgent attention, including reform of the inner palace, instruction of the heir apparent, selection of ministers, improvement of official discipline and social customs, reform of taxation, and the military system. Then he concludes:

> None of these six points can be neglected, but they all have their root in Your Majesty's mind-and-heart. If the mind-and-heart is correct, then these six things cannot go wrong. But if even one iota of selfish-mindedness or selfish desire is allowed to intervene, then no matter how much mental effort or physical exertion go into the rectifying of these matters . . . the empire still cannot be well managed. Therefore this root of empire is also the most urgent of all urgent needs and cannot be put off even for a little while. . . .[106]

Enough has been cited from this considerable body of Neo-Confucian political literature to illustrate the following points concerning the application of the orthodox tradition to the problem of rulership:

1. The "precariousness of the human mind" points to the fallibility of the ruler and the dangerous consequences from the misuse of power if the ruler does not engage in self-examination and rectification of his mind-and-heart.

2. The ruler has a heavy personal responsibility which he cannot evade, but he can share it with scholar-mentors learned in the political literature of the past and familiar with the practice of government, who can help him to learn the essentials for himself.

3. The *Great Learning* contains the essence of that literature which can be applied to the myriad transformations of human life in different contexts.

4. That essence lies in rectifying the mind, here especially the ruler's and minister's minds.[107]

Thus the cumulative outcome of the orthodox tradition is actually the compression of that learning or teaching into a key text among the Four Books, namely the *Great Learning*, and a key formula in that text, the rectifying of the mind. The more formal elements and practices of this type of imperial instruction-and-discussion based on the classics were summed up in two fascicles of the encyclopedic *Sea of Jade (Yü hai)* by one of the leading Ch'eng-Chu scholars of the late Sung, Wang Ying-lin (1223–1296), under the heading "Learning of the Emperors" (*Ti-hsüeh*). [108]

Though a sufficient scriptural basis for the above points may be found in the Sung texts cited, it would be a mistake to think that the tradition stopped growing with Chu Hsi. The next scholar-statesman to be cast in the heroic role of rescuing the Way from oblivion, Chen Te-hsiu, carried on both sides of this tradition. His major compilation, the *Extended Meaning of the Great Learning (Ta-hsüeh yen-i)*, not only resumes all of the above, but also provides a wealth of corroborative material from the classics and histories which gives the classical essence its contemporary application in different historical settings. The work thus exemplifies in content and style earlier expositions of the orthodox tradition, the lectures from the classics mat (which he himself gave to the emperor), and the combination of principle and practice which had been embodied in the genre of Learning of the Emperors. [109]

Presented by Chen to the Emperor Li-tsung and by others in the Yüan to the Emperor Jen-tsung (r. 1312–1320), the *Extended Meaning of the Great Learning* was translated in abridged form into Mongol for the edification of those unable to read classical Chinese. A much shorter work by Chen, the *Classic of the Mind-and-Heart (Hsin ching)*, contained a convenient selection of his sayings on rectification of the mind. [110] Together these two works of Chen's may be taken as links in passing on this tradition from Chu Hsi to the mentors of Khubilai.

In the Yüan the tradition of the classics mat was revived, both informally and formally, as a principal means for discussing the relevance of Confucian principles and Chinese institutions to the problems of the day. Indeed, so influential did it become as a means of sinicizing or Confucianizing Mongol rule that one leader of a nativist reaction eventually tried to suppress it.[111] Khubilai, for his part, took a strong interest in such lectures and saw to it that his heir apparent also benefited from this type of instruction.[112] Among his advisers Tou Mo is credited with exemplifying this tradition at its best in his forthright criticism of the policies of the high official Wang Wen-t'ung (?–d. 1262), then at the height of his power.[113] Khubilai, when he finally realized the correctness of Tou's admonitions, was much impressed with the value of such courageous, principled advice, which Sun K'o-k'uan associates with the finest traditions of the classics mat.[114] The underlying spirit of that tradition is conveyed in Tou Mo's first interview with Khubilai. Tou told him that "in the Learning of the Emperors and Kings, what is most esteemed is 'rectifying the mind and making the will sincere.' If the ruler's mind is correct, then none will dare to be incorrect."[115]

Yao Shu, in one of the major policy papers mentioned earlier which contain numerous specific recommendations for reform, prefaced these with a typical Neo-Confucian appeal to Khubilai's conscience and the *Great Learning's* doctrine of mind-cultivation. The latter was still crown prince at the time, formulating the goals of his administration, and Yao Shu urged him to aim high; he should not think it too much to emulate the sage-emperors' and kings' pursuit of learning, their practice of government, and the establishment of an era of great peace and order in the world. The essentials of this learning consisted of the practice of self-cultivation, encouragement of study, respect for the worthy, affection for one's kin, fearing Heaven, loving the people, and keeping aloof from sycophants.[116]

Hsü Heng performed the function of mentor to the emperor both through his memorials and through his services as adviser and tutor to the heir apparent. Hsü's Five Point Memorial is believed by Sun to have been drafted originally for presentation from the classics mat.[117] As tutors to the heir apparent, Hsü and Wang Hsün combined the study of historical works and political manuals such as Ssu-ma Kuang's *General Mirror for Aid in Government (Tzu-chih t'ung-chien)* and the *Essence of Government in the Chen-kuan Era (Chen-kuan cheng-yao)* with discussion of the orthodox principles of the Learning of the Emperors and Kings and the method of preserving the mind.[118]

In his memorial of 1266 to Khubilai Hsü asserted the moral basis of the ruler-minister relationship by using the words of Confucius to express the thought of Ch'eng I and Chu Hsi: "If one cannot serve the ruler in accordance with the Way, then one must withdraw [from his service]" (*Analects* 11:23). Throughout the memorial Hsü repeatedly exhorts the emperor to take the *Great Learning* as his guide to rulership. "In ancient times, according to the Way of the *Great Learning*, self-cultivation was the basis of government. One word or one action set before the people could become the model for all the world; one reward or one punishment could draw together the public spirit of all-under-Heaven."[119] This is because the emperor, in his position, could serve as a model for the *Great Learning's* "fulfilling of the highest good" by all, in their respective positions.[120] Since the essential Confucian hierarchy is defined in terms of self-imposed limitations on the exercise of power, restraint on the pursuit of private or selfish ends *(ssu)*, and an obligation to promote the public interest *(kung)*, the emperor's example of self-examination and self-restraint, emulated by all, would become a means of governing through universal self-discipline.[121] This is the meaning of "governing men through self-discipline" *(hsiu-shen chih-jen)*.

In the same memorial Hsü emphasized the need for the ruler to "win the hearts of the people" through his manifestation of love and impartiality *(kung)*, and explained how this could be done in relation to the issues of the day. The fidelity of the memorial to the essential spirit of the classics mat and the Learning of the Emperors is found in its emphasis on the awesome responsibility of one whose power affects millions of lives, and of his need for humility and modesty, for becoming a servant of the people, if that power is not to be abused.

Elsewhere Hsü explains,

Everything depends on the ruler's setting an example for those below. . . . If those on high do not treat those below with proper respect and deference, those below will not exert themselves to the utmost.[122]

It was because Yao rectified his own mind that he recognized in Shun a person who rectified his own mind and was thus willing to yield the throne to him . . . and it was because of this willingness to yield on the part of Yao that all-under-Heaven had yielding, non-contentious, sharing, and reciprocating hearts.[123]

In teaching men the essentials of the *Great Learning,* Confucius taught them the essentials of the correct and proper mind. . . . [Thus] rectifying the mind is the excellent method of the *Great Learning.*[124]

Further, Hsü explains, "renewing the people," as taught by this text, means for the emperor to "extend this mind to the common people," showing them how to renew themselves through a constant process of self-examination and self-correction, that is, by dispelling the obscurations of selfishness and partiality, clarifying their own virtuous natures *(ming ming-te),* and enabling each to achieve the highest good for himself.[125]

We shall see later how Fan Tsu-yü, Ch'eng I, Chu Hsi, and Chen Te-hsiu made the *Great Learning's* "rectifying of the mind" and "clarifying of luminous virtue" (the originally good nature) the focal point of imperial instruction (pp. 131–47 below). Hsü Heng does the same. When he lectures to Khubilai he talks about Confucius and the *Great Learning,* not about Ch'eng and Chu, but his exposition is informed throughout by the spirit of the last two and by their new encapsulation of the classical tradition. On several scores Khubilai was apt to be suspicious of or uncomfortable with the Neo-Confucians, and there are limits beyond which Hsü would not go in directly challenging him on this, but in effect Hsü's presentation of the classical teaching is one reshaped and reinterpreted by the School of the Way. It is also, in its utter simplicity and conciseness, adapted to serve as the lowest common denominator among men—rulers and ruled, Chinese and Mongols—a lesson in public morality and impartiality *(kung)* through mind-rectification for all.[126]

The Examination Debate under Khubilai

In their concern for moral self-cultivation, the Neo-Confucian reformers did not neglect consideration of the complex political and intellectual issues of the day. Their record is replete with discussions of such questions.[127] This Neo-Confucian version of moral rearmament should not be seen as a form of anti-intellectualism, or as a tendency to reduce political problems to moral ones. Rather it was an effort by the Neo-Confucian mind to counter-balance and cope with that complexity, and to achieve an objectivity that was not value-free. What prompted their reassertion of the moral claims of Confucian humanism was not only the enervating effect on civic morality they saw in Buddhism and Taoism, but, in the political context, pragmatic realism on the part of the Mongols and their fiscal technicians, whose main aim was to maximize the conqueror's power and resources. As critical decisions were being made, someone had to raise the question of what human ends were to be served by this vast mobilization of power and wealth.

In the background of the Neo-Confucian discussion of selfish interest versus public interest lies the question of the employment of worthy, humane men able to defend the long-term public interest against those who seek only immediate gains for the state. This is a particular concern of Hsü Heng in his memorial of 1277 on the people's livelihood.[128] Again, it is the age-old issue of virtue versus technical competence in office, ideological fitness versus expertise—familiar even today in Communist China, but never really a simple matter.

In 1267 a proposal was made by the Hanlin academician Wang O (1190–1273),[129] a leading scholar among the survivors from the Chin and a *chin-shih* degree winner in 1224, that the civil service examinations should be reintroduced. Wang cited the precedents of earlier dynasties from the Chou and Han down through the Liao and Chin, as well as the example of Ögödei's examinations in 1237. He argued that if such a system were not available, there would be no ladder of advancement for able and ambitious men to follow. In the absence of such they would be easily diverted into less worthy callings, either becoming subofficials whose expertise had not benefited from a classical training, or attaching themselves to the service of local satraps, or perhaps even using their talents as merchants and artisans rather than as officials at court or in central administration.[130]

This might seem a good Confucian position to take, and in a sense it was, but Khubilai besought the opinions of other Confucians, as often he did before coming to a decision. One such opinion came from Tung Wen-chung (d. 1281),[131] a member of a distinguished military family long in the service of the Mongol court, who advocated, albeit indirectly, a more typical Neo-Confucian position. Without claiming any great authority in the matter, and deprecating his own learning, Tung replied to Khubilai: "I only know that 'at home one devotes oneself to the service of one's parents and abroad one exerts oneself in the service of one's prince.'[132] I know nothing about the composition of *shih* poetry."[133]

Tung's seemingly offhand dismissal of *shih* poetry is really calculated to stigmatize the old-style examinations for their preoccupation with the purely literary side of things, and when Tung counterposes practical moral conduct to literary frills, he is invoking classical Confucian authority in favor of a neoclassical, Neo-Confucian position. He says nothing about Ch'eng I or Chu Hsi, but anyone familiar with Chu's writings would know of his strong criticism of the T'ang and Sung examinations for their overemphasis on the composition of *shih* and *fu* poetry at the expense of a more meaningful understanding of the classics.[134] The unspoken implication of Tung's disclaimer is that such knowledge is hardly worth having. Khubilai, apparently, was persuaded by this not to go ahead with the proposal.

At any rate, nothing was done, and the idea reemerged four years later from T'u-tan Kung-lu,[135] another prominent member of the Hanlin Academy who had drafted the edict proclaiming the dynastic name of the Yüan in 1271.[136] This time, the available accounts present the argument for reviving the old-style examinations as quite calculating and contrived. T'u-tan apparently believed that he could exploit Khubilai's known preference for a more traditional doctrinal Buddhism over Ch'an Buddhism, by making a similar distinction between the original Confucianism supposedly incorporated into the old-fashioned examinations and the School of the Way, which was to be discredited by association with Ch'an. Khubilai saw through this ploy immediately, and resorted to his usual tactic of inviting counsel from others apt to disagree. Again Tung Wen-chung was called in, as well as Yao Shu and Hsü Heng (though the direct comments of the latter two are not recorded). Khubilai apparently regarded Tung as an unacknowledged partisan of the School of the Way because he was always citing the Four Books (a clear indication that it was the mark of the Neo-Confucians to stress these particular texts), and Khubilai tried to smoke him out on this. But Tung replied:

> Your Majesty has often said that those who neglect the study of the classics and do not ponder deeply the Way of Confucius and Mencius, but rather engage in composition of *shih* and *fu* poetry, have no concern for self-cultivation and nothing of benefit to offer the governance of the state. Therefore, scholars throughout the land wish to engage in studies that are solid and practical *(shih-hsüeh)*. What I cite are the works of Confucius and Mencius; I make no claim to knowing about the School of the Way. But some scholars cling to the ways of fallen dynasties [i.e., the Sung and Chin] and talk like this to mislead Your Majesty. I fear that this is not in accord with Your Majesty's intention of setting a proper model on high and maintaining self-discipline among those below.[137]

Here Tung attempts to discredit the proposal on grounds of the alleged uselessness and frivolity of poetry composition, and also by associating such examinations with recent dynasties whose leadership, recruited on that basis, had failed to assure the viability of their regimes. One notices too that either side puts forward its own ideas as if they were the emperor's own.

Also recorded are the views of Yang Kung-i, colleague of Hsü Heng and Tou Mo, who is said to speak for them as well as himself in response to T'u-tan Kung-lu's proposal. Yang reviews the whole history of the examinations in a manner reminiscent of Chu Hsi's earlier analysis.[138] First he cites the exemplary system of the ancient dynasties that appointed persons on the basis of their virtuous character and mastery of classic arts. In the Han, filiality and integrity were still considered important qualifications, along with a knowledge of the classics. In the Wei and Chin, literary skills began to dominate. From the Sui and T'ang the composition of *shih* and *fu* gained exclusive attention, and candidates who took the examinations virtually prostituted themselves in the scramble for office. This was continued down through the Mongol's predecessors. Thus the system established was actually a perversion of the original and not genuinely representative of orthodox tradition.

If Khubilai really wanted to remedy the situation, said Yang, he should discard the *shih* and *fu* as so much empty verbiage and have officials recommend men on the basis of irreproachable character and genuine understanding of the classics and histories, rather than make them demean themselves by submitting to a corrupt examination system.

These men should then be examined both on their understanding of the larger significance and precise meaning of the Five Classics and Four Books and on their knowledge of history as it relates to contemporary problems. If this is done and they engage in studies of a practical sort *(shih-hsüeh)*, then the whole climate and style of scholarship will be improved, the people's customs will be enhanced, and the state will obtain men of talent who know how to govern.[139]

That Hsü Heng would have subscribed to these views is not at all unlikely. We recall his youthful expression of skepticism about the value of the old-style examinations. In an interview he pointedly disavowed any interest or competence in the kind of studies required under the old system.[140] His condemnation of the evils of the T'ang and Sung examinations is clearly stated in his writings.[141]

Whether Khubilai fully accepted this view or not, he went along with it to the extent of not carrying out the proposal before him.[142] No doubt he had reasons of his own for not pushing ahead with any kind of examination system, even though he is recorded as favoring the idea. In the politics of the situation he could expect that his Mongols would be opposed. They would have the greatest difficulty competing with the Chinese on the latter's own cultural ground, especially in the niceties of literary composition. Hence their own control as a regime based on conquest would be directly threatened. Nor would those who served the immediate power interests of that dynasty, as Khubilai's financial experts and resource managers, find examinations of either the literary or the classical type to their liking. Khubilai himself must have felt, at the very least, some ambivalence.[143]

In any event, as an issue among Confucians, these particular proposals highlighted the differences between the two groups whose ideological and scholarly styles can be traced back to opposing sides in the Sung, typified by Su Tung-p'o and Chu Hsi. Though they were proponents of a change in the existing situation, the Hanlin backers of the old system spoke essentially for a restoration of the Sung and Chin system unchanged. In this respect Wang O and T'u-tan Kung-lu represented a conservative position, and stated it as such. They spoke for the type of Chinese institutions already reestablished under the Mongols, and spoke too for the reproduction of their own species—the heirs of the literary culture in the Northeast who had entrenched themselves early in the bureaucracy (especially in the Hanlin Academy) through their success in the examinations of 1237 and through their undoubted capability in drafting state documents.[144]

Though vested interests were at stake, however, it would be misleading to imply that this debate was conducted purely along lines of vested interests, factional alignments, or class background. One of the leaders of the Neo-Confucian reform movement, Hao Ching, was, as we have seen, reared in the Chin literary tradition of the Northeast,[145] and yet this only made him the more conscious of what was at stake:

> What the world thinks of as Confucian scholarship is only letters. That is what is used for instruction by parents and teachers; it is what scholars occupy themselves with and what official careers are determined by . . . but it does not correspond to what made a scholar a scholar in ancient times. Really letters are only the outer branches of scholarship; it is moral action and virtuous conduct *(te-hsing)* that constitute the root and core of scholarship.[146]

By *te-hsing* Hao Ching meant not simply fastidious conduct and the avoidance of impropriety but an active effort to carry out the way.[147] In other words, underlying the Neo-Confucian position in the debate is the same concern for active self-cultivation stressed in the *Great Learning's* "rectifying of the mind" and "clarifying of luminous virtue" and in the teachings of Hsü Heng and others from the classics mat, which linked individual morality to public concerns.[148]

The debate ended in a draw, probably because of Khubilai's uncertainty over whether the benefits were worth the political costs, but perhaps also because of the Neo-Confucians' own ambivalence about examinations. In the past the most they had been willing to concede on this score was that they were not necessarily opposed,[149] but they certainly had less faith in them than in judgments of personal character—that is, as Yang Kung-i suggested, recommendations or sponsorship should be based on observation of a man's conduct and learning.[150] For Neo-Confucians the highest priority went to the precondition of any effective recruitment system at all— education in character formation and public morality.

Neo-Confucian Education under Khubilai

From the earliest days of their collaboration under Khubilai, his reform-minded advisers agreed on the importance of universal education, a principal aim of Sung thinkers earlier.[151] Liu Ping-chung, the pivotal figure in the early administration of Khubilai, is said to have had doubts about the civil service examinations but not about the need for schools.[152] In their early memorials Yao Shu, Tou Mo, Hao Ching, and Hsü Heng all urged action to this end. The last especially featured this as one of his Five Points, linking provision for the people's sustenance and for education as the indispensable conditions for the uplifting of public morality (as Mencius earlier had taught).[153]

In the preface to his Commentary on the *Great Learning*, Chu Hsi had traced the origins of schools from the days of the sage-kings. His account of education in those times parallels his account of the genesis and transmission of the orthodox tradition presented in the preface to his Commentary on the *Mean*. Thus these key Neo-Confucians texts put before the reader succinct statements of the guiding principles and ideals of Neo-Confucian education. The two prefaces, as almost the first things to be seen by anyone studying Chu Hsi's version of the Four Books, had a wide impact on those exposed to the Learning of the Way (*tao-hsüeh*). It is not surprising, then, that Hsü Heng, in his famous memorial of 1266, in his *Essentials of the*

Great Learning (Ta-hsüeh yao-lüeh),[154] and in other writings, should reflect this same vision of a universal school system and curriculum, based on Chu's interpretation of the *Great Learning,* which stressed the study of principle, rectification of the mind, and self-cultivation as the basis of the political and social order.

In this preface, however, Chu Hsi also pointedly refers to the elementary education which laid the groundwork for the higher education of the *Great Learning.* In this way he introduces a concept of education which he further developed in his compilation of the *Elementary Learning (Hsiao-hsüeh).* Its contents, as basic training adapted to the everyday life of the common man, were suitable for use as a primer in a system of universal schooling. What is most extraordinary is that Hsü Heng should have judged that this basic approach was also suited to the education of Mongols, and that the *Elementary Learning* should have become a fixture of Neo-Confucian education in Korea and Japan as well.

In Hsü Heng's memorial, having first besought Khubilai to end the merciless exploitation of agriculture which his revenue agents engaged in, he put before the emperor the prospective benefits of instituting this type of universal education:

> If schools are set up from the capital district down to the local districts so that the young, from the imperial princes on high to the sons of the common people below, can engage in study; if day by day the great moral relationships of parent and child, ruler and minister, are explained, along with the great Way that begins with the [*Elementary Learning's*] "sweeping up and responding to questions" and extends to the [*Great Learning's*] pacifying of the world, then after ten years those above will know how to guide those below and those below will know how to serve those above them. With those above harmonious and those below cooperative, it would be far better than what you have now.
>
> If you can do these two things [provide for the people's livelihood and education], a myriad other things can be accomplished. If you cannot do these two things, then nothing can be expected from any of the other things you try to do.
>
> This is the Way of Yao and Shun. The Way of Yao and Shun fostered life and promoted unselfishness. If you can do these things, they will foster life and promote unselfishness. Mencius said, "Anything other than the Way of Yao and Shun I would not dare propose to my king." [2B:2][155]

Here Hsü Heng speaks as a mentor to the ruler (echoing Fan Tsu-yü's advice to his emperor),[156] as a teacher in the tradition of Confucius and Mencius, and more specifically as a Neo-Confucian educator in the line of Chu Hsi. Chu had given much thought to the problems and methods of education, especially to what the proper content and sequence of instruction should be at each level of human development, and it is this major contribution of the Sung philosopher which provided Hsü Heng with the basis for the characteristic Neo-Confucian curriculum that became established under the Mongols and later was widely extended throughout East Asia.

The universality of this education is also to be understood in terms of its essential message, which was the same for all. Self-rectification and mind-culture should be directed at nourishing the innate goodness of each man's moral nature, and then by extension to developing the moral nature in others through "clarifying their own luminous virtue." If all were aided in removing the obscurations of their originally pure virtue, the principle of "governing men through self-discipline" would become the basis of the political order.[157]

Though this doctrine insisted on rigorous control over selfish desires and on vigilant defense against the corrupting influences of heterodox teachings, it expressed great confidence in man's moral and intellectual powers to deal with such defects. It was basically an optimistic view, encouraging men to believe in their own potential for sagehood or the ruler's potential for becoming a sage-king. In this very common sense of the term, *sheng-tao*, often translated as "Way of the sages," meant for Neo-Confucians "Way to sagehood," or "Way of becoming a sage."

Individual commitment and acceptance of personal responsibility were the starting point for advancement in this Way, unceasing self-discipline the means. But its premise, the underlying unity in principle *(li)* of man's moral nature *(hsing,* or *te-hsing)* was also seen as the basis of an ordered human community. Hence the educational effort implied by a universal school system must look to collective fulfillment in a moral and spiritual communion among all mankind—indeed among all things—provided only that one dealt first with the weakness and fallibility of men.[158]

In these terms the Neo-Confucian doctrine of human nature

(hsing-li) could be seen as the natural successor to the Mahayana doctrine of the universal Buddha-nature, which earlier had contributed not a political philosophy but a moral and spiritual formation to accompany the processes of political unification in China, Korea, and Japan seven centuries earlier. Though the prospect of sagehood had meaning primarily for the educated, and sagehood as the embodiment of the new learning of the Sung was something of an elitist ideal, the potential in all men for the fulfillment of virtue and advancement in the Way was a plausible basis for everyone's enlistment in the new educational program, Mongols as well as Chinese. In his writings, as the Ch'ing editors of the Imperial Library Catalogue noted, Hsü Heng sought to communicate this basic teaching in simple, unadorned language. He did not strive for originality or stylistic effects, but only to get the message across, to convert and enlist human talents in the service of the Way.[159]

It may sound somewhat paradoxical to say that Hsü Heng had great faith in the practicality of this doctrine, but his sense of conviction certainly had this religious quality to it. He believed that the Learning of the Way dealt with man in his actual condition, cultivated his inherent powers, and assisted a natural process of growth.[160] In his personal instruction this self-identified farmer-teacher, with the rugged character of the peasant, communicated his earnest conviction to all, even to his imperial "students." He was deeply dedicated to the teaching of Mongols and firmly convinced that a Neo-Confucian education was the best way to develop their native intelligence as well as to insure the survival of the tradition.[161]

Khubilai was much impressed.[162] His motives, as the ruler of a conquest regime, may well be suspect; they were probably not unmixed in sponsoring a doctrine susceptible of manipulation by the state for its own ends. But as an aspirant to hegemony over a multinational empire, Khubilai had much to gain from the spread of such a universalistic doctrine.[163] Some additional measure of commitment is implied by the fact that he entrusted the Confucian education of the heir apparent Jinggim to Yao Shu, Tou Mo, Wang Hsün, and Hsü Heng,[164] and by the decision to include his own Mongols in the new educational program, rather than extend into it a wall of cultural separation which would have insulated the Mongols from

Chinese culture and reinforced the dyarchical principle in government.

Among the many educational measures of Khubilai's long reign, two principal developments stand out. First is his early commitment to the idea of universal schooling, as repeatedly urged by Tou Mo, Yao Shu, and Hsü Heng.[165] This was done through a general proclamation of 1261 in which Khubilai stressed the need for a resumption of educational activities in the conquered territories after the years of disruption. To implement this he ordered the establishment of schools on the local level and appointed regional superintendents of education to oversee the effort.[166]

Second was the reestablishment of the Imperial College[167] at the capital in 1271 and after, first under Hsü Heng and then Wang Hsün, again on an interracial basis.[168] Neither the school system nor the Imperial College seems to have been fully implemented at first, but went by fits and starts. Given Khubilai's grandiose ambitions in many directions, his continuing campaigns of conquest, and his dependence for funding on fiscal experts not always sympathetic to the new educational schemes, one can, without attributing to him either hypocrisy or vacillation, easily imagine his problems of resource allocation and bureaucratic obstruction.

In any case, both these efforts grew in time. Whether we credit official reports that place the number of local schools over 23,000 by 1290 or discount these as paper figures[169] makes little difference. We have no reason to doubt that imperial sponsorship contributed substantially to Neo-Confucian education from this time on. Hsü Heng's followers were heavily represented among the teachers in the Imperial College and the education officers in the provinces. In fact, they became as strongly entrenched in this area as the literary group had been in the Hanlin Academy,[170] and even Neo-Confucians from the South found their outlook somewhat narrow and partisan.

The curriculum on both levels was based squarely on the "new" classics, i.e., the Four Books with Chu Hsi's commentary and the *Elementary Learning,* along with the more traditional classics: the *Odes, Documents, Record of Rites, Rites of Chou, Spring and Autumn Annals, Changes,* and *Classic of Filial Piety.*[171] The aims of this education were stated by Hsü Heng and Wang Hsün, as libationers (chancellors) of the Imperial College, in terms of the eight items in the "curriculum" of the *Great Learning* and *Elementary Learning*, emphasizing moral, intellectual, and political concerns at the expense of the literary.[172] As Hsü's closest disciple Yao Sui (1238–1313) put it, "His teaching took the *Elementary Learning* and [Chu's version of the] Four Books as the gateway to virtue, discussing the essential unifying principles before going on to the *Changes, Odes, Documents,* and *Spring and Autumn Annals*."[173]

In this light the new attention given to the *Great Learning* and *Elementary Learning* goes one step beyond Chu Hsi's own digesting of the Four Books and represents Hsü's use of these basic primers to reach the lowest common denominator of educated leadership among Mongols, Central Asians, and Chinese, it being understood that graduates of this system would enter official service, i.e., were being trained for practical employment in government and not as speculative philosophers.[174]

Actually, even in the absence of more consistent support of the government program, the mere fact of imperial encouragement gave impetus to private or semiofficial efforts in the local academies (*shu-yüan*).[175] It was in these academies that the School of the Way had found its first institutional base and its first formulation as a working orthodoxy. Everything indicates that Neo-Confucianism had its own power to attract adherents as long as no obstacles were put in its way. Even without a major investment by the state, just to have official cooperation with individual or community efforts gave them added stimulus. An early example is found in the establishment of the Academy of the Supreme Ultimate (*T'ai-chi shu-yüan*) at Yen-ching (Peking) in 1238, which sprang from the personal initiative of Yao Shu and Yang Wei-chung (1206–1260), but obviously had official sanction. Along with the Imperial College as later established, it symbolized the coexistence under the Yüan of semiprivate and official education, both of them now in the service of Neo-Confucian teaching.[176]

Thus a relatively loose government policy, decentralized control, and even benign neglect could be conducive to a flourishing development of Neo-Confucian schools on the local level. Records indicate that this occurred on a considerable scale and in a variety of ways, especially in the South, as displaced or alienated scholars, unassimilated into the Yüan bureaucracy or official schools, found other outlets for their talents, especially in the sanctuary of local academies or in cultural services to other religions.[177] The spread of printing at this time reinforced the trend by facilitating the distribution of books and their collection in local centers.[178] The number of local academies rose to 390 that were sustained or built in 14 provinces in Yüan times (1260–1368). This rapid proliferation, which compares favorably to the range of 266 to 382 private schools reported by Chaffee for the 152 years of the Southern Sung period (1127–1279) and is only approached during the next great wave of Neo-Confucian teaching led by Wang Yang-ming, testifies to the cultural expansion that took place under the unlikely auspices of this "barbarian" dynasty.[179]

Khubilai's "Bakufu" (Mu-fu) and the New Orthodoxy

Within a few decades this educational movement produced a new generation of scholars and officials many of whom readily supported the next major move in Neo-Confucianism's rise, the decisive step Khubilai had been unwilling to take: incorporation of the new curriculum into a civil service examination system.

I have elsewhere distinguished among several types of Neo-Confucian orthodoxy, official and unofficial, and within the former, between the "Mandarin orthodoxy" of Ming and Ch'ing China, closely identified with the state bureaucracy and its key institutions, and the orthodoxy sponsored in Japan by the Tokugawa shogunate or Bakufu (see pp. 188–92 below). The term "Bakufu orthodoxy" describes a looser, more decentralized and pluralistic pattern of education, while "Mandarin orthodoxy" refers to a more rigid and centralized system of bureaucratic training and recruitment, with greater pressure toward ideological conformity and standardization of thought.

In the case of Khubilai there is more than a superficial resemblance between his patronage of Neo-Confucian scholars and Tokugawa Ieyasu's (1542–1616) patronage of Hayashi Razan, as noted by Professor Yoshikawa Kōjirō, who likened the two rulers in their readiness to innovate as founders of new regimes.[180] There is also more than a coincidence in name between Ieyasu's Bakufu and Khubilai's *mu-fu* military government,[181] alternative pronunciations of the same Chinese characters. Khubilai's Bakufu at Chin-lien ch'uan set the pattern of rule and masterminded the policies that dominated the Yüan regime in China. Both rulers, though Buddhists and counseled by Buddhist monks (Liu Ping-chung and Hayashi Razan, both nominally Buddhist monks, donned Buddhist robes for their formal appearances at court),[182] saw the need for civil and secular rule, as well as an ethical code and the educational system to support it, if they were to make the transition from conquest on horseback to stable, peacetime rule. This Buddhism could not offer and Neo-Confucianism did. Consequently, both rulers gave strong support to the promotion of Neo-Confucian studies, but both held back from establishing the kind of meritocratic civil service system which would have undermined the position of the hereditary military elite.

Khubilai's failure to support Neo-Confucianism completely or to reestablish the examinations leaves him in an anomalous position from the ordinary Chinese point of view, some strange hybrid of a half-sinicized ruler. From the Japanese point of view there was nothing unusual at all in Ieyasu's failure to do this, nothing to detract from his unqualified success as the founder of an enduring, stable regime. More than one observer of the Japanese scene has noted how the relatively decentralized pattern of political and cultural life under the Tokugawa manifested a diversity and dynamism apparently lacking under the more comprehensive but less flexible control of the centralized bureaucracies which emerged in China after Khubilai's time.[183]

If this is so, or even possibly so, it poses a question: might not Neo-Confucianism have fared differently in China had it kept its distance from the dynastic state, and not let orthodoxy become enmeshed in the web of a bureaucratic system? It is a fair question to ask, since Neo-Confucians themselves asked it and held more than one view on the subject. As we have already seen, Khubilai's Neo-Confucian advisers as well as the ruler himself were of two minds on the merits of the examination system. Even at the time of the climactic decision to go ahead, there was opposition to it from scholars as distinguished as Wu Ch'eng, who invoked the authority of Chu Hsi and other Sung patriarchs in an unsuccessful attempt to avert it.

Nevertheless, when in 1313–1315 one of Khubilai's successors finally took steps to "reintroduce" the system, the precedents of both Khubilai and Hsü Heng were cited in its favor.[185] To some extent this may be a contrivance of court politics and of the increasingly assertive School of the Way, invoking and exploiting the prestige of the honored dead for their own purposes. Already Khubilai and Hsü had entered into the contemporary hagiography, as we see in the fulsome tomb inscription for the emperor written by Ou-yang Hsüan (1283–1357).[186] Likening Khubilai to the sage-kings of old, Ou-yang says of him:

> With his heavenly endowment he resumed the lost teaching of the sage-emperors and kings, while Hsü Heng, with the gift of heavenly talents, was able to repossess the untransmitted teaching of the sages and worthies, linking up with the tradition of the Duke of Chou, Confucius, Tseng Tzu, Tzu-ssu, Mencius, and the other noble men who came after them, to become a minister of unparalleled stature in those times. The aspirations of ruler and minister matched perfectly, and all that was enunciated in the emperor's name served to uphold the perfect norm of rulership, set up proper guidelines for the people, resume the lost teaching, and usher in an era of great peace—all as if a myriad ages were fulfilled in one day.[187]

Ou-yang Hsüan was no ordinary hack, writing a conventional eulogy on order, but one of the most celebrated statesmen and historians of his day. Nor was he alone among Chinese in his admiration for Khubilai.[188] Even making allowances for this as a pious tribute to his predecessor as libationer of the Imperial College, we can see how it expresses some of the dominant ideals of the mandarins of the age—the heroic mythology of sage-king and sage-minister, the rediscovery of the lost teaching (with pointed inclusion of the authors of the Four Books and omission of the philosophers), the reconvergence of the orthodox tradition with the practice of kingship to usher in a golden age. Here at last were brought together the "orthodox tradition" and the "Learning of the Emperors" in the person of ruler and minister, exactly as Neo-Confucians had long dreamed.

Other views were held of this pair, of course, much less complimentary. Liu Yin, whom Ou-yang Hsüan also had occasion to eulogize,[189] was highly critical of Hsü's eagerness to serve at court. (Significantly, in their legendary encounter, Hsü defended himself on the ground of his personal responsibility to advance the Way, while Liu insisted on a primary obligation to uphold the purity of the Way.)[190] Ch'iu Chün (1420–1495) in the Ming and Yamazaki Ansai (1618–1682) in Japan were among those who later condemned Hsü on nationalistic grounds.[191] The great Ch'ing historian Chao I challenged the image of Khubilai as a benevolent monarch, excoriating him over his ungovernable appetite for military conquest and his rapacity in exacting revenue from the people.[192] But whether Khubilai is viewed as more of a shogun than a sage-king,[193] or Hsü is seen as easily coopted by him, there is not much question that ruler and reformer collaborated to produce the new situation. By converting the Mongol conquest to Chinese bureaucratic institutions, they rendered it probable that a new civil service system would emerge from the rationalization and routinization of recruitment procedures. By promoting, alongside this, the spread of Neo-Confucian teaching, they posed implicitly the question of how Neo-Confucian values would relate to Mongol power. There would be a persistent disposition among those participating in the system to see these joined—to see fulfilled the long-held ideal of reuniting sage wisdom and imperial power.

Herein lies the basic difference between Khubilai's transitional regime and the more enduring Tokugawa Bakufu in Japan, which easily took the teachings and left the political trappings behind. In the Chinese case, however, it remains to be seen how the Mongols could have been led to accept a civil meritocracy so potentially subversive of their own military rule, and how the Neo-Confucians could be reconciled to an examination system they had so long opposed, as Wu Ch'eng, the leading Neo-Confucian philosopher of that day, still did.

The New Mandarin Orthodoxy

In the *Yüan History's* account of the events which led up to the instituting of the new civil service examinations in 1313–1315, the rescript of Emperor Jen-tsung (Ayurbarwada) in 1313 credits Khubilai with four steps, taken after the Mongol conquest, which naturally led up to the new development: his "establishing of the various offices of [Han Chinese] administration," his "employment of Confucian scholars at court," his "setting up of schools as a training ground for men of talent," and his "plan to maintain a recruitment system."[194] The logical connection among these and with the further step of instituting the examinations is clearly made in the mind of the author of this historic document.[195] It goes on to assert that Khubilai had given his approval to a new system of schools and examinations proposed by Hsü Heng, which would eliminate the composition of *shih* and *fu* poetry and emphasize study of the classics instead, but it is reticent as to the reasons why this plan was never carried out, though it remained ostensibly the intention of Khubilai's successors as well.[196]

A foreshortened account is then given of the Neo-Confucian version of how the recruitment of scholars was conducted in the past, glossing over some of the stickier issues:

Since the Three Dynasties each age has had an examination system with a definite order of priorities. In the recommendation of scholars virtuous conduct is the chief consideration and in the testing of skills proficiency in the classics should come first, with the composition of prose and poetry subordinated to that. The frivolous and fanciful we do not need.[197]

In the discussions at court which led to the drawing up of the new system, its proponents, including Hsü's followers in the Imperial College, emphasized that "the method of selecting scholars should embody the study of the classics with a view to

self-cultivation for the governance of men. The composition of *tz'u* and *fu* poetry is only artful display.[198] Since the Sui and T'ang dynasties there has been exclusive emphasis on the *tz'u* and *fu*. Therefore scholars have become accustomed to superficiality. Now what we propose . . . will emphasize virtuous conduct and an understanding of the classics. If scholars are chosen in this way, they will all be the right kind of men.[199]

Among the members of the Secretarial Council, the ministerial body which backed the change and was asked to work out the details of its implementation, was Ch'eng Chü-fu (1249–1318),[200] a southerner who had become one of the most successful recruiters of scholarly talent for the Yüan dynasty. Ch'eng made specific reference to Chu Hsi's thoughts on the matter. While expressing reservations as to how much of Chu's own prescriptions would be feasible in the given situation, he affirmed the importance of basing the examinations on the classics and interpreting them according to the commentaries of the Ch'eng-Chu school, instead of perpetuating the evils of the T'ang and Sung systems.[201]

Events just prior to this reinforce the impression that the teachings and texts of the Ch'eng-Chu school, as transmitted by Hsü Heng and his group, had reached a new height of influence by the reign of Jen-tsung.[202] In the same year that the new examinations were proposed, Hsü was enshrined in the Confucian temple as a representative of the honored tradition of the Sung masters from Chou Tun-i down to Chu Hsi and Lü Tsu-ch'ien (co-compiler of the *Reflections on Things at Hand*), linking this tradition to the educational and examination system.[203] Increasing emphasis on the Four Books, and in particular the *Great Learning*, was shown by the formal presentation to the court, at the time of Jen-tsung's designation as heir apparent, of Chen Te-hsiu's compilation the *Extended Meaning of the Great Learning (Ta-hsüeh yen-i)*, an abridgment of which was translated into Mongol. In terms reminiscent of past imperial encomiums, the future emperor and sponsor of the new examination orthodoxy said of this work, with its emphasis on "self-cultivation for the governance of men," that "this one work is sufficient for the governing of all-under-Heaven."[204]

The new system as actually promulgated in 1315 had both noteworthy features and notable omissions. For example, though a great deal of outward tribute was paid to virtue—the hallowed Neo-Confucian idea of the selection of candidates on the basis of character—there is little to indicate that this was more than a preliminary screening device.[205] A significant innovation was a quota system for Mongols and Central Asians which insured that the two together would comprise half the graduates and Chinese the other half.[206]

There was a precedent for this in the official schools of Khubilai's time,[207] but it was new to the examination system. From a modern egalitarian, or even typically Chinese, point of view, this could be seen as discrimination in favor of the elite minority and against the Chinese, whose "equal representation" was out of proportion to their numbers in the population.[208] Seen, however, as an effort to achieve minority participation in the majority culture or the established system, it might be thought of as roughly analogous to "affirmative-action quotas" in contemporary welfare legislation. The same could not be said, however, for the provision which placed Mongols one grade higher if they succeeded in passing the more difficult examination for the Chinese. In any case this preferential treatment was of no lasting importance; a political trade-off to win Mongol support, it did not become a permanent feature of the later system.

Far more significant was the content of the new examinations held on the metropolitan and provincial levels. Mongol and Central Asian candidates took these in two sections. The first consisted of questions on Chu Hsi's versions of the *Great Learning, Analects, Mencius,* and the *Mean* (listed in that order in accordance with Chu Hsi's recommendation;[209] the second consisted of a question on contemporary issues, to be answered with an essay of 500 characters.

For Chinese the requirements were far more difficult. The first part dealt with the Four Books in a manner similar to the above, but an additional section dealt intensively with one among the *Odes, Documents, Changes, Spring and Autumn Annals,* and *Record of Rites,* each with approved commentary by Chu Hsi, Ch'eng I, or some other Sung school scholar (except that for the *Record of Rites* one would still use the old commentaries). Answers for the Four Books would be 300 characters in length, those for one of the classics would be 500 characters. One had to show a knowledge of text and commentary, and conclude with one's own opinion. The Chinese had a further section dealing with documentary forms and old-style *fu,* as well as a section on the classics and histories in relation to contemporary problems, the latter to be answered in an essay of 1,000 characters.[210]

Taking the long view again, the much simpler requirements for the Mongols and the Central Asians than for the Chinese are of consequence only insofar as they encouraged many of the former to participate in the system during the remaining decades of the dynasty's life. Of greater significance for later centuries is the fact of simplification itself and how it was done, that is, how priority was given to the Four Books, how the problem of commentaries was reduced to just one authoritative version, and how these two together became the one common element in both types of exams. That element is the equivalent of the "lowest common denominator" in the Neo-Confucian teaching as defined for practical purposes by Hsü Heng in the official program of instruction.

Already in the official schools and academies the basic curriculum of elementary education had tended to follow this pattern because of the ease with which the student could master the Four Books with Chu's commentary as compared to the difficulty of the more voluminous text and commentary for the Five (or Six) Classics.[211] Thus Chu Hsi's and Hsü Heng's sense of what was educationally practicable probably had a significant bearing on the outcome.

If we may judge the types of questions asked in these examinations from some specimens that have been preserved, they would seem to have required of the candidate a reasonable familiarity with the thought content of the classics (as distinct from rote memorization of texts), an ability to relate this judgmentally to contemporary problems of a concrete sort (such as water control), and some sense of the orthodox tradition as a set of enduring values that must be reactivated in each age.[212] There is, understandably, a greater emphasis in examinations for would-be officials on the kind of problems which would be encountered in the ruler-minister relationship than on the family relationships so stressed in the *Elementary Learning*. In this respect they confirm the tendency to draw most heavily on that side of the orthodox tradition expressed in the Learning of the Emperors, while in the process pitching the curriculum at a level which would minimize the cultural differences between Chinese and non-Chinese participants.

A measure of the reduced scale and compression of the orthodox tradition which the above represents is to be found in Chu Hsi's own detailed recommendations for the examinations. Without attempting to give a full account of the comprehensive knowledge which Chu would have his aspirants for office command, the following may suffice to make the point.

In addition to the classic texts and commentaries required of the Chinese candidates, Chu would have expected a familiarity with the commentaries of nine or ten other scholars of the Sung alone on each of the major classics, such as the *Changes* or the *Documents*. Chu included even the views of such scholars as Wang An-shih and Su Shih (1036–1101), usually anathema to the Ch'eng-Chu school. It is important, says Chu, to read the original texts for oneself; however,

The words of the sages and worthies are profound and highly refined; they cannot be easily fathomed. Their systems, nomenclature, practices, and sense of priorities are all beyond our ordinary experience today. Therefore in studying the classics one must have regard for the considered views of former scholars and extrapolate from them, aware that they are not necessarily conclusive but must be weighed as to what they understood and what they missed; then finally all this must be reflected upon in one's own mind to verify it.[213]

Among the nonorthodox philosophers of early China whom Chu would include are Hsün Tzu, Yang Hsiung, Wang Ch'ung, Han Fei Tzu, Lao Tzu, and Chuang Tzu, as well as the various Sung thinkers.[214] "We cannot fail to learn from their strong points or confront their weaknesses."[215]

With regard to the histories, the discussion should include the successive changes from past to present, the rise and fall of dynasties, the periods of order and disorder, and the successes and failures. Among contemporary problems, the major ones are rites and music, governmental systems, astronomy, geography, military strategy, penal systems, and all the needs of the time that require attention.[216]

Among the relevant texts to be included in these discussions are the *Tso Commentary on the Spring and Autumn Annals*, the *Dialogues of the States (Kuo yü)*, *Records of the Grand Historian*, the *Histories of the Former and Latter Han*, the *Three Kingdoms*, *History of Chin*, *History of the Southern and Northern Dynasties*, the *Old* and *New T'ang History*, and the *History of the Five Dynasties Period*. A similarly copious body of documentary literature is cited as relevant to the discussion of contemporary problems.[217]

Perhaps this much will suggest what a store of learning Chu Hsi expected candidates to possess. In the language and layout of the Yüan curriculum for Chinese there is just enough similarity in details to Chu's plan (for instance, in the subject categories, the length of the answers, and the importance of concluding with one's own views) for us to surmise that the Yüan authors are looking over their shoulders at Chu's model, as Ch'eng Chü-fu's earlier statement implied. To adopt that model whole, however, was out of the question, as Wu Ch'eng, the principal critic of the new system, himself recognized when he came up with his own abridgment of the Sung masters' views on the subject. In the skirmishing at court which preceded the adoption of the Yüan system, Wu objected to it on both curricular and procedural grounds, citing Chu Hsi's "Personal Proposals on Schools and Examinations" as well as the views of Hu Yüan (993–1059)[218] and Ch'eng Hao in support of his own position. We have only a brief account of Wu's digest to go by and a synopsis of his educational curriculum,[219] which do not permit a full comparison with Chu's plan, but Wu's ideas appear to have been similar to Chu's in form and spirit, especially in his deemphasis on literary composition and his stress on an understanding of the classics and history, a knowledge of practical affairs, and exemplary conduct.

Like Chu, Wu is catholic in his acceptance of a variety of commentators; he does not call for exclusive reliance on the interpretations of Chu Hsi or the Sung school (as the new system did). Like Chu and earlier Neo-Confucians in the Yüan who considered competitive examinations degrading, Wu has a fundamental aversion to the competitive character of the examinations; he prefers a series of achievement tests, based on a fixed curriculum, that would also provide an opportunity to observe the conduct of the candidate in his personal relations with his parents, family, clan, friends, community, and people in general. There is no suggestion of making any special concessions to Mongols or Central Asians.

If in these respects Wu can be considered more faithful to Chu Hsi and the earlier Neo-Confucians, he and the new system are at one in adopting the Four Books into the canon. In the further inclusion of the *Elementary Learning* Wu follows Hsü Heng's curriculum for the Imperial College, as the new system does not. Thus to some extent both Wu and the new system reflect later adaptations of the Learning of the Way already found in Hsü's curriculum. In other respects Wu offers an authentic Neo-Confucian alternative to the new Mandarin orthodoxy, inasmuch as he would resist the most impersonal and dehumanizing features of the competitive system, which, by putting a premium on a literal command of classic texts at the expense of personal realization of their truths, were to alienate later Neo-Confucians.

For Wu, as for Chu Hsi, these were matters of deep principle. We may wonder, and wish we knew from Wu Ch'eng, how a more personalized approach could ever be adapted to the needs of a large, relatively egalitarian bureaucracy without making some compromises. In any event, failing to win acceptance of his own position, Wu chose to withdraw from the government.[220] In this he may be considered to typify the spirit of other Neo-Confucians, with at least as much claim to speak for orthodox tradition as the new mandarins, who continued to offer an authentic alternative outside the official system.

For their part, the authors of the Yüan system took such latitude as Chu Hsi himself had allowed when he said that "reform must be adapted to the times in order to effect a gradual return to the ancient system,"[221] or when he stated that the first priority must always lie with the *Great Learning's* teachings of self-cultivation to develop the moral nature and the proper way of human conduct embedded in one's own heart-and-mind. "If the scholar can truly apply himself to this, then not only can he cultivate his own person but by extension he can govern others as he governs himself."[222] If only this could be done, even a system less than ideal could be lived with; Chu's selections in *Reflections on Things at Hand*[223] recognize that if one is truly committed to the Way one's learning need not be impaired by participation in the examinations.

The Dubious Triumph of Neo-Confucian Orthodoxy

If some sort of compromise was inevitable, a case can be made that the content of the new examinations, simplified though it undoubtedly was, emerged as the product of a long process of distillation in the School of the Way and a concomitant adaptation to the requirements of the Yüan situation. In 1315 we are worlds away from the high culture of the Sung which Chu Hsi so majestically presided over as a scholar and philosopher.[224] When Chu projected his own ideal system, he prescribed for the leisured and cultured Sung gentleman who would represent the full range of thought and sophisticated scholarship in his time. Chu's curriculum was a mirror image of his whole approach to learning in its amplitude, structure, balance, and integration; consciously orthodox but not narrowly doctrinaire; deeply serious but not cramped and crabbed; idealistic perhaps, but not so far-fetched that later scholars of broad tastes and even different philosophical loyalties could not regard it as a fitting and practicable model for those who would be entrusted with heavy responsibility for the conduct of affairs.[225]

It was no less characteristic of Chu that he should have anticipated even more basic educational needs than these and should have provided the wherewithal for his followers in the Yüan to advance the Way in a very different set of cultural circumstances, one in which Confucian humaneness, surrounded by the ruins of a civilization and vast human tragedy, would have to settle for a minimum of scholarly refinement. Hsü Heng had the unusual experience for a Confucian of having to learn a barbarian tongue in order to communicate his message to a ruler who knew little Chinese,[226] of having to practice Confucian reciprocity in a multiracial, multicultural context. This basic fact of his experience of life, plus his own zeal for the Way, made him a rare case of a Confucian with a mission who served as a missionary in the more typical religious sense, something like the Buddhist Kumarajiva in fourth-century China or the Jesuits later at the Ming and Manchu courts.

Against this background we can appreciate how the new mandarins fell short of fulfilling Chu Hsi's ideal and how their new curriculum would seem to be only a stripped-down version of Chu's. What is truly extraordinary about this new orthodoxy, however, is that it proved capable of surviving the vicissitudes of Mongol politics and even the Mongols' downfall. When a nativist backlash among the Mongols brought the shelving of the examinations in 1335, it was the support of Mongols and Central Asians, along with the Chinese, which helped bring the system back into effect within a few years. As John Dardess has said: "There was no other cause, no alternative principle, no competing movement that could serve to bind the ethnic classes together and permit the Yüan bureaucracy to function normally once again."[227] Quite apart from the functioning of the bureaucracy, there is much evidence in the studies of Ch'en Yüan and in the recent literature that Neo-Confucian ideals had taken deep root among Mongol and Central Asian converts, and were a moving force among self-motivated individuals who proved capable of taking leadership even in situations where the bureaucracy had ceased to function effectively.[228] The extraordinary number of examination graduates who sacrificed their lives for the Yüan dynasty at its fall belies any thought that their Neo-Confucianism was skin deep.[229]

The Yüan system had limitations as a method of recruitment. It provided only a fraction of those employed in Yüan officialdom, the others gaining access by other types of appointment. Nor as an orthodoxy was it so pervasive. The Yüan did not attempt to achieve ideological conformity of the kind which was to make the Ming and Ch'ing systems far more repressive. In these senses the Mongols fell short of establishing a full-fledged Mandarin orthodoxy. They did, however, provide the model and content for what was to follow.

The successor Ming dynasty would have no need for ethnic quotas or interracial consensus, but its peasant founder, Chu Yüan-chang, shared Khubilai's low esteem for literary refinement, while feeling no less of a desire than Khubilai for a curriculum and examination system which would promote basic literacy and practical virtue rather than produce pundits. Instead of scrapping the Mongol examinations, he favored something much like them for the Chinese themselves, settling essentially for the Four Books and Chu's commentaries.[230]

This confirmation of the Yüan pattern in the early Ming took place in a climate of thought relatively free of scholastic partisanship or pressure for ideological conformity, which only developed later.[231] The new curriculum had come to be widely accepted, and there is no sign of its being contested at this time. In setting up the system that was to last into the twentieth century, the Ming founder Chu Yüan-chang (Ming T'ai-tsu) simply reaffirmed a consensus view (and enjoyed what prestige might accrue to him from sharing the same surname as Chu). He was not imposing his own creed in an atmosphere of intolerance and repression, or indulging in an excess of Han chauvinism.

Thus Ming T'ai-tsu's proclamation in 1370 reestablishing the examinations adopts essentially the same stance as Jen-tsung in the Yüan. To have some kind of definite system was the traditional practice, the proclamation says, though the system of each earlier dynasty had its own merits and demerits. In the Han, T'ang, and Sung the trouble lay in overemphasis on literary composition to the neglect of classical study and practical virtue. In the early Yüan the old system was reestablished momentarily, but powerful families and self-seeking individuals quickly exploited it for their own benefit, and worthy men, ashamed to join in such a scramble for office and emoluments, hid themselves in the mountains and forests. Nothing is said in this connection about Chinese unwillingness to serve a foreign dynasty, about the reform of 1313–1315, or about the debate which preceded it. These are all dead issues, and T'ai-tsu proceeds to reinstitute exactly the same system as the late Yüan's without acknowledging it. He will see to it personally that men are selected for their practical virtue and understanding of the classics, and will guarantee that no office, civil or military, will be awarded except through this uniform system. Thus the proclamation appears to range the emperor on the side of the Neo-Confucians who disdain sordid competition, but it implies that this is a defect attaching to its former sponsors, not to the system itself. It will be enough now for the emperor to guarantee equity, and to issue a stern warning, as he does in the conclusion of the proclamation, against the pursuit of power and privilege by self-seeking individuals, who will meet with strong condemnation and heavy punishment.[232]

Actually, T'ai-tsu had second thoughts about the value of the system in turning out men of practical ability, and suspended it for over ten years, but none of his doubts had to do with the content of the exams, which was even more squarely focused on the Four Books and Chu Hsi after its resumption in 1384.[233] Later, when the official Ming position was codified in the *Compendia on the Four Books, Five Classics, and Human Nature and Principle (Ssu-shu, Wu-ching, Hsing-li ta-ch'üan)*, the discussion of the examination system contained therein said nothing of Chu's "Personal Proposals Concerning the Schools and Examinations," or of any of the issues in the Yüan debate, but confined itself to the quotations found in the *Reflections on Things at Hand* and Chu's other writings to the effect that the system itself should not be blamed if the motivations of the individual scholar rendered him susceptible to corrupt influences.[234]

Much later a leading eighteenth-century historian, Ch'ien Tahsin (1728–1804), reviewing this phase in the development of the examination system, found it necessary to point out the significance of what had happened in these formative years. He noted that in the Yüan the Chinese were still expected to answer questions on the Five Classics, and that to be examined on just the Four Books, which were much easier to understand, was originally a special concession to the non-Chinese, intended as part of a sequence from the easier to the more difficult and not meant to displace the Five Classics, as became the case in the Ming and Ch'ing.[235]

By Ch'ien's time that concession had long since become the norm for all, not only because of its simplicity, practicality, and bureaucratic convenience, but no doubt also because the lowest common denominator of ethical cultivation and public morality, as set forth in relation to the Four Books and the *Great Learning* in particular, had proven itself serviceable to many people, including, as was subsequently shown, the Koreans and the Japanese as well as the Mongols and Manchus.[236]

If one were inclined to think of tradition as merely an accretion from the past, the formulation and reformulation of Neo-Confucian orthodoxies would show that in this case it was even more a process of distillation and compression, a fundamentalist effort to identify and reassert the irreducible ethical core of the teaching. What further marks this effort as Neo-Confucian, i.e., a new teaching, is that even in the case of Chu Hsi, the grand synthesizer of all previous philosophy, his contribution was most distinctively made in formulating a new basic education and educational philosophy for Confucians. As we have seen, this centered increasingly on the Four Books, the *Great Learning* among the Four Books, and the eightfold formula for self-cultivation within the *Great Learning*.

But further, even where Chu Hsi had held in the final balance both the investigation of things and the rectification of the mind, both scholarship and moral discipline, his immediate successors were compelled to strip down further, to give primary attention to the moral mind at some expense to the objective investigation of principles in things. First there was the need to muster the moral energy required to repossess and reassert the Way, to "find the Way for oneself." Then in the Yüan there was the need to find it in other men, across linguistic and cultural barriers. The moral mind was the key, and the moral nature the basis for any consensus as to social or political action.

We have seen how this belief in the common moral nature was expressed in Hsü Heng's educational efforts among the Mongols and how his instruction of the emperor was predicated on the applicability to Mongol rulers of the same "mind-rectification" Chu Hsi and others had urged on Sung rulers. This was no less true of the principal proponent of the new examination system, Ch'eng Chü-fu, who subscribed to the same basic doctrine. The goodness of the moral nature in all men and the educability of all men were the true basis of government, which Ch'eng cited directly as grounds for maintaining the school and examination systems.[237] Along with them went the ruler's obligation to cultivate and rectify his own mind.

The mind is the ruler of the self and the root of all affairs. . . . Thus the sage-emperors and kings attached prime importance to the clarifying of the mind *(ch'ing hsin).* . . . If the mind is clear, corruption and deceit will not dare show themselves . . . laws and systems will operate unhindered, and public discipline will be upheld. There will be a surcease from calamities and the world will be at peace.[238]

Wing-tsit Chan has noted with surprise how little attention is given in the Yüan to the other half of the Ch'eng-Chu equation, the investigation of principle to the utmost *(ch'iung-li).*[239] This is not because principle is forsworn,[240] but because principle as manifest in the moral nature and the rectification of the mind preempt scholarly study and the pursuit of principle in bookish learning. In other words the School of the Way was at this time still as much a school of mind as of principle, and the two had not yet become separated along sectarian lines.

This common denominator of mind correction and cultivation was as much the property of the schools as of the official system. Indeed, as we have seen, in the Yüan it had its first formulation in the schools, and from there successfully penetrated the system. (Hsiung Ho, writing in 1307 to commemorate Chu Hsi's teaching at the K'ao-t'ing Academy somewhat more than a century before, speaks of this teaching as having been carried and become accepted throughout the land, much more rapidly than even Confucius' teaching had become accepted.)[241] But if this was success for the orthodox tradition, just who succeeded in the matter of the civil service examinations remained unclear. The Mongols, as a dynasty, were not thereby saved. The Neo-Confucians at court were not spared from the demands which their commitment to it made upon them.

In the schools and in the minds of independent scholars the compromises and concessions of those associated with the new Mandarin orthodoxy continued to be judged, as they would have been by Chu Hsi himself, according to the highest standards of the tradition as a whole. Fortunately for that tradition, there was room in it for more than just the hard core of rigorists, and bureaucratic control had not yet extended itself, as far as it attempted to do in the Ming and Ch'ing, over all the schools and solitary scholars who pursued other lines of thought. To this question we shall return after considering in Part II the background of the intellectual issues which would come increasingly into dispute as the early consensus evaporated.

Part II: THE NEO-CONFUCIAN LEARNING OF THE MIND-AND-HEART

It was some years ago, on a visit to Korea, that I first climbed up to the Potter's Mountain Academy *(Tosan sowon)*, and spotted among the books in the library of Yi T'oegye (1501–1570) the title of a book in Chinese, the *Hsin ching*. Not long before this I had made a visit to the famous Korean Buddhist monastery of Hae-in sa, earlier identified with the Three Treatises and Flower Garland schools but more recently with Zen. There the woodblocks of the Korean Tripitaka are kept, and the visitor is given as a souvenir a printed copy from a woodblock of the scripture known as the *Heart Sutra (Hsin ching)*, one of the most celebrated texts of Mahayana Buddhist philosophy. With this experience so recently in mind, it was natural for me to associate the *Hsin ching* in T'oegye's library with the *Heart Sutra*, but no less natural for me, knowing T'oegye's reputation as a champion of Neo-Confucian orthodoxy and foe of Buddhism, to register some surprise that he would have kept a copy of this "heretical" work on his shelves.

One look at the contents, however, cleared up the mystery. This *Hsin ching* was a work by the late Sung scholar-official Chen Te-hsiu (1178–1235). It presented what might be considered a Neo-Confucian alternative to the *Heart Sutra;* that is, it offered a different view of the nature and cultivation of the "mind-and-heart," as we must render the Chinese word *hsin* to convey both its cognitive and affective functions. As a concise anthology of selected passages from the Confucian classics and from works of later philosophers of the Confucian school (especially of the Sung period), it made some claim to represent canonical scripture. Thus we may consider the title to signify, within this tradition, the *Classic of the Mind-and-Heart* or, for short, the *Heart Classic*.

Perhaps a better claim for its place as a classic in the Western sense would be that it came to be viewed as a classic statement among Neo-Confucians of a spiritual ideal and approach to mind-cultivation that dominated the orthodox Ch'eng-Chu school for many centuries in China, Korea, and Japan. Though almost unnoticed in this century and rarely mentioned in modern works on the history and thought of East Asia, this *Heart Classic* had a prominent place in Neo-Confucian academies down into the nineteenth century, was frequently lectured on at court in Korea, and was greatly admired by Confucian activists in late Tokugawa and early Meiji Japan.

In the context of Chen Te-hsiu's thought as a whole, and its place in the development of the Ch'eng-Chu school in its formative years, the *Heart Classic* and Chen's other major works open up dimensions of Neo-Confucian thought hitherto ignored or misunderstood, and suggest solutions to problems that have long gone unsolved. Through these works one may gain access to the larger Neo-Confucian "Learning of the Mind-and-Heart," which preceded the divergence of Neo-Confucianism into schools of principle and of mind, and which represents the original matrix from which emerged the thought of Wang Yang-ming (1472–1529). It is also a key to understanding how Chu Hsi's thought became formulated into an "orthodoxy." Finally, it contributes to a proper evaluation of the influence of Buddhism on Neo-Confucian mind-culture.

Chu Hsi had conceded that before the time of Ch'eng I, Confucianism lacked a true science of the mind, a way of dealing with the inner world of the spirit, while Buddhism had lacked the means which Confucianism always possessed for dealing with the outer world of human affairs. According to him Ch'eng I, drawing on the resources of the classical tradition, had succeeded in reconciling the two by his discovery of a method of spirituality and mental discipline which was expressed in terms of reverent seriousness *(ching)*. The modern scholar Ch'ien Mu speaks of Ch'eng's synthesis as a way of dealing with both "the ground of the mind-and-heart" and the external world.[1] To meet this need arose the Learning of the

Mind-and-Heart of which Chen's *Heart Classic* became a quintessential expression.

This learning arose in eleventh- and twelfth-century Sung China as one among several trends of thought which converged into the Ch'eng-Chu teaching. Closely identified with it were such concepts as the "Learning of the Emperors and Kings," the "Emperors' and Kings' System of the Mind-and-Heart," and the "Art (or Practice) of Governing the Mind," all relating to the ruler's cultivation of the mind-and-heart as the principal means of governance. It was believed that universal self-cultivation through rectification of the mind was the best way to "govern men" or "govern the state."

Another formulation of this learning was the doctrine of the substance *(t'i)*, functioning *(yung)*, and literary expression *(wen)* or transmission *(ch'uan)* of the Way. This meant that the enduring principles of the Way should be made manifest in human activities, while the written testimony of the sages' Way would insure their perpetuation. As the Learning of the Mind-and-Heart assumed greater importance in the Ch'eng-Chu school, the transmission from mind to mind, through the insights of inspired individuals morally and spiritually attuned to the mind of the sages, came to overshadow the earlier emphasis on the written record as an expression of the Way. In this view, the light of revelation, instead of inhering in classic texts themselves, had to leap over the centuries from Mencius to the Ch'eng brothers before the texts and the Way could be brilliantly illumined again. Still another formulation of this idea, found in Chu Hsi's exposition of the *Great Learning*, spoke of the "whole substance and great functioning" of the Way. This brought out the mind-and-heart's full potential for practical activity that would conform to the Way and benefit mankind.

These ideas were articulated in lectures on the classics at court by prominent Sung scholar-statesmen (see Part I), in the memorials of the Ch'eng brothers and Chu Hsi, and in the introductory matter for Chu Hsi's key commentaries on the *Mean* and the *Great Learning*. In the last they were closely associated with Chu's concept of the orthodox tradition or transmission of the Way. These concepts gained prominence as Chu's Commentaries on the Four Books became standard texts in Neo-Confucian academies, and became prominently identified with the School of the Way. Thus in the early years of the movement after Chu's death, the Learning of the Mind-and-Heart was almost synonymous with the School of the Way or the Ch'eng-Chu school.

Originally this learning was put forward as an alternative to Buddhism, and especially to Ch'an. From the beginning it had a political and social orientation and was not derivative from Buddhist teachings and practices concerning the mind. Illustrative of this is the term "System of the Mind-and-Heart" *(hsin-fa)*, often used synonymously with the "Learning of the Mind-and-Heart." Though it may sound Buddhistic, *hsin-fa* is of Sung Neo-Confucian origin, and its usage in this sense was, as we shall see, probably taken up by Buddhists after the term had gained wide currency among the educated class of Sung China.

As the Neo-Confucian movement grew and became differentiated, attempts to systematize this learning produced works of a more specialized character, placing heavy emphasis on methods of mind-rectification, disciplining of the desires, reforming of human weaknesses. In their pursuit of the high ideal of sagehood and service to mankind, Neo-Confucians insisted on firm assertion of the moral will, strict self-control, and the practice of an extreme self-denial which gave this early formulation of Neo-Confucian orthodoxy a stern, rigoristic quality. While this last trait was characteristic in general of the early followers of Chu Hsi, it was especially true of Chen Te-hsiu, the preeminent intellectual and political leader of the Neo-Confucian movement in the early thirteenth century. An active, committed statesman and an enormously productive scholar, in whom there is no trace of Ch'an quietism or anti-intellectualism, Chen gave classic expression to this moralistic doctrine in his works the *Extended Meaning of the Great Learning* and the *Classic of the Mind-and-Heart*.

Neo-Confucianism in this form, far from representing a conservative ideology or defense of the status quo, was at once traditionalist and reformist. It drew from its severe, moralistic religiosity the dynamism of an intense faith and a commitment which carried the early movement through political repression, social ostracism, and subjection to barbarian conquest. Many converts to the movement in the thirteenth century became activists at the Mongol court, and their leader Hsü Heng (1209–1281) articulated the doctrine in a form understandable to non-Chinese peoples and mundane rulers little interested in the metaphysical subtleties of the Sung philosophers. These reformers succeeded in displacing the old literocratic "orthodoxy" of the Sung and Chin dynasties, and established basic texts of Chu Hsi as the core curriculum in official schools and later in the new civil service examinations.

The study of texts and the use of lectures and discussions at court gave the new teaching an explicit formulation which provided the basis for a public philosophy. This in turn functioned as the ideal and ethos of the Confucians serving the Mongol state. After surviving the challenge to their leadership role under the Yüan, they became strengthened in their bureaucratic functions as mandarins of the successor Ming state and won confirmation of the new teaching as its official ideology.

In one sense this process of institutionalization reasserted Chinese tradition by reaffirming Confucian doctrine in its more ample Ch'eng-Chu formulation, while the Chinese imperial bureaucracy too was being reestablished in a more mature form. But it is important to recognize that the new teaching, while representing the quintessence of Neo-Confucian thought, had transcended its cultural limits and achieved a certain universality by emphasizing the lowest common denominator in its philosophy of human nature; that is, it taught a belief in the inherent moral nature of man irrespective of cultural differences, his perfectibility through self-cultivation, and the achievement of an ordered human community through universal self-improvement. Thus while the Sung philosophy had articulated the concept of sagehood as the dominant ideal of the educated leadership class in its struggle for survival, the new ideological "orthodoxy," through the process of adaptation to non-Chinese conquerors and later to the peasant tastes of the Ming founder, attained a broader base and outreach.

On this basis the Learning of the Mind-and-Heart expressed not only the mind of the sages but the mind-and-heart of a common humanity, and stressed the obligation of the ruler to identify with both. It was egalitarian as well as elitist, ecumenical as well as orthodox. It was, if not all things to all men, at least founded on a consensus rather than being exclusivist. To the extent that it spoke to the common mind-and-heart, this learning could be adopted by non-Chinese, as well as Chinese, and the adaptation it made in the Yüan period anticipated the adjustment which Neo-Confucianism would make later to the other non-Chinese peoples of East Asia.

In its most concrete form this new "orthodoxy" was represented by the Four Books with Chu Hsi's commentaries, supplemented by other Neo-Confucian writings such as the *Elementary Learning* and *Reflections on Things at Hand*. These were understood to express the mind of the sages, but as interpreted through the minds of other would-be sages in the persons of scholars, teachers, and rulers. It was in this arena that the utter simplicity and adaptability of the learning showed its own limitations. The pragmatic views and despotic actions of rulers evoked covert, and sometimes overt, opposition from principled scholars and teachers. The "mind-and-heart" which was to become the ground for asserting the Oneness of the Three Teachings (Buddhism, Taoism, and Confucianism) in the early Ming came into conflict with those followers of Chu Hsi who upheld the Master's rejection of facile syncretisms and pragmatic philosophies.

Embedded in Neo-Confucian tradition and reactivated by later thinkers, in response to local circumstances and temporal needs, were both the conservative and liberal—and sometimes indeed fundamentalist or even radical—views of this "learning." In more peaceful and prosperous times, the high idealism of the early movement, which evoked heroic commitment to the Way in periods of crisis, encountered resistance to the extreme demands for self-sacrifice which it made upon the individual.

In the subsequent development of the Learning of the Mind-and-Heart, in the Yüan, Ming, and Ch'ing periods, in Korea and in Japan, there was continuing debate between those who held to the letter of the sages' teaching as found in scripture and those who exercised their own minds over the sages' prescriptions for action and self-reflection. It is a sign of this fretful ambiguity at the heart of orthodoxy that the Learning of the Mind-and-Heart continued to be a wellspring of creative thought and action among both those who avowed that orthodoxy and those who, disavowing it, were challenged to go beyond it.

In the Ming period one of the most creative interpreters of this doctrine was Wang Yang-ming (1472–1529), with whose name and teaching this learning came to be prominently identified, his views resembling in certain respects those of Lu Hsiang-shan (1139–1192) in the Sung. The two have become known as the Lu-Wang "School of the Mind" (*hsin-hsüeh*), though there was in fact no "school" connecting them. But it is rather with the earlier development of the Ch'eng-Chu Learning of the Mind-and-Heart that I shall deal here, tracing it from Chen Te-hsiu in the late Sung, through Hsü Heng, the leader of this school in the Yüan period, into the fourteenth and fifteenth centuries, when it became fully established as both the official ideology and the orthodox teaching of Ming China.

The Synthetic "Classic of the Mind-and-Heart"

Chen Te-hsiu's *Heart Classic*,[2] we must admit from the start, is a pastiche of quotations from the Confucian classics and Neo-Confucian philosophers. In this sense it is unoriginal, and some observers would quickly dismiss it as merely a ritualistic invocation of the past—nothing at all new or noteworthy. Nevertheless, Chen's highly selective arrangement of these texts has produced a concise statement with its own distinctive emphases, recapitulating key Neo-Confucian doctrines and highlighting some that would otherwise have played a less crucial role in the movement.

The opening passages illustrate Chen's method. With no prologue or preface declaring his intentions, Chen starts out by citing a relatively obscure passage from the *Book of Documents*, attributed to the sage-king Yü: "The mind of man is insecure, the mind of the Way is barely perceptible. Have utmost refinement and singleness of mind. Hold fast the Mean!"[3] Though obscure in itself, the passage had already been given great prominence by Chu Hsi in his preface to the *Mean (Chung-yung)*, and Chen proceeds to quote the latter as direct commentary on this line:

The mind-and-heart as the empty spirit and consciousness is one and undivided, but there is a difference between the human mind and the moral mind, depending on whether it arises from the selfishness that is identified with the physical form or originates in the correctness of the innate moral imperative, in accordance with which consciousnesses differ. The former may be precarious and insecure, the latter so elusive as to be barely perceptible. All men have this physical form and even the most intelligent invariably possess the human mind, while even the most stupid possess the mind of the Way. If these two are mixed in the human heart and we do not know how to control them, the insecure will become even more insecure, the barely perceptible [Way] will become even less perceptible, and the impartiality of Heaven's principle [in the moral nature] will have no way of overcoming the selfishness of human desires.

"Refinement" means to discriminate between the two and not let them get mixed. "Singlemindedness" [Oneness] means to hold on to the correctness of the original mind and not become separated from it. If one pursues this task without the slightest interruption, making sure that the mind of the Way is always master and the human mind heeds its commands, then what is insecure will become secure, what is barely perceptible will become more manifest, and whether in action or in quiescence one will not err through going too far or not far enough.[4]

The significant aspects of this selection are manifold. One becomes immediately aware that the classical quotations chosen are pretexts for the propounding of Neo-Confucian moral philosophy, and not necessarily representative of the original classics themselves. The commentary bears the message and focuses directly on the mind and human nature. Here Chu Hsi presents in sharp contrast the fallibility and instability of the human mind, barely able to perceive the true Way, and a Heaven-bestowed nature that is good and potentially perfect. Recognizing his own susceptibility to selfish desires, man must struggle to assert the command of the moral will over this divided mind.

Nowhere in the classics themselves is the problem of selfish desire so prominently featured. We recall, however, the initial formulation of Buddhism in the Four Noble Truths, which identify desire and selfish craving as the essential human problem, and we realize that Chen is pressing the claim for a Neo-Confucian solution to the same problem, but one which will not, like Buddhism, call into question ethical commitments and obligations. To a lesser extent this same approach is made to the secondary theme of action and nonaction, the classic problem of Taoism, for which the Neo-Confucians offer a new spiritual integration embracing action and quiescence. Instead of just reciting an ancient litany, Chen is marshaling the resources of the classical tradition in response to these specific challenges.

Chen's next selections, from the *Odes* and the *Changes*, stress singleness of purpose, an undivided mind, and a moral firmness which comes from complete integration of the person with fixed principles.[5] Deeply rooted in constant values, one can achieve a moral freedom that is not contingent on social approval or disapproval, that is unaffected by economic circumstance and independent of political pressure. To be free within from all hypocrisy, to lead no double life, to be rid of false pretensions are the requisites for those who would achieve true sincerity, and thus be at peace, at ease, with themselves. There is an overriding insistence on moral and spiritual realities, realities one must confront when alone with oneself. Here the representative quotation is from the *Mean* (*Chung-yung* 1) and *Great Learning* (*Ta-hsüeh* 5): "The noble man is watchful over himself when alone." It is accompanied by passages from the *Odes* and *Changes* affirming the unseen presence of immutable values and the reality of an invisible spiritual order, manifesting themselves in the observable character and conduct of the person.[6]

Other quotations from early classics speak of the sage-kings and noble men of the past who maintained an attitude of reverent piety, living constantly on a high spiritual plane. There are passages in which the Confucian virtue of *ching* may be understood as an intense seriousness and concentration on the matter at hand, but others, in keeping with the teaching of the Ch'eng brothers and Chu Hsi, which invoke the ancient piety toward Heaven-and-earth as an undifferentiated reverence toward the whole creative power of the universe. To the Neo-Confucians this attitude of constant mindfulness is the essential link between man and the universe, the point of integration between the creativity of Heaven-and-earth and man's vital essence.

Mindfulness is one and undifferentiated, as well as being single-minded, in the sense that its reverence is directed toward no specific object of worship but holds all things in proper respect. That is, it holds all things to the highest standard by which they should be respected. "The noble man is ever reverent"[7] is an utterance, attributed to Confucius in the *Record of Rites,* cited by Chen and recited innumerable times by later Neo-Confucians. It conveys the sense that one should deal with all persons as if they had a high dignity and all things as if they had an infinite value. This is a matter not merely of recognizing inherent qualities but of enhancing their value by bringing something to them from one's own creative consciousness—joining the value principles in one's own mind to the principles inherent in things.

Another important quotation is from the *Book of Changes,* cited by Ch'eng I as the key to the noble man's integration of his interior life with his activity in the world: "He is reverent in order to make his inner life straight, and righteous [dutiful] in order to make his outer life square."[8] Ch'eng I's gloss on this text, cited here by Chen, identifies *ching* or reverence with the state of interior integration which is the precondition for the natural expression of man's humaneness in the specific outward forms which duty or propriety dictate in given cases.[9]

The constant mindfulness of the noble man also expresses itself in a responsiveness to the needs of others, and requires of him that he exercise unremitting care in regard to the effects of his own actions upon others. It is a matter of deep seriousness how one's actions affect one's fellows, and this shows itself in a heightened sense of responsibility, especially for leadership and the exercise of power.

In practice this reverence/seriousness is to be expressed in personal modesty and self-restraint, lest one abuse oneself or others. A deep humility too will recognize and correct one's errors before they become habitual and their harmful consequences are greatly magnified. It is natural to err, says the *Changes,* and for this there need be no remorse, but serious fault is incurred by a failure to admit error and correct it.[10] Continual self-correction thus becomes another major theme of this manual of Neo-Confucian cultivation. The high standard here is one attributed to Confucius as quoted in the *Changes*, when he said of his disciple Yen Hui, "If he has a fault, he never fails to recognize it. Having recognized it, he never commits the error a second time."[11]

Confucius' negative formulation of the Golden Rule, "Do not do to others what you do not want done to you" (*Analects* 15:23), provides another pretext for quotations from Ch'eng I and Chu Hsi emphasizing a constant reverence as the antidote to the poison of selfish desires. "If one holds the self in constant reverence and extends a ready empathy for others, selfish desires will be held back and the virtue of the mind-and-heart will be complete."[12]

From Chen's other work we know that the *Great Learning* was perhaps the most important of the classics for him, and it is interesting that he quotes it only twice in this work, once, as we have seen, to urge "self-watchfulness in making the will sincere," and again to assert that "self-cultivation lies in rectification of the mind-and-heart."[13] Rectification of mind proves to be a central feature of Chen's system. Since for him the desires are not inherently evil but only become so if they are selfish, the Neo-Confucians generally do not urge their total elimination but stress instead the importance of discriminating between selfish and unselfish desires. Here "rectification" takes the form of Chu Hsi's moral discrimination in judging the desires, while "making the will sincere" involves mobilizing the moral will in steadfast support of such judgments.

Mencius figures prominently in this compilation because of his special attention to the mind-and-heart and because of the importance Neo-Confucians attached to his doctrine of the goodness of human nature. Chen, by the choice and order of his quotations from Mencius,[14] draws special attention to humaneness (*jen*), both as the totality of human virtue and as a sensitivity to the sufferings of others. Again, this was a key issue vis-à-vis Taoism and Buddhism, which were seen as trying to rise above suffering rather than cope with the reality of it. For the Neo-Confucians it was the mark of the humane man that he could *not* endure the sufferings of others, but felt compelled to take action to remedy them. As one might expect, Mencius' episode of the child about to fall into a well and of the instinctive human impulse to save it (*Mencius* 2A:6:3) is cited by Chen as an illustration of the goodness of man's moral nature,[15] which is to be nourished and developed into the fullness of human virtue.

This prominence given to Mencius, while unsurprising, has some significance. In the absence of any more overt structure, the thematic development of Chen's work depends heavily on the juxtaposition of two opposing ideas, human waywardness and the promise of human perfectibility. The juxtaposition is highlighted by the quotations from Mencius, with appropriate Neo-Confucian commentary. At this point, however, Chen shifts from the classics and turns to Neo-Confucian texts as authoritative scripture in their own right. Having posed the question of a decision between the path of self-indulgence and the path of sagehood, Chen invokes the Sung thinkers, not as metaphysicians but as moralists. From Chou Tun-i (1017–1073) he draws the assurance that selfish desire can be conquered and man's nature can be fulfilled in the achievement of sagehood:

> "Can sagehood be learned?"
> "It can."
> "Is there some essential way?"
> "There is."
> "Please explain."
> "Singlemindedness is the essential way. Singlemindedness is having no desires. Having no desires, one is empty in quiescence and straightforward in action. Being empty in quiescence, one's mind is clear and hence penetrating. Being straightforward in action, one is impartial, and being impartial, one is all-embracing. Being clear and penetrating, impartial and all-embracing, one is almost a sage." [16]

In the absence of direct commentary by Chen, it is perhaps not warranted to draw the inference that he favors Chou's doctrine of "having no desires" *(wu-yü)* over Mencius' doctrine of limiting or reducing the desires *(kua-yü)*. Nevertheless, in a work preoccupied with the restraint of desires, a strong final impression is left with the reader that Chou's model sage has no desires. Though this does not necessarily represent Chen's theoretical position, its practical effect is noteworthy as an expression of the developing tendency toward an extreme Neo-Confucian rigorism, going well beyond Chu Hsi's philosophical stance.

Chen concludes with some short, philosophically insignificant pieces by Sung masters, containing prescriptions for moral and spiritual praxis. One from the Ch'eng brothers cites Confucius' response to Yen Yüan's inquiry about the practical steps in the practice of humaneness: "to look at nothing contrary to decorum, listen to nothing contrary to decorum, say nothing contrary to decorum, and do nothing contrary to decorum (*Analects* 12:1)." [17] The Ch'engs elaborate on these as detailed steps in the achievement of sagehood. Three other pieces from Chu Hsi in the form of inscriptions (*ming*) or admonitions (*chen*) deal with the practice of reverence, "recovering the lost mind" (as in *Mencius*), and "honoring the moral nature" (as in the *Mean*). [18]

From this summary of the contents it may be seen that the *Heart Classic* is almost totally preoccupied with a type of spiritual orientation, moral discipline, and religiosity that seems highly refined and specialized in comparison to the wider range of human concerns discussed in the classics and, indeed, even in the Sung writings. Whether the resulting product is Confucian or some kind of hybrid is arguable, but for the moment we simply note its special intensity and the singling out of certain classical concepts which can be reformulated into a new system of ethical cultivation and spiritual praxis.

What would appear here to be almost a puritanical view of the desires is not in fact unrepresentative of Chen's thought generally. Thus, in a discussion of the orthodox tradition (*tao-t'ung*), he states:

When one has committed himself to this Way, to what should he then devote his practice of it and apply his effort? If we look to remote antiquity, we can see that in the one word "reverence" as passed down through a hundred sages is represented their real method of the mind-and-heart (*hsin-fa*). The practice of principle in the world takes the Mean as the ultimate standard of correctness and sincerity as the ultimate norm. However, reverence is that whereby one achieves the Mean, and without reverence there can be no achieving of the Mean. Only if one is reverent can he be sincere, and without reverence there is no way to achieve sincerity. The violence of the physical passions surpasses that of runaway horses; reverence is like lassoing them in. The wildness of the feelings is worse than a river in flood; reverence is like dikes to hold it back. Therefore, for Master Chou to speak of "concentrating on quiescence" (*chu-ching*) and for Master Ch'eng to teach "concentrating on oneness *(chu-i)* were most apposite to the condition of man. And Master Chu was careful to reaffirm the same point.

If one who pursues learning knows to devote effort to this, one will be certain to exercise caution and apprehension in the state of premeditation, and when actively involved with things and affairs, will be certain to approach them in a humble and respectful manner. The active and quiescent states will lead into each other, with no interruption, so that heavenly virtue may find completion and human desires may be overcome. . . .[19]

In another passage there are overtones of an almost Manichean struggle between light and darkness in the conflict between the desires and the virtuous nature. The following comes in response to a question about moral firmness versus sensual desire:

. . . Master Heng-ch'ü [Chang Tsai] said, "If the light of yang prevails, the moral nature functions. If the darkness of yin prevails, the desire for things *(wu-yü)* has its way." The moral nature is our inherent nature of humaneness, righteousness, decorum, and wisdom. The desire for things arises from the senses' coming into contact with things. If he who would be a man is resolute in holding to firmness and light, then principle will be preserved and desires will be destroyed. Therefore to say that "the moral nature functions" means that the moral nature dominates in the use of things. If a man allows darkness and turbidity to envelop him, desires will dominate and principle will be destroyed. Therefore, "the desire for things has its way" means that the desire for things dominates and goes unchecked. The light and transparent, the dark and turbid are both present in our physical endowment, but one can learn to reverse the passions and return [to one's better nature]. If a man is willing to make the effort himself, then weakness can be turned to strength and darkness can be enlightened. If man cannot learn this, then strength may turn to weakness and what is enlightened rapidly turns to darkness.

Master Chang's words were meant to encourage men to transform their physical natures through the effort of learning, so that the light of yang prevails, the moral nature will always function, and the desire for things will not have its way.[20]

In an essay on "Dedication to the Way" Chen likens the struggle to armed conflict:

If selfish desires are given free rein, principle is obscured by desires and inhumaneness follows as a matter of course. Thus in the seeking of humaneness what is of first importance is to "conquer the self" *(k'o-chi).* . . . What, then, does it mean "to conquer"? It is like attacking and vanquishing in battle. When selfish thoughts first appear and the original mind has not yet been lost, then principle and desire stand opposed to each other, like two armies ranged in battle. If what is straight wins, what is crooked loses. If principles dominate, desires must be subordinate. The violence of armed conflict and the dangers of war are well known to all, but unless one knows the Way he will not be prepared to guard against the danger of selfish desires, which wound more grievously than a double-edged sword and burn more fiercely than the hottest fire. Therefore, if one is dedicated to the Way, he will value nothing more than the seeking of humaneness, and in seeking humaneness he will put nothing before conquering the self. . . .[21]

Taken together, these statements and Chen's *Heart Classic* probably represent a more extreme view of human desires as evil, and a more austere, straitlaced ideal of human conduct than can be found in the Ch'eng brothers or Chu Hsi.[22] In Chu's writing one can find statements deprecatory of human desires, and there is some ambiguity too in Chu's treatment of the evil in man as arising from obscurations in the psychophysical makeup of the individual, so that later critics are not without some grounds in asserting that Chu held a "puritanical" view of the psychophysical nature as in some sense evil.[23] Nevertheless, it remains true, as Fung Yu-lan and others have pointed out, that there is no warrant for this interpretation in Chu's philosophy as a whole, and there is repeated stress on the goodness of human nature.[24] Chen too, as Chu's faithful follower, reaffirms this position. But given the increasingly moralistic tone of Chen's writing (the *Heart Classic* was presented to the emperor in 1234 as almost the last testament of Chen), we are faced by the seeming inconsistency of this "puritanical" view of human desires coexisting with an optimistic view of human nature—indeed, one which took issue with Buddhism for denying the substantial reality and physical nature of the human person.

For such reasons we should qualify use of the term "puritanical" in the Neo-Confucian context. "Rigorism" as a form of extreme scrupulosity in the West is perhaps a better approximation of the phenomenon we are dealing with here. Whatever label we give it, however, we are left with the problem of how this extreme attitude arose, how it became accepted as orthodox Chu Hsi teaching, and how it affected the subsequent development of the movement.

The full answer is not to be found in the *Heart Classic* alone, nor indeed in Chen Te-hsiu alone, but it is nonetheless true that Chen's *Classic* had a significant role in spreading this rigoristic form of Neo-Confucian teaching. Presented to the throne in the last days of Chen's service at court, it was spoken of admiringly by the Emperor Li-tsung in a colloquy with a minister lecturing on the classics the following year.[25] The *Classic* was printed in 1242 and an early bibliographic notice of it comes from the eminent institutional historian and indirect follower of Chen, Ma Tuan-lin (1254–1325), who appears to have been much influenced by Chen's scholarly outlook and method.[26] Perhaps because of the particular esteem in which it was held by Yi T'oegye, the leading exponent of the Ch'eng-Chu school in Korea, the *Heart Classic* became a standard text for lectures at the Korean court, ranking along with the Four Books, the Five Classics, and major works of Chu Hsi such as *Reflections on Things at Hand (Chin-ssu lu)* and the *Elementary Learning (Hsiao hsüeh).*[27] Having been reprinted in several Korean editions, it found its way to Japan and was influential among members of the Chu Hsi school such as Kaibara Ekken (1630–1714), Yamazaki Ansai (1611–1682), and later representatives of the Kimon school.[28] In the Tokugawa (Edo) period too it went through several Japanese editions.[29]

One of the distinctive features of this *Classic* is that, except for a final hymn of praise *(tsan)* by Chen, it consists entirely of quotations from earlier sources, and, somewhat in contrast to the frequent Chinese practice of quoting without attribution, Chen clearly identifies each passage as to original source. Indeed, it was only on this basis that he would have dared to call his work a classic, for such a claim could not have been made for a more overtly personal statement. By the same token, however, there is an inherent difficulty in judging the full extent of its influence, since the work, however often cited, would never be quoted. Its contents, being derivative, would be identified by their original source.

In any case the *Heart Classic* was not Chen's major work, and we can arrive at a proper estimate of its significance only in the context of Chen's larger contribution to Chinese history and thought.

Chen Te-hsiu: The Neo-Confucian as Teacher to the Ruler

Chen Te-hsiu was born into a family of the lower gentry which had migrated from Nanking to Nanchang (Kiangsi) and Lung-ch'üan (Chekiang) before settling down in P'u-ch'eng (Fukien), the home region of Chu Hsi. The biographical sources[30] speak of his great precosity in learning and his prodigious memory at an early age; it is said that by the age of thirteen he had already come to a considerable mastery of the Confucian classics, philosophers, and histories, and this is plausible in view of his subsequent achievements. But he was left fatherless at the age of fourteen, and his mother had a difficult struggle to continue his education. With the help of a friend in the locality who recognized Chen's extraordinary talent, he was able to prepare for the civil service examinations, pass them at the provincial level by the age of seventeen, and succeed in the metropolitan examinations for the *chin-shih* degree by the age of twenty-one (in 1199).

During these same years Chu Hsi and his school had been subjected to fierce repression by enemies at court. "By 1196 government attacks on Neo-Confucianism as 'false learning' had become intense. The teachings of Ch'eng I and others were proscribed. A powerful censor impeached Chu Hsi for ten crimes, including 'false learning,' and an official candidate even petitioned for his execution."[31]

Under such circumstances Chen's preparation for the examinations, based on the long-established, officially approved learning, and his study of the new teachings of the outlawed Ch'eng-Chu school had to proceed on somewhat different tracks. Presumably Chen pursued them in parallel, successfully launching an active official career while he was also, as a student under one of Chu Hsi's disciples, Chan T'i-jen (1143–1206),[32] learning the new philosophy and enlisting in the cause of the so-called School of the Way.

After brief service in a subordinate local position, in 1205 (at age twenty-seven) he took the special examination in "broad learning and literary versatility" *(po-hsüeh hung-tz'u),* which certified him as a man of exceptional scholarly attainments and led to service at court in the Imperial College and other posts which made use of his unusual capacities for expressing himself in writing and in speech. By 1208 as a professor *(po-shih)* of the Imperial College, he was already making himself known for his courage and outspokenness in challenging the repressive measures against the Ch'eng-Chu school. He also criticized the monopolization of power which discouraged criticism at court, the defamation of worthy scholars and officials, and the perversions of truth which produced a confusion of values and frustrated all attempts to practice the true Way of government.[33] By this time Chu Hsi's chief persecutor at court, Han T'o-chou (1151–1202), had fallen from power and the process of rehabilitation had begun. In 1209 the first step was taken to exonerate Chu by granting him the posthumous title of "Cultured" *(Wen).* The campaign to promote Chu and his teaching, which spanned Chen's active career, eventually led to honors being paid to Chu and other Sung masters in the Confucian temple the year before Chen's death (1234).[34]

In the meantime, Chen's own career had suffered repeated setbacks. His forthrightness at court, his calls for more open discussion of public issues, his vigorous advocacy of strengthening defenses in the North through the development of colonies of farmer-soldiers, and his attacks on evils in the government as a greater danger than external enemies, drew upon him the enmity of the prime minister, Shih Mi-yüan (1164–1233)[35] and led to Chen's reassignment in 1215, at his own request, for service in the provinces. By all accounts his effectiveness in successive local assignments was outstanding, demonstrating that he could be a doer as well as a talker. From 1216 to 1219 as prefect of Ch'üan-chou, long an important port on the coast of Fukien but then in a state of decline, he reduced oppressive taxes so as to encourage legitimate trade and discourage smuggling. By these means and by taking strong measures against piracy, he was able to increase shipping many-fold and restore the port to prosperity. In Lung-hsing prefecture (Hunan), from 1219 to 1222, he distinguished himself in pacification efforts, and in T'an-chou (modern Ch'ang-sha in Hunan province) from 1222 to 1225 he engaged in numerous efforts to improve the people's livelihood, especially by reforming and extending the public granary system (which also, we might note parenthetically, had been a contribution of Chu Hsi's).[36] Local administration had always included judicial functions, and Chen also gave close attention to improving the administration of justice and the handling of litigation—one of the conventional marks of a good official.

During these same years Chen displayed a special interest in promoting education and scholarship. He took seriously his obligation to provide moral instruction for the general populace,[37] and himself lectured regularly to his disciples and subordinates on the teachings of the Neo-Confucian masters Chou Tun-i, Hu An-kuo (1074–1138), Chu Hsi, and Chang Shih (1133–1180). Chen is said to have been particularly mindful of his master Chan T'i-jen's precepts concerning the Confucian's service in government, which he summed up in the motto: "To expend fully [all the resources of] one's mind-and-heart, and to be fair-minded [or evenhanded]. If one gives fully of his mind-and-heart, he will have no reason to be ashamed; if he is fair-minded, he will not be guilty of favoritism."[38] As precepts for his subordinates in T'an-chou, he is said to have offered: "Incorruptibility, humaneness, impartiality, and diligence":

> Discipline the self by incorruptibility [refrain from graft].
> Pacify the people by humaneness.
> Preserve the mind by impartiality.
> Perform your duties with diligence.[39]

The relationship of these precepts to Chen's Learning of the Mind-and-Heart is not difficult to discern, and as we shall see later, virtually all his experience of administration, practical as well as pedagogical, had a bearing on his philosophy.

In 1225 the situation changed at court with the accession of the Emperor Li-tsung. Chen was invited back to the capital, where he served in the Secretarial Council *(Chung-shu sheng)* and Board of Rites, and was soon engaged in lecturing the emperor on the need "to take the ancient sage-kings as his models and mentors" and to "rule in the interests of all, not just of one man and his family."[40]

Chen performed in the capacity of "lecturer from the classics mat," a function which had become especially honored in the Sung because of the high distinction of the scholar-statesmen who took on this duty of expounding the meaning and significance of the classics as they related to historical cases and contemporary problems (see pp. 29–34 above). Among the figures who had excelled in this role were Fan Tsu-yü (1041–1098), the younger Ch'eng, Ssu-ma Kuang (1019–1086), Fan Ch'un-jen (1027–1101), and Chu Hsi. The last had made a special point of taking the *Great Learning* as his basic text. Chen took up where Chu had left off, no doubt relishing the opportunity to carry on the work of his illustrious predecessor.

The spirit in which Chen approached this work, and its relation to the Learning of the Mind-and-Heart is suggested by a quotation in the memorial tribute written by his scholarly colleague, Wei Liao-weng (1178–1237), who was another leading follower of Chu Hsi. In urging the emperor to believe in his own innate virtue and make the effort to achieve sagely rule, Chen had said, "Only study can nourish the mind; only reverence can preserve this mind; only by befriending noble men can you give support to the mind." [41]

Twenty-three texts from his lectures on the *Great Learning*, delivered on sixteen different occasions, have been preserved in Chen's *Collected Writings*, as have the texts prepared by Chu Hsi for his lectures. [42] It is a testimony to the remarkable continuity, consistency of format, and thematic unity of these two series of lectures that a Japanese publisher in the Tokugawa period was inspired to republish them in a combined edition as *Kei'en kōgi* (Lectures from the Classics Mat), [43] denoting the collaboration across time of these two outstanding Neo-Confucian teachers.

Unfortunately, although the emperor was not unsympathetic to Chen, the continuing hostility of Shih Mi-yüan, who still dominated the court, soon led to Chen's dismissal and return home. In 1232, however, he was reassigned to Ch'üan-chou, where his previous accomplishments had so endeared him to the populace that they gave him a hero's welcome: "welcoming throngs packed the roads, the aged came out hobbling on their canes, and the city resounded with the joyous tumult." [44] Later he was reassigned to be prefect of Fu-chou, but in the capital the death of Shih Mi-yüan opened the way for Chen's recall to court. He was appointed minister of revenue in 1233, and subsequently was placed in charge of edicts and pronouncements at the Hanlin Academy. The following year (1234) he presented to the throne his monumental work, the *Extended Meaning of the Great Learning (Ta-hsüeh yen-i)*, which he had been compiling over the years in his spare time, mainly while in the provinces, as an extension of his lectures from the classics mat.[45] The emperor is said to have exclaimed, "This one book of the *Extended Meaning* is sufficient as a guide and model for the ruler."[46]

By this time the Mongols had overrun the Chin dynasty in the North and posed a new threat to the ailing Sung dynasty. Li-tsung, in an apparent fit of consternation and self-reformation, bestirred himself to proclaim a new era name, Tuan-p'ing, expressing the thought that a fresh start was being made to achieve the sagely ideal of peace and order.[47] The new era was formally inaugurated in 1234, and Chen was appointed associate director of political affairs *(ts'an-chih cheng-shih)* at the beginning of the following year.[48] However, he was already suffering from the illness that would take his life later that year, and he could not take a very active role. It would not have surprised, though no doubt it would have saddened him that after his death in 1235 nothing came of Li-tsung's promised new order.

Chen was honored with the posthumous title Junior Tutor to the Heir Apparent *(T'ai-tzu shao-shih)*, and was raised to Grand Preceptor *(t'ai-shih)* in 1362. In 1438 the Ming Emperor Ying-tsung (r. 1436–1465) had his tablet installed in the Confucian temple, and in 1467 he was accorded the honorary title of nobility, Earl of P'u-ch'eng (his home town).[49] As we shall see, many other tributes, official and unofficial, were paid to his major work, the *Extended Meaning of the Great Learning*.

In his memoir *(shen-tao pei)* of Chen, Wei Liao-weng lauded his high-mindedness, his strength of character, and his signal contribution to rescuing the True Way, a tribute repeated in the official Yüan history of the Sung, the *Great Compendium on Human Nature and Principle (Hsing-li ta-ch'üan)*, and many other works.[50] Describing the persecution under Han T'o-chou, the ban on the writings of the Sung masters, and the near-extinguishing of the Way by the time Chen appeared on the scene, the *Sung History* says that Chen "singlehandedly took upon himself the responsibility for [preserving] 'this culture' [using the language of Confucius in describing his own mission]. Thus, with the proscription lifted, it was largely through his efforts that the true learning could be made clearly known throughout the land and to later generations."[51] We recognize here the same language in which Ch'eng I and Chu Hsi had eulogized earlier champions of the Way, and it was rapidly becoming a convention (see pp. 14–17 above), but since it is confirmed by Wei himself, who had suffered through these difficult times and had reason to appreciate his friend's personal qualities, it ill behooves the modern historian to dismiss them as mere clichés.

By traditional standards Chen was a diligent and hard-working official, but the Confucian life-style allowed for, and indeed encouraged, cultural activities alongside official duties. Chen was an indefatigable writer, and a considerable body of his voluminous output has survived. Among his more important works are the *Collected Writings* in 51 fascicles *(chüan)*,[52] which include the usual variety of poetry, memorials to the throne, letters, essays, prefaces, memoirs, inscriptions, etc.; his *Collected Commentaries on the Four Books (Ssu-shu chi-pien)*,[53] an early example of the kind of compilation which later became codified in the *Great Compendium on the Four Books (Ssu-shu ta-ch'üan)* as the standard texts for official purposes in the Ming; *Models of Literary Form (Wen-chang cheng-tsung)*,[54] containing exemplary specimens of different literary forms in 30 *chüan*, with a 12-*chüan* supplement; *Reading Notes (Tu-shu chi)* in 40 *chüan*;[55] and the *Classic on Government (Cheng ching)*,[56] in addition to the aforementioned *Heart Classic* and *Extended Meaning of the Great Learning*.

Of the above, the *Classic on Government* and the *Reading Notes* deserve some mention. The former is somewhat similar to the *Heart Classic* in that it contains passages from the classics and philosophers on basic principles of government, with emphasis on practical administration, while it differs from the *Heart Classic* in that it also includes historical cases and examples drawn from Chen's own experience, as well as official documents by Chen himself dealing with many specific problems encountered in his own performance of official duties, especially in local administration. The work was begun by Chen in his last years, and may have been conceived as a functional complement to the *Heart Classic*, showing how the conduct of government went hand-in-hand with self-cultivation. In any case, these two "classics" were printed together in 1242 and circulated in a single edition in the late Sung and after, in Korea and Japan as well as in China.

The *Catalogue of the Imperial Manuscript Library*, in commenting on this work, raises questions concerning its compilation and date. The *Catalogue's* editors surmise that the work was left unfinished by Chen but was completed by one of his followers, who added writings by Chen himself and then passed it off as a "classic" in the same mold as the *Heart Classic* (though the latter consisted entirely of quotations from earlier sources and had nothing of Chen's own in it). Chen, they say, held high ambitions as a scholar and a lofty conception of his own political mission, but he would never have had the temerity to call a work with so much of his own writing in it a "classic."[57]

They may well be right about the misappropriation of the term "classic." From our point of view, however, it is Chen's own writings that make the work significant. Though its subject lies outside the scope of this study, the existence of the work helps us understand Chen's intentions. For him it is another way of fulfilling his role as a loyal minister, loyal especially in the Confucian sense that it is the minister's obligation to inform and instruct his sovereign. Unable for long years to perform this function at court, Chen applied himself to bringing humane administration to people at the local level, and to recording for the benefit of the court what he had learned. The spirit of the *Classic on Government* is very much that of the lectures on the classics at court, but the locale is shifted to the countryside. Chen seeks to make the emperor aware of the actual circumstances and difficulties of the people, so different from what he would be apt to hear in the bland, reassuring reports of those seeking to ingratiate themselves with the court. Thus the imperial *Catalogue* says: "Chen's days at court were few, and his experience of administration was largely in posts outside the capital. Hence he had an intimate knowledge of the sufferings of the people and so wrote this work."[58] To Chen it was vital that the emperor know the people's lives and their actual feelings toward government. "The little people of the vil-

lages," he says at one point, "dread petty bureaucrats like wild ti-
gers. Having a petty bureaucrat come into the village is like letting a
tiger into one's house."[59]

Chen's *Reading Notes* have a bearing on his Learning of the
Mind-and-Heart because they constitute a larger whole of which the
Extended Meaning of the Great Learning was originally a part. Like
nearly all his works, the *Reading Notes* were regarded by Chen as
having political relevance. When the work was completed in 1225
with the help of his students, he said to them: "This is the gateway
to the ruler's conduct of government."[60] The contents, however, are
varied, covering a wide range of classical learning and organizing it
topically according to the method which became Chen's trademark:
quotations from the classics, comments by the philosophers, specific
historical cases, and finally Chen's own observations.[61] One discerns
in these notes a consistency of views and tendencies, reinforcing the
basic tenets of the *Heart Classic* and the *Extended Meaning.*

In forty large fascicles and over one hundred headings and
subheadings, the material may be characterized as follows:

1. Basic metaphysical and psychophysical concepts relating to
   human nature and the mind.
2. The cardinal virtues.
3. The basic human relationships.
4. Learning and teaching.
5. The classics: how to read and understand them.
6. The orthodox tradition—how it was passed on, became lost, and
   was rediscovered—from the ancient sages down to the Sung masters.
7. Dealing with different circumstances and life situations.
8. Cosmology.

The editors of the Imperial Manuscript Library *Catalogue* paid
warm tribute to the work. They comment on the breadth of Chen's
learning, his systematic approach to the organization of the material,
his diligence in searching out relevant evidence and analyzing it,
and his unusual combination of attention to underlying principles
and practical details. "Among the works of the Sung scholars," they
note, "these have genuine practical value."[62]

This is significant praise. For us it indicates that the depth of Chen's moral and spiritual concerns was matched by a wide learning and empirical scholarship. Chen does not fit the usual stereotype of the Chu Hsi schoolman as either narrowly pedantic or preoccupied with his own inner consciousness—an impression one might well receive from the *Heart Classic* if one read it alone.

The Learning of the Emperors

The *Extended Meaning of the Great Learning,* a part of the *Reading Notes* which took on independent life, represents a distinctive synthesis of its own, a special product of the chemistry of the times as catalyzed by this extraordinary agent.

The elements which came together in the process were many and not all of them obvious. Despite its title, this work is not just a lengthy commentary on the *Great Learning*. In fact it is not the usual phrase-by-phrase commentary at all. Following the method of the *Reading Notes* as a whole, it includes a variety of materials—classical, philological, philosophical, historical, and even personal. Indeed, the appeal of the *Extended Meaning* has been greater than that of the *Heart Classic* because of Chen's added comments. Chen's own mind and writing style exhibit a lucidity, coherence, and passion surpassing most of the other writings he includes. Notwithstanding its seeming subordination to the *Great Learning*, Chen's work is an intensely personal statement, fully deserving of consideration as an independent contribution to Neo-Confucian thought.

Yet it is no less true that Chen does draw special attention to the *Great Learning*. Among the classics he had discussed in the *Reading Notes* and his *Collected Commentaries,* Chen had already given more prominence to this short work than to other, longer ones and still he had something more to say about it, in a manner quite distinctive to him. He drew on all the resources of his learning and personal experience and put them at the service of this one classic, though one could say equally well that he used the *Great Learning* as the vehicle for his own most trenchant thinking.

One cannot say, however, that this use of the *Great Learning* was unprecedented. The Sung period as a whole had witnessed a steady rise in the attention commanded by this brief chapter in the old *Record of Rites,* [63] a trend evident from the outset of the period in the early Sung scholars' admiration for Han Yü and his disciple Li Ao (fl. 798). The two had given a special place in their writings to the *Great Learning,* as Chen Te-hsiu was well aware. [64] For leaders of the reform movement in the Northern Sung, including Fan Chung-yen (989–1052) and Ou-yang Hsiu (1007–1072), it was an inspirational text. Ssu-ma Kuang stressed its importance in his memorials, and was apparently the first scholar to separate the *Great Learning* from the *Record of Rites* and comment on it. [65] In fact, what is well known as the canonization of the Four Books through the influence of Chu Hsi can be regarded as only the most spectacular manifestation of the *Great Learning's* rise in the Neo-Confucian firmament. A measure of this is to be found in the importance Chu attached to it by his own work of commentary, and in his famous Jade Mountain lecture, widely regarded as the culmination of his teaching career. [66] In his *Recorded Conversations (Yü-lei)* and *Questions on the Great Learning (Ta-hsüeh huo-wen),* Chu asserted that this text was essential to interpreting the *Analects* and *Mencius,* and that the *Mean* too could not be understood without it. "Hence those who discuss learning cannot but start with the Four Books, and among the Four Books, one cannot but put the *Great Learning* first." [67] It was no doubt on this high authority that later, in the official examinations and the authorized versions of the classics, the *Great Learning* was listed and placed ahead of the *Analects* and *Mencius* (see pp. 48–49, 55–56).

Another measure of the high place of the *Great Learning* in the thought of the time is its central position in the developing tradition of the lectures from the classics mat. Successive lecturers at court, among them Fan Tsu-yü (1041–1098), Fan Ch'un-jen (1027–1101), and the Ch'eng brothers had already recommended it as a guide to the ruler before Chu Hsi made the *Great Learning's* method of self-cultivation the focus of his own lectures at court and his sealed memorials to the throne. These developments I have touched on in the first essay, but in connection with the Learning of the Mind-and-Heart, we should observe how Chu identified the *Great Learning* with the teachings of Yao and Shun concerning "refinement," singleness," and "holding fast to the Mean." "From of old what the sages passed on by word of mouth, communicated from mind-to-mind, and rendered visible in their actions was none other than this [teaching of the *Great Learning*]."[68]

Here Chu identifies the *Great Learning* with the "refinement" and "singleness" which are hallmarks of the sages' teaching "communicated from mind-to-mind." Later Chen Te-hsiu quoted these same passages on "refinement" and "singleness" in the opening lines of his *Heart Classic*, and in the *Extended Meaning of the Great Learning*, thus confirming the linkage of these ideas with the teaching of the *Great Learning* as the central theme of both the Learning of the Mind-and-Heart and the lectures from the classics mat.

No less significant, however, was the role of the *Great Learning* in another developing genre of imperial instruction in the Sung period, the "Learning of the Emperors and Kings" (*Ti-wang chih hsüeh*) or, for short, the Learning of the Emperors (*Ti-hsüeh*), already discussed in Part I. This branch of Sung learning, largely lost sight of in recent times, was so deeply implicated in Chen's work that we cannot ignore it here. From its inception in the early Sung this special genre of Neo-Confucian teaching had an intimate association with both the lecturing on the classics at court and the text of the *Great Learning*.

The prototypical work in this genre is the *Learning of the Emperors (Ti-hsüeh)*[69] by Fan Tsu-yü.[70] It consists of eight fascicles of material prepared in connection with Fan's lectures from the classics mat, and represents the historical documentation for the type of advice and instruction given by Fan to the Emperor Che-tsung (r. 1086–1093). A one-time associate of the statesman Wang An-shih (1021–1086) and a collaborator with the historian Ssu-ma Kuang in the compiling of his monumental *General Mirror for Aid in Government (Tzu-chih t'ung-chien)*, Fan was also the author of the *Mirror of the T'ang (T'ang chien)*, a manual of political advice based on events of the T'ang dynasty. Highly respected for his learning and courage in counseling the emperor, Fan was, like the Ch'eng brothers and Chu Hsi, a victim of the bitter factional struggles of the Sung. Ch'eng I said of his *Mirror of the T'ang*, "There has been no such discussion since the Three Dynasties"; and Chu Hsi was to list him among the exemplary scholars and martyred leaders of the Sung school.[71] Chen Te-hsiu frequently quotes Fan's works (as well as Ssu-ma Kuang's) in his *Extended Meaning*, and we have reason to believe that the *Learning of the Emperors* set a basic pattern for Chen's exposition of the principles of the *Great Learning*.

Unfortunately, Fan's work was almost lost in later centuries, perhaps being overshadowed by the great success of Chen's. For some time only rare manuscript copies survived in China and Japan,[72] a circumstance which may explain why this tradition of political learning, closely associated with the rise of Neo-Confucianism, has been largely neglected. Its importance in the late Sung is attested, however, by the outstanding historian Ma Tuan-lin, who notes the existence of Fan's work in the bibliographical treatise of his encyclopedic institutional history,[73] the *Wen-hsien t'ung-k'ao*, and by the eminent scholar Wang Ying-lin (1223–1296), himself a product of the Chu Hsi school and influenced by Chen Te-hsiu, who devoted a section of his *Sea of Jade (Yü-hai)*, just preceding his discussion of imperial writings and general bibliography, to the "Learning of the Emperors" as an institution at court and a genre of instruction.[74]

The *Catalogue of the Imperial Manuscript Library* also notes Fan's work, saying that it deals with the emperor's obligation to advance his own learning and with the need for him to "rectify his own mind-and-heart and engage in self-cultivation."[75] Fan, it says, was known for his directness of speech, command of historical precedents, and detailed knowledge of relevant documents.

The concept of the Learning of the Emperors was ancillary to the Sung Confucians' aim of promoting the Way of the sage-kings as a model for the emperor. This way of government had been passed on by the sage-kings as something to be studied and practiced by their successors, but somehow by the time of Confucius and Mencius it had ceased to be implemented and survived only as a way of learning, thanks largely to Confucius' efforts to recover what he could of the lost tradition. This great breach in the natural order, sundering the way of the ruler from the way of teaching and learning, was described by Ch'eng I in the tribute to his brother: "Even without good government, scholars could explain the way of good

government for the benefit of mankind and transmit it to later generations, but without true scholars the world fell into darkness and
people lost their way. . . ."[76]

Here Ch'eng I distinguishes the ancient ideal of the ruler-
teacher from the historical reality of a separation between these two
functions, and underscores the importance of salvaging at least the
tradition of learning and teaching, if not the way of rulership. Fan,
for his part as mentor to the ruler, faces the problem in a somewhat
different form. Like other Sung reformers he still hopes to convert
the emperor to sagely rule, but he encounters resistance which cannot be overcome by merely dwelling on the past achievements of the
sage-kings. Ch'eng Hao, as minister at the Sung court, had faced
similar resistance when he tried to talk to the Emperor Shen-tsung
(1068–1085) about the way of governing according to the ancient
ideal, and Shen-tsung, much to Ch'eng Hao's vexation, rejected the
idea that he should be expected to measure up to the ideal of Yao
and Shun.[77]

Chinese rulers, if they did not suffer delusions of grandeur,
had difficulty identifying with sage-kings. Fan recognized the fact
and sought to deal with it. Thus his *Learning of the Emperors* eschewed further talk about generalized ideals and concentrated on the
problem of the ruler's motivations, especially as they were centrally
involved in the ruler–minister-mentor relationship. His argument,
developed through a series of classical and historical cases, ran like
this:

1. The early kings did not rely on their innate virtue alone,
superior though that was, but made an effort to learn from wise
teachers. In doing so they established the practice of regularly consulting learned counselors and studying what was transmitted to
them from their sage predecessors.

2. Later rulers often failed to make this effort or refused to
listen to wise counsel. Those few who did study the classics or listened to the learned went down in history as great rulers; those who
failed to do so brought ruin upon themselves and their dynasties.

3. Because of the lapse in the transmission of the true Way
and the confusion of divergent teachings in later times, rulers did
not always have wise counsel available to them, and sometimes even

their own good intentions became misdirected. Thus it was important to discriminate between true and false teachings.

4. The Han and T'ang dynasties, though they had a few outstanding rulers aided by able ministers, suffered greatly from the corrupting effects of heterodox teachings and the unscrupulousness of ambitious ministers who usurped power. But the Sung, Fan was glad to believe and tactful enough to state, had been blessed with the natural benevolence of its rulers and the revival of true Confucian teachings. The Emperor Jen-tsung (r. 1023–1064) in particular had listened to wise men and demonstrated how sagely rule could still be practiced in these times. Hence, instead of feeling remote from the sage-kings, the reigning emperor should feel the assurance of a practical example near at hand.

All this Fan laid out in a series of case histories, first drawn from antiquity and then from the later dynasties, assessing the rulers' intentions, evaluating the advice of the ministers, and pointing to the consequences for good or ill in each case. Among other things, his distribution in time is worth noting: one fascicle devoted to the early kings, another to sovereigns from the Han through the T'ang, and the remaining six to the Sung, from the founder through Shen-tsung. In this way he asserts the classical principles but achieves greater realism by dealing for the most part with recent examples that cannot be dismissed as irrelevant or too high to reach. Moreover, he avoids the tactical error of seeming to pit ancient ideals against recent dynastic practice. Instead he ranges the founding fathers of the Sung on the side of the Confucian saints.

Generally Fan is willing to let the facts of history (as recorded by the historian) speak for themselves, and when he intervenes with his own observations they are usually significant. A few illustrations follow:

Even the first of the sages, Fu Hsi, faced the necessity to learn. He had to read and study the signs of Heaven before he could establish models and norms on earth.   [1:3ab]

Commenting on Yao and Shun, Fan states unequivocally that the "Learning of the Emperors and Kings was the *Great Learning*."

Then he quotes the opening passages of this text, linking the steps in self-cultivation to the governance of the state and the manifesting of luminous virtue throughout the world. These, he says, "are none other than the Way of Yao and Shun" (1:13b–14a).

The Sung founder's respect for learning and eagerness to advance in the Way laid the basis for later generations. He invited scholars to hold discussions at court and encouraged lectures on the classics. He even provided for the education of the military. "Can his posterity afford to ignore this example?" (3:6b–7a).

Never was there a ruler in the past who loved learning, befriended scholars, and encouraged discussions at court as much as Jen-tsung. Every word and deed of his exemplified humaneness [the *jen* in his name] and had a beneficent effect on all. This was due simply to his pursuit of learning.   [6:25a–26b]

From this we can see that the Learning of the Emperors meant several things. It was the learning of the sage-emperors and kings, the learning later emperors were obliged to study, and the learning about rulership which ministers had a responsibility to impart to their sovereigns. It was also a learning essentially expressed in the *Great Learning* as a text, in lectures on the classics at court, and in other admonitions or exhortations to the throne by wise counselors. In dwelling on the lessons of history, it sought to persuade the emperor that there was no way to escape the consequences of his decisions or indecisions, and only those who sought out informed advice could make wise decisions.

All this was included in Fan's legacy of instruction at court, to which Chen Te-hsiu later succeeded. This continuity is shown not only in Chen's frequent quotation of Fan and his further treatment of the *Great Learning* as a basic text, but also in the concern shown in the *Extended Meaning* for the ruler's motivation and in the way Chen develops his argument through a combination of classical texts, historical cases, and personal comment. There is, however, one way in which Chen chooses not to follow his predecessor. He avoids direct discussion of the record of Sung emperors, referring to them only occasionally and very indirectly as footnotes to earlier cases. The reasons for this are not clear, but perhaps by this time so great was the disparity between ideal and actuality in the matter of imperial conduct that Chen, unwilling either to resort to hypocrisy or appear contumacious, avoided outright confrontation.

There is one other respect in which Chen's work differs substantially from Fan's. Between Fan's time and his there had been important developments in Ch'eng-Chu philosophy, and in drawing upon this tradition, Chen is able to give a much deeper meaning to his subject.

Chu Hsi's Doctrine as Taught by Chen Te-hsiu

Chen Te-hsiu is known, if at all, as a faithful follower of Chu Hsi. Historians and biographers speak of his championing Chu's cause at its nadir; later Chu Hsi schoolmen hail his fidelity to orthodoxy; modern writers, with few exceptions, dismiss him as merely repeating what Chu had said. Actually, however, Chen's success as a teacher and writer lay in choosing certain ideas to expound from among the many in Chu's system, and in focusing attention on them as the working doctrine of the Neo-Confucian movement. Among them four have a particular relevance to Chen's purpose in writing the *Extended Meaning* and are major themes in Chen's writing as a whole. These themes are (1) Chu's concept of the orthodox tradition *(tao-t'ung)*; (2) the doctrine of the "whole substance and great functioning" *(ch'üan-t'i ta-yung)* of the Way as found in man's nature; (3) the primary virtue of reverence or seriousness *(ching)*; (4) the nature and importance of empirical learning. All four derive from the Ch'eng-Chu teaching, and each is shared to greater or lesser degree with Chen's late Sung contemporaries in the Chu Hsi school, most notably with Huang Kan (1152–1221),[78] Ch'en Ch'un (1153–1217),[79] and Wei Liao-weng, but perhaps no one expressed them with such force and clarity as he.

1. The orthodox tradition *(tao-t'ung)*. Chu Hsi, the principal formulator of this concept, was much influenced by Ch'eng I's view of the Confucian tradition. Usually thought of as "the transmission of the Way," *tao-t'ung* almost literally has the sense of "the linking or stitching together of the Way," that is, actively putting it together

rather than just passively receiving it and handing it on. In fact, Chu Hsi emphasized the discontinuities in the tradition almost more than the continuities, and underscored the contributions of inspired individuals who rediscovered or "clarified" the Way in new forms.[80]

The Way itself is understood by Chen under the three aspects cited by Hu Yüan (993–1059) in the early Sung: as substance (*t'i*) it is immutable and imperishable; as function (*yung*) it is adapted to and applied in different circumstances; as literary expression (*wen*) or as "transmission" (*ch'üan*) it is passed on to successive generations, often in fragmentary and obscure form, sometimes brilliantly illuminated, as it was in the Sung when new masters had their own unique insights (*tzu-te*), thus contributing to the advancement and amplification of the Way.[81] Hence tradition in the form of *tao-t'ung* represents immutable truth but also dynamic growth.

Drawing on Chu Hsi's account of it in the preface to the *Mean*, Chen brings out its implications even more clearly in a memoir of Ch'eng Hao:

what Yao transmitted to Shun was "Hold fast to the Mean" and no more. Shun, transmitting this to Yü, added the three phrases [the mind of man is insecure, the mind of the Way is barely perceptible, and one should have utmost refinement and singleness of mind]. When he spoke of the human mind, he meant human desires. When he spoke of the mind of the Way, he meant heavenly principle. Keeping to refinement and preserving singleness, one can hold fast to the Mean. The Mean is the normative rule of Heaven's principle, without the slightest interference from the selfishness of human desires. The *Great Learning, Analects,* and *Mencius* all accord with this idea, but they do not express it in terms of Heaven's principle, which only appears in the *Record of Music (Yüeh-chi)* section of the *Record of Rites.* . . .

Thereafter the Way became obscured for more than a thousand years until our dynasty. . . . when Chou Tun-i appeared and was able to grasp the long-lost secret. Master Ch'eng Ming-tao [Ch'eng Hao], when he came upon this, recognized it immediately, penetrating the surrounding darkness and shedding further light. Now, reading what is contained in his surviving works, we can see that when he spoke about learning, he upheld "fulfilling heavenly virtue" as the main thing, and when he spoke about government he upheld practice of the kingly Way as the key point. Only when one has fulfilled heavenly virtue can one then speak of practicing the kingly Way. Heaven and man, inner and outer, there is "one thread uniting them" and no difference between them as regards practice of the Way. Therefore Master Ch'eng once said to students, "Although there are things I have learned from others, as regards Heaven's principle, what I have set forth is based on my own experience." [82]

Further on in the same memoir Chen pursues the point that Heaven's principle is only barely mentioned in the *Yüeh chi* and nowhere else in the classics. It is to the great credit of Ch'eng Hao that he made this discovery himself and explained it with such clarity that "the secret of a thousand ages past was at last revealed and the misconceptions of a myriad ages were finally dispelled. Thus his contributions to 'this Way' can truly be called abundant. . . ." [83]

This progressive revelation of truth originally implicit in the Way is further explained by Chen in another memoir which expressed in awed terms the wondrous creativity of Heaven as manifested through the inspired work of outstanding individuals.

Relaying and re-creating, each in turn, they provided the full teaching both in essence and in elaborated detail. Thenceforward men could know that the nature of man was inseparable from the values of humaneness, righteousness, decorum, and wisdom, so that what was evil or mixed could not be called the true nature; that the Way was inseparable from daily practice and concrete things, so that empty nothingness could not be the true Way; and that the teaching was inescapably based on the relationships between ruler and minister, parent and child, husband and wife, older and younger brother, so that suppression of human relations could not be the true teaching. Do we not have here the full revelation of the sagely learning, the dispelling of the blindnesses of this generation of men, and the correct succession to the orthodox teaching handed down from a thousand ages past? Indeed, has not Heaven shown the most extraordinary favor to this Way? [84]

This creative interaction between Heaven and certain inspired individuals I have discussed earlier as a "prophetic" element in Neo-Confucianism (see the first essay). Without dwelling further on it here, we may proceed to the corollary doctrine of substance and function in Chen Te-hsiu.

2. The "whole substance and great functioning" *(ch'üan-t'i ta-yung)* of man's humaneness. In the following passages Chen explains that man's humaneness, his Heaven-given nature, is the manifestation of the ever-loving, life-giving power of Heaven, and that the goodness of human nature, which is grounded in the fundamental affinity/empathy among all creation, expresses itself in sympathetic, loving activity in the world. The "whole substance" is the full human potential for communion and co-creation with Heaven, as activated through all of the faculties of the mind-and-heart—rational, moral, affective, and spiritual. "Great functioning" is the greatest possible exercise of those capabilities for benefiting mankind and fostering life in concrete situations and practical ways. Although this functioning takes tangible, definable form, the essential nature remains open-ended, reflecting the illimitable creative power of Heaven. Only in part is the individual socially determined and delimited by his past, for his nature includes the capacity for self-transcendence.

These passages are from Chen's response to the question, "What is the meaning of humaneness" *(jen)*:

The Way of Humaneness is great. It includes the five constants [humaneness, righteousness, decorum, wisdom, and good faith]; it is the integrating thread among all the forms of goodness. This is why one word cannot exhaust its meaning. In the Han and after scholars used *ai* [love] to explain *jen*, but did not realize that while *jen* expresses itself chiefly through love, love does not exhaust the meaning of *jen*. Mencius said that the commiserating heart was the seed of *jen*. Commiseration, however, is just the mind's natural feeling of sympathy for others, that is, of love for them. It is still only the first sign or inception of *jen*.

Han Yü spoke of *jen* as unbounded love [in his *Inquiry into the Way*]. Master Ch'eng I rejected this, saying [*I-shu* 18:1a]: "*Jen* in itself is the nature. Love in itself is feeling. To take love as *jen* is to take feeling as the nature." No truer words have been spoken! Master Chu Hsi described it in six characters [*Lun-yü chi-chu* 1:2], "principle of love and virtue of mind." That is to say, speaking of *jen* as the principle of love does not limit *jen* to love even while it still serves as its principle. In terms of substance, the way of *jen* is great and all-inclusive, but when it expresses itself as function it does so principally as love (*jen* is the substance of love and love is the function of *jen*). . . .

Origin is to Heaven what *jen* is to man. Origin represents the totality of heavenly virtue; even so *jen,* as the underlying reason of the virtue of the mind, expresses itself as love. The reason *jen* can express itself as love is that the mind of Heaven-and-earth is creative, and man, receiving this mind from Heaven-and-earth, expresses it chiefly as love. The idea expressed in the six characters "principle of love, virtue of mind" was something no earlier scholar discovered; Master Chu first did so. How matchless is his contribution to learning! How could we fail to appreciate it! [85]

This same thought is pursued in a letter by Chen to his son explaining the meaning of the name, Dedicated to the Way *(Chih-tao),* which he had given him.

The Way and humaneness are not separate pursuits. In the teaching of the sages when they speak of "dedicating oneself to the Way" at the same time they speak of "following humaneness" [*Analects* 7:6], and when they speak of cultivating oneself in accordance with the Way [*Mean* 20] they also feel compelled to speak of "cultivating the Way in accordance with humaneness" [*ibid*]. The Way is a general term for the totality of principle, and humaneness is the whole virtue of the mind-and-heart. . . . Humaneness is like finding your way home to the familiar ground whereon you can apply your efforts on behalf of others. When the ancient sages spoke of humaneness they always stressed its essential importance. *"Jen* means to be a man"* [*Mencius* 7B:16]. *"Jen* is the mind of man"* [*Mencius* 6A:11). In other words, they explained it by directly citing the complete substance. . . . [86]

Chen Te-hsiu also gave particular emphasis to the inseparability of substance and function, especially as applied to learning:

As we read in the *Record* [*of Ritual, She-i*], in ancient times the people were taught virtuous conduct and the arts of the Way. There was nothing in the daily lives of the people, whether in activity or repose, eating or drinking, that was not a subject of study . . . for among the ancients study and practice were one. They discussed principles with a view to their practical applications [function] and took advantage of practical applications as a means to exalt virtue. In later ages study and practice have been two different things. Those who profess to seek the Way regard concrete forms and implements as gross excrescences, and those who manage affairs look on moral principles as so much empty talk. This, then, is the difference between past and present.

In the learning of the sages . . . substance and function [principle and practice] were never separate. Among the philosophers, Lao Tzu and Chuang Tzu talked about principles without touching on human affairs, and thus the world had substance without function. The early Legalists Kuan Tzu and Lord Shang talked about affairs but did not touch on principles, so that the world had applications [function] based on no substance. The reason the sages found fault with the practices of the heterodox lay precisely in this.[87]

3. Reverence. In the *Heart Classic* alone there is ample evidence of the importance of reverence in the thought of Chen Te-hsiu, as in that of the early Ch'eng-Chu school generally. But one encounters it everywhere in Chen's works as the basis for both self-cultivation and social action—even, for instance, in the opening passage of the *Classic on Government*, for all its secular concerns.[88] The following excerpt explains how this type of religious awareness, as a reverent respect for life, involves no discontinuity from rational, moral, or affective consciousnesses such as is found in Buddhism and Taoism, but is a continuum including both quiescent and active states. The following is from a memoir of a friend's studio named "The Studio of Reverent Thoughtfulness."

Reverence is oneness and constitutes the continuum between action and quiescence. As to the difference between taking thought and not taking thought, when the seven emotions [joy, anger, sorrow, fear, love, hatred, desire] remain unaroused, heavenly principle is whole and undifferentiated. To preserve the mind in this state, nothing is needed but holding and nourishing. At such a time there is nothing to think about. But when the emotions become aroused, there is a difference between good and evil, and if fine distinctions are not made, a slight miscalculation leads to incalculable error. At such a time thinking is indispensable. To be without [predetermined] thought is for establishing the basis; to have thought is for engaging in practical action. Action and quiescence are interdependent; their efficacy is as one. But what the sages and worthies have been most insistent upon is quiescence. . . .

"To be ever reverent" [in the *Record of Rites*] refers to the combination of action and quiescence. "To be stern in thought"[89] refers just to quiescence. But in the midst of quiescence, what is there to think about or deliberate over? What can it mean, then, to be "stern in thought"? It is just like a mirror: even when there is nothing for it to reflect, the mind radiates principle, which is never absent. The mind, empty and spiritual, penetrates within and without, and even when it is not actively engaged in thought or deliberation, all principles are contained within. Even when one is sitting motionless and erect, with one's garments straight and one's demeanor composed, the radiation of one's spiritual intelligence is as if one were engaged in thought. When one experiences this deep within the self, ideas and images spontaneously arise in the mind. Chuang Tzu would "make the body become like withered wood and the mind like dead ashes." [90] Our kind of no- [predetermined] thought is meant to establish the ground for thought. Chuang Tzu's kind of no-thought is intended to render the mind useless and purposeless. This is typical of the way deviant doctrines mislead men. . . .

The Great Appendix [to the *Changes*] says, "Tranquil and unmoving, when it responds to things it penetrates all-under-Heaven." Only when discussion reaches this level of the sage will it be free from any defect. I hope [our friend] Chin-po will personally realize this, so that in moving successively from quiescence to action everything will be done with reverence. Thus when there is thought, it is a responsiveness which follows from tranquillity and when there is no thought, it is the tranquillity which follows from responsiveness. . . . [91]

4. Empirical learning. As we have seen, despite Chen Te-hsiu's strong religious orientation and moral rigorism, he does not neglect intellectual concerns or the study of the external world. The following passage is from Chen's answer to the question "Why does the *Great Learning* speak only of the 'investigation of things' and not of 'fathoming principle'?" Here the term *ch'i* (lit. "implements") refers to concrete embodiments of the Way as discussed in the *Changes*. [92]

Concrete things have form. The Way is formless principle. Master Ming-tao [Ch'eng Hao] said, "The Way is concrete things and concrete things are the Way." [93] The two are never separate. All things under Heaven which have form or shape are concrete things. Their principles lie within them. Even such great things as Heaven and earth are physical. The male and female principles are metaphysical. . . . Sun, moon, and stars, wind, rain, frost, and dew are all physical; their principles are metaphysical. Speaking of the body, its form is physical; speaking of the nature or the principle of the mind-and-heart, they are metaphysical. With all objects and implements it is the same. Lamps and candles are implements; that they can shine is their metaphysical principle. Beds and stands are implements; their functions are principles. In the world there are no implements without principles and no principles without implements [embodying them]. . . . If you set aside implements and search for principles, you cannot escape empty theorizing, which is not the real, practical learning of our Confucian school. The reason the *Great Learning* teaches the investigation of things and the extension of knowledge is that principles are always found in things. Scholars should have the solid ground of reality on which to exert their efforts and not let their minds chase off into realms of empty nothingness.[94]

A recent account of the life of the classicist and historian Wang Ying-lin (1223–1296), after discussing the relative influence of Chu Hsi and Lu Hsiang-shan upon him, concludes that perhaps the greatest influence upon his encyclopedic scholarship was Chen Te-hsiu: "No doubt the breadth of Wang's writings provide some justification for both claims [on behalf of Chu and Lu], but perhaps it would be more accurate to say that he was deeply influenced by the example of Chen Te-hsiu, because in his desire to prepare for the *po-hsüeh hung-tz'u* examination, he compiled a vast amount of material from all branches of knowledge without which later generations might have lost the threads of cultural growth broken by China's absorption into the Mongol empire."[95] This would seem to suggest that Neo-Confucian reverence and a concern for the moral nature need not preclude, and might indeed motivate, pursuit of learning over a wide range. The *Extended Meaning of the Great Learning* exemplifies exactly this combination.

From this brief discussion it may perhaps be appreciated how Chen Te-hsiu brings to the Learning of the Emperors a body of philosophical discourse which goes well beyond the level on which Fan Tsu-yü had presented that learning. Of particular importance is the concept of "whole substance and great functioning," which relates the manifold faculties of man to an active effort for the achievement of a humane world order.

The Extended Meaning of the Great Learning
(Ta-hsüeh yen-i) [96]

In the classical context, "to extend the meaning" *(yen-i)* means to enlarge upon the significance of the Way of humaneness and righteousness.[97] This would also apply to the Sung style of classical interpretation—not the literal, phrase-by-phrase dissection of a text (though both Chu and Chen had done some of that), but the drawing out of its larger significance and contemporary application. What was most relevant to Chen and most germane to his particular line of approach had already been indicated when he first presented the *Great Learning* for discussion at the classics mat. Chen knew he faced a problem—the same problem as earlier lecturers like Fan Tsu-yü, Ch'eng Hao, and Chu Hsi—about the emperor's recognizing and living up to his own humanity. Commenting on passages in the *Book of Documents* concerning the clarifying or "illumining" of the virtuous nature *(ming-te)*, he said:

luminous virtue is something shared by all men. What makes the difference between their becoming sagely or stupid lies only in whether they are able to illumine that virtue or not. The ordinary man's inability to clarify it derives either from a weakness of his psychophysical endowment or from the obscuration of the desire for things. Despite this obscuration, however, if one day he experiences a feeling of remorse and wants to clarify his own virtue, then there is no reason why he cannot do it. If he should have doubts about his own capacity to achieve it and cannot bring himself to try, there is the saying of Confucius: "If I wish to be humane, humaneness is already right there." [*Analects* 7:30][98]

Chen's intentions, both philosophical and personal, are further expressed in the memorial accompanying his presentation of the *Extended Meaning* to the throne in 1234, where he first speaks of its relation to classical tradition and Sung teaching:

I have heard that in the Way of the sages there is substance and function. To root it in the self is substance; to extend it to the world is function. Yao, Shun, and the Three Kings' conduct of government, the Six Classics, and Confucius' and Mencius' conduct of teaching did not go beyond this. The *Great Learning* is most clear and complete in its presentation of substance and function, root and branch, and their order of priorities. Therefore, recent scholars [the Ch'engs and Chu Hsi] have said that today, for perceiving the ancients' method of learning one need only rely on this work, with the *Analects* and *Mencius* to supplement it. What are spoken of as the "investigation of things," the "extension of knowledge," the "making of the will sincere," and the "cultivation of the person"—these are the substance. "The regulating of the family, ordering of the state, and pacifying of the world" are its function [application]. The learning of the ruler must be based on these if he is to understand the fullness of substance and function.[99]

He gives a further statement of purposes in his preface to the work itself, which includes his own outline of the contents. I give it here in full.

Preface to the Extended Meaning of the Great Learning

When your minister first read the *Great Learning*, he became aware that there is an order of importance and sequence of priorities among the investigation of things, the extension of knowledge, the making of the will sincere, the rectifying of the mind-and-heart, the cultivation of the person, the regulating of the family, the ordering of the state, and the pacifying of all-under-Heaven. As I fondly perused its contents I exclaimed to myself, He who would be a ruler among men cannot fail to study the *Great Learning*. He who would be a minister among men cannot fail to study the *Great Learning*. The ruler who fails to comprehend the *Great Learning* lacks the means to arrive at a clear understanding of the source of governance. The minister who fails to comprehend the *Great Learning* lacks the means to fulfill his duty of correcting the ruler.

Only when one has inquired into the governance of the emperors and kings of antiquity, and found that they invariably take the human person as its basis and extend this to all-under-Heaven, can one appreciate that this book represents an essential text in transmitting the mind-and-heart of the hundred sages, and is not just the personal utterance of Confucius alone. After the Three Dynasties this learning of the emperors and kings was lost, and although this text survived it was no more than a brief outline. Where then could one go if he sought to inquire into good government or sought to expound it to the prince?

Only Han Yü and Li Ao in the T'ang took up this teaching, as may be seen from their essays "On the Way" and "Returning to One's True Nature,"[100] and yet even they were unable to recognize in it a full-fledged theory and program of government. Thus after the Ch'in and Han dynasties only Han Yü and Li Ao showed some respect for this book, and since even they were unaware of it as the true source of sagely learning, how much less could one expect others to be aware of it.

It has long been my humble view that this one book, the *Great Learning*, could serve as a model and standard for a prince's governance of the world. If this were taken as the basis, the establishment of order would be assured; if it were flouted, disorder would be the certain consequence. The great scholar of recent times, Chu Hsi, wrote *Words and Phrases in the Great Learning* and *Questions Concerning the Great Learning* in order to analyze and clarify its meaning. At the beginning of the reign of Ning-tsung (1195–1224), he was called to serve at court and lecture on the classics. Often he presented this text for discussion. He who would govern well, Chu said, if he examined this work carefully and understood it thoroughly, would find in it a clear and systematic exposition of the emperors' and kings' order of priorities in the conduct of government, as well as the basis for conducting his own learning.[101]

Now your minister makes bold to say that he has ventured to give some thought to supplementing this work. Therefore he has taken some passages from the text, amounting to 205 words, and put them in this compilation, prefacing them with the teachings found in the "Canon of Yao" (*Yao tien*), the "Counsels of Kao" (*Kao-yao mo*), and "Instructions of I Yin" (*I hsün*) [in the *Book of Documents*], as well as passages from the *Odes* of Ssu-ch'i and the *Chia-jen* hexagram of the *Book of Changes*. From this one can see that the precepts of the sages [in these classics] do not differ from those of the *Great Learning*. Following these are the views of such later scholars as Tzu-ssu, Mencius, Hsün Tzu, Tung Chung-shu, Yang Hsiung, and Chou Tun-i, from which we can see that the theories of later worthies too are in accord with it. (The foregoing represents the emperors' and kings' priorities in governing.)

The learning of Yao, Shun, Yü, T'ang, Wen, and Wu was the purest form of the *Great Learning*. The learning of Kao-tsung of the Shang and King Ch'eng of the Chou came close to it. By the Han and T'ang dynasties, even in the case of the more worthy rulers it was no longer possible for their learning to avoid contravention of this learning in some ways, but the learning of the Emperors Hsiao and Yüan of Han and many rulers thereafter was involved either with mere technical contrivances or philological niceties and could not but fall into serious error. (The foregoing represents the emperors' and kings' pursuit of learning.)

For several thousands of years, early and late, order and disorder and the rise and fall of dynasties have all followed from this, and it is therefore my decided opinion that these teachings should serve as rules and regulations for anyone seeking to govern. Nevertheless, in the learning of the ruler it is necessary to know what is most essential if one is to know where to apply one's efforts. For the ruler what is most essential in the investigation of things and the extension of knowledge is that there should be a clarification of the practice of the Way, that there should be careful discrimination in the judging of human talents, that there should be careful consideration of the forms of rule, and that there should be attention to ascertaining the feelings of the people.

(Clarifying the practice of the Way consists of four items: [recognition of] the goodness of the heavenly nature and the human mind; the correctness of Heaven's principles in human relations; the difference between our Way and deviant doctrines; and the difference between the kingly way and the way of the despot.)

(Judging human talents also consists of four items: the sages' and worthies' methods of observing men; how the emperors and kings got to know men; the techniques by which clever scoundrels usurp the state; the passions exploited by those who would ensnare the ruler.)

(Consideration of the forms of rule consists of two things: distinguishing the order of priorities in the exercise of virtue and the application of punishments, and assessing the relative weight of righteousness and profit.)

(Ascertaining the state of the people's feelings also consists of two items: according with the people's sensibilities; and learning the facts of life in the countryside.)

The most essential things in making the will sincere and rectifying the mind-and-heart are exalting reverent awe and restraining wayward desires.

(Exalting reverent awe consists of six items: the reverence which is manifested in cultivating the person; the reverence which is manifested in serving Heaven; the reverence manifested in dealing with the people; the reverence manifested in dealing with affairs; the effort of preserving the mind and engaging in self-examination; the assistance of admonition and warning [from others].)

(Restraining wayward desires consists of five items: restraining drunkenness; restraining lewd desires; curbing wasteful amusements; curbing extravagance; the above are preceded by a general discussion concerning the consequences of failure to restrain these four.)

The most essential things in the cultivation of the person are to be careful in word and deed, and to maintain a proper demeanor and bearing. (These being one, there are no subtopics here.)

The most essential items in regulating the family are taking the matter of wives seriously, being strict in dealing with the inner court; settling the dynastic succession, and providing proper education for the conjugal relatives.

(Taking the matter of wives seriously consists of four items: care in the selection and installing of wives; the benefits of listening to sound advice; differentiating legal wives and consorts from others; the error of disestablishing legal consorts.)

(Strictness in dealing with the inner court consists of four items: strict separation of inner and outer courts; curbing the inner court's interference in affairs of state; the blessings of loyal and conscientious admonition on the part of ministers in the inner court [eunuchs]; the misfortune of ministers of the inner court interfering in state affairs.)

(Settling the dynastic succession consists of four items: planning for the installation of the heir apparent should be done in advance; provision for the system of instruction should be planned for; the differentiation between legal wives and concubines should guard against the danger of disestablishing [the heir apparent].)

(Providing proper education for the conjugal relatives consists of two items: the blessings of modest and respectful comportment on the part of the conjugal relatives, and the unfortunate consequences of arrogance and overweening ambition on the part of conjugal relatives.)

If these four ways can be followed [corresponding to the four major topics above], then the ordering of the state and pacifying of the world will require nothing more than can be found therein. Under each heading are given the luminous instructions of the sages and worthies, and then historical examples from former times. In these success and failure are clearly mirrored.

In former times I served as lecturer at court and dedicated myself to this task; in recent years whenever I could spare time from my duties I studied the classics and commentaries and succeeded in collecting this compilation. This then is what I have to show for my loyal dedication [to the emperor's interests] even when away from court, quietly pursuing the task of compilation while awaiting the time when I might present this to the throne. The guidelines for this book are all in the *Great Learning*, the first two parts setting forth the general principles and the last four parts giving the details, so as to bring out the extended meaning and significance of the *Great Learning*. Therefore I have entitled it *The Extended Meaning of the Great Learning*.[102]

From the foregoing one may get a sense of the difference between Chen's work and the *Great Learning* or its usual commentaries. He is not elaborating upon the general significance of the text for individual cultivation. He does not even address the issues much debated in the Sung about the intellectual and ethical priorities in the education of the Confucian scholar, much less the larger philosophical questions which surround these. Nor does he concern himself with political questions of the type dealt with in his *Classic on Government*. He rather speaks to the ruler's mind-and-heart, his intentions as ruler, and his practice of rulership. These are, of course, the typical concerns of the lectures on the classics at court and the Learning of the Emperor.

The *Catalogue of the Imperial Manuscript Library* testifies to this, when, after summarizing the contents and noting Chen's method of exposition, it observes:

The overall gist of it was to rectify the ruler's mind-and-heart, to be stern with the inner palace, and to reprove imperial favorites who abuse authority. The Emperor Li-tsung, though paying lip-service to the teaching of the Way, inwardly cherished excessive sensual desires. Powerful ministers and imperial relatives intrigued together to abet his licentiousness, leaving him debilitated and exhausted. For over fifty years this sort of thing went on until the Sung was destroyed.[103]

We may note too that the editors of the *Catalogue*, writing in the Ch'ing period when much of Sung scholarship was called into question, concluded that Chen's teachings offered a practical guide to the problems of rulership. "It is not just empty talk about the mind and human nature."[104]

Though the outline of contents given in Chen's preface has its own interest for what it reveals of his overall conception, some explanation may help to bring out the significance of his headings in the light of the actual contents and the line of argument he develops in his personal comments at the end of each section. From the *Great Learning* Chen borrows only the most general concepts. He also draws to a limited extent on the conceptual framework and terminology of Chu Hsi's "Articles of the Academy of the White Deer Grotto," which state the general principles and order of priorities to be followed in education, under such headings as "The Order [of Precedence, or Priority] in the Pursuit of Learning" *(Wei-hsüeh chih hsü);* "The Essentials of Cultivating the Person" *(hsiu-shen chih yao);* "The Essentials of Handling Affairs" *(ch'u-shih chih yao);* "The Essentials of Dealing with Others" *(chieh-wu chih yao).*[105] The similarities between these and Chen's headings are sufficient to indicate that Chen is prescribing a program of education in keeping with Chu Hsi's. Otherwise the structure, development, and details of the *Extended Meaning* are of Chen's own devising.

On the most general level, the contents are divided into six parts of disparate length. The first part, in just one fascicle, is the only one that could be construed as an interpretation of the *Great Learning* itself. It attempts to show that the approach to self-government through self-cultivation is implicit in the earlier classics and was accepted by the leading philosophers of the later Confucian school. In other words this teaching constitutes the essence of the Way of the emperors and kings as a way of government.

The second part, in three fascicles, describes the emperors' and kings' way of learning, i.e., what they studied and from whom they sought instruction. This is the part that corresponds most closely to Fan Tsu-yü's *Learning of the Emperors.*

The third part, under the overall heading "The Investigation of Things and the Extension of Knowledge," consists of twenty-two fascicles, more than half the work. The contents are so heterogeneous that one might question whether the *Great Learning's* rubrics provide a coherent rationale for them, but the basic idea seems to be that these are all appropriate subjects for the ruler to study and therefore part of his intellectual cultivation.

The fourth part, under the heading "Making the Will Sincere and Rectifying the Mind-and-Heart" consists of seven fascicles discussing moral and spiritual cultivation, with heavy emphasis on reverence and restraining the desires. The fifth part, entitled "Cultivating the Person" is in just one fascicle and deals with the ruler's personal comportment: how he measures his words and maintains a proper demeanor as an example for his subjects to emulate. These two parts dealing with moral cultivation are only one-third the length of the part dealing with intellectual cultivation, but the difference in emphasis is more apparent than real, since so much of what is to be studied in the latter pertains to moral questions.

The sixth and last part, headed "Regulating the Family," has little to do with family relations of the usual sort but is specifically directed to the problems of the ruling family as a dynasty.

Those familiar with the Eight Items *(pa t'iao-mu)* of the *Great Learning* will notice that the last two of the eight are not represented here. In the Ming period, when the *Extended Meaning* was to have an especially great vogue, a leading scholar-official and follower of the Chu Hsi school, Ch'iu Chün (1420–1495), shared in the prevailing esteem for this work, but noting the absence of the items "Ordering the State" and "Pacifying the World," he compiled another massive work, the *Supplement to the Extended Meaning of the Great Learning (Ta-hsüeh yen-i pu),* to correct the ostensible deficiency.[106] Actually there is no reason to believe that Chen felt his work to have been left unfinished. Five years had elapsed between its completion and its submission to the throne, ample time in which to fill any gaps. Therefore, we may take him at his word when, in the preface, he says nothing more would be needed for ordering the state and pacifying the world than the steps already outlined for cultivating the ruler's person. Ch'iu's supplement, then, may be considered an independent contribution, "sheltering under" the prestige of Chen's *Extended Meaning* just as the latter exploited the extraordinarily high standing of the *Great Learning* in the late Sung. Ch'iu's purposes had to do with the conduct of state administration and governmental institutions, something Chen had dealt with in the *Classic on Government* but considered secondary to his main purpose in the *Extended Meaning.* For he seems genuinely to have believed that these institutional problems would take care of themselves if the primary problem of the emperor's personal orientation to rulership could be dealt with.

Chen's opening quotation from the Canon of Yao sets the tone and direction of his own approach to that problem. It says of Emperor Yao that

he was reverential, intelligent, accomplished and thoughtful—naturally and without effort. He was sincerely courteous and capable of all complaisance. The display of these qualities reached to the four extremities of the empire and extended from earth to heaven. He was able to make illustrious his lofty virtue and thence proceeded to the love of the nine classes of his kindred, who all became harmonious. He also regulated and polished the people of his domain, who all became brightly intelligent. Finally he united and harmonized the myriad states of the empire and lo, the black-haired people were transformed. The result was universal concord.[107]

Chen takes this as confirming the essential message of the *Great Learning* that self-cultivation is the basis of government and can be universalized so as to achieve world peace. His comment on this passage is:

Natural virtue is what all men possess in common. Originally there is no differentiation of wise and foolish among them, but in conjunction with the physical endowment, they may become obscured by selfish desires and their virtue cannot manifest itself. They must then follow a ruler of divine sageliness whose manifestation of virtue is an example to all the world. Only then can they be returned to their original state. . . .

Thus the governance of the sage-emperors was never more flourishing than it was with Yao, and it all started with his self-conquest and the clarifying of his own inner virtue. Hence the *Great Learning* takes the clarifying of luminous virtue as the starting point of renewing the people, but the Canon of Yao is the honored forefather of the *Great Learning*.[108]

Chen then proceeds to another quotation from the Plans of Kao Yao in the *Book of Documents:*

Oh! let him be careful about his personal cultivation, with thoughts that are far-reaching, and then he will expect a generous kindness and nice observance of distinctions among the nine classes of his kindred; all the intelligent will exert themselves in his service; and from what is near he may reach in this way to what is distant.[109]

Chen comments on this:

> The person of the ruler is the true root of the empire and
> dynasty, and, in a word, "careful circumspection" is the root of
> cultivating the person. One who is concerned about the [dynasty's]
> enduring, wishes it to last and not expire; one who wishes to be a
> ruler of men cannot but know that he should cultivate his person. If
> one is to be careful, he must be constantly reverent and not heedless;
> and if he is to be thoughtful, he must preserve his mind and not let
> it get lost. In this the way of cultivating the person is replete. . . .
> From one's own family this can be extended to the state, and from
> the state to all-under-Heaven.[110]

Two quotations from the later philosophers will illustrate how
Chen appropriates them too to his purpose. First from Tung Chung-
shu (c. 179–c. 104):

> The ruler rectifies his mind-and-heart in order to rectify the
> court. He rectifies the court in order to rectify the hundred officials;
> he rectifies them in order to rectify the myriad peoples; he rectifies
> them in order to rectify all in the four directions. . . .[111]

Chen comments:

> Since Mencius no one has said it so well as Tung. The court is
> the basis of the empire, the ruler the basis of the court, and the
> mind-and-heart the basis of the ruler. . . . It all goes back to the
> mind-and-heart of the ruler.[112]

The second quotation is from Yang Hsiung (53 B.C.–A.D. 18):

> Although the empire is large, its governance lies within the
> Way, which makes it small. Although the four seas are distant, their
> governance lies in the mind-and-heart, which makes them near.[113]

Chen's comment:

> The Way is principle. Although the empire is vast it is all one
> principle. If the ruler follows principle in what he does, there is
> order; if he flouts principle, there is disorder. Therefore it is said,
> "Order depends on the Way." Though the four seas are vast, if the
> ruler's mind-and-heart are rectified, there is order; if not, there is

disorder. Therefore it is said, "Order lies in the mind-and-heart." [114]

From these four examples out of twelve in this section we see how Chen asserts self-cultivation as the basis of rulership and then rectification of the mind-and-heart as the basis of self-cultivation. Thus the Learning of the Mind-and-Heart is the key to the Learning of the Emperors.

In the second part of the book, entitled "The Learning of the Emperors and Kings," his procedure is similar. The initial quotation is the now familiar one from the *Book of Documents:* "The mind of man is insecure; the mind of the Way is barely perceptible. Have utmost refinement and singleness of mind. Hold fast the Mean!" This is followed by Chu Hsi's explanation of it, already cited, and Chen's comment:

> The sixteen characters beginning with "The mind of man is insecure . . ." are the system of the mind-and-heart handed down from Yao, Shun, and Yü, and the source of the sages' learning for all generations. If the ruler wishes to study Yao and Shun, he need only study these texts. And although former scholars have offered a host of interpretations [of these texts] that of Chu Hsi alone represents the utmost in clarity and precision.
>
> What is referred to [by Chu Hsi] as the "selfishness identified with physical form" indicates the desires arising from the senses of sight, sound, smell, and taste. The "correctness of the innate moral imperative" refers to the principles of humaneness, righteousness, decorum, and wisdom. The sense desires all arise from the ether *(ch'i)* and represent the "mind of man." The principles of humaneness, righteousness, decorum, and wisdom are all rooted in the original nature of man and represent the mind of the Way.
>
> Now speaking of this in the person of the ruler, he has the desire to enjoy the comfort and security of the palace, the desire for fine food and beautiful garments, the desire to be served by lovely ladies, the enjoyment of outings in the countryside—all of which arise from the mind of man. If this mind dominates him and he cannot exercise proper judgment and control, then desires for things proliferate and he is close to going the way of [the wicked kings] Chieh and Chou. To know that ambitions for wealth and rank are not to be trusted and to guard against them with scrupulous care; to know that arrogance and extravagance cannot be allowed free rein,

but must be controlled by humility and frugality; to know that fine wines and delicacies are deadly addictions that ensnare the mind, and to give thought to abstaining from them—these all arise from the mind of the Way. If this mind dominates and there is no slackening or loss of control, then moral principles will be replete and one will not be far from going the way of Yao and Shun. . . .[115]

Here we have Chen's essential definition of the Learning of the Emperor. All that follows is an elaboration upon or illustration of it. Later in this section, discussing the "clarifying of luminous virtue," he explains that since goodness has no fixed substance, one must have singleness of mind and constant watchfulness in responding to the promptings of the mind-and-heart.[116] "If one is concerned with virtue, one must make goodness the master of the mind, and for choosing goodness, singleness must be the master."[117]

This being the case, says Chen, the essential transmission of learning from the sage-emperors consists in control of the mind.

When King Ch'eng of Chou inaugurated his rule, the Duke of Chou was concerned that the former might learn the system of government from King Wen but not his system of the mind-and-heart. Therefore he wrote the document entitled "Establishing Government" [in the *Book of Documents*],[118] which set forth all matters concerning the appointing of officers and the employment of men, but he insisted on giving first priority to the stabilizing of the mind.[119]

Just as goodness is not a fixed thing but requires reverent attentiveness and impartiality to follow it, so in the Learning of the Emperor there is need for constant effort.

The reason for seeking much learning is only to handle affairs. Learning must deal with affairs if it is to be useful. Otherwise one may learn a great deal and nothing will come of it. . . . But in learning one must find the Way in and for oneself *(tzu-te)* if it is to be effective. Otherwise the Way remains itself and I remain myself, as if there had never been any learning going on. . . .

One must learn from the past and renew it in order to advance the Way and advance in the Way. There must be an accumulation of good, day by day, until the Way and the self eventually become an inseparable unity. This is a process of "creating principles one by one."[120]

Having established that self-rectification of the mind is the substance of the Learning of the Emperors, Chen goes on to evaluate successive rulers and ministers by that standard. His cast of characters is much the same as Fan Tsu-yü's. The near-heroes, by comparison to ancient sages, are the founders of the Han and T'ang dynasties. Few other rulers approach their wisdom and virtue; the well-intentioned, but weak and self-indulgent, abound. The most pathetic of the latter is T'ang Hsüan-tsung (or Ming-huang, r. 712–756). Among usurpers Wang Mang (29–23 A.D.) in the Han is the classic villain. Empress Wu (r. 691–704) in the T'ang also gets much attention for her usurpation, though her abilities are also grudgingly admired. Examples of worthy ministers are Tung Chung-shu under the unworthy Emperor Wu (r. 140–88 B.C.) of the Han; Wei Cheng (589–643) and others under the worthy T'ang T'ai-tsung (r. 627–649), Lu Chih (754–805) under the unheeding Te-tsung (r. 780–804) of the T'ang, etc. The list of unworthy rulers and ministers is, of course, a long one. There are also many mixed cases and mismatches—rulers originally well disposed but misled and corrupted by crafty ministers; noble ministers victimized by slander and abandoned by their sovereigns, etc.

Chen's evaluation implicitly judges teachings as well as emperors. Thus in Emperor Kuang-wu (r. 25–57 A.D.) of the Latter Han, Chen recognizes many of the qualities of a leader and scholar; but, for want of ministers with a true understanding of the classics who could help him rectify his mind-and-heart, he was led into many improper actions, such as putting to death a remonstrating minister, dispossessing the designated heir apparent, setting aside the legitimate empress, etc.[121] Similarly, with T'ang Hsüan-tsung, the implied criticism of his scholarly advisers is that they represented a sterile, pedantic classicism or a dilettantish belle-lettrism. He was fond of letters, but his ministers' scholarship did not go beyond the literary and philological. So literature and art flourished under him but did not prevent him from being ensnared by a beautiful woman and deceived by treacherous ministers. "Hence the learning of the ruler, if it does not take the sages and kings as one's teachers and put cultivating of the person and rectifying of the mind first, will come to no good."[122]

Chen's exposition of the basis of rulership sets the overall direction of the work. There follows, in the major part of the work entitled "The Investigation of Things and Extension of Knowledge," a discussion of things it is essential for the ruler to learn, most of them relating to his self-cultivation. These fall into five general categories:

Goodness of human nature—This doctrine is the fundamental assumption for both self-cultivation and public morality. For the fulfillment of this goodness the ruler bears a heavy responsibility through his conduct of education:

> If you take human nature to be evil and forcibly try to teach men to be good, they will rebel and not conform [to their own best nature]. . . . The Way and human nature are one. . . . To conform to one's [true] nature is to rest in the Way. . . . The parent rests in compassion [for the child]; the child rests in filiality. Only when one knows what must be so and cannot be changed, what is meet and proper so that one cannot just have one's own way, can one be at rest.[123]

> If one takes one's own nature to be evil and does not attempt to govern the self according to the Way of the sages, this is to do violence to oneself. And to take the nature of man to be evil and not govern him according to the Way of the sages, is to do violence to all-under-Heaven.[124]

Humaneness—"What is humaneness? It is 'to conquer self and return to decorum [ritual].' This is the substance of humaneness. To love men and benefit things is its function. For the ruler this means that inwardly he eschews the selfish desire for things and sees to it that in everything he sees, hears, or says, or does there is nothing not in accord with decorum."[125]

Filiality—Love and respect for one's own parents and family should be extended to all the people. The rulers of later times, however, did not extend this love and respect beyond their own family (i.e., their dynastic house), and by bringing misfortune upon the people, they eventually jeopardized their own kith and kin and endangered their ancestral altars (i.e., the life of the dynasty).[126]

Human relations—As in the foregoing, Chen's discussion of human relations is in the special context of the emperor's own relations, particularly with his wives and ministers. It is essential for the emperor to maintain his own self-respect and not let himself be dominated by others.[127] At the same time he must respect the dignity of his ministers. In the Han the ruler assumed too exalted a position and the minister came to be treated as a menial servant. Thus a great gap opened up between ruler and minister, and the intimate understanding between the two became impaired.[128] It reached the point where rulers regarded truly loyal and conscientious ministers, who did their duty in remonstrating with him, as enemies.[129] If they cannot agree on correct principles, the minister must withdraw from service to the ruler. This is true love for the ruler. A servile and compliant attitude represents the height of disrespect for the emperor.[130]

Orthodoxy and heterodoxy—Again the discussion focuses on the ruler's self-cultivation by the method of "utmost refinement and singleness, and by holding fast to the Mean." Because the emperor occupies such a crucial position, affecting the lives of all the people by his exercise of power and the influence of his example, he must meet and set the highest standard for humaneness and filiality. Chen especially notes the personal contribution of Chu Hsi on this point. "Out of his own deep wisdom Chu contributed something he had learned for himself, speaking for the first time ever about the ruler's setting the preeminent standard, so rulers would know that, being at the head of the people, all of their self-cultivation and political actions must set the highest standard."[131]

The only way for the ruler to achieve this is for him to "subdue one's self and return to decorum." Ch'eng I is quoted as calling this the "essence of the system of the mind-and-heart as transmitted by the sages."[132] " 'Self' here means the selfishness of human desires. If they are not made subject to decorum, they will dominate principle and destroy it. Human desires injure men. That is why the word 'conquer' or 'subdue,' the language of warfare, is used [by Confucius]: because human desires are enemies of man."[133]

In his discussion of heterodoxy Chen cites a long list of rulers deceived by practitioners of the occult, seduced into indulging their own weaknesses, or encouraged in their excessive lust for power.[134]

Such are the topics developed in Chen's first section of "The

Investigation of Things and Extension of Knowledge." They represent the classic subject matter of Confucian study as interpreted in terms of Neo-Confucian philosophy and as illustrated by examples from the histories. The second section under this same general heading has to do with practical judgment in evaluating human character and the ways of men in relation to the uses of power. There is extensive discussion of the misjudgments of emperors who put their trust in clever men, eventually shown to be unscrupulous in their pursuit of power for unworthy ends, or who refused to heed the advice of honest ministers, trying in vain to warn the ruler of threatening danger. The tactics and stratagems of usurpers are exposed in detail. In age after age wily scoundrels observed the weaknesses of rulers and played up to them. Chen quotes Fan Tsu-yü: "Unworthy men never fail to encourage the ruler's selfish desires so that they may advance their own selfish desires." [135]

Among the devices of such schemers cited by Chen are flattery of the emperor, slander and calumny of worthy ministers, the use of alluring women or attractive young men to seduce the ruler, calculated efforts to estrange the emperor from the empress or from his son and heir apparent, or to exploit divisions in the imperial family; enticing the emperor with schemes that will greatly increase his personal wealth or appeal to his lust for power, etc.

A third section deals with what the emperor should know about the limits of reliance on power and coercion. It contrasts the sage-kings' limited use of punishments with the excessively harsh laws of the later Ch'in and Sui dynasties. This is followed by a discussion of the pursuit of virtue or profit as ends of government, and another stressing the importance of the emperor's ruling in the interests of all and ascertaining the state of the people's feelings, sharing with them his joys and their worries (as Mencius had put it). Good government, says Chen, originates in sentiments of reverential awe and serious concern; disorder arises from arrogance and contempt on the part of the ruler and his officials. The emperor should constantly "have the little people on his mind," and be aware of their difficulties and sufferings, lest they become overburdened by the exactions of officials. The Duke of Chou expressed such concerns to King Ch'eng of Chou in the *Odes* and *Documents*. "This is how he communicated the essentials of the system of the mind-and-heart handed down from the emperors and kings."[136]

On this note Chen concludes this lengthy and important part of the *Extended Meaning*. From his many scriptural quotations, philosophical explanations, and historical cases, he draws out what it is most essential for the emperor to learn: that his mind-and-heart should be constantly attentive to the needs of the people and responsive to them.

But Chen goes further to point out how this result can be achieved: by the encouragement of open discussion at court. If there is an atmosphere which encourages the airing of all issues and charges, the truth will emerge for the emperor to see. Flattery, slander, cliquishness, and misappropriation will be exposed. Corruption cannot stand the light of open discussion. In this connection the great virtue of T'ang T'ai-tsung is often cited by Chen for his encouragement of outspoken debate at court, his willingness to accept criticism, and his readiness to correct his own mistakes.

The part of the work entitled "Making the Will Sincere and Rectifying the Mind" extends this line of thinking to the area of spiritual and moral cultivation. Here one finds emphasized the same themes we have already encountered in the *Heart Classic:* the attitude of reverent seriousness and the restraining of desires. Two quotations from Chen's commentary will suffice to illustrate this:

> Yao, Shun, Yü, T'ang, Wen, and Wu were all sages who followed Heaven, and the *Odes'* extolling of their virtue starts with their reverent attitude. Now reverence is the ruler of the one mind, the root and source of all that is good. What the scholar takes up for study and what the sage takes for sageliness do not lie outside this. . . . If the ruler wishes to take the emperors and kings as his teachers, must he not apply himself to this?[137]

> From the time of Yao and Shun on down, what has been passed on from generation to generation is just this one thing, reverence. What has made the difference between great sageliness and great wickedness is reverence or irreverence, that is all.[138]

There is more, but it is all to the points already noted in the *Heart Classic:* reverence as singleness of mind, reverence as the continuum between action and quiescence; preserving, recovering, or rectifying the mind-and-heart; constant self-watchfulness; and the value of the court lectures on the classics for the furtherance of these efforts on the part of the emperor.[139]

Restraint of the desires is treated at length and in considerable detail. In four thick fascicles Chen draws out the sorry record of imperial decadence and debauchery: drinking to the point of debility; sex to the point of exhaustion; extravagant entertainment; wasteful outings and excursions; destructive hunting parties; over-expenditure on luxurious palaces, etc.—all to the mournful accompaniment of warnings from Confucian ministers who go unheeded by irreverent and inattentive sovereigns.[140]

The concluding portions of the *Extended Meaning*, having to do with the emperor's management of his own household, illustrate the dangerous consequences that follow from not limiting the number and power of those kept in the inner palace—wives, concubines, and eunuchs, especially—who exploit the weaknesses of the ruler and utilize the stratagems that lead to his undoing. The more positive side of these discourses has to do with proper selection of wives for their virtue and wisdom, protecting the rights of legitimate wives, arranging for the legitimate succession and defending it from attempts to subvert it, and providing for the education of the imperial family.[141]

The Extended Meaning *and the Learning of the Mind-and-Heart*

The contents of Chen's *Extended Meaning of the Great Learning* reveal it as a major expression of the Learning of the Mind-and-Heart, as well as the culmination of several converging lines of thought and activity in the late Sung:

1. The rising importance of the *Great Learning* in the Ch'eng-Chu school.
2. Its special role in the lectures on the classics at court and in the developing genre of the Learning of the Emperors.
3. The Learning of the Mind-and-Heart viewed at this time as the essence of the orthodox tradition handed down from the sages.
4. Chen's own distillation of the Ch'eng-Chu teachings.

5. Chen's personal experiences as an official in the Sung court and in the provinces.

The *Extended Meaning* expounds the same underlying philosophy and advocates the same method of self-cultivation as the *Heart Classic*, but focuses these on the imperial institution. Like Fan Tsu-yü's *Learning of the Emperors*, it draws upon the literature and practice of the lectures from the classics mat, but is much broader in scope and, given the resources of Ch'eng-Chu thought available by this time, far richer in philosophical content. On the other hand, viewed as an extension of the Ch'eng-Chu Learning or System of the Mind-and-Heart, it gives the latter its most practical application to human institutions. So understood, the *Extended Meaning* is highly significant for the later development of both Neo-Confucianism and Chinese political thought.

To the extent that Chen's work had a strong influence on the formulation of Neo-Confucian orthodoxy, its original orientation becomes highly relevant to an understanding of its meaning. The human weaknesses Chen attacks so vigorously are not at all typical. They are those of rulers and dynasties, and by extension, of the ruling class who assist them, magnified in proportion to the power they hold. Plausibly the educated elite might recognize themselves in such characterizations, and depending on the historical and cultural circumstances, respond to the challenge of such a lofty ideal of service. On the other hand, a morality prescribed for such an elite leadership class would have its own limitations. One might anticipate signs of strain and rejection if it were generalized and prescribed among persons who could not see themselves in the same role or failed to find in themselves the weaknesses or excesses which had called for such a stern rigorism in the first place.

Before we leave this subject, a word or two is in order about the later history of the *Extended Meaning*. Printed by Chen in 1229, it was presented in 1234 to the Emperor Li-tsung, who paid much lip-service to it and ordered another printing for official distribution.[142] By the late 1250s at least it was circulating in Mongol-occupied North China. As heir apparent, Khubilai, prior to the proclamation of the Yüan dynasty in 1260, received in audience the learned scholar Chao

Pi (1220–1276). Impressed by Chao's scholarship, Khubilai assigned ten Mongol students to study Confucian texts with him and asked Chao to study the Mongol language so that he could translate the *Extended Meaning* into Mongol.[143] What became of the translation is unclear. In any case, on the accession of the Emperor Wu-tsung (Haishan) in 1308, his heir apparent Ayurbarwada (later to become Emperor Jen-tsung, r. 1312–1321) ordered the collection, preservation, and publication of classical writings; among them the *Extended Meaning* was especially honored. The future emperor ordered that an abridgment be made of it and translated into Mongol. He said of the *Extended Meaning,* with "its teaching of self-cultivation for the governance of men" that "this one work is sufficient for the governance of all-under-Heaven."[144]

It was also Jen-tsung who took the initiative in the official recognition of Neo-Confucianism. Hsü Heng, the leading Neo-Confucian teacher of the age, was enshrined along with the Sung masters in the Confucian temple in 1313.[145] That same year Jen-tsung ordered the resumption of the civil service examination system, but now using Chu Hsi's version of the Four Books as the basic texts for the first time, a pattern that was to endure into the twentieth century. During Jen-tsung's reign too another translation of the *Extended Meaning* into Mongol was ordered, presumably because previous attempts at translation were abortive, incomplete, or unsatisfactory.[146] Jen-tsung made gifts of the work to his ministers, and in 1318 had copies of a new printing of selected passages distributed to court officials.[147] Just after the accession of the Emperor Ying-tsung (Shidebala) in 1320, a new translation of the *Extended Meaning* was presented to the throne and he responded with another encomium of Chen's work as unsurpassed for its teaching of "ordering the state through self-cultivation" *(hsiu-shen chih-kuo).*[148] Under the reign of the Emperor T'ai-ting (Yesun Temur) from 1324–1327 great importance was given to lectures from the classics mat by both Mongol and Chinese scholars, with the *Extended Meaning* serving as one of the basic texts of instruction, along with the *Imperial Pattern (Ti-fan)* of T'ang T'ai-tsung, *The Essence of Government in the Chen-kuan Era (Chen-kuan cheng-yao),* and the *General Mirror for Aid in Government (Tzu-chih t'ung chien).*[149]

Thus the *Extended Meaning* and Chen Te-hsiu attained extraordinary prominence during precisely the same years in which the Ch'eng-Chu teaching was becoming established as the official teaching of the state and the new system of civil service examinations was setting the pattern to be followed by later ages in China. Chen's work had no direct part in the examinations, but the wide influence of his writings at this time suggests that they played a substantial role in the interpretation and promotion of Chu Hsi's teaching and in the intellectual development of the scholar-officials responsible for the establishment of the new state ideology.

Buddhism and the Learning of the Mind-and-Heart

Chen Te-hsiu's *Heart Classic*, as we have seen, offered a Neo-Confucian view of the mind in which a deep reverence and moral seriousness, combined in the Chinese term *ching*, were central virtues. The *Extended Meaning* showed how these virtues should be exercised in meeting the Confucian responsibility for leadership and public service. Together they expressed a new religiosity and social idealism which became a powerful inspiration in the rise of Neo-Confucianism.

Hitherto it has been commonplace to view Neo-Confucian religiosity as almost a direct adaptation from Buddhism. Almost any reference to the cultivation of the mind was suspected of having a Buddhist coloration. Moreover, as we have seen earlier, Chu Hsi had acknowledged the lack of any Neo-Confucian system of mind-culture until the appearance of the Ch'eng brothers in the Sung, and one easily assumed that they were incorporating Buddhist attitudes into a new hybrid Confucianism. Almost any attention to the "mind" was immediately interpreted as a sign of infiltration from Ch'an Buddhism.

Sorting out what is distinctively Confucian in the Ch'eng-Chu teaching, and what is influenced by Buddhism, is not easy. To start with, there had been a virulent reaction against Buddhism in the Sung school, which saw its critique of human values as prejudicial to urgently needed political and social reforms. Yet this dominant practical concern of the Neo-Confucians, though juxtaposed to the transcendental or "empty" view of Buddhism, should not be construed to mean that Chu Hsi and his school were wholly rationalistic and secularistic in their outlook, as has sometimes been assumed. Rather this school looked to the Chinese' own pre-Buddhist tradition for a religiosity fully compatible with their humanistic concerns. Chu Hsi himself was a deeply religious person, not at all insensitive to the powerful appeal of Ch'an, but he sought a spirituality that would be integral with moral cultivation and from the very beginning affirmative of social action, not just belatedly reconciled to it.

In the type of spirituality which the Ch'eng-Chu school developed, the practice of quiet-sitting and a new preoccupation with self may be seen as influenced by Ch'an Buddhism.[150] Yet the original context of the Learning of the Mind-and-Heart, as presented by Chu Hsi and more fully elaborated by Chen Te-hsiu in the two works just discussed, demonstrates that this Neo-Confucian view of the mind-and-heart has a strong ethical and social orientation, and that the reverent seriousness which became the most characteristic Neo-Confucian virtue is explained as a direct expression of humaneness constantly attentive to the needs of human life, rationally anticipating the threat of human suffering and actively responding to it. Reverence as constant mindfulness, as humane concern, is an expression of the goodness of man's nature. Mencius, as we noted earlier, had spoken of the natural apprehension aroused in a man who sees a child about to fall into a well and rushes to save it. In the *Extended Meaning* such concern is raised to the level of heightened awareness appropriate in a ruler, whose exercise of power may have incalculable consequences for mankind. In the philosophical language used by Chen this doctrine of reverent seriousness can also be formulated as the key agency linking the "whole substance" of man's mind and its "great functioning," i.e., activating the total capacity of the mind-and-heart so that it becomes fully realized in the world of human affairs.

Characteristically this high seriousness of the Neo-Confucian takes the form of a strenuous effort to curb selfish desires; but in contradistinction to Buddhism, which was more concerned with the problem of enlightenment than with the social order, this restraint is directed primarily at self-indulgence on the part of those who exercise power. In other words, seriousness is "high" in proportion to the elevated station of those upon whom it is enjoined, and the dedication it demands is solemn in proportion to the great weight of responsibility which should be borne by the ruling class. Thus, while Chu and Chen attempt to reckon with the larger spiritual dimensions of the human problem here, they do not espouse a religiosity which renounces the world. Instead of a cloistered, ivory-towered withdrawal, it calls for active engagement in a problematical human situation.

Similarly, although there are frequent references in Neo-Confucianism to human desires as prone to err, there is nothing to suggest that human nature is radically evil or fundamentally corrupt. On the contrary, the goodness of human nature is affirmed as the basis for a high-minded dedication to the struggle against evil. One must understand its moral rigorism, then, not as a puritanical rejection of man or the world as evil, but as something more nearly akin to the modern revolutionary idealism and discipline which calls for the sacrifice of individual gratification in the higher interests of the common cause.

In the expression "System of the Mind-and-Heart" *(hsin-fa)*, often spoken of by Neo-Confucians as virtually equivalent to the "Learning of the Mind-and-Heart" *(hsin-hsüeh)*, we have another example of possible confusion with Buddhist concepts. The second half of the compound, *fa*, has many connotations in Chinese, the principal ones being "way," "method," "law," or "doctrine." We have already seen how Chen Te-hsiu identified this *hsin-fa* as a systematic but humane alternative to the power systems or coercive institutions identified with the early Legalist school in China. Accordingly, to translate *fa* as system here may convey some of its connotations as both the teaching and practice of mind-cultivation, which was to be developed in Neo-Confucianism on a more systematic basis than ever before.

The compound *hsin-fa* does appear as a way of cultivating or cleansing the mind in the poetry of Po Chü-i, but it becomes a standard philosophical term, in the sense intended here, only in the Sung.[151] Buddhist use of the term in exoteric and esoteric doctrine had to do with distinctions between physical *(se)* and mental *(hsin)*, or sensate and spiritual, components of reality.[152] Ch'an use of it as a discipline of the mind is almost certainly a later development, probably reflecting its currency in Sung Neo-Confucian circles.[153] We should not assume that the term or concept of *hsin-fa*, as used by Neo-Confucians, had to derive from Buddhism.

Among Sung Neo-Confucians Shao Yung (1011–1077) appears to have been the first to use the term for cultivation of the mind in its a priori or pre-conscious state. In his *Supreme Principles Governing the World (Huang-chi ching-shih shu)* he speaks of the "learning of the mind in its a priori, undifferentiated state as the system of the mind-and-heart" *(hsien-t'ien chih hsüeh hsin-fa yeh)*. And the commentary of Shao Po-wen (1057–1134) explains this in turn as the Mean or Supreme Ultimate, probably identifying it with the metaphysical doctrine expounded by Chou Tun-i in his *Diagram of the Supreme Ultimate Explained.*[154] Ch'en Ch'ang-fang (1108–1148) in his "Essay on the Learning of the Emperors" *(Ti-hsüeh lun)* speaks of the ruler's practice of the "rectification of the mind," taught in the *Great Learning,* as the "ruler's system of the mind-and-heart" *(jen-chu hsin-fa).*[155] Thus Neo-Confucian use of the term had by this time developed an ethical and political connotation along with its earlier metaphysical use by Shao Yung.

Chu Hsi in the opening lines of his Commentary on the *Mean,* quotes "Master Ch'eng" to the following effect: "This work [the *Mean*] represents the system of the mind-and-heart as transmitted in the Confucian school. Tzu-ssu feared that in time it would become misunderstood, and so he wrote it down in this work so as to pass it on to Mencius. This book was the first to explain that the unitary principle . . . when dispersed reaches out to the ends of the universe, and when gathered in is concealed in mystery. Its significance is inexhaustible. It is all real learning."[156] Actually this "quotation" is a concatenation of several different phrases appearing in the extant writings of the Ch'eng brothers,[157] but Ch'eng I's reference to the "system" as the essential method of the *Mean* appears to be the primary source for later reference to the term.[158]

As it appears in Chu's work, the "quotation" identifies the "system of the mind-and-heart" with the transmission from Tzu-ssu to Mencius and also with the "real learning" of Confucianism under both its numinous and its practical aspects. It follows almost immediately after Chu's discussion in his preface to the *Mean* of the famous doctrine of the "orthodox tradition" *(tao-t'ung)*:

> Why was the *Mean* written? Master Tzu-ssu wrote it because he was worried lest the transmission of the learning of the Way become lost. When the divine sages of highest antiquity had succeeded to the work of Heaven and established the Supreme Norm, the transmission of the orthodox tradition *(tao-t'ung)* had its inception. As may be discerned from the classics, "Hold fast the Mean" is what Yao transmitted to Shun. That "the mind of man is insecure" and "the mind of the Way is barely perceptible," that one should "have utmost refinement and singleness of mind" and should "hold fast the Mean" is what Shun transmitted to Yü. . . .[159]

The passage continues with Chu's account of Confucius' contribution in reviving the Way and passing it on down to Tzu-ssu, but the essential elements are those given above. We have already seen them prominently featured by Chen Te-hsiu, who likewise refers to them as the "emperors' and kings' system of the mind-and-heart." It is the same with Hsü Heng later, who was well aware that this formulation was original with Chu Hsi. "The term *tao-t'ung* does not appear in ancient texts but first arose in recent times. When Chu Hsi wrote his preface to the *Mean,* he was much troubled over the nontransmission of the orthodox way and deeply concerned over what would happen to later generations."[160]

To sum up, then, this "system of the mind-and-heart" had close associations in the original context with the orthodox tradition *(tao-t'ung)* and the Learning of the Emperors and Kings, the content of which derived from Chu Hsi's interpretations of the "insecurity of the mind of man," the "imperceptibility of the mind of the Way," "refinement and singleness of mind," and "holding fast the Mean." Although we may understand it in a general way as reflecting Chu Hsi's belief that Ch'eng I had "discovered" this doctrine of the mind-and-heart, which had gone unnoticed before, there is no basis for thinking that it is a Neo-Confucian adaptation of an originally Buddhist concept, while there is good reason to regard it as a Sung creation stimulated by the interaction of Confucianism, Taoism, and Buddhism at that time.

The Yüan period, when Neo-Confucianism was first put forward as the basis for state education and the civil service examinations, represented a new phase in this interaction among the Three Teachings. All three enjoyed the patronage of the Yüan dynasty, which officially adopted an ecumenical stance aimed at keeping the peace among them. Nevertheless, their differing conceptions of the mind made competing claims for attention, with Buddhism and Neo-Confucianism especially contesting the central ground of the mind at issue between them. In this situation another leader of the School of the Way, Hsü Heng, often paired with Chen Te-hsiu as the next great scholar-statesman of the Ch'eng-Chu school, had to convert the Mongols to an acceptance of the new teaching for official purposes. To Hsü then we now turn as the second great protagonist of the Neo-Confucian Learning of the Mind-and-Heart.

Hsü Heng (1209–1281) as Teacher to the Mongols

Hsü Heng[161] was born into a family who had been peasants for generations and into times as dangerous as any China had known. His birthplace, Hsin-cheng in Honan Province, had served as a refuge for his family in time of war. North China was then the scene of violence and famine as one "barbarian" conqueror, the Mongols, overran and overthrew an earlier non-Chinese dynasty, the Chin. In these circumstances, the young Hsü had difficulty getting an education. Books and good teachers were scarce, and it is testimony to both his native talent and his personal determination that he overcame these handicaps and, though largely self-educated, became recognized as the leading scholar of his time.

Hsü, it will be recalled, when told that the purpose of book-learning was "to take the civil service examinations and advance to official rank," asked, "Is that all?,"[162] a question which implied, more than mere skepticism of conventional standards, an aspiration which reached higher. Sufferings yet to come, when he was a captive of the Mongols for two years, added to the hardship of his early years, no doubt tempered his resolve and engendered in Hsü an unusual combination of high idealism and earthy realism.

Thus Hsü was looking for something more than either book-learning or official advancement when, after moving north in 1247, he met the scholars Tou Mo and Yao Shu at Su-men. These gentlemen shared with Hsü new books of the Ch'eng-Chu school which Yao had obtained from the scholar Chao Fu, a captive of war, when he persuaded him to come north and spread the new learning. By this time Hsü was a mature scholar and regarded as something of an expert on the *Book of Changes*, but Ch'eng I's commentary on the *Changes* and Chu Hsi's on the Four Books struck him almost as a religious revelation and induced a deep conversion to a new way of life and teaching.[163]

Such conversions were not uncommon among scholars drawn to the School of the Way in those times. A high level of Confucian scholarship had been attained under the Chin, and when the writings of Chu Hsi finally became available North China was eager to receive them. No doubt too the atmosphere of crisis—personal, political, and cultural—added to the desperate desire for a philosophy that could give meaning to the suffering and tragedy many men experienced in those days. It may also explain why many of these same scholars were willing to serve under the Mongols. Their Confucian consciences, sensitized as Chen Te-hsiu's had been by Ch'eng-Chu teaching, would not let them be indifferent to the needs of their people, however detached they might indeed be from personal ambition.

Hsü eventually joined an extraordinary group of scholars in the service of Khubilai and became their acknowledged intellectual leader. I discussed in Part I some of the significance of his political involvement. Here I confine myself to points which are germane to the development of the Learning of the Mind-and-Heart.

Hsü and his colleagues, as ministers to Khubilai, faced the necessity of converting the Mongols to Chinese ways of government. The problem for them was not the decadence of a Li-tsung, who needed personal moral reformation, but the inexperience of nomads in managing a mature, agrarian society through complex bureaucratic institutions. Hsü Heng and his colleagues in Khubilai's

Chinese brain trust were activists trying to "rescue the times" *(ch'iu-shih)* by engaging in studies of "practical use in governing the world" *(ching-shih chih yung).* [164] They submitted numerous memorials to Khubilai on a wide range of institutional reforms, which became the basis for an extensive sinicization of the government and had lasting effects on cultural policy. [165]

In this context it is not surprising that Hsü too should have placed great importance on laws and institutions. His most famous memorial on governmental reform, the so-called Five Point Memorial of 1266, gave prime attention to the importance of establishing proper laws and institutions *(li-fa).* [166] If one contrasts this with Chen's *Extended Meaning* in its relative depreciation of governmental systems as compared to the pursuit of moral ends and the practice of self-cultivation, one might conclude that Hsü is more of a utilitarian or legalist than a true Neo-Confucian, whereas in fact this only reflects a difference in his and Chen's circumstances, not one in basic outlook. In the same memorial Hsü affirms the equal indispensability of moral men and good laws: "It is laws that govern men but men that guard the laws; men and laws mutually sustain each other." [167]

Throughout the memorial Hsü exhorts the emperor to take the *Great Learning* as his guide to rulership, in language similar to that of Chu Hsi and Chen Te-hsiu: "In ancient times, according to the way of the *Great Learning,* self-cultivation was the basis of government. One word or one action can become the model for all the world. One reward or one punishment can draw together the public spirit of all-under-Heaven." [168]

Accordingly Hsü recommends that Khubilai establish a system of universal education. In this too he is following Chu Hsi, who had spoken of the sage-kings' provision of schooling for all the people in the preface to his commentary on the *Great Learning.* [169]

In an early interview with Khubilai, Hsü had identified himself as a farmer and teacher, but disavowed any competence in the types of literary learning upon which the earlier civil service examinations had put such a premium. [170] This contempt for belles-lettres and strong preference for education in the classics which would develop moral character and socially useful learning were attitudes Hsü shared with other Neo-Confucians at court. As we have already seen, Chen Te-hsiu too had repeatedly identified purely literary learning as unorthodox and had cited rulers in the past for whom this distraction from true learning had proved to be their undoing. This became a major issue at court when advocates of the old-style civil service examinations pressed Khubilai for their reestablishment. Hsü and other Neo-Confucians opposed the old-style Confucians on this, and after a running debate over several years, succeeded in getting the matter shelved for the time being.[171]

In the meantime Hsü had become established as the leading scholar at court, as tutor to the heir apparent, as libationer of the Imperial College, and as head of the new educational system which he had urged upon Khubilai, with commissioners sent out from the capital to promote and supervise the development of a nationwide system of instruction. Hsü was more than conscientious in the performance of these duties. He devoted himself tirelessly to the education of the heir apparent and to his lectures from the classics mat (the modern scholar Sun K'o-k'uan believes that much of Hsü's writing, including the material in the Five Point Memorial, was prepared in connection with his lectures on the classics.)[172] The broad themes of instruction were the Learning of the Emperors and Kings as formulated especially in the *Great Learning*, the preservation and rectification of the mind, the moral constants of the Five Human Relationships, and the illustration of these in historical cases.[173]

Beyond this Hsü took a special interest in the education of the Mongols and their Central Asian aides, as had been recommended by his friends Tou Mo and Yao Shu.[174] Indeed, Hsü became well known for his patience and dedication in this respect. It was a demonstration of his belief in the potentiality of all men for fulfilling their common moral nature. He had great faith in the native ability and educability of young Mongols and Central Asians, and in their capacity to serve in Chinese-style civil administration if given proper training.[175] This was, of course, one aspect of his more fundamental belief in the perfectibility of human nature generally.

To perfect that nature, however, Hsü recognized the need to address the weaknesses in men. Indeed, the point of education was to identify and reform such defects. In this respect he even made a distinction between the educating of men and the employment of them. "Teaching men and employing them are exactly the opposite. In employing men one should be attentive to their strong points; in teaching them one should be attentive to their weak points."[176] Accordingly, Hsü took special pains in adapting his teaching to the weakness of the Mongol's and Central Asians in mathematics and to their unfamiliarity with the Confucian ritual, wherein differences in cultural background would be a handicap.

All this special care is testified to in a memoir written by one of Hsü's Central Asian students, the sinicized Ch'i-tan Yeh-lu Yu-shang (1236–1320), who speaks of Hsü's high sense of duty, his integrity in refusing gifts or special attentions from his students (even a present of wine on his birthday), and his extraordinary combination of fatherly concern and statesmanlike rectitude.[177] There is evidence that Khubilai himself was no less impressed with Hsü's personal qualities as a teacher—his rugged character, directness of speech, and deep sense of commitment to the Way, qualities which an active ruler might appreciate more than scholarly learning or polite letters.[178] Nor were Hsü's efforts lost on the non-Chinese. From them Hsü often received crucial support at court, which is said to have been a major factor in extending his influence.[179]

In principle there is nothing here that differentiates Hsü from Chen Te-hsiu, whose "teaching to the weaknesses" of Li-tsung led him to develop the Learning of the Emperors in the way he did in the *Extended Meaning*. Hsü Heng confronted a different situation. To apply or advance the Way in his time meant speaking to the condition of the Mongols, not just the Chinese. The question became whether Confucian or Neo-Confucian teaching was for all peoples, whether it embodied universal values that could touch the minds-and-hearts of the conquerors, or whether it was indeed so identified with Chinese culture that other peoples could see in it only a threat to their own identity and survival.

In responding to this challenge, and finding the common ground between Mongols, Central Asians, and Chinese, Hsü anticipated the future adaptation of Neo-Confucianism to the Manchus, Koreans, and Japanese. Implicitly, in devising a curriculum for Mongol China, he was making himself a teacher to all of East Asia.

Hsü Heng's Learning of the Mind-and-Heart

The essential content of Hsü Heng's instruction had already been determined in the aftermath of his dramatic conversion to the School of the Way. Then he had told his students to throw away the books they had been studying and apply themselves just to the basic works of Chu Hsi, especially his version of the Four Books and his *Elementary Learning (Hsiao-hsüeh)*.[180] The latter, compiled under Chu's direction as a primer to be studied in preparation for the Four Books, became a key text in the early Neo-Confucian movement. It stressed the importance of moral training through early initiation into social decorum, within the family and local school, before serious study of the classics began. This would set the pattern for the individual's later participation in the larger community, by establishing the basis for his self-development in higher studies. The code words for this early training were "sprinkling and sweeping," "responding to questions and requests," and "advancing and retiring," phrases taken from the *Analects* (19:12) where the idea is put forth of a sequence from the rudimentary to the higher stages of learning, in contrast to the notion of grasping for the wisdom of the sage all at once.

For Chu Hsi and Hsü Heng the *Elementary Learning* in combination with the *Great Learning* represented a progression in education from the performance of the humblest household duties on up to participation in government and the achieving of "great peace in the world." As we have seen, this orderly sequence had already impressed Chen Te-hsiu and now struck Hsü with great force. Abandoning all scholarly pretenses and preoccupations, he insisted on his students' starting their education all over again by practicing these humble rituals, and set an example for them by performing them himself. Instead of standing on his dignity as a teacher, he dignified himself by truly serving as a teacher. The fundamentalist approach of the *Elementary Learning* struck a deep chord in Hsü's down-to-earth peasant soul, evoking a reverential response. In a letter of 1266, recommending the *Elementary Learning* and the Four Books to his second son, Hsü said: "I revere and have faith in . . . [these books] as if they were divine."[181]

Thenceforward Hsü's scholarship and teaching were marked by this sense of religious conviction and an almost populist fundamentalism. He was bent on communicating his message to all, regardless of class or cultural background, and he devoted himself to the simplest exposition of the basic texts. Hsü shared in the general admiration for Chen Te-hsiu's writings, which were remarkable to him for the clarity and simplicity of their prose,[182] but in his own expository work he avoided anything like Chen's extensive reference to past commentaries and histories or his compiling of all relevant glosses on a text. Instead he tried to abridge the message in the most economical way. Thus his teaching manuals had titles like "The General Significance of the *Elementary Learning*" *(Hsiao-hsüeh ta-i)*; "The *Great Learning* Reduced to Its Essentials" *(Ta-hsüeh yao-lüeh)*; "A Straightforward Explanation of the *Great Learning*" *(Ta-hsüeh chih-chieh)*; and "A Straightforward Explanation of the *Mean*" *(Chung-yung chih-chieh).*[183]

Many of these writings were in vernacular Chinese, which would aid the comprehension of those without substantial classical learning (including Mongols like Khubilai, who generally used interpreters but knew enough vernacular Chinese so that he could follow Hsü's oral presentations and sometimes anticipate or correct the translation).[184] If Hsü found a reference in a text to Chu Hsi or the Ch'eng brothers, instead of presuming on the reader's familiarity with them as most writers would do, he identified them, e.g., " 'Master Ch'eng' here refers to Ch'eng I, a great scholar of the Sung dynasty."[185]

Hsü's other works include his *Recorded Dialogues (Yü-lu)* and a compilation entitled *Master Hsü Lu-chai's System of the Mind-and-Heart (Hsü Lu-chai hsien-sheng hsin-fa),*[186] which is actually a collation of quotations from his *Dialogues* that pertain to the metaphysics and cultivation of the mind-and-heart. Despite its title, this work cannot be taken as a self-contained, systematic presentation of the subject, but must be interpreted in the light of other writings of Hsü. Because of the *Elementary Learning's* crucial role in the conversion of Hsü to Chu Hsi's teaching, and because of his insistence upon it as the starting point of all learning, we do well to begin with his "General Significance of the *Elementary Learning*," [187] which establishes the basis for the Learning of the Mind-and-Heart.

In ancient times every child, from the sons of the king and the nobility down to the common people, entered elementary school at the age of eight, and were taught the essentials of "sprinkling, sweeping, responding to inquiries and requests, advancing and retiring," as well as the polite arts of ritual, music, archery, charioteering, reading, writing, and arithmetic. At the age of fifteen the crown prince and other princes, the sons of nobility and great officers, and the most talented sons of the common people all began [higher education] in the *Great Learning,* wherein they were instructed in the way of governing through fathoming principle to the utmost, rectifying the mind-and-heart, and cultivating the person.

The reason for having this distinction between the elementary learning and the great learning was that, if they did not receive training in the elementary learning in their younger years, they would have no means of judging moral issues or taking responsibility for the handling of affairs.

Their starting first with elementary learning was intended to establish the basis for the great learning, and advancing to the great learning was to reap the benefits of the elementary learning. In the flourishing days of the Three Dynasties all ability and intelligence were developed and the customs of the people enriched by making the most of this Way. But after the Ch'in's burning of the books, the classics and records of the sages were no longer complete and there was no way to ascertain the proper sequence by which the ancients carried on their education. . . .[188]

Hsü then recounts the confusion and disarray in later times and the successive efforts of Han Yü, the Ch'eng brothers, and Chu Hsi in reviving education on the basis of the text of the *Great Learning,* and finally the compilation of the *Elementary Learning* under Chu's direction. The main divisions of this work are "Setting Up Instruction," "Clarifying Moral Relations," and "Reverencing the Person." [189] Hsü sums up the essence of each in turn.

"Setting Up Instruction" means the Way in which the sage-kings of the Three Dynasties taught men. The innate mind of man is originally without imperfection, but after birth through the interference of the physical endowment, the blinding desire for things, and unrestrained selfishness, imperfections arise for the first time. The sages therefore set up instruction to help men nourish the original goodness of their innate minds and eliminate the imperfections which came from selfishness. . . .

What the early kings set up, however, was not simply their own idea. Heaven has its principles, and the early kings followed these principles. Heaven has its Way, and the early kings carried out this Way. Following the natural course of Heaven's imperative, they made it the proper course of human affairs, and that was what was called instruction. . . .

What then is this Way? It is the moral relation between parent and child, prince and minister, husband and wife, elder and younger, friend and friend. Therein lies the Heaven-bestowed moral nature and the Way for man. . . .

"Clarifying Moral Relations"—"Clarify" means to make manifest. "Moral relations" means moral principles. In the moral nature endowed in man by Heaven, each has his proper norm, as in the intimate love between parent and child, the moral obligation between prince and minister, the sex differentiation between husband and wife, the order of precedence among older and younger, and the relation of trust between friends. These are the natural relations.

In the Three Dynasties, when the early kings established schools to teach all-under-Heaven, it was only to clarify and manifest these relations and nothing more. Men who cannot clarify these human relations cannot bring order into distinctions of noble and base, superior and inferior, important and unimportant, substantial and insubstantial, controlled and uncontrolled . . . and when it comes to this, disaster and disorder follow upon one another until everything lapses into bestiality. . . .

"Reverencing the Person"—the preface [to this section] cites Confucius' saying [in the *Record of Rites*], "The noble man is ever reverent." [190] To reverence the person is the important thing. The person is the branch [outgrowth] of parental love. How can one not reverence it? Not to reverence the person is to do violence to parental love. To do violence to parental love is to do violence to the trunk [of the tree of life]. Harm the trunk and the branch will die. [191]

The sage uttered this as a warning. He who would be a man cannot for a single day depart from reverence. How much more should one reverence his own person, which is truly the trunk of all things and affairs? Err in this, and all things go awry. How could one then not be reverent?

Reverencing the person consists of four things: directing the mind, proper bearing, clothing, and food and drink. If the direction of the mind within is correct and one's outer bearing is correct, then one has achieved the most substantial part of reverencing the person. Clothing and food are meant for the service of the person. If one does not control them properly and regulate them according to decorum, then what is meant to nourish man will, on the contrary, bring him harm.

We can distinguish among these by saying that the direction of the mind and proper bearing have to do with the cultivation of virtue [the moral nature], while clothing and food and drink have to do with conquering the self. Taking them together, we can say that they are all essential to the reverencing of the person. Therefore it will not do if in the conduct of the relations between parent and child, prince and minister, husband and wife, older and younger, friend and friend, there is not this reverencing of the person. That is why the ancients insisted on reverence as the basis for the cultivation of the person.[192]

In the foregoing we have a most revealing statement for our understanding of Hsü Heng's approach to the mind-and-heart. Certain of Hsü's points will be obvious as doctrines already emphasized by Chen Te-hsiu: the struggle in the mind between selfish desires and moral principles, the need for constant reverence, and the basic goodness of man's nature. Particularly to be noted here, however, is the stress on early training and development of the moral, social, and affective relations, establishing their sequential priority over cognitive activities. This is not new among the Neo-Confucians, who had always spoken of the human mind as socially and morally conscious both in its origin and in its essence (as opposed to the enlightenment of the Buddhists, which was supposedly free of personal attachments and moral obligations).

Hsü, following Chu Hsi, goes further to ground the process of socialization in the fundamental reality of creative love, and to center it in the human person as the offspring of an intimate relation as deeply rooted and inviolable as life itself. Despite the defective logic of the opening quotation, which raised doubts in the minds of some commentators as to its authenticity,[193] the passage from the *Record of Rites* about reverencing the person is given special weight by both Chu Hsi and Hsü Heng (being the lead-off quotation for Chu and the only one cited by Hsü in his precis). This seems to suggest that the very circularity of the argument conveys the sense of life as a sacred continuum of affective relations, from conjugal love to parental concern and filial devotion, all centering on respect for the personhood of the individual.

Thus Chu and Hsü structure the educational process in a concept of human personhood which avoids the polarization of individual versus society. The conventional view of Neo-Confucianism has it relying heavily on conformity to ritual and repression of the individual within a system of hierarchical relations preserving the status quo. Hsü, however, actually makes these relations subserve the development of the human personality, while the mind that is to direct this development has acquired its moral sensitivity through the experiencing of loving relations with others, not through subjection to cognitive disciplines and rote learning.

Of the books which Hsü had said he "believed in as if they were divine"—the *Elementary Learning* and the Four Books—the other two he particularly spoke to were the *Great Learning* and the *Mean*. His treatment of the former is quite different from that of Chen Te-hsiu, who made it serve his own purposes with respect to the instruction of the emperor. Hsü adheres closely to the text of the *Great Learning* and explains almost every phrase in the plainest language. His favorite passages have to do with "clarifying luminous virtue" *(ming ming-te)*, "loving the people" *(ch'in-min)*, "cultivating the person" *(hsiu-shen)* and "rectifying the mind-and-heart" *(cheng-hsin)*. His comments on these follow.

> Clarifying luminous virtue—"Clarify" means to make clear. "Luminous virtue" is the radiant virtue originally inherent in our mind-and-heart. The Master [Chu Hsi] said that in ancient times the method of learning as taught in the *Great Learning* was that one should apply one's efforts first to the clarifying of one's own radiant virtue so as not to allow it to become obscured.[194]

> In the learning of clarifying luminous virtue the first thing is to hold to reverence *(ch'ih-ching)*. If there is reverence, body and mind can be collected and concentrated so that the psychophysical nature cannot become obstreperous. . . .[195]

> "Loving the people"—"People" refers to the common people. When the great man has pursued this study so as to clarify his own luminous virtue, he should extend this mind to the common people

so that each of them can rid themselves of any blemish from former impurities and clarify their luminous virtue. Thus all in common would be free of obscuration.[196]

[On Chu Hsi's glossing of "loving the people" as "renewing the people" (hsin-min)]—"Renewing the people" means for the sage to teach people to renew themselves through a constant process of self-examination and self-correction. For those who serve at court, "renewing the people" means to fulfill to the utmost what an official should be by being reverent and conscientious. In the presence of one's parents to be filial and complaisant is the right way to fulfill the principle of being a [true] child. For parents to be compassionate and loving towards their children is to fulfill to the highest degree what it is to be a parent. . . ."[197]

[On "cultivating the person"]—The most essential and urgent matter in the *Great Learning* is cultivating the person.[198]

Confucius taught that cultivating the person lies in rectifying the mind-and-heart. The mind is the master of the person. When the mind's control is right, the person's conduct cannot go astray.[199]

In the Way of Confucius cultivation of the person lies in rectifying the mind-and-heart. This is the excellent method of the *Great Learning*. If one can rectify the person, one can regulate the family . . . govern the state . . . and pacify the world. "Making the will sincere, investigating things and extending knowledge all follow upon this [rectifying of the mind]". . . . Chu Hsi's teachings on the Six Classics, the Four Books, and the various philosophers all sprang from his being a man who rectified his own mind.[200]

It was because Yao rectified his own mind that he recognized in Shun a man who rectified his mind, and thus he was willing to yield the throne to him. It was because of this willingness to yield on the part of Yao that all-under-Heaven had yielding, noncontentious, sharing, and reciprocating hearts. . . . And it was because of his correct mind's making use of the right man that all-under-Heaven and later generations spoke of him as a wise and humane ruler. [Therefore] in teaching men the essentials of the *Great Learning*, Confucius taught them to practice this correct and proper mind. . . . Thus rectifying the mind is the excellent method of the *Great Learning*.[201]

[On the "sudden and total penetration of the pervading unity" (huo-jan kuan-t'ung) referred to by Chu Hsi in his special note on the "extension of knowledge" in his *Words and Phrases in the Great Learning* (Ta-hsüeh chang-chü)]—

[Chu Hsi:] After one has made an effort for a long time, all at once one penetrates the totality.

[Hsü:] *Huo-jan* has the meaning of breakthrough or opening up to enlightenment. When the learner has fully searched out the principles of things and affairs, searching out one matter today and another tomorrow, his successive efforts will culminate one day in a sudden opening [of the mind] to enlightenment which is thoroughly penetrating.

[On the "whole substance and great functioning" *(ch'üan-t'i ta-yung)*]—

[Chu:] When knowledge has been extended to all things and affairs, inward and outward, fine and coarse, my mind's whole substance and great functioning are totally clarified and made manifest.

[Hsü:] "Outward" means "external" and refers to principles easy to see; "inward" is "internal" and refers to principles difficult to see. "Fine" refers to the most subtle of principles; "coarse" refers to the coarsest and most superficial of principles. For a man's one mind to be full of principles is to have the "whole substance," and for it to respond to all things is the "great functioning." If a man reaches the point of a sudden breakthrough, then in relation to the principles of all things, manifest or hidden, fine or coarse, there is none which is not understood. The whole substance and great functioning of such a mind is without any obscuration whatever.[202]

It was because of the special attention drawn to this last doctrine by Chu Hsi in his commentary on the *Great Learning* that Hsü Heng (like Chen Te-hsiu) took this formulation of the "whole substance and great functioning" as the culmination of Chu's teaching on the mind-and-heart. When we turn to Hsü's exposition of the *Mean* we find that there too repeated reference is made to it. First, however, Hsü introduces the text in characteristic fashion; explaining that "Tzu-ssu," the author, "is the grandson of Confucius," and "Master Ch'eng," the commentator, refers to "Ch'eng I, the great Sung scholar." Then he proceeds:

Master Ch'eng said that this one book represents the "wondrous system of the mind-and-heart passed down by the teachers and disciples of the school of Confucius." Confucius transmitted it to his disciple Tseng Tzu and Tseng Tzu to Tzu-ssu. In those days there was only oral transmission, and Tzu-ssu feared that as time passed further and further from Confucius, it was inevitable that there should be discrepancies [in what was transmitted]; so he took what had been communicated in ordinary speech and wrote it down, passing it on to the other disciples and Mencius. The *Mean* was the first work clearly to state that man's nature and the moral imperative originated with Heaven and that there was just one principle diffused among all things and imparted to them all without exception. . . .[203]

Here, as well as in his *Dialogues* and in the *System of the Mind-and-Heart*,[204] Hsü's view of the mind, its substance, and its functioning is much influenced by the doctrine of the "unity of principle and its diverse particularizations" *(li-i fen-shu)*, which Chu had received from Ch'eng I through his teacher Li T'ung (1093–1163). In this view the substance of the mind is unitary, corresponding to the "oneness" or "singleness" to be preserved by "holding to reverence,"[205] while its functioning takes manifold forms when responding to the multiplicity of human affairs. Doctrinally, Hsü places equal emphasis on the unity of the principle in the mind and the diversity of its applications, but pedagogically he stresses the practicality of its functioning, its responsiveness and adaptability to the ordinary daily needs of man, and its exemplification in the humble tasks with which all cultivation of the person must begin.[206]

Nevertheless, a fundamental tenet with him was still to preserve the unity and integrity of the substance of the mind in its unexpressed, unmanifest state, wherein resides the moral nature. "The principles of all things and affairs proceed from this substance of the Way [in the mind of man]."[207] "Holding to reverence," as Ch'eng I and Chu Hsi had recommended, or "stressing quiescence," as Chou Tun-i had spoken of it, were disciplines, often practiced in the form of quiet-sitting, which preserved the composure and balance of the mind so that the substance of the mind could be fully aligned with the mind of Heaven-and-earth, and the mind's natural functioning would express to the maximum degree the principles inherent in it.[208]

"The original substance of the mind-and-heart is broad and great. The noble man does not allow even one iota of selfish desire to obscure it, and is careful to see that not even the slightest error or deviation is made from this lofty and clear state of the original mind."²⁰⁹ "The whole substance of the mind is the great basis for all human relations," says Hsü, speaking of it in terms of brightness, clarity, radiance, and luminosity—terms expressive of the rationality and coherence of the moral nature.²¹⁰ On the other hand, under its numinous aspect it is sometimes described by him as "hidden," "mysterious," "elusive," and "barely perceptible";²¹¹ that is, it partakes of the infinite, wondrous creativity of Heaven-and-earth, which is also the inexhaustible source and indefinable essence of the person's true dignity and freedom.

A leading disciple of Hsü Heng, the historian and statesman Ou-yang Hsüan (1283–1357), summarized Hsü's teaching as follows:

> The master's teaching stressed "clarifying the substance [of the mind-and-heart] and fulfilling its function" as the main thing. In cultivating the person the essential thing is to "preserve the mind and nourish the nature." In the service of the ruler, one's duty is to urge upon him what may be difficult to accomplish and put before him models of excellence [as Mencius says at 4A:1] The teaching of men begins with "sprinkling, sweeping, responding to questions and requests, advancing and retiring" [as in the *Analects* and *Elementary Learning*] and ends with the [*Book of Changes'*] "refining moral principles and entering into their spiritual essence" (*ching-i ju-shen*).²¹²

This concise characterization aptly conveys both the centrality of the mind-and-heart in Hsü's teaching and his emphasis on its practical functioning, both the everyday, down-to-earth character of his teaching and his awareness of the deeper reaches of the human spirit. In these respects he may indeed be called "a faithful follower of Chu Hsi," as the conventional label has it, but if one is aware of the extraordinary demands imposed by fidelity to such a comprehensive, delicately balanced view of man and the universe as Chu Hsi's is, one may appreciate how its interpretation and application to Hsü's own time could be an achievement of great magnitude and leave a profound impression on his contemporaries.

What Ou-yang says is no doubt also a fair expression of Hsü's teaching as it was imparted to his many students, themselves to become influential scholars and teachers of the Yüan period. The texts Hsü adopted for his own students—the *Elementary Learning* and the Four Books—also became the basis for his instruction at court and at the Imperial College. As libationer of that college he employed his former students as tutors, and as head of the Directorate of Education, supervising the new system of regional and local schools, he also had many of his followers in key positions from which they carried Hsü's version of the Ch'eng-Chu teaching into the provinces. While Hsü was discouraged by Khubilai's failure to provide adequate financial support to carry out his educational plans, he could hardly have been disappointed at the results of his own efforts, for there is almost unanimous testimony to the wide extent of his influence as a teacher.

Finally, that influence is shown in the adoption of his curriculum, through the efforts of his followers in the next generation, as the basis for the new civil service examination system established after Khubilai's departure from the scene. Whether Hsü would necessarily have gone along with the system itself is by no means certain, since he had opposed resumption of the old system on some grounds that would also apply to the new one, but in any case the form of the curriculum to be studied and tested was essentially his (and not what Chu Hsi had advocated for this purpose), so the historic importance of Hsü's own contribution cannot be denied.

Before leaving Hsü Heng, we should take note of one relatively inconspicuous omission in the body of his work. He contributed little to what had always been a major branch of Confucian studies, the ritual system or rules of decorum. It is true that he had prepared a court ritual for Khubilai and recognized in general the importance of ritual, both as a form of discipline and as the set of objective norms by which to judge the individual's achievement of the highest good for himself. But it is precisely this theoretical assumption which should have led to some further specification of the system beyond the relatively simple formulas of the *Elementary Learning*. The practical implication seems to be that once one had received his basic social and moral formation on the level of "sprinkling and sweeping," one was ready to move on to the higher level of leadership dealt with in the *Great Learning*. Having entered into the spirit of ritual and decorum, one could leave further determination of proper conduct to individual judgment through the constant practice of mind-rectification.

Others of Chu Hsi's early followers paid far more attention to ritual matters and institutional forms, and contributed to a large body of scholarship on ritual, rendered necessary by the recognition that in this area too the "orthodox tradition" had lapsed as seriously as in the ethical, political, or philosophical realms.[213] Without extensive research and skillful adaptation it could not be reconstituted. Under the Chin dynasty conservative Confucians in North China had devoted themselves to such an effort,[214] but Hsü Heng's new type of down-to-earth education and scholarship for everyman gave ritual a high priority mostly in theory. Hsü went on talking about "the conquest of self and returning to ritual," but his own experience in trying to educate the Mongols and Central Asians in the rules of Chinese decorum may well have left him with a sense of their limits. Considering the violent disruption of cultural traditions in that age of conquest, it was only natural for the conservative instinct to cling to ritual tradition, but it was also only realistic to recognize that in this age new forms of cultural life were displacing the old.[215]

It may have been just such realism which identified the orthodox way with the more simplified and flexible "system of the mind-and-heart," and held in abeyance the question of whether the ancient ritual could ever be fully recovered and applied. Perhaps too this is why Hsü, in his discussion of the *Elementary Learning,* focused the prime practical virtue on the "person" *(shen)* and personal relations *(lun),* rather than on ritual and social rules.

The Learning of the Mind-and-Heart as Living Orthodoxy

The climax of Hsü Heng's educational efforts came after the turn of the fourteenth century, with the ascendancy at court of the new-style Confucians trained or influenced by Hsü. The Imperial College, to which he had devoted so much of his effort, finally received proper quarters, adequate financial support, and a much larger quota of students.[216] At court the dominant figure in cultural affairs was Ch'eng Chü-fu (1249–1318), who wrote a commemorative inscription at the time of Hsü's enshrinement in the Confucian temple in 1313, paying tribute to his dedication as a teacher, his belief in the educability of all men, and his foresight in drawing up plans for the college. This was, Ch'eng says, in accord with the sage-kings' realization that "the world can be won by military might, but it cannot be governed by military might."[217]

Hsü's role in converting the Mongols to an acceptance of Chinese institutions and support of Neo-Confucian education was also eulogized by Ou-yang Hsüan, who likened Khubilai and Hsü to sage-king and sage-minister:

With his heavenly endowment [Khubilai] resumed the lost teaching of the sage-emperors and kings, while Hsü Heng, with the gift of heavenly talents, was able to repossess the untransmitted teachings of the sages and worthies, connecting up with the tradition of the Duke of Chou, Confucius, Tseng Tzu, Tzu-ssu, Mencius, and the other noble men who came after them, to become a minister of unparalleled stature in those times. The aspirations of ruler and minister matched perfectly, and all that was enunciated in the emperor's name served to uphold the perfect norm of rulership, set up proper guidelines for the people, resume the lost teaching and usher in an era of great peace—all as if a myriad ages were fulfilled in one day.[218]

Tribute was also paid to Hsü Heng at the time of the adoption of the new civil service examination system that same year. Ch'eng Chü-fu, the principal proponent of the new system, invoked the authority of Hsü as virtually a latter-day sage when Ch'eng recommended that a new curriculum and set of criteria for selection be set up. Ch'eng also spoke in familiar terms when he subscribed to the idea that the *Great Learning* and the *Mean* were the key texts in transmitting the sages' Learning of the Mind-and-Heart, and to the view that mind-culture was the essence of rulership. In counseling the emperor he spoke of the importance of clarifying or cleansing the mind in a memorial on "Portentous Matters" for the emperor's consideration:

The mind-and-heart is the ruler of the person and the root of all affairs. The eyes' seeing, ears' hearing, mouth's speaking, hands' holding, feet's walking—these all serve the mind. If the mind-and-heart attains correctness, then in contact with things and responding to affairs, the seeing, hearing, speaking, and moving all attain correctness, and there is no danger of loss or error. How much more, given the vast impenetrability of the world and the difficulty of perceiving all that transpires therein, do all in the empire look up to the one man for guidance and he to the mind-and-heart?

Now water must be still if it is to reflect things and images; the mind must be clear if it is to discriminate beauty from ugliness. Therefore the emperors and kings attached prime importance to clarifying the mind. To clarify means to preserve undisturbed unity in quiescence. Thus the pleasures of sound and color, the delights of drinking and feasting, which should not be done away with, by control and moderation can be kept from disturbing the clarity of the mind.

If the mind is clear, then the vast obscurity of the world will not go unlighted, and a myriad barely perceptible signs will not go unobserved. Bright and clear, the mind will see through everything and achieve implicit understandings in silent accord. Slander and calumny will not gain credence; corruption and deceit will not dare come forward. The hundred officials, under proper surveillance, will be secure each in his own position and need not fear meddlesome strictures. The system will work of itself and laws take effect smoothly. Public discipline will be upheld. There will be surcease from calamity and the world will be at peace. The *Analects* [1:2] says: "When the root is established, the Way lives and grows." Thus the sage-emperors and kings' clarifying of the mind-and-heart is the root, and most truly it is the essence of the Way of comprehensive self-control and the maintenance of authority.[219]

From this one can see how the Learning of the Mind-and-Heart was closely associated with the orthodox teaching of the emperors and kings which Ch'eng was imparting to the ruler and hoping to incorporate into the body politic through the examination and recruitment system. Educational issues arose among Neo-Confucians at this time which were to separate Ch'eng Chü-fu from his boyhood friend Wu Ch'eng (1249–1333), the leading philosopher and classicist of the day, who opposed the new examination system,[220] but there was no issue of orthodoxy which called into question the centrality of the mind-and-heart. This all parties accepted, and it was only the question of how the mind-and-heart was to be cultivated which came increasingly into dispute. Thus in these years and for some time to come, the Learning of the Mind-and-Heart remained the heart of orthodoxy.

This is so, indeed, irrespective of official sanction and sponsorship, or what had long preceded it, voluntary subscription to this "learning" in independent schools and academies. From Chu Hsi's leading disciple Huang Kan through Ch'en Ch'un, Ho Chi (1188–1268), Wei Liao-weng, and Hsiung Ho (1253–1312) and on down into the late Yüan there is a steady succession of teachers, largely independent of official patronage, carrying on this form of Ch'eng-Chu learning, often with special emphasis on the doctrine of "the whole substance and great functioning" of the mind-and-heart.[221]

It should hardly need to be mentioned that Wu Ch'eng too was among those who represented this view of the orthodox tradition as essentially a Learning of the Mind-and-Heart transmitted from the sage-kings down through Confucius and Mencius to the Sung masters.[222] Wu took a liberal, expansive view of this tradition, however, and like other early successors of Chu Hsi, including Huang Kan, Chen Te-hsiu, and Hsü Heng, in his time tried to minimize the differences between Chu Hsi and Lu Hsiang-shan (and in Chen's case, even between Neo-Confucianism and Buddhism, as long as the latter did not prey upon the superstitions and weaknesses of rulers).[223] But Wu's efforts to reconcile Chu and Lu made his orthodoxy suspect in the eyes of some who took a narrower view, and to avoid begging this question, the discussion is limited here to those whose Ch'eng-Chu credentials are unquestioned or without whom there could have been no Ch'eng-Chu school at all.

Writing in these same years of seemingly total triumph for Neo-Confucianism under the Yüan dynasty, Hsiung Ho,[224] a Ch'eng-Chu scholar in the line of Huang Kan, commemorated Chu Hsi's teaching in the K'ao-t'ing Academy in a memoir of 1307. He likens Chu's role in preserving and propagating the Four Books to Confucius' earlier efforts to save the Six Classics as a record of the Way of the sage-emperors and kings. Chu's teaching he characterizes as "The Learning of the Sages Concerning the Whole Substance and Great Functioning [of the Mind]."

If it is rooted in one's person and one's mind-and-heart, then it can be carried out in virtuous action; if it is propagated throughout the land, it becomes a model for all. Its substance lies in the nature that follows humaneness, righteousness, correctness, and the Mean; its functioning lies in the instrumentalities of government, education, agriculture, rites, arms, and punishments; its literary expression is found in the *Elementary Learning, Analects,* etc. . . .[225]

But it was only in the later years of his teaching at the K'ao-t'ing Academy, says Hsiung, that Chu imparted to his students the full depth of his teaching as he had heard it earlier from his own teacher Li T'ung, with emphasis on a deep personal realization of the Way and a spirit of reverence that pervaded and integrated the states of action and quiescence. "This," he says, "was the ancients' transmission of the system of the mind-and-heart, the profound subtlety of which could not be appreciated by those sunk in the superficial learning of the mouth and ear."[226]

Among those who carried on their teaching and scholarship at a considerable remove from the court was Tu Pen (1276–1350),[227] a scholar known for his wide learning and reclusive life, whose friend the historian Yü Chi (1271–1348) left a memoir of Tu's Studio of Thoughtful Learning *(Ssu-hsüeh chai),* which explained the nature of his "thoughtfulness" in terms of Confucian learning as opposed to Buddhist and Taoist enlightenment:

what was known as "learning" among the ancients was simply the Learning of the Mind-and-Heart and nothing else. The substance of the mind is commensurate with Heaven-and-earth, and the effort to apply it can carry on and complete the work of Heaven-and-earth in ways that the latter alone could not accomplish. Apart from this there is no learning, and to seek for it in externals is not the learning of the sages and worthies.

This being so, its essentials do not lie outside the fixed values of humaneness, righteousness, decorum, and wisdom. No matter how manifold and differentiated the world of our external experience, it does not lie outside the moral relations of parent and child, husband and wife, ruler and minister, elder and younger, and friend and friend. Thus sagehood is spoken of simply as the perfection of human relations.

But sagehood is perfection and we are imperfect, and therefore study is indispensable. And how are we to know the sages? Just by their words and actions. Speak as they spoke, do as they did.

Thus when we reflect in our minds and see that there is something which remains unattempted, or on our persons, that there is something which remains unachieved, if we give thought to it, the mind will not be without a master or allowed to run wild. . . . If, on the contrary, we cut ourselves off from moral relations and treat the mind as if it were a blank wall, waiting for some sudden awakening to come in a flash of enlightenment, is this not dangerous? [228]

With the spread of Neo-Confucian teaching and with the inducement to study offered by the new examination system, a number of Mongols and Central Asians were attracted to the new learning either by the advantageous terms on which they could compete in the examinations or by the inherent appeal of the teaching itself. Among those of whom some record exists, one Sams, said to be a native of Arabia with the Chinese name of Shan-ssu,[229] was, for a person of foreign extraction, an extraordinarily prolific writer and classicist. He had studied under a disciple of Yüan Hao-wen (1190–1257) and gained a reputation both for the breadth of his learning and for his ability to put it to practical use. When the examinations were held by the Yüan court for the first time in 1315, he refused to compete (whether for personal reasons or for reasons of principle, shared with other Neo-Confucians, we do not know). But when invited to court in 1330 and assigned to duties in the Hanlin Academy, he had an interview with the emperor. The latter asked him if he had written anything, and "the very next day he submitted a work entitled 'The Emperor's and King's System of the Mind-and-Heart' "[230] (*Ti-wang hsin-fa*). This work is no longer extant, but the title itself and Sams' known concern for the study of rulership suggest that it may well have been a blend of the kind of learning represented by Chen Te-hsiu's *Extended Meaning of the Great Learning* and Hsü Heng's *System of the Mind-and-Heart*.

In any case, Sams' subsequent career exemplified precisely those qualities of mind and character so stressed by Chen and Hsü. In addition to his breadth of learning, he gained a reputation as an official for his incorruptibility, his fearlessness in exposing injustice, and his conscientious concern for the welfare of the people. Perhaps the most convincing evidence of his success in thoroughly assimilating this learning into his own person and living by it is the fact that, notwithstanding the opportunities to enrich himself in office, it could be said that "His family was very poor and sometimes did not have enough even for simple meals, but he carried on his study of the classics very happily."[231]

This gives us early evidence that the Learning of the Mind-and-Heart was able to establish itself as an ethicoreligious system which could be meaningful and practicable for many peoples of different ethnic origins and social statuses, for lonely scholars far from the centers of power as well as for Confucians heavily engaged in political struggles and official duties.

The Ruler as Sponsor and Sage: Ming Repercussions

Given its wide spread and the deep root it had taken in the minds of many scholars within a century and a half after Chu Hsi's death, his teaching was already well established by the time its Mongol sponsors began to lose their own hold on power. Whatever benefits may have accrued from its endorsement by the Yüan dynasty, the Ch'eng-Chu learning had a life of its own, sturdy enough to survive the collapse of Mongol rule. Chu Hsi's followers were everywhere, and when the Ming founder, Chu Yüan-chang (Ming T'ai-tsu, r. 1368–1398), succeeded in putting together a new regime, he had in his service representatives of this school who played a leading role in setting the cultural direction of the new dynasty.[232] They included Hsü Yüan, who "would not read anything but the Five Classics and Four Books and would not teach anything but the learning of the Ch'eng-Chu school," and whose father Hsü Ch'ien (1270–1337) had emphasized learning "the mind-and-heart of the sages" as revealed in Chu Hsi's version of the Four Books:[233] Chang I (1314–1369),[234] spoken of as someone holding the highest respect for Chu Hsi's teachings; Chu Lien, a deep student of Chu Hsi's *Classified Dialogues (Chu Tzu yü-lei)*;[235] Sung Lien (1310–1381), widely known as "an ardent admirer of Chu Hsi";[236] Wang Wei (1323–1374),[237] who held to the orthodox tradition from the Sung school; and Liu Chi (1311–1375),[238] who though not formally identified with this school, was influenced by its Learning of the Mind-and-Heart.

Indeed, so strong was the continuity with Yüan scholarship and so general the acceptance of Chu Hsi that resumption of the examination system in essentially the Yüan form, with a prominent place for the Four Books and Chu's commentaries, became almost a matter of course. Already by the third year of his reign (1370), Ming T'ai-tsu, advised in this matter by Liu Chi (according to the *Ming History*),[239] issued a proclamation confirming and reestablishing the former system without acknowledging any debt to the Yüan for it. There is no sign of any debate at the time, no long controversy such as had protracted the matter in Khubilai's time. And while T'ai-tsu himself had some doubts about the practicality of this form of recruitment, the content of the examinations and Chu Hsi's place in them were never at issue.

Yet the very lack of ideological struggle is significant. Since Chu Hsi's installation as the authorized interpreter of the new classics had gone uncontested, no alternative was consciously considered and rejected. "Orthodoxy" won without a struggle and there was no need to define or stigmatize heterodoxy. In fact, as the consensus' choice, instead of representing an exclusive position, the new learning could be viewed as an inclusive, catholic view open to broad interpretation. Ming T'ai-tsu himself no doubt preferred it this way. Like the Mongols before him, and most other dynastic founders, he saw a policy of religious toleration as in keeping with his own political interests. This was a time for reconciliation and reconstruction. The new regime did not need sectarian strife or scholarly polemics. Indeed, far from enforcing a single view of truth, Ming T'ai-tsu declared himself for a policy of unity in diversity, issuing a succession of pronouncements affirming that "the Three Teachings [or Religions] are One," which became the precedent and policy for Ming rulers thereafter.[240]

In this atmosphere, among scholar-officials there was a similarly tolerant and relaxed atittude. The "liberal" view of the Learning of the Mind-and-Heart which had been espoused by Wu Ch'eng was well received. Sung Lien, perhaps the most representative scholar of the day, had received his early training in the Chu Hsi school. He once had criticized Lu Hsiang-shan as less than orthodox, but in these years and in the prevailing ecumenical atmosphere he took a much more tolerant view of him.[241] From the start Sung had believed that "learning is for the preservation of the mind-and-heart, and it is in preserving this mind that principle is preserved."[242] From this standpoint, which took the mind-and-heart and principle as on a par, it is not surprising that Sung should have come to believe that "the six classics are all the Learning of the Mind-and-Heart," and should speak of reviving the latter as "the most urgent need of the times."[243] But later he even went on to quote Lu Hsiang-shan favorably to the effect that "should a sage arise in the Eastern Sea, this mind would be the same, this principle the same," and also to assert that "My mind is the Supreme Ultimate."[244] Moreover, as Professor Araki Kengo has shown, Sung Lien extended this view of the Learning of the Mind-and-Heart to include Buddhism, affirming the essential complementarity of Confucianism's "preserving the mind-and-heart and nourishing the nature" with Buddhism's "enlightening the mind and seeing the Buddha-nature."[245]

Noting this combination of Confucianism and Buddhism in Sung Lien, the Ch'ing scholar Wang Ta-shen also observed the resemblance between Sung Lien in his relationship to Ming T'ai-tsu and Hsü Heng in his earlier relationship with Khubilai. "Hsü Lu-chai educated Khubilai in Confucianism and succeeded in raising the cultural level of that whole age. Sung Lien likewise assisted Ming T'ai-tsu in the learning of Confucianism and Buddhism and in the promotion of scholarship and education. He was the standard bearer for the whole Ming dynasty. In this the two were true followers of Master Chu."[246]

Wang Wei, who worked with Sung Lien under Ming T'ai-tsu and had a special admiration for Hsü Heng's practical efforts in behalf of the Way, also joined in the ready acceptance of Chu Hsi's teaching as the basis for instruction in the schools and for the examinations. For him the indispensable essence of this teaching was the Learning of the Mind-and-Heart:

What is most subtle and refined in the human person, and yet most broad and great, is the mind-and-heart. It ranges out to Heaven-and-earth, connects past and present, coordinates human principles, and binds together human affairs through all their vicissitudes—indeed, there is nothing to which thought does not extend. Thus the sages and worthies had the learning of the Mind-and-Heart: first "seeking the lost mind," then nurturing it, and in due time making the utmost use of it. Therefore were there no learning of the mind, it would be as if man's possessing a mind made no difference to him. Without [the learning] there is no way to direct the person, and the person becomes a mere thing, undeserving of the name "man."[247]

Wang Wei subscribed to Wu Ch'eng's position that "honoring the moral nature" *(tsun te-hsing)* and "the pursuit of scholarship" *(tao wen-hsüeh)* were equally necessary, implying that there was room for both Chu Hsi and Lu Hsiang-shan within Neo-Confucian orthodoxy.[248] Wang also took a relatively benign view of Buddhism, asserting that it "had substance but not function," as if to say that it lacked something Confucianism offered in the way of moral activism but was not positively antithetical to Confucianism in matters of underlying principle.[249]

From this it may be seen that there was considerable flexibility in the Learning of the Mind-and-Heart as it was understood by these early Ming scholar-statesmen. It could seem to afford continuity between a pragmatic present and a principled past, between the new state orthodoxy of the examinations and the "orthodox tradition" of the Ch'eng-Chu school. It could also lend itself to reinterpretations which might seek common ground with other teachings and cultures. It was the kind of consensus view which drew upon the distillation of Ch'eng-Chu teachings by Chen Te-hsiu, Wei Liao-weng, Hsü Heng, and others in the century after Chu's death,[250] the simplification of which for educational purposes left it readily adaptable to different needs in changing circumstances.

I discussed earlier in this book how the teachings of Hsü Heng and his followers in the Yüan sought out the lowest common denominator of public morality and self-discipline for a multinational state, a process which paralleled the steady compression of the Confucian classics, first into the Four Books, then into the *Great Learning*, next into the eight-step method of self-cultivation in the *Great Learning*, and finally into the practice of mind-rectification as the essence of the cultivation of the person, which was seen as the basis of the polity. This simplification of tradition dispensed with a great deal of cultural baggage and rendered it usable by busy rulers like Khubilai and Ming T'ai-tsu. It also lent itself to the kind of religious toleration which both of them practiced.

In Sung Lien's case Professor Araki has offered the view that his receptivity to other religions was inherent in the freedom Sung allowed himself as a literary man, engaged in creative work (especially poetry) inherently open to new experience.[251] This suggests that he was an almost classic example of the literary inspiration or aesthetic appreciation undermining the moral will, comparable indeed to the "heterodox" learning which Chen Te-hsiu had condemned in earlier rulers like T'ang Ming-huang whom he saw as corrupted by a facile and decadent belle-lettrism. On this basis one can recognize that latent in this early Ming situation was the possibility that stricter consciences might find such accommodations unacceptable to their own sense of orthodoxy.

In terms of Sung Lien's relationship to the ruler, however, there was a more portentous and far-reaching development in the outcome of his efforts to educate Ming T'ai-tsu. Once T'ai-tsu asked Sung what were "the essential works for an understanding of the Learning of the Emperors and Kings, and Sung immediately suggested Chen Te-hsiu's *Extended Meaning of the Great Learning.* As a consequence of this recommendation and the impression the *Extended Meaning* made upon him, T'ai-tsu had passages from it inscribed on the walls of his palace so that his ministers might have the teachings of the sages and the lessons of history as a constant reminder. T'ai-tsu also asked Sung Lien to lecture on the *Extended Meaning,* and the latter did so, commenting especially on a passage from Ssu-ma Ch'ien's *Records of the Historian (Shih-chi)* which described Emperor Wu of Han's credulousness toward the magical arts of the Huang-Lao cult of immortality.[252] Sung also lectured the emperor on the importance of "the ruler's using rites and righteousness as the means to govern his own mind, and using education in the schools as the means to govern the people."[253]

The incident marks more than just the Ming's reinstatement of the *Extended Meaning* to the same prominent position it had held in the Yüan as a basic text of Confucian instruction at court. Where the purpose of that instruction had been to make the ruler conscious of his responsibility as teacher to the people, T'ai-tsu understood and acted upon it in a sense different perhaps from what was intended by either Chen Te-hsiu or Sung Lien. It took only a slight shift in focus for the emperor's self-examination and rectification of mind—putting a generous interpretation upon it—to direct itself toward the conscientious fulfillment of his duty to edify his subjects by something more than personal example. He would provide guidelines for his heirs, his ministers, and his people similar to those which Chen Te-hsiu himself had provided for the ruler. Thus he set about preparing and promulgating a series of imperial instructions, some offering generalized moral guidance and others with a high degree of specificity and functional differentiation. Like Chen's work, these made much use of historical examples for emulation and admonition.[254] One of them published in 1375 (the eighth year of the Hung-wu period) included guidelines for the conduct of rulers, ministers, commoners, scholars, farmers, artisans, and merchants. Others dealt with the "preservation of the mind," with filiality, admonitions to women, officials, military officers, etc.[255] T'ai-tsu also adopted strong measures to keep the women and eunuchs of the imperial household out of the civil administration, a point particularly underscored by Chen Te-hsiu in his *Extended Meaning*.

At the height of his power T'ai-tsu's increasing megalomania and paranoia, revealed in his purge of the prime minister Hu Wei-yung and suspected accomplices in 1380, also showed themselves in the more and more autocratic tone of these instructions and their growing preoccupation with the conduct (or misconduct) of ministers.[256] The greater his sense of insecurity, the more desperate T'ai-tsu's dictatorial decrees, even to the point of his exercising dogmatic authority in the expurgation of *Mencius* to remove passages considered subversive of imperial rule.[257]

It would be a mistake, however, to treat this as merely the aberration of an aging autocrat. T'ai-tsu's effective successor, the third emperor Ch'eng-tsu (r. 1402–1424), showed that the exercise of such authority had a rationale and momentum of its own. Ch'eng-tsu too felt the need to set standards for the conduct of his heirs and subjects. If Chen Te-hsiu believed it important for the Learning of the Emperors and Kings to be spelled out in prescriptions for the conduct of the court, Ch'eng-tsu could do the same from his own unique vantage point. Thus he took it upon himself to compile and promulgate in the seventh year of his reign (1409) a substantial work called *The System of the Mind-and-Heart in the Learning of the Sage* (*Sheng-hsüeh hsin-fa*) in four large fascicles.[258] Although another set of imperial precepts from this period, *Essentials of the Transmission of the Mind-and-Heart* (*Ch'uan-hsin yao-lüeh*) has been lost,[259] original copies of Ch'eng-tsu's *System* have survived.[260] We cannot undertake a detailed analysis of it here, but we should note its marked similarity to Chen Te-hsiu's *Extended Meaning* in the organization of the material, the topical headings, and the manner in which quotations are drawn from the classics and philosophers. Moreover, frequent quotations fom Chen Te-hsiu (the *Extended Meaning* and *Reading Notes),* as well as from Chen's model Fan Tsu-yü (the *Learning of the Emperors* and *Mirror of the T'ang*), make it clear that the imperial author is following in the genre and style of the Learning of the Emperors as represented in the works of these two Sung authors.

Ch'eng-tsu's precepts, like the earlier instructions of T'ai-tsu as founding head of a dynasty, are ostensibly addressed to the members of his family and to his posterity. Nominally too there are sections dealing with the Way of the parent, the Way of the child, and the Way of the minister—all lacking in Fan's and Chen's works. Yet in fact Ch'eng-tsu does not devote much attention to these subjects, but concentrates on rulership, even slighting or avoiding matters of concern to the imperial household dealt with by Chen Te-hsiu. Also, perhaps with a view to avoiding the forbidding length of Chen's work and keeping the whole within manageable proportions, he has largely omitted historical examples. An alternative explanation of this omission, not necessarily to the exclusion of the former, would bring out the difference in Ch'eng-tsu's motivations from those of Chen. The latter's case histories dwelt at length on the failings of past rulers, but Ch'eng-tsu's pretentions to imperial sageliness did not fit well with the recitation of such a sorry record of fallibility and delinquency.

Finally, in order to give himself some scope for pointing up the moral lesson in the same way Chen and Fan had done in their personal comments, the emperor appended didactic comments of his own at the end of many sections, speaking ex cathedra under the rubric of "The Learning of the Mind-and-Heart." From this and from the overall title of the work it seems unmistakable that Ch'eng-tsu was trying to incorporate into a work modeled in general on the *Extended Meaning* some of the features of the System of the Mind-and-Heart and perhaps also Chen's *Heart Classic*.

The greater part of the work is devoted to the Way of rulership, but is clearly intended for the guidance of all. The first section stresses those virtues and principles which the ruler is supposed to exemplify for his people: conformity to principle, restraint of selfish desires, the practice of reverence, and rectification of the mind-and-heart. The final portion of this first section includes quotations from the *Extended Meaning* of Chen Te-hsiu: "If the ruler's heart is nourished with principle and right action, it is bright and clear; if it is obscured by the desire for things, then it is deluded. . . . If one really has a mind for the cultivation of virtue, then there will be the fact and deed of cultivating virtue. Only if one really has a mind-and-heart for loving the people will there be the fact and deed of loving the people. There is no such thing as having the reality of the fact if there is not first the reality of this mind-and-heart." Ch'eng-tsu echoes Chen and Ch'eng Hao (*Wai-shu* SPPY 3:la):

"Heaven-and-earth have in mind to give life to things"; the sages and worthies have in mind to give life to the people. . . . Rulers all wish to see the world at peace, but their hearts and minds must be at peace before they can govern peacefully. . . . The ruler's ordering of the world must be rooted in principle and right action. Principle is the whole substance of the mind-and-heart; right action is its great functioning. Principle cannot but be bright and clear; right action cannot but be refined. . . . From the Three Dynasties down to . . . the Yüan it has never been the case that a dynasty's rise did not come from the ruler's mind-and-heart being set on principle and right action, or that its fall did not come from his mind-and-heart being sunk in desires for personal gain.[261]

The classical and philosophical sources drawn upon are not very different from Chen Te-hsiu's, but in the absence of historical illustration a quite different tone is conveyed. Here the moral message is persistent and unrelieved, while the sins or weaknesses of the emperors are not in evidence. The total impression then is one of undiluted idealism, seriousness of moral purpose, and the bland unanimity of past authority.

The second section is entitled the "Learning of the Ruler" and is probably meant to parallel the second division of Chen's *Extended Meaning*, which deals with the manner in which the emperor should go about educating himself. Here again the emphasis is on the same substantive virtues and their cultivation in the mind. Ch'eng-tsu appears to take seriously the obligation to study and practice self-discipline, both on his own part and that of others. It is not at all clear, however, that he wishes to dwell to the same degree on the major role which Fan Tsu-yü and Chen Te-hsiu envisaged for the minister as mentor and the scholar as teacher to the emperor. Instead of citing the many historical cases in which emperors failed to heed good advice or succumbed to obsequious and corrupt ministers, Ch'eng-tsu is content to recapitulate the teachings allegedly transmitted from the sages. He says: "Hold fast the Mean, preserve utmost refinement, and [preserve] singleness of mind are the three essentials of the emperors' system of the mind-and-heart for all ages of time." Indeed, so much the essence of the Way are they that "even Confucius' 'one thread which runs through all his teaching,' Tzu-ssu's 'Mean' and 'Harmony,' Mencius' 'humaneness and righteousness' are all contained within Yao and Shun's singleness, refinement, and holding to the Mean." [262] Thus again the impression is conveyed of unanimity and continuity in the teaching of the sages from past to present.

In this context it is not surprising that Ch'eng-tsu should be relatively comfortable with that aspect of the Learning of the Emperors which enjoined reverence and obedience to Heaven, as if Heaven were his parent, while he gave somewhat less consideration to the need for following anything other than his own conscience in this respect. He could quote any number of Sung scholars, including Chu Hsi and Chen Te-hsiu, on the subject of revering and serving Heaven, and then conclude by saying that "to do this one must search within himself, not outside." [263] Understandably, in one whose legitimate succession to the throne was more than questionable (since he had overthrown T'ai-tsu's successor), Ch'eng-tsu was perhaps disinclined to put much stress on following the example of one's forebears *(fa-tsu),* which he disposes of in a very brief section with no personal comment.[264] No need to limit unduly the free exercise of the sage-emperor's mind-and-heart!

This attitude extended also to his ready endorsement of the idea that the ruler should be free of preconceptions, "should not have fixed likes and dislikes." Rather, "he should like what should be liked and dislike what should be disliked," responding to things as they are, not as he would wish them to be.[265] For this it was important that the ruler preserve his equanimity and impartiality, for "of the seven feelings anger is the most dangerous to him and the hardest to control." Hence there is a constant need for him to guard against the collective assault of the selfish desires.[266]

In the third part of the work Ch'eng-tsu does finally give attention to the need for wise counsel, sound teaching, and impartial advice. Here his quotations draw heavily on Fan Tsu-yü and Chen Te-hsiu. He is by no means insensitive to the advantages of having disinterested and honest admonition, or to the value of having ministers of genuine character. He quotes Chen: "In evaluating men the ruler looks not for literary proficiency but virtuous conduct, not for empty praise but for solid accomplishments, not for the 'goodness' that consists in agreeing with one's own opinion, but for the loyalty that lies in correcting one's own mistakes."[267] Ch'eng-tsu lets this quotation stand by itself, adding no comment of his own, but he proceeds in the next section, which deals with the sovereign's relations with his ministers, to make absolutely clear in his own words where sovereignty and authority lie:

Ranks are Heaven's ranks, offices are Heaven's offices, emoluments are Heaven's emoluments. All those respects in which the ruler employs men and confers offices or ranks upon them should be in accord with Heaven. . . . All reward and punishment should also accord with Heaven. If the Learning of the Mind-and-Heart is not set forth clearly and the handling of affairs is not in accord with propriety, then there is no distinction between worthy and unworthy; if the meritorious are not employed, the guilty are not perceived, and if rewards and punishments are not what they should be, then things are not in accord with Heaven's Way. Whether things conform to Heaven's Way or not is the key to order and disorder and the thread on which hangs the continuance of the mandate of Heaven. . . .[268]

Lastly in the section on the way of the minister there is heavy emphasis on loyalty. Ch'eng-tsu's own summation underscores the basic accord which the minister must have with the ruler. He cannot serve unless his heart is one with the prince's and there is single-minded commitment to the latter, as well as complete openness with him. "If the minister's mind-and-heart is clear, it will be settled; if it is concealed or obscured, there will be disorder. If the mind-and-heart is settled, all affairs will be settled; if it is disordered, all affairs will be disordered. . . . The minister's service of the prince is like serving Heaven. . . . There can be no lack of reverence [respect] for him even for an instant. . . ."[269] On this basis, Ch'eng-tsu is prepared to state that the exchange of views between prince and minister should be mutual. Every matter should be discussed freely, fully and honestly so that the best conclusion can be arrived at. In all matters there should be no lack of full consideration. "In everything there must be a reverent seriousness, with nothing lax or remiss. Men's minds must be brought into accord and follow Heaven."[270]

Years after its promulgation, this work was commented on by the editors of the *Catalogue of the Imperial Manuscript Library* in highly significant fashion. After describing its contents, they note:

According to the *Veritable Records (Shih-lu)* for the seventh year of Yung-lo [1409] . . . the emperor presented this work to the Hanlin scholars Hu Kuang [1370–1418] and others, saying: "In my spare time I have made notes on the sayings of the sages and worthies, and now have compiled a book of them. I ask you, my lord ministers, to examine them and if there are any infelicities or mistakes, please revise what I have written."

After Hu Kuang and the others completed their examination of it, they memorialized the throne as follows: "The essentials of the emperors and kings are complete in this book. Please have it printed and distributed." The emperor agreed, eventually giving it the title of *The System of the Mind-and-Heart in the Sages' Learning (Sheng-hsüeh hsin-fa)* and having it printed by the Directorate of Rites *(Ssu-*

li chien). The emperor personally wrote a preface for it. Thus this book was actually compiled by Ch'eng-tsu himself and was not put together and presented by his assistants.[271]

Having drawn attention to the unusual character of this work, the editors, despite their reputation among some modern writers as enforcers of the state ideology, castigate Ch'eng-tsu for presuming to speak as a sage, rather than, as the ruling authority, simply giving his imprimatur to what more competent scholarly authority had prepared. They even complain about the undue length of his personal preface; in letting himself run on so long, he showed no sense of modesty or shame. They note the blood spilled in his rise to power, the harshness of his rule, and the many who suffered unjustly from his arbitrary decrees and excessive punishments, all in sharp contrast to the benevolent professions of the work in question, and conclude: "Men of later generations would not be taken in by this hypocrisy."[272]

Ch'eng-tsu's next major effort to codify official teaching came with his order to Hu Kuang and other scholars in 1414 to compile complete collected commentaries on the Five Classics and Four Books by Chu Hsi and other Sung scholars, as well as selected philosophical writings of the Sung masters on the philosophy of human nature. These were completed within a year's time and presented to Ch'eng-tsu in 1415.[273] The collection was entitled *The Great Compendia on the Five Classics, Four Books, and Human Nature and Principle (Wu ching, Ssu-shu, Hsing-li ta-ch'üan)*,[274] though the Four Books, because of their important role in the examination system, were often cited first among the three, or cited separately under the title *Great Compendium on the Four Books*.

Several factors lay behind the compiling of these works. By this time the "new" civil service examination was well established,[275] as was the curriculum of the Four Books and Five Classics in the schools which prepared men for the examinations. But the whole system was a much bigger business in the Ming than in the Yüan. It was a more comprehensive means of recruitment, drew from a wider field of candidates, and offered more opportunities. Above all, it was more competitive, and this put strains on the educational system which were more than just scholarly. Though Chu Hsi had been declared the highest authority in interpretation of the classics, there were different editions of his various commentaries circulating. One such edition, we are reminded by the introduction to the *Compendium*, was Chen Te-hsiu's effort to collect all Chu Hsi's authentic comments on the Four Books in one edition.[276] Chen's was among the first of such efforts; others followed.[277] Students wished to know which was authorized for official use. If their aim had been simply to understand the classics or Chu Hsi, slight differences among these versions would not have posed much of a problem. But most of them were bent on passing the examinations, not so much on gaining personal understanding, and success often seemed to depend on literal proficiency more than general comprehension. Standardization of texts was the obvious solution to the demand for this kind of authoritative guidance—an institutional answer to an institutional problem.

One official step had led inexorably to another: adoption of the Four Books in the official instruction of the Yüan, to adoption of them in the examinations, to promulgation of an official version of the texts. In the process Chu Hsi's preference for the *Great Learning* as the first among the Four Books also became institutionalized.[278] Both the Yüan and Ming examinations had listed the *Great Learning* first, and now it appeared first among the texts in the standard edition of the classics as well. The *Great Learning* had become a prime fixture of the official system.

Less directly relevant to the examinations was the third in this series, the *Great Compendium on Human Nature and Principle (Hsing-li ta-ch'üan)*.[279] This compilation reflected Ch'eng-tsu's own belief in the important contributions of the Sung philosophers, and his disposition to regard their writings as almost classics in themselves. Thus his original commission to Hu Kuang noted the "discoveries" of the Sung masters and called for their inclusion with the classics and commentaries.[280] Implicit in this notion was a view of the orthodox tradition as not something wholly fixed in the remote past but susceptible of later expansion.

This view of the orthodox tradition as living and growing, rather than static, should perhaps, in all fairness to Ch'eng-tsu, be taken into account in judging his alleged sin of presumption in writing the *System of the Mind-and-Heart in the Sages' Learning (Sheng-hsüeh hsin-fa)*. To his mind there was room for further contributions, whereas for later Ch'ing critics, more caught up in problems of authenticity, there was less allowance for expansion or improvisation.

As an exercise in defining a developing orthodoxy for the fifteenth century, however, the *Great Compendia* had other implications. Ch'eng-tsu took a strong interest in the project and expressed his own great faith in the value of the *Compendia*'s contents as a summation of all true learning. Since their completion and presentation, he says, "I have been studying them and have greatly benefited from it." [281] In the original edition of the *Great Compendium on Human Nature and Principle (Hsing-li ta-ch'üan)* and copied into the *Veritable Records* of his reign, there is a preface by Ch'eng-tsu (lacking in the other two compendia). Herein Ch'eng-tsu stresses the importance of the ruler's obligation to make the Way known to his people. After recounting the genesis and vicissitudes of the Way of the sage-kings, he says:

> In later times the Way was not always practiced and so misgovernment arose. This is not because the Way had failed but because men had failed to set it forth clearly and carry it out. Those who know this Way have a responsibility to make it clear and see that it is carried out. . . .
>
> With the passing of the sages, the Way is now preserved in the Six Classics. If the Way of the Six Classics is made clear, then the mind of Heaven-and-earth and the sages can be seen by all and the benefits of good government can be achieved. If the Way of the Six Classics is not made clear, then men's minds will not be put to correct use, and if the use of men's minds is not correct, depraved thoughts will run wild. . . .
>
> But if men can see for themselves the fullness of the Classics and the richness of the sages' teaching, they can fathom principle to the utmost, clarify the Way, set up sincerity as the basis of their self-cultivation, practice the Way at home, use it in the state, and extend it to all-under-Heaven, thereby regaining the perfect order of the sages. . . . [282]

With these noble professions Ch'eng-tsu had the *Compendia* distributed widely to government officials, intending that they should replace the assorted earlier commentaries and establish a reliable standard for education and examination.[283] The Imperial Library *Catalogue* later observed of the *Compendium on the Four Books:* "The source and basis of the learning of scholar-officials throughout the whole Ming period lay in this work."[284]

In 1426 the Emperor Hsüan-tsung (r. 1425–1435) presented a set of the *Compendia* to the Korean king, saying: "The Way of the sages and whatever has been preserved of it since former times are all contained here."[285] In Korea, where the Chinese example was greatly honored (often to the extent of trying to outdo it), this compilation also had an authoritative character and similar influence. The Manchus too held it in high esteem, reprinting it and also getting out a handier abridgment.[286] In their reprint of 1673, however, Ch'eng-tsu's preface yielded to that of the Ch'ing Emperor K'ang-hsi, who said in part:

> In ancient times the means by which the sage-kings succeeded to Heaven and established a polestar to guide the world and rule the myriad peoples lay not only in setting forth the system of government but also in delineating the system of the mind-and-heart and the true Way. The original instruction to "hold fast the Mean" was followed in the teaching of the sage-emperors and of the kings from T'ang to Wu without exception. When they spoke of the mind-and-heart, they said "the mind of man is insecure and the mind of the Way is barely perceptible.". . . The governance of the Two Emperors and Three Kings was based on the Way, and the Way was rooted in the mind-and-heart. For analyzing the principles of the mind and human nature and for enhancing the exposition of the Way of the sages in the Six Classics, no one was so clear and explicit as were the scholars of the Sung. Thus in the Ming, during the Yung-lo period, the scholar-ministers were commanded to compile the work entitled the *Great Compendium on Human Nature and Principle (Hsing-li ta-ch'üan).*[287]

From this it is evident how the Learning of the Mind-and-Heart became established as the official orthodoxy of successive dynasties, both non-Chinese and Chinese, and yet with consequences far beyond what might have been envisaged by its original sponsors. Ch'eng-tsu's intentions, allowing for his sincerity and genuine zeal in the matter, were perhaps not that different from Chen Te-hsiu's, but still for him to act on them as he did in promulgating the *Great Compendia*, even conceding that in this case it was within the bounds of imperial decorum and not liable to the charge laid against his *System of the Mind-and-Heart*, had incalculable effects and repercussions. Although Ch'eng-tsu had adopted an expansive rather than a static view of the orthodox Way and taken the liberty of contributing to it himself, the effect of his own actions was contrarily to fix that Way and impede its natural growth.

The great seventeenth-century classicist and historian Ku Yen-wu (1613–1682) had good reason to take note of the extraordinary significance which attached to this compilation and its imperial sponsorship. In his *Record of Daily Knowledge (Jih-chih lu)* he speaks of the successive collections of Chu Hsi's commentaries compiled from the time of his disciple Huang Kan up to the time of Ch'eng-tsu, and says that, because there were so many variant versions, "Confucian ministers were ordered to prepare the *Compendium on the Four Books,* which was distributed to education officers and the other works were dropped."[288] Ku concludes with an anguished lament over the disastrous effect which this had on the study of the classics thereafter, since no one paid further attention to commentaries other than the approved ones and there was no point in scholars' devoting themselves to serious critical efforts which might come to conclusions other than the approved ones. "Truly, the abandonment of classical studies all started with this."[289]

Already in 1436 even a high minister of state could have grave doubts about the educational consequences. "Nowadays Confucian students everywhere, instead of reading the classics, Four Books, and histories, just memorize the commentaries in the *Great Compendia,* aiming solely at success in the examinations."[290] Others, concerned over the chilling effect of the *Compendia* on the conduct of classical studies themselves, observed the awkwardness they felt in correcting errors found in the *Compendia* and in putting forward alternative interpretations once the *Compendia* had made such questions issues of imperial authority.[291] Prior to this, for a scholar to offer a differing opinion only contributed to the advancement of scholarship; once the emperor had spoken, even though it might be with the best of intentions, either the debate would be ended or the imperial authority would have to be challenged.

In the Yüan dynasty Hsü Heng and his followers had envisaged a system of universal education, based on a relatively simple Neo-Confucian curriculum, to produce men of practical learning and good moral character for service in government. Schools were to be the training and recruiting ground; Chu Hsi's teaching was to produce the model servants of the state. Given the inconsistencies of Mongol policy and inefficiencies of their administration, however, this ideal was never quite put to the test in the Yüan. In the early Ming, with the consolidation, rationalization, and routinization of the system, elements of Chu Hsi's teaching became incorporated into a single pattern of approved instruction which supposedly led from early schooling to eventual employment in government and ostensibly would put power into the hands of those qualified to exercise it. Behind the system the resources of the state bureaucracy were mobilized and the full authority of the emperor invoked to enforce a more precisely defined orthodoxy than had existed before. Seemingly the ideal would become fully embodied in Ming practice.

It was here, then, that the test really came. Would the new system yield the promised result? Would this "humanistic" education and efficient recruitment bring benevolent rule? As it turned out, Chu Hsi "orthodoxy" in this form did not produce sages, and instead the noblest men among the adherents of the Ch'eng-Chu school often suffered grievously at the hands of would-be sage-rulers,[292] the most celebrated case being that of Fang Hsiao-ju (1357–1402), the disciple of Sung Lien whose father had already been martyred by T'ai-tsu and whose family all died with him at the hands of Ch'eng-tsu. Under the new system, without any deep commitment to learning or moral cultivation, one might still succeed in rising to office; but with such commitment, one might only find one's principles in hopeless conflict with the emperor's conduct. There had always been discrepancies between Confucian ideals and Chinese dynastic practice, but now, with Neo-Confucian teaching so identified with the ruler, it too could become contaminated by his actions and implicated in his crimes.

In this way the very "success" of Neo-Confucianism in winning imperial sponsorship and the very perfection of the Ming system created a new dilemma for the orthodox tradition. Its whole credibility was at stake, its adherents faced with the loss of their integrity if they participated in a brutal system and with the seeming default of their obligation to public service if they did not. A new strain was thus put on the former consensus which went by the name of the Learning of the Mind-and-Heart. As we found it in Chen Te-hsiu and Hsü Heng, this learning had remained optimistic with regard to the incorruptibility of the original nature of man and the possibility of fulfilling one's virtuous nature through firm and disciplined exercise of moral will. No doubt such an idealistic faith still sustained those who dared to resist the emperor, yet in the Yung-lo period (1402–1424) and after there was a more intense pre-occupation *within* the Ch'eng-Chu school over the preservation of one's purity from the taint of political success. One cannot say that this situation was wholly unprecedented, since Confucian con-sciences had faced such conflicts with the state before, but now they were estranged from a world contaminated by the poison of Neo-Confucian "orthodoxy" itself as interpreted by imperial "sages." With this, the classic moral struggle between inner integrity and selfish desire became translated into a conflict between fidelity to the true teaching and submission, out of worldly ambition, to false sages.

Thus, as orthodoxy became more formalized and codified by the state, Confucian consciences showed increasing signs of aliena-tion. The aspiration for genuine sagehood and the hope for official success parted ways. The striving for "sincerity," which had been seen as the essential pursuit of the sage, went underground, there to encounter the subterranean depths of human deviousness and hy-pocrisy in subtler forms. Yet it could equally well be said that for some minds, no less deep an impression was left on them by the formidable intractability of human institutions.

In these circumstances, new forms of interiority and subjec-tive idealism appeared, but also, concomitantly, new forms of exter-nal involvement and objective study. In the scholarly sphere, though critical study of the classics could be inhibited by publication of the imperial *Compendia,* it could not be totally suppressed. In fact, over the long haul the effect of installing the new classics of Neo-Confu-cianism in such a prominent position in the life of the nation was to compel greater attention to them. When Ku Yen-wu, in his comment

on the promulgation of the *Compendium on the Four Books*, complained of its depressing effect on classical scholarship, he spoke of
this scholarship as the true, real, and practical learning *(shih-hsüeh)*
of the Confucian school.[293] In this he betrayed the extent to which
"the proper study of mankind" had come to be defined and delimited in relation to the Confucian classics, a tendency reinforced by
the system itself.

In one way or another scholars were left to ponder the meaning of this formally established "neoclassical" tradition in relation to
the classical. Wang Yang-ming's special attention to the new prominence of the *Great Learning* and its reinterpretation by Chu Hsi is
one example.[294] Lo Ch'in-shun's rejection of Wang's view, and his
rebuke to Wang on grounds of empirical scholarship, is another.[295]
Both show how irrepressible was the controversy stimulated by the
"success" of Neo-Confucianism. Another illustration is found in Ku
Yen-wu's criticism of the Learning of the Mind-and-Heart itself. In
a passage devoted to this in his *Record of Daily Knowledge* Ku demonstrates his awareness that this "learning," the *hsin-hsüeh*, did not
originate with Wang Yang-ming, of whom he is highly critical in
other portions of his work, or even with Lu Hsiang-shan (to whom
Wang was often linked as his predecessor in the *hsin-hsüeh*), but
with Chu Hsi himself. That is to say, he knows that this "learning"
lies at the heart of the Ch'eng-Chu school. Citing the very lines from
the *Book of Documents* which Chu Hsi had fixed upon in his preface
to the *Mean*—"the insecurity of the mind of man and the imperceptibility of the mind of the Way," "singleness," "refinement," and
"holding fast the Mean"—he explains how such expressions had
been taken out of context to formulate the new doctrine of the mind-
and-heart.

By Ku's time this teaching had become almost entirely centered on a "mind" cultivated in isolation from the concern for mankind and governance of the world toward which they had originally
been oriented in the *Book of Documents*. It is now a mind preoccupied
with its own inner nature. This we recognize as considerably removed from the Learning of the Mind-and-Heart Chen Te-hsiu had
written about in the context of imperial rule. By Ku's time it has
come to have a more specialized meaning, reflecting the intensifica-

tion of one tendency among many in the original synthesis of the Ch'eng-Chu school, shaped and tempered by the Ming experience. We might say that this is the "learning" as found in Chen's *Heart Classic (Hsin-ching)*, separated off from his *Classic on Government* and the dominant political orientation of the *Extended Meaning*.

Ku says in part:

Nowadays those who delight in talking about the Learning of the Mind-and-Heart disregard the original context and concentrate only on the mind of man and the mind of the Way. The worst of them just seize upon the two words "Way mind" and proceed to speak of the mind as the Way. This is to fall into Ch'an Buddhism and not realize that one is departing far from the basic mandate transmitted by Yao, Shun, and Yü.

Ts'ai Chiu-feng [Ts'ai Shen, 1167–1230], when he wrote his commentary on the *Book of Documents*,[296] cited Master Chu's words as follows: "When the ancient sage-kings passed on the empire to their successors, they never failed to pass on with it the method for governing it." We can say that this truly conveys the basic meaning of this passage. Although by this Chiu-feng meant to set forth clearly the "mind of the emperors and kings," for him it was the mind-and-heart for governing the state and pacifying the world. This view is solidly grounded in principle.

Those who later came forward to present this text and commentary to the court as conveying the Three Sages' transmission of the mind-and-heart, pointed to these sixteen words [of the *Book of Documents*] as the essence of the transmission of the mind, and those pursuing the study of Ch'an borrowed this as support for their own views. In my humble opinion the mind does not depend on any such transmission. What prevails in Heaven-and-earth, links past and present, and is universal and common, is principles. These are implanted in our minds, and when tested in things and affairs, it is the mind which asserts control of these principles, distinguishing truth and falsehood. Wisdom and imprudence, right or wrong in the conduct of affairs, order and disorder in the world, are all determined here. This is why the sages discriminated the "insecurity," "imperceptibility," "refinement," and "singleness" of the mind and transmitted the Way of "holding fast the Mean," so that all matters might be conducted in accordance with principle and there would be no distortion of excess or deficiency.

In Ch'an principle is considered an obstacle [because of its fixity] and Ch'an Buddhists point only to the mind [of nondiscrimination], saying that one should not try to define things in words but just transmit the implicit "seal" of the mind. . . .

In Chu Hsi's Commentary on the *Mean* he cites the words of Ch'eng I, saying this section [of the *Record of Rites*] represents the system of the mind-and-heart *(hsin-fa)* as transmitted in the Confucian school. This too is borrowing the language of Buddhism. . . .[297]

What Ku says here about the *hsin-hsüeh* shows him to be well aware of its Ch'eng-Chu origins, and it is the School of the Way's "transmitting of the mind of the sages" that he finds Buddhistic. A somewhat similar view of the matter is found in Ku's contemporary, Huang Tsung-hsi (1610–1695), who sees an affinity to Buddhism in the Ch'eng-Chu school's distorted preoccupation with the mind. Finding it addicted to highly refined "discussion of the mind and human nature" and "concerned with nothing but self," Huang advocates a more activist, public-spirited brand of Neo-Confucianism, exemplified by Fan Chung-yen (989–1052) in the Sung and by Fang Hsiao-ju in the early Ming. Of the Ch'eng-Chu schoolmen who had been enshrined in the official cult of Confucian worship, Huang says, "If what you want are those who close up their eyes, dull their senses, and reduce the mind to a state of unimaginable purity—a never-never land of consciousness—that is the teaching of the Buddha, and your candidates for enshrinement would have to be found among those who transmit the lamp [of the Ch'an masters]."[298]

How the Ch'eng-Chu teaching could have come to be so perceived in the seventeenth century is partly a question of how the Learning of the Mind-and-Heart itself had evolved in the intervening centuries, and especially in the Ming. To some extent the altered perception of it by Ku and Huang in the seventeenth century reflects a massive shift in focus as other developments in Ming thought diverted attention away from the interiority of the mind and toward the external field of empirical study or outward engagement in the affairs of the world. This became a recurrent pattern in the evolution of Neo-Confucian "practical learning" in Korea and Japan (see the next essay), recapitulating the Ming experience.

For present purposes we may simply note that what Ku Yen-wu speaks of as the original social and political orientation of the classical passages cited is not in fact different from Chen Te-hsiu's understanding of the matter. Moreover, despite Chu Hsi's alleged lapse into the language of Buddhism, in his case too the original orientation of Learning of the Mind-and-Heart was to the responsibilities of rulership, not to some isolated essence of the mind. It is significant too that Huang Tsung-hsi held in high regard not only Chen Te-hsiu, but Hsü Heng in the Yüan and those Neo-Confucian statesmen like Sung Lien and Liu Chi at the founding of the Ming dynasty who exemplified a public-spirited conception of the Way and saw to its active perpetuation, whether under foreign conquerors or under native autocrats.[299] The strong implication, in Huang Tsung-hsi's view of it, is that the Learning of the Mind-and-Heart had worthy champions and exemplars in precisely those teachers, writers, and leaders whom we have identified here as the principal early exponents of this mainstream orthodoxy. Presumably the warping of it into an introverted, self-centered, and "Buddhistic" doctrine came with a subsequent polarization of Ming thought, while the initial impulse was originally quite at variance with Buddhism.

With all its intense purism and rigorism, this type of Neo-Confucian spirituality had arisen out of a primary belief in and commitment to the dignity of man and a corresponding commitment to the service of the Way in human society, precisely at a time when such a faith had been called into the greatest question. In an age of crisis and decline it asked that man hold himself to the highest moral standard, keep strict watch on his own conduct, and hold himself in a constant state of alertness for meeting his human obligations, ever ready to engage in active struggle when the circumstances were right.

That such an idealistic faith should have become channeled into an intense moral rigorism which made extreme demands on the individual, without, however, asking him to renounce the world, has a rough analogue in recent experience. In the Cultural Revolution in the 1960s, one can see how the high social idealism of the radical Maoists too became expressed in more and more extreme demands for personal austerity, moral rigor, and ideological purity. The analogy is imperfect of course, considering the very different views of man and society held by Neo-Confucians and Maoists, but at least it may suggest how an almost religious intensity would be generated from a commitment *to* the world rather than from a desire to escape from it.

Some New Classics Recycled

As the early Ming consensus on the Learning of the Mind became unraveled, leading thinkers and scholars pursued different of its implications, each in his own way. Significant new formulations of Ch'eng-Chu orthodoxy appeared as a result. Ts'ao Tuan (1376–1434), Wu Yü-pi (1392–1469), Hsüeh Hsüan (1389–1464), and Hu Chü-jen (1434–1484) all represented typical Ming forms of the Learning of the Mind-and-Heart.[300] Each can be seen as an outgrowth of the Ming inheritance from the Yüan and yet also as a distinctive reflection of the intellectual situation in his own time. Thus they also represent a continuing, incremental growth in the development of Neo-Confucian thought, which carries beyond the limits of the present study.

To mark the threshhold of this new stage, however, we may return to certain of the texts influential in the first phase of this development and observe the new significance they took on at this point in the Ming. When Han Shih-ch'i *(chin-shih,* 1502) had Hsü Heng's *System of the Mind-and-Heart (Lu-chai hsin-fa)* reprinted in 1522, it may have strained credulity for him to imply that he was thereby saving Hsü's work from oblivion,[301] but this was not his only motive, as may be discerned in his preface, which reads in part:

What gives man distinction among the creatures of Heaven-and-earth is his mind-and-heart, and what gives distinction to the mind-and-heart is having a system [for its cultivation and use]. The transmission of the system of the mind-and-heart began with Yao and was expanded by Shun. Emperor Yü, Kings T'ang, Wen, Wu, the Duke of Chou, our Confucius and Mencius, all dedicated themselves to its perpetuation. The various streams of Sung thought, from Chou Tun-i to Chu Hsi, however divergent in their respective teachings, came together in fundamental agreement on the system of the mind-and-heart. Unless Master [Hsü] Lu-chai had attained a profound grasp of it, could we ever have had this record of it?[302]

Here is Han's reaffirmation of fundamentalist belief in the essential Ch'eng-Chu teachings (as found in Hsü's work), along with the scholastic reassertion of the authoritative succession. There is also an implication that the core of the tradition represents common ground among thinkers otherwise diverse in their views. Whether this be read as nostalgia for an idealized past or as a yearning for renewed agreement on fundamentals, Han Shih-ch'i seems to reflect a recurrent view of orthodoxy as not only the hard core of truth but also the main line, the ground where divergent teachings can still meet and shared values can be reaffirmed. This is much in the spirit of Hsü Heng's or Wang Wei's fundamentalist faith, and their belief that the Learning of the Mind-and-Heart represented the value consensus on which a new political order could be erected in their time.

A similar spirit is found in a work completed in 1534 by one Wang Ming,[303] entitled *Record of Chu Hsi's Learning of the Mind-and-Heart (Chu tzu hsin-hsüeh lu).*[304] This is an anthology of Chu Hsi's sayings and writings in much the same style as Chen Te-hsiu's *Heart Classic* or Hsü Heng's *System*. It emphasizes that Chu Hsi's "learning was the Learning of the Mind-and-Heart" and "took the ground of the mind as primary." Much attention is given to the teachings of Chu's master Li T'ung concerning the mind-and-heart. Otherwise the contents of this work stress many of the same doctrines as Chen's *Heart Classic*. We may take it, like Han's reissuing of the *System*, as essentially a conservative effort to perpetuate the Ch'eng-Chu learning by reproducing the writings of the old masters, as distinct from the production of new writings by Ch'eng-Chu thinkers in the Ming —like Ts'ao Tuan, Wu Yü-pi, and others cited above.

A somewhat more liberal tendency is found in another, ostensibly conservative effort in the same genre. This is the reissuing and supplementing of Chen Te-hsiu's *Heart Classic* in a work entitled *The Classic of the Mind-and-Heart, Supplemented and Annotated (Hsin-ching fu-chu),* compiled by Ch'eng Min-cheng[305] (1445–1499+) and published in 1492.[306] A Hanlin scholar, classics mat lecturer at court, and prolific writer himself, Ch'eng was a dedicated Neo-Confucian whose sense of orthodoxy showed itself, on the one hand, in a rather strict view of who should be honored in the Confucian temple, and on the other hand in his acceptance of Chen Te-hsiu's and Wu Ch'eng's view that there was no irreconcilable opposition between Chu Hsi and Lu Hsiang-shan in their views on the mind.

In his preface to this work Ch'eng pointed out that the concluding selection in Chen's *Heart Classic* was a piece by Chu Hsi on "honoring the moral nature," which was also central to Lu Hsiang-shan's teaching.[307] Ch'eng accepted the doctrine of the "whole substance and great functioning" of the mind-and-heart, as had Chen Te-hsiu. Nevertheless, he rejected the notion of some writers that Chen's *Heart Classic* represented substance and his *Classic on Government* functioning. Ch'eng argued that Chu Hsi, in his *Commentary on the Great Learning,* had characterized the mind as both substance and function.[308] On this basis he proceeded to supplement Chen's *Heart Classic* by including additional passages from the latter's *Reading Notes (Tu-shu chi),* and from Chu Hsi, the Ch'eng brothers, Huang Kan, Wu Ch'eng, and others in his annotations. This produced a considerably expanded work in four fascicles, presenting a view of the Learning of the Mind-and-Heart broad enough to serve as the consensus of the major late Sung, Yüan, and early Ming Neo-Confucians. His interpretation of Chu Hsi's view of the mind as both substance and function also pointed in the direction Wang Yang-ming was to take soon afterward.[309]

Recognizing as we do that in the fundamentalist view of orthodoxy there was already a persistent tendency to see the Learning of the Mind-and-Heart as a common denominator, we can understand how delicate was the balance between conservative and liberal interpretations of this central doctrine. When Ch'eng's version of the *Heart Classic* reached Korea, Yi T'oegye at first accepted it as virtually Neo-Confucian holy writ, holding it in veneration along with Chu's commentaries on the Four Books and *Reflections on Things at Hand (Chin-ssu lu)*—in fact, he likens his own faith in the *Heart Classic* to Hsü Heng's reverence for the *Elementary Learning.* Yet later in an epilogue to the work dated 1566 he expressed serious doubts about Ch'eng as making unacceptable concessions to Lu Hsiang-shan.[310] Given both the centrality of the issue and the ambivalence of its interpretation, it is not surprising that the position taken by Ch'eng was to become a pivotal one in the discussions in Japan between Fujiwara Seika and Hayashi Razan on the orthodox Neo-Confucian view of the mind (see the next essay). Indeed there is good reason to believe that both Chen's *Heart Classic* and Ch'eng's *Supplement* had a formative influence upon Korean and Japanese understandings of Chu Hsi orthodoxy.[311]

In the Ming itself Ch'eng's more liberal consensus view was to afford the seeming sanction of orthodoxy—insofar as Chen Te-hsiu's reputation as a champion of Chu Hsi orthodoxy could be so invoked—to the more active and creative development of the Learning of the Mind-and-Heart. Chief among the contributors to this new activity, of course, was Wang Yang-ming, who appears to have been much stimulated by Ch'eng's *Supplemented* edition of Chen's *Heart Classic*, and came to a similar view of the unity of substance and function in the mind.[312] Just as Ch'eng thought this view wholly orthodox, so too did Wang Yang-ming believe it to be genuinely faithful to the Ch'eng-Chu teaching in the deepest sense. Another less celebrated case in the sixteenth century, in its own time a widely influential interpretation of the liberal view in the name of Ch'eng-Chu orthodoxy, was that of Lin Chao-en (1517–1598),[313] whose "system of the mind-and-heart" *(hsin-fa)* developed into a full-fledged syncretism of the three religions: Confucianism, Buddhism, and Taoism. This too made a claim to Neo-Confucian orthodoxy plausible enough for Fujiwara Seika and other Tokugawa Confucians to take Lin's teaching seriously as such.[314]

All this shows how the supposed main-line orthodoxy, with its appeal to consensus, was as susceptible to "liberal" interpretation as it was to reformulation by imperial ideologues like Ming T'ai-tsu or Ch'eng-tsu. Indeed, late Ming syncretists of the "Three Teachings are One" school took full advantage of T'ai-tsu's precedent for this liberal view of orthodoxy. Against these, in China, more conservative positions were quickly staked out, representative of other values in the original consensus. But by the sixteenth and seventeenth centuries new complications had arisen which would preclude any simplistic categorization in "liberal-conservative" terms. One was the static which arose from interference in the intellectual dialogue on the part of the imperial authority and its bureaucratic agencies, resistance to which might come from either scholarly camp. Another was the onrush of time and the shifting ground of debate, which might, at a given moment or on a given issue, make those conservative of certain values in the synthesis "progressive" in relation to past or future trends.

Illustrative of this is a third type of outcome for the Learning of the Mind-and-Heart which returns us, finally, to Chen Te-hsiu's *Extended Meaning of the Great Learning.* To this "classic," in the early Ming, great tribute had already been paid by Sung Lien, while his colleague Wang Wei had cited it as the preeminent model for lectures from the classics mat when they were resumed under Ming T'ai-tsu.[315] Subsequently, the high honors paid to this work by the Emperors T'ai-tsu and Ch'eng-tsu were reaffirmed by their successors, especially in the Cheng-te (1506–1522) and Chia-ching (1522–1567) reigns.[316] The Manchus too, in their turn, confirmed the canonical status of the *Extended Meaning.* In an imperial edition of this work a poem and postface dated 1737 in the name of the Ch'ien-lung Emperor paid lavish tribute to Chen's contribution: through this guide to the ruler's self-cultivation, he had insured the continued transmission of the mind-and-heart of the sage-kings and the counsels of wise ministers down through the ages.[317] A translation of the *Extended Meaning* into the Manchu language was ordered and eventually published in 1856.[318]

Chinese use of it as a favorite text for lectures from the classics mat was, if anything, outdone by the Korean court of the Yi dynasty. There discussion of it and the *Heart Classic* was intensive, systematic, and prolonged, especially in the late seventeenth and early eighteenth centuries.[319] In Japan too we know that the *Extended Meaning* was studied carefully by members of the official Hayashi school.[320] But here the dynastic situation was wholly different, since actual power was held by the Tokugawa shoguns, and a text intended to educate the emperor to the active and responsible exercise of power simply had no place. It was unthinkable in this situation for anyone to urge upon the reigning emperor such an idealistic view as Chen's of the emperor's personal responsibility for virtually everything that went wrong in his empire.[321] Hence its net effect for Tokugawa Confucians was perhaps no more than to reiterate the religious and moral message more concisely stated in the *Heart Classic,* which was less encumbered than the *Extended Meaning* by the institutional baggage of China so largely irrelevant to the Japanese situation.

But even in the case of China, for all the difference in the dynastic pattern, one wonders if a certain unreality did not attach to the pious attention shown to Chen's work. True, any number of scholars, including representative Ch'eng-Chu schoolmen like Hsüeh Hsüan and Hu Chü-jen, paid sincere homage to Chen and his work for his exposition of Chu Hsi's twin doctrines of "abiding in reverence" and "fathoming principle." [322] But perhaps the most significant tribute to the *Extended Meaning* came from another quarter of the Ch'eng-Chu constituency. This was in the person of Ch'iu Chün (1420–1495), a scholar and statesman whose career closely followed the path of his predecessors in the teaching and practice of the Learning of the Emperors"—i.e., service as a Hanlin academician, court historian, lecturer from the classics mat, libationer of the Imperial College, and high minister to the throne. [323] Ch'iu was devoted to Chu Hsi and became a severe critic of the subjectivism represented by the independent-minded Ch'en Hsien-chang (1428–1500) at that time. Ch'iu was also an admirer of Chen Te-hsiu, on whose *Extended Meaning* he had often expatiated in his lectures from the classics mat. [324] To Ch'iu this work exemplified Chu Hsi's and Chen's doctrine of the "whole substance and great functioning," meaning that it activated the full resources of the human mind and spirit in addressing the needs of mankind.

Eventually Ch'iu compiled and presented to the throne another massive work entitled *Supplement to the Extended Meaning of the Great Learning (Ta-hsüeh yen-i pu).* In his preface Ch'iu took note of the fact that Chen's *Extended Meaning* only covered six of the eight steps of the *Great Learning,* stopping with the "regulation of the family" and including nothing directly on the "governing of the state" and "pacifying of the world." [325] It was Ch'iu's intention to remedy this lack and supply materials on these latter subjects. In the process he dealt with a wide range of practical and institutional questions. His work has been aptly characterized as "a comprehensive handbook of public administration, dealing with every aspect of governmental function, including military defense, public finance, personnel management, transportation, water control, etc. Under each entry the historical background is presented, different approaches to every problem are discussed, the author's opinion is enunciated, and, wherever possible, considerable numerical data are appended. Aside from its practical use, the work is noted for the painstaking research behind it and for its historical value. Being widely read, it exerted a genuine impact on Ming scholarship."[326]

From this it will be evident that Ch'iu's work is quite different in content from Chen's, and there is a question as to the precise relationship between the two. Was it a kind of false modesty which led Ch'iu to subordinate his new work to the *Extended Meaning*, as if it were a mere appendix, or did Ch'iu actually attempt to exploit the high prestige of the earlier classic for his own purposes? A full answer with regard to Ch'iu's intentions would require a more thoroughgoing analysis of his life and work than I can attempt here, but in relation to Chen Te-hsiu's work certain observations can be made.

Ch'iu knew from Chen's preface that the latter had in fact considered the *Extended Meaning* to be complete. Fulfillment of the first six of the eight steps, he had said, would suffice to dispose of the last two.[327] In the context of the *Great Learning* itself this was a plausible position to take, for there self-cultivation by the ruler was the key to good government. Ch'iu acknowledged this in his own preface when he said that Chen had based his approach on the self and the family and then extended it to the state and world at large, whereas Ch'iu was approaching it from the opposite direction, assessing the requisites for ordering the state and pacifying the world and referring them back as proper subjects for the ruler's self-cultivation.[328] No doubt he was also aware that Chen had done something like this on a smaller scale in the writings which appear in his *Classic on Government*. In any case, he regarded the two approaches as complementary, not opposed.

Ch'iu also explains that Chen dealt primarily with self-cultivation and did so on the basis of broad general principles, whereas he, though dealing with a larger sphere of action, emphasizes facts and precise details.[329] It is tempting, but probably unwarranted, to interpret this to mean that making a distinction between principles and facts, or substance and function, differentiates these two works. This would be going too far, for Ch'iu understands Chen's work to combine both "the whole substance and great functioning" and affirms that his own work is meant to do the same.[330]

It would seem then that Ch'iu is bringing his own experience of government and his own study of history to bear on the analysis of the same problem, and with the same assumptions that Chen made regarding the interpretation of principle and fact, the interdependence of substance and function, and the inseparability of self-cultivation and rulership.[331] For we must remember that neither Chen nor Ch'iu is discussing ethical values in the abstract, disconnected from the actual political situation of his own time. Each is talking, in his own way and his own circumstances, about the Learning of the Emperors: what it is specifically that the emperor needs to know, not what can be said in general about the subject.

Ch'iu believed, like Chen, that the Learning of the Emperors and Kings was also the Learning of the Mind-and-Heart. In his time he had to be concerned about the threatened distortion of the latter by Ch'en Hsien-chang's new teaching with its undue exaltation of the self, so bent was Ch'en on subjecting the world of fact to the domination of the autonomous mind. Ch'en's view, developed in isolation from the court and the actual exercise of power, could be dangerous if implanted in the mind of a ruler only too prone, in his time as in Chen Te-hsiu's, to neglect the business of study and to rely on his own intuitions.

In Ch'iu's view, for the ruler or for any scholar who would assist the ruler, the study of history was an essential task, and this included the kind of book-learning so deprecated by Ch'en Hsien-chang. Indeed, scholarly study went hand-in-hand with the cultivation of the mind and with the learning of the Way of the sages as communicated through the *Great Learning* and passed on down from Tseng Tzu to Ch'eng Hao, Chu Hsi, and Chen Te-hsiu.[332] Ch'iu speaks in much the same terms of this learning as embodied in another classic, the *Spring and Autumn Annals:* "This one book of the *Spring and Autumn Annals* was the means by which the sages transmitted their mind-and-heart. If one does not grasp this book, one does not comprehend their mind-and-heart, and if one does not comprehend their mind-and-heart, how can one transmit their Way?"[333]

When Ch'iu speaks of the true Learning of the Mind-and-Heart as inseparable from the study of facts in the historical record, he is trying to bridge the threatened gap between principles in the mind and principles in things, i.e., between the mind and things. The problem had not yet become one of principles versus the mind, that is, the School of Principle (*li-hsüeh*) versus the School of the Mind (*hsin-hsüeh*), for in his comments on Chen Te-hsiu he affirms that the latter was much concerned with principle while he himself sought to complement Chen with further study of facts, both in the name of the Learning of the Mind-and-Heart. Ch'iu's view may also be distinguished from the "orthodox" Ch'eng-Chu schoolman in Tokugawa Japan, Satō Naokata (1650–1719), who complained that Chen Te-hsiu was Buddhistic in his preoccupation with the mind at the expense of principles,[334] while others were criticizing the early Ch'eng-Chu school as Buddhistic because of its preoccupation with principles as opposed to things.[335] Ch'iu's view was still essentially that expressed earlier by Chen when he said that "principles are always found in things," and scholars should "not let their minds chase off into realms of empty nothingness."[336]

Ch'iu's particular stress on the empirical aspect of learning must be understood against the background of the rising preoccupation with the self in Ming times. This may have been influenced very indirectly by Ch'an Buddhism, but the especially intense preoccupation with the state of one's own conscience or soul owes much more to the Neo-Confucian concept of the self advanced as an alternative to Buddhism. More specifically, it relates to the view of sagehood as an attainable ideal and to the methods of self-cultivation adopted to achieve it. Was there not here an inner conflict in the Learning of the Mind-and-Heart, which had been latent in the consensus view of the early Ming, between the idealistic demands for the full development of one's nature and authentic self—the fulfillment of the "whole substance and great functioning"—and on the other hand the demand for cooperation with the state system in the form of loyalty to the ruler, acceptance of the official orthodoxy, and participation in the civil service system? In the reaction of scholars to this counterfeit orthodoxy, many conventional values were called into question, including scholarly objectivity and the validity of all external knowledge. Ch'en Hsien-chang reflects this intense search for the authentic self and the distrust of external canons of value, which was already showing itself embryonically in the thought and conduct of his teacher Wu Yü-pi.[337]

Against this trend Ch'iu Chün seeks to redress the balance in favor of objective realities—the facts of history, the facts of power, and above all the facts of institutional life which condition the ruler's (or ruling class's) exercise of authority. Ch'iu could even come to a less optimistic view than Chen Te-hsiu's of the ruler's ability to rectify things simply by the exercise of the moral will. It is not that the facts as cited in the *Extended Meaning* were wrong or inapplicable to rulership, but only that they were insufficient in the light of recent experience. As one who had preached Chen's text from the classics mat, and was well aware of the great lip-service given to it since the early Ming, he could no longer innocently believe that this text alone was "sufficient for the governance of all-under-Heaven," as so many emperors had avowed earlier. Certainly its message had not been adequate to cope with the growing problems of the Ming dynasty, which already, in Ch'iu's lifetime, had seen its emperor taken captive by the Mongols at Tu Mu[338] and almost brought down by the neglect of basic institutions.

From this standpoint Ch'iu was not abrogating or displacing Chen's work, but true to Chu Hsi's dictum of the "investigation of things and the fathoming of principle," was seeking to inform his ruler of the current facts without which his self-cultivation would be groundless. The aim was still, in the light of those facts, to activate "the whole substance" of the ruler's mind-and-heart and to achieve its "great functioning" in the world of men. But that world was not a static one, and the followers of Chu Hsi, whether in their investigations of things or their applications of principle, had to move with it.

How they did so in later times is beyond the scope of this study. With the passage out of this early stage of incubation, however, the Learning of the Mind-and-Heart propagated itself and proliferated in manifold forms, some of them still making a claim on their original Sung inheritance, others no longer even recognizing their common parentage. As thinkers or schools, they might, with great effort and inspiration, manage to keep body and soul, "substance and function," together, but to contemplate a grand reunion on the scale of Chu Hsi would now constitute a challenge of greater magnitude than the Master himself had had to meet.

Part III: NEO-CONFUCIAN ORTHODOXIES AND THE LEARNING OF THE MIND-AND-HEART IN EARLY TOKUGAWA JAPAN

In Professor Masao Maruyama's *Studies in the Intellectual History of Tokugawa Japan,*[1] Neo-Confucianism is presented as a closed and unvarying system of thought which had served as the orthodoxy of an unchanging dynastic state in China. Influenced by an Hegelian (and what subsequently became a Marxian) view of Chinese history and the state as stagnant and unchanging, Professor Maruyama abstracts from Chu Hsi's philosophy and presents a highly structured model of Neo-Confucian orthodoxy which corresponds closely to the pattern of an authoritarian state and social order.

It is a view lent some credence both by the long association of Confucianism with the Chinese state and by that state's efforts to define Confucian orthodoxy for its own purposes. This is especially true of later Neo-Confucianism, a mature, highly developed form of the teaching which grew up alongside of, and indeed in the shadow of, a similarly mature and highly developed system of state power. By extension from this relative stability of dynastic institutions a similar fixity of Neo-Confucian doctrine was often assumed.

In Maruyama's view, however, such a monolithic system was ill adapted to the different historical situation of Japan. Dynamic and undergoing constant change, Japanese society would never conform for long to such a rigid pattern. The outcome of any attempt to impose such an orthodoxy on Japan was predictable: Neo-Confucianism could only break up and disintegrate. Its rigidity could not withstand the shocks of Japan's tectonic instability, and the restless Japanese would not hold still for such a static world view.

Even in the Chinese case, however, the comparative stability of dynastic institutions was insufficient to guarantee the integrity or fixity of state orthodoxy. It is true that for over half a millennium, from the Ming to the Manchus, the civil service examinations were perpetuated with remarkably little change, with Chu Hsi nominally installed as the authoritative interpreter of the classics. Despite this, however, the leading seventeenth-century scholar Ku Yen-wu fulminated at length over the infiltration and subversion of the examinations by the heterodox teachings of Wang Yang-ming and his school. At this point one may discern the helplessness of any formal system, however firmly entrenched, to resist by simple inertia the spread of vital thought processes set in motion not so much by heterodox thinkers as by "orthodox" philosophers themselves. Wang Yang-ming, after all, was both a traditionalist and a reformer, struggling with the problems left him by Chu Hsi. Even Chu Hsi's philosophy, nonconformist in respect to the official view of his time, won acceptance as orthodox in spite of the establishment.

In the Japanese case, moreover, the specific forms of Neo-Confucianism which became influential in the seventeenth century did not themselves represent a direct inheritance from the Sung. The Chu Hsi school, despite its later reputation for rigidity, had grown and in some ways changed. It may have "sat still" but did not stand still. More than just a dogma serving the purposes of the state, or a hierarchical system upholding the status quo, it was a system of ideas inspiring further thought, reflection, and reinterpretation. The Japanese exposure to it in the sixteenth and seventeenth centuries was strongly affected by the more developed forms in which Neo-Confucian teachings reached them from Ming China and Korea.

Here I wish to underscore certain general features of the changes which had taken place, inasmuch as seventeenth-century Neo-Confucianism in Japan tends to recapitulate Ming thought— learning and "catching up" with the latest developments from abroad as the Japanese have so often done throughout their history.

In Ming China, Neo-Confucian orthodoxy appeared in not just one but three distinguishable types. First, there was the official state orthodoxy or ideology, which adopted Ch'eng-Chu doctrine chiefly in the form of commentaries on the classics as a standard for civil service examinations, and promulgated selected Sung texts as authoritative doctrine while ignoring much else in Chu Hsi's teaching.

Second, there was the philosophical orthodoxy upheld by nonofficial schools which identified themselves with Ch'eng-Chu teaching and practice, engaging most notably in the combination of scholarly study and mind-cultivation (especially quiet-sitting). Often the exponents of this second type of philosophical orthodoxy were critical of prevailing attitudes or at odds with the state authority, as Chu Hsi himself had often been. Thus we find nonconformity to the official system or to current convention as a not infrequent feature of this kind of orthodoxy; Wu Yü-pi in the early Ming and the neo-orthodoxy of the Tung-lin school in the late Ming are examples of this.[2]

Third, there was the sense of orthodoxy upheld by many later Confucians who did not identify the authentic tradition with either the state system or the Ch'eng-Chu school as a sectarian doctrine, and yet, as spokesmen for what they considered to be the mainstream of Neo-Confucian thought, argued for a broader and more liberal view of orthodoxy. This group included many who criticized the Ch'eng-Chu school for its want of political activism and commitment. Admittedly, this third view was less fixed and doctrinaire, but it remains an identifiable alternative tradition *within* the Neo-Confucian movement. Liu Tsung-chou and Huang Tsung-hsi exemplify this in the seventeenth century, and it would be granting too much to his critics not to allow some such claim to Wang Yang-ming, who sought to fulfill the aims of the Sung school and believed himself faithful to the import of Chu Hsi's mature thought. We may also include Lin Chao-en (1517–1598) in this classification; while an avowed syncretist, he based himself on the Neo-Confucian mental discipline *(hsin-fa)* and ethical system, and conceded nothing on the score of orthodoxy.[3] Lin's continuing influence in Japan constitutes a link between the various forms of the Learning of the Mind-and-Heart *(shingaku)*, from Fujiwara Seika (1561–1619) to Nakae Tōju (1608–1648) and Ishida Baigan (1685–1744).

Within both the second and third types we find individual thinkers whose doctrinal emphases or interpretations give a different tone or direction to these philosophical orthodoxies as they pass from one generation to another. And the same is true of their passage to Japan, where all three of the above types of orthodoxy reappear. First, there is the Chu Hsi orthodoxy which became established doctrine through its sponsorship by the Tokugawa shogunate or *bakufu*. The same texts are given authoritive status as in the Ming: the Ch'eng-Chu commentaries on the Four Books and Five Classics; to a somewhat lesser degree, the *Great Compendium on Human Nature and Principle (Hsing-li ta-ch'üan)* containing selected texts of the Sung masters on metaphysics, ethical and spiritual cultivation, and ritual matters; *Reflections on Things at Hand (Chin-ssu lu)*; the *Elementary Learning (Hsiao-hsüeh)*; and the *Outline and Digest of the General Mirror (T'ung-chien kang-mu)*, Chu Hsi's edited and condensed version of the general history of China by Ssu-ma Kuang.

As the term "Bakufu" indicates, however, the Tokugawa maintained an essentially hereditary military government, and this difference from the civil bureaucratic system of Ming and Ch'ing China suggests a need for distinguishing between two types of official Neo-Confucian orthodoxy. For this purpose, the Chinese type might be termed "Mandarin orthodoxy," inasmuch as it represented the ideology and ethos of the bureaucratic Mandarin class, and its formal mastery for purposes of the civil service examinations constituted an important qualification for entrance into the ranks of officialdom. In Japan, this examination system did not exist except barely in name, and the largely hereditary officers of the military government or feudal aristocracy did not actually depend on such mastery for their status or success. Neo-Confucian texts served rather as the basis of the curriculum in the official schools at Edo and in the various domains, and for the training of the Confucian advisers and teachers employed by feudal rulers. To identify this type of official teaching we might use the term "Bakufu orthodoxy," distinguishing the military and feudal character of its political setting from the more bureaucratic, meritocratic Mandarin orthodoxy of China. Illustrative of the Japanese case is the hereditary nature of the Hayashi family's position as the official teachers of the Bakufu—something unthinkable in China.

There is much irony in both situations, of course, as regimes so diverse adopted the Ch'eng-Chu texts for educational purposes while largely ignoring the political views of the Ch'eng brothers and Chu Hsi. In China, as a consequence, the texts became enshrined in a bureaucratic examination and recruitment system, of which most Neo-Confucians did not theoretically approve, and in Japan the teaching was entrusted to professional Confucians who had a very limited political role, and were precluded, by the very feudal system they upheld as the ideal, from any kind of political activism.

The Mandarin and Bakufu orthodoxies held in common traditional forms of canonization and ritual observance associated with Confucian temples in both countries. The enshrinement of Confucian sages and worthies was another mode of upholding values for general emulation, and thus of propagating official doctrine. In Japan, which lacked the incentives of an official reward system channeling education along orthodox lines and attracting ambitions into well-defined roles, the ceremonial aspects had relatively greater importance as educational instruments.

Even so, Bakufu orthodoxy, as compared to Mandarin, was probably less pervasive in influence, less routine in its workings, and less uniform in its effects. It operated more through personal relationships, at first quite informal, rather than through institutional arrangements. Hence, even among official orthodoxies sharing certain traditional ritual observances and a common scriptural basis, there are significant differences in institutional setting and style.

As a reflection of these institutional differences, there is also in Japan a somewhat different relationship between the official orthodoxy and the philosophical orthodoxy. The Japanese setting gave more scope to the individual teacher or school as educator and less to routine preparation for examinations as a system. In this circumstance, accidents of personal history and preference came more into play. Sometimes, indeed, they had a decisive influence on what was taught, what was thought, and what was pursued in the way of scholarly studies. The two leading figures in the original Tokugawa establishment of Neo-Confucianism, Fujiwara Seika and Hayashi Razan, despite their own teacher-disciple relationship, contrasted markedly in personality and outlook. They also responded quite differently to ideas reaching Japan from Korea at the turn of the sixteenth and seventeenth centuries, as the researches of Professor Abe Yoshio and others have indicated.[4]

Professor Abe identifies these two types as parallel transmissions of Neo-Confucianism down through the Tokugawa period, the one stressing principle *(ri)* and the other ether *(ki)*. In the former case, however, principle is not to be understood as static, abstract, or rational principle, but as the unitary principle or the dynamic integration of the conscious mind. As such it comes to function as a powerful religious or mystical element, generating a moral and spiritual energy which flows down through this line of transmission into the late Tokugawa period. By contrast, the rationalistic tendency sometimes identified with principle *(ri)* is actually to be found more often associated with the empirical study of principles in their concrete physical manifestation and, here too, in a dynamic, developmental state.

In terms of the twin Neo-Confucian aims of "abiding in reverence" and "exploring or fathoming principle" *(chü-ching ch'iung li; kyokei kyūri),* we can see how these two strains of Tokugawa thought might evolve not so much from separate lines of pedagogical transmission as from the further exploration and adaptation of polar values in the Ch'eng-Chu teaching itself. Principle, having both its objective and subjective aspects, might be studied or pursued in relation to the differentiated worlds either of physical nature or of human affairs, in which case *ch'iung-li/kyūri* could well mean "exploring principle," with the emphasis on extensive investigation, wide experience, or broad learning; or it might be pursued in depth, subjectively or experientially, in which case the term could be understood as "fathoming principle," stressing the attainment of truth through a more profound interiority or reflective contemplation, whether active or passive. By the same token, "abiding in reverence" could represent an intense concentration, dwelling on the unity of principle, in which case it might become a powerful force activating the individual psyche; or it could express the sense of communion with cosmic forces and the human community as manifestations of the Way, with somewhat less stress on the individual's self-mastery. If, however, Tokugawa thinkers exhibit these differing tendencies in varying degrees, it is usually in some combination which still reflects the basic polarities.

Finally, we note that these alternative interpretations of Ch'eng-Chu teaching have an equal claim to "orthodoxy," as represented by its founding fathers in Japan, Seika and Razan. Each fulfills in different ways the possibilities inherent in the Ch'eng-Chu synthesis. In consequence of this fruitful duality, Neo-Confucian orthodoxy in the Tokugawa Bakufu could serve to engender a wide range of Confucian activities in the seventeenth and eighteenth centuries, much as Mt. Hiei with its Tendai synthesis of Buddhist philosophy and religious practice had served earlier as the fountainhead of the new movements which dominated the medieval period.

Most previous characterizations of the so-called "Chu Hsi orthodoxy" in Japan, like Maruyama's, have assumed that it was "pure" at the start of the Tokugawa period—with connotations of dogmatic "purity" and a "medieval" conformity to one fixed authority—and that it subsequently became modified or undermined by modernizing tendencies.[5] In fact, Chu Hsi orthodoxy was pure mainly in the sense of being faithful to the ambiguities of the Neo-Confucian tradition and carrying forward the development of the two main lines of thought which had already appeared in Ming China.[6] It was already furnished with many of the elements of criticism and reevaluation which have been misconceived heretofore as being antithetical to Neo-Confucianism rather than as being in a state of dynamic tension within it.

Though both had Tokugawa sanction, the two main lines of transmission of Ch'eng-Chu philosophy were not confined within the official Hayashi school. The school of Yamazaki Ansai (1611–1682) carried on the orthodox Learning of the Mind-and-Heart under the patronage of a branch of the Tokugawa family in the Aizu domain, and Ishida Baigan (1685–1744) propagated a popular form of this *shingaku* among the townspeople. Both in its "samurai" and its "commoner" forms this teaching exhibited the strain of rigorism which had become a mark of Ch'eng-Chu orthodoxy in its spiritualistic and moralistic discipline, formally practiced in both the Ansai *(Kimon)* and Baigan *(Sekimon)* schools through quiet-sitting.

The continuing importance of this moralistic and spiritualistic type of orthodoxy is shown in its sharp interaction with the alternative transmission of a more intellectualized Neo-Confucianism and empirical scholarship, and also in its activist ideology at the end of the Edo period. In fact, both the moralistic and the intellectual tendencies have an element of "practicality"—the one experiential and the other empirical—and neither can be lost sight of in any discussion of the Learning of the Mind-and-Heart and practical learning in Neo-Confucianism.

Alongside these trends—"orthodox" in the first and second senses cited above—grew up the brand of *shingaku* which considered itself, and not the Chu Hsi school, the authentic orthodoxy according to the broader canons of the third type. This movement became identified with the Neo-Confucianism of Wang Yang-ming, but as represented by Nakae Tōju it emerged directly out of and in reaction to the Chu Hsi teaching. Tōju, in effect, rediscovered Wang Yang-ming only after making his own exodus from the formalistic disciplines of the mind along the same spiritual path Wang had traveled in the Ming. While this school was true to much the same sense of "practical learning" as Ch'eng-Chu *shingaku,* it was less sympathetic to the Ch'eng-Chu ideals of broad learning and empirical investigation on the one hand, and to the practice of reverence through quiet-sitting on the other.

Included in these transmissions of Neo-Confucian thought to and within Japan are three active ingredients: one is the original complex of Ch'eng-Chu teaching; another is the extension, clarification, and reformulation of this teaching in the hands of Ming Chinese and Yi dynasty Korean thinkers; and the third is their continuing development in Japanese hands. We must bear in mind, however, that none of these elements existed in unmixed form, and there was no direct or pure transmission of Chu Hsi philosophy at the beginning of the process. One cannot say that "to present the views of the Tokugawa Chu Hsi scholars would merely be to repeat the statements of the Chinese Chu Hsi philosophers."[7]

The subtleties of the problem are typified by Fujiwara Seika, who, at the outset of the Neo-Confucian movement in Japan, recapitulated in his own life and personal synthesis the successive developments in Sung and Ming Neo-Confucianism: (1) as a former Zen monk, he represents the abandonment of a medieval religiosity for a new spirituality with a strong ethical emphasis; (2) as a sufferer from the violent final paroxysm of the Warring States period, he feels a compelling need for a philosophy and way of life on which to establish peace and construct a new polity; (3) as a consequence of both his personal situation and his exposure to the works of Ming thinkers, he stresses practical utility in everyday life and the subjection of all learning to the test of personal experience; (4) as both ex-Zen monk and Confucian convert, he expresses the need for a synthesis of religious and moral disciplines which would reconcile the claims of moral duty and spiritual freedom *(ching/kei* as both seriousness or concentration and undifferentiated reverence), and (5) as one involved in the international relations of his day (with China, Korea, Annam, and the West), he manifests the universalistic drive to find the common human ground in all teachings and thus to arrive at a deeper humanism.

Seika's synthesis is all the more remarkable in one who stands at the inception of the movement in Japan rather than at its climax or culmination. As a personal achievement his synthesis is indeed impressive. Yet it falls short of attaining a perfect balance among the elements in Chu Hsi's synthesis, and it was left to his follower Hayashi Razan to develop the broad range of scholarly acitvities, empirical studies, and official duties which had equally been concerns of Chu Hsi.

Seika's conversion to Neo-Confucianism arose from his increasing conviction that it represented "real" or "practical" learning *(jikkō no gaku)* in contrast to the "emptiness" and insubstantiality of Zen. "The Buddhists take the nature to be empty. . . . We Confucians take it to be real, to be principle, as in the saying [of the *Mean*]: 'what Heaven decrees is called nature,' which is the unmanifest state."[8] The basis for this view lay in Neo-Confucianism's moral concept of man's nature, its applicability to human relations, and its daily utility. But Seika was also aware that the subjective intentions of the individual had a determining effect on what would prove to be "real":

Even the study of "empty words," if pursued with a view to self-discipline for the governance of men so that its effects extend to concrete things and affairs, may represent real action and not mere empty talk. Conversely, even the study of "real action" *(jikkō no gaku)*, if it is merely given lip-service and superficial thought and is not subjected to the test of practical experience of one's own, becomes empty words and not real action.[9]

In this passage one may see the criterion for practical learning being set by Seika, as it was by other Neo-Confucians of his persuasion, in terms of personal motivation and effective action rather than bookish learning or scholarly investigation. On the basis of this criterion we can understand how even the contemplative practice of quiet-sitting might have been viewed as a valid exercise, preparatory to effective action and more "practical" than any amount of book-learning. Actually, however, Seika's practical learning has little to show for itself in terms of either empirical studies or direct political action, and one might even argue that quiet-sitting was not, after all, very far removed from *zazen* as a practical method. Nevertheless, in the total context of Neo-Confucian humanism and the broad spectrum of values it sought to reconcile, we can still appreciate the historical contribution made by Seika in adapting the latest developments in Ming thought to the many Japanese uses of practical learning *(jitsugaku)* in the seventeenth century.

In general, one may characterize Seika's teaching as centered on a tradition of mind-cultivation and spiritual discipline which underlay both the Ch'eng-Chu school and the so-called Lu-Wang School of the Mind. Both these were indeed "schools of the mind," as Seika well recognized, but this fact has since become obscured by the attention given to rationalist tendencies in the Ch'eng-Chu School of Principle *(li-hsüeh)* and its seeming anthithesis in Lu-Wang "intuitionism," rather than being viewed as a matter of differing emphasis between two schools which shared the rational and intuitive approaches in different ways.

There is an intended ambivalence in Neo-Confucian teaching between reason and intuition, objective and subjective learning, observation or contemplation of the world and active involvement in it. A balance was sought among the intellectual, moral, and spiritual claims on one's self-cultivation. Values and facts, the principles of things conceived in both normative and descriptive terms, were seen as complementary or converging aspects of truth. Yet for all this, the tensions among them were very real, whether in self-cultivation, philosophical speculation, or scholarship. Seika's effort to achieve a personal synthesis of these elements was not uninfluenced by centuries of debate in China and Korea over such issues in Ch'eng-Chu doctrine. New access to the work of Yi T'oegye, the commanding figure in Chu Hsi orthodoxy in Korea, and also to that of the Ch'eng-Chu school philosopher Lo Ch'in-shun and the syncretist Lin Chao-en in Ming China, was an historical development of crucial significance for both Seika and Razan, and for many other Neo-Confucians in Japan, as Professor Abe and others have shown.

T'oegye's synthesis of Ch'eng-Chu teachings stressed the moral and spiritual aspects of principle as subjectively realized in the mind. Seika was strongly drawn to this view, though for him, as for most Neo-Confucians, it was not an issue of mutually exclusive principles, since he affirmed the need to apprehend principle in both the mind and things.[10] To Seika, indeed, an essential mark of Confucian orthodoxy was its hold on the proper balance between the unity and diversity of principle, or in other words, between unitary principle in the mind and the manifold principles found in affairs and things as the differentiated world of facts and events came into being through the individuating and actualizing agency of ether or material force *(ch'i; ki)*.

As Seika said to Hori Kyōan:

The True Way of learning in making ethical distinctions, takes "the unity of principle and the diversity of its particularizations" *(li-i fen-shu)* as its basis. There is a unity of principle pervading the multiplicity of things and facts. Between self and things there should be no separation. To insist only on the unity of principle is to follow in the way of Buddha with his leveling of things and his purely expediential view of them, or in the way of Mo Tzu with his undifferentiated universal love. [On the other hand] to dwell exclusively on the particularity of things inevitably leads to the egoism of Yang Chu. Unable directly to benefit from the personal instruction of the sages, we turn to their books and enter into their minds so that we may be converted to the truth of "the unity of principle and the diversity of its particularizations" and free ourselves from all error and defect.[11]

Seika believed in the possibility of latter-day saints and sages, and the sages he has in mind here are the Sung masters. When he speaks of "the unity of principle and the diversity of its particular-izations," he invokes a doctrine which came to him from Chang Tsai and Ch'eng I through Chu Hsi's teacher, Li T'ung.[12] In Chu Hsi's *Dialogues with Yen-p'ing (Yen-p'ing ta-wen)*, a text republished in Korea with commentary by T'oegye and a work particularly signifi-cant for Seika, this expression appears to represent the quintessence of the Confucian experience of truth as expounded by Li T'ung and as exemplified by Li's lofty and pure character.[13] The personal reali-zation *(t'i-jen)* of this truth was described by Li T'ung as "a total realization of oneness" *(hun-jan i-t'i)*, and by Chu Hsi as a "sudden and total penetration of the pervading unity" *(huo-jan kuan-t'ung)*, a holism overcoming the dichotomies of internal and external, subject and object, one and many, latent and manifest nature.[14]

As a method or exercise *(kung-fu; kufū)* most conducive to the attainment of this illumination, Li T'ung favored quiet-sitting, and Seika, adopting this practice, saw it as the prime means for the personal realization of truth in an experience of enlightenment which Li T'ung had described as "untrammeled spontaneity" *(sa-lo; sharaku)* and which Seika (like Li T'ung) sharply distinguished from the amorality of Zen.[15] In such an experience Seika found a basis for reconciling the divergent philosophies of Chu Hsi and Wang Yang-ming. Though this can be characterized as an eclectic view, Seika's profound personal synthesis of these teachings, manifested in his notable independence of mind and strength of character, belies any suspicion of a facile or soft-minded eclecticism on his part, and stands instead as an impressive example of the integrative power of Neo-Confucian cultivation.[16]

In this way Seika became identified with one basic strain of Ch'eng-Chu orthodoxy as transmitted through Yi T'oegye. It re-flected the specific character of a Korean orthodoxy markedly reli-gious in tone. Its aims are summed up in the expression "abiding in reverence and fathoming principle" *(chü-ching ch'iung li; kyokei kyūri)*. "Abiding in reverence" is a term we have seen deriving from Ch'eng I and Chu Hsi, whose combination of moralistic and rationalistic tendencies justifies using for *ching* ("reverence"), the alternative translations of "seriousness," "concentration," or "devotion." In practice, for T'oegye and Seika, the method of "abiding in reverence" was chiefly the quiet-sitting so strongly recommended by Li T'ung. Along with it came, from T'oegye to Seika, a philosophical formulation meant to clarify the metaphysical basis of self-cultivation. This formulation dealt with the accepted Neo-Confucian equation of human nature and principle. On the one hand, it identified the "four seeds" or "sprouts" of virtue (spoken of by Mencius as the basis of the goodness of human nature) with principle, and on the other, it explicitly identified the "seven emotions" *(ch'i-ch'ing)* with the physical nature of man *(ch'i-chih)*. [17] Since these emotions were seen as the source of selfish desires and a potentiality for evil, a practical implication of the doctrine for those engaged in quiet-sitting was to employ it as a kind of self-watchfulness over evil thoughts and impulses associated with the physical, sensual nature. In the stilled mind man's original nature or principle, unobstructed by disturbing psychophysical activity, emerged clearly as the effortless controller of the mind-and-heart—principle in this state being conceived as naturally dominant over ether.

According to the studies of Professor Kanaya Osamu, Seika's rigorism was reinforced by the specific influence of Lin Chao-en, whose system of mind-culture became for Seika a discipline to purge the mind of the "stain of worldly desires." "*Butsu* or worldliness is dust [on the mirror of the mind]. As the mirror becomes clear and bright when no speck of dust dirties it, so lucid wisdom will come to us if we renounce the worldliness of our mind." [18] Professor Kanaya stresses that for Seika, as for Lin Chao-en, this mental discipline was strongly oriented toward moral activism and away from quietistic contemplation, and the same is true of the influence of Lin on other thinkers such as Nakae Tōju and Kumazawa Banzan.

From this one can see how attitudes associated very early with the practice of quiet-sitting might engender a strong tendency toward moral rigorism. Though not a necessary deduction from Chu Hsi's philosophical position, neither was it without some basis in Chu's doctrine concerning the physical nature. T'oegye's theory of the "four sprouts of virtue and the seven emotions" served simply to formulate in more explicit terms a rigoristic view which in China very early became associated with Ch'eng-Chu orthodoxy and was already present or latent in Li T'ung's teaching. [19] The formulations of Chen Te-hsiu and Yi T'oegye heightened this tendency, and communicated to certain Japanese "orthodox" Neo-Confucians a "reverence" with a moral "seriousness" about it. Indeed, recent studies of specific late Ming influences on early Tokugawa thought and ideology,[20] including those of Lin Chao-en and the *Ming-hsin pao-chien*, have reinforced the view that Japanese Neo-Confucianism exhibited an intense theistic and moralistic quality which is not wholly identifiable with Chu Hsi's philosophy but only expresses certain tendencies or options available within it.

Hayashi Razan (1583–1657), on the other hand, rejected T'oegye's view, adopting an alternative one of Ming provenance, likewise with a history of philosophical and polemical dispute attaching to it. The debate in Korea had given prominence to the views of the Ming thinker Lo Ch'in-shun and his work, the *K'un-chih chi*, freely translatable as "Knowing Pains" but more literally "Record of Knowledge Attained through Painful Effort." Lo's view of the physical nature is discussed in *Principle and Practicality* by Irene Bloom, and his influence in Japan has been described by Professor Abe.

Lo represented a strong countertrend in the Ming and within the Ch'eng-Chu school resisting the idea that the physical nature was evil and asserting that principle, including human nature, could not exist apart from its actual embodiment in ether (physical or psychical *ch'i*). Wang Yang-ming had said something similar when he spoke of principles not existing apart from the mind, but Lo questioned the subjectivity of Wang's view and stressed instead the objective "investigation of principle in things and affairs." By emphasizing the reality of ether and the physical nature, Lo countered the tendency to think of the desires as anything but natural. Hence, his view may be termed "naturalistic" insofar as he affirmed the reality of man's actual nature and the necessity of accepting it as sharing in the goodness of the moral nature. At the same time, since ether was the individuating, concretizing agent in the actual world, Lo's philosophy directed attention to the principles in things as concrete facts to be observed. In this sense his view may be said to have a strong empirical bent, establishing the need for evidential inquiry.[21]

Though this naturalism and empiricism were increasingly in

evidence as a general trend of late Ming thought, their emergence within the Ch'eng-Chu school is significant. Lo believed that he was only amending and not revoking the essential Ch'eng-Chu tradition, which he sought to defend against an excess of moralistic idealism. A major point in the Neo-Confucian case against Buddhism had been its reaffirmation of the physical world. In accepting Lo's view, Razan had no reason to believe that Lo was anything but faithful to the original Neo-Confucian intention, or that his contribution was other than a needed clarification of what Chu Hsi had meant. At the same time, we recognize it as a clarification which led in one possible direction out of several. Indeed, Lo's empirical approach was a possibility which Wang Yang-ming himself had recognized in Chu Hsi and consciously reacted against, i.e., the possibility of a value-free objectivity in regard to external matters, or "the investigation of things good and evil purely as external objects."[22] In resisting this tendency, Wang claimed that he was actually following Chu Hsi's own thought to the revised conclusions Chu Hsi ultimately arrived at.

Razan's identification with Lo Ch'in-shun arose from two objective needs in his own situation. First was the need for a strong stand against Buddhism, which had dominated shogunal courts for centuries and was virtually an established religion. To serve as an adviser to the shogun Razan had to submit to the tonsure and serve as if he were a monk. This indignity for a Confucian made Razan all the more appreciative of Lo Ch'in-shun's keen critique of Buddhism, which exhibited both a sophistication and an articulateness Razan must have envied.

Second, Razan's strongest qualification was his encyclopedic learning. It was his stock of knowledge that Tokugawa Ieyasu (1603–1616) found so impressive and so useful to his administration.[23] Lo's philosophy likewise underscored the value of a knowledge of facts as well as texts, and in this it fulfilled the aim of Chu Hsi to achieve "broad learning" *(po-hsüeh)*. Razan's own activities as a cultural and diplomatic adviser to the shogunate extended to a wide variety of fields, and his published works reflected his interest in law, diplomacy, military affairs, medicine, pharmacopoeia and herbology, religion, philosophy, and institutional and cultural history. Professor

Abe's studies bring out the impetus Razan gave to his disciples' wide range of scholarly activities and research, including empirical studies in the natural sciences.[24]

Moreover, Razan had a strongly rationalistic, skeptical cast of mind and reserved judgment on many questions pending further evidence. Far from being a credulous fanatic in the service of a blind orthodoxy, he demonstrated a questioning attitude and insatiable curiosity in regard to many points which others took on faith or accepted authority. Thus Lo's philosophy, which set a high value on objective learning and evidential research, was well suited to the presentation of Chu Hsi's teaching under two of its aspects most likely to meet the needs of both Razan's temperament and his situation.

Behind these differences in received transmissions, there were differences in the personal backgrounds and temperaments of Seika and Razan which affected their respective philosophical approaches. Seika was retiring and introverted. After spending almost a lifetime in the practice of Zen, even after his conversion to Neo-Confucianism he was drawn to the mental and spiritual disciplines which constituted the *shingaku* of the Chu Hsi school, especially in the form of quiet-sitting and in Lin Chao-en's Taoistic method of practicing the *I ching's* "stilling in the back" *(ken pei)*. Razan's more extroverted personality, which had never been subdued by the practice of *zazen*, did not take to quiet-sitting, was diffident about the nonrational elements in the Chu Hsi school, and felt more at home in studies of a rationalistic and empirical sort.[25]

In an essay on "Tokugawa Feudal Society and Neo-Confucian Thought," Professor Ishida Ichiro has sought to correct two misconceptions among modern scholars: first, that Neo-Confucianism was merely an ethical system with a strong secular orientation; and second, that its moralistic tendency inhibited the development of an interest in natural science and empirical research.[26] Ishida points to the pervasive religious element in Neo-Confucianism, centering on the concept of Heaven, and he simultaneously affirms the Tokugawa Confucianists' philosophical disposition toward a naturalistic empiricism and "love of scientific learning."[27] He offers a detailed account of Confucian religiosity toward Heaven, which was combined with a scholarly interest in secular problems and scientific study. These he encompasses in a characterization of "Chu Hsi-Confucianism" as a secularized medieval religion.[28]

According to Ishida, there was a close correspondence between this religion, the basic principle of which was the sovereignty of Heaven governing all things through natural law, and the fundamental reality of Tokugawa feudal society.

Japanese Chu Hsi-Confucianism emphasized the power of Heaven not only because this idea was germane to Chu Hsi-Confucianism as it was originally formulated, but also because it was inherently demanded by the ideals and reality of Tokugawa society. The life experience of the people who lived under the absolute autocracy of the feudal system was such as to enable them to respond sympathetically to the doctrines of Chu Hsi-Confucianism even though these were of foreign origin. . . . [It] met a need of the times by giving formal expression to the life experience of feudal society.[29]

Professor Ishida's explanation of the ideological uses of Neo-Confucianism in Tokugawa Japan gives a good account of those aspects of the teaching which offered a rationale for the exercise of feudal power. However, his attempt to link Neo-Confucian "secular religion" to the "consciousness of feudal life (particularly in the castle towns)," and to see it as giving "formal expression to the life experience of feudal society" and becoming the "supporting 'theology' of the Tokugawa system,"[30] is subject to some qualification. Neo-Confucianism served much the same functions in the very different political and social circumstances of China and Korea. The Japanese castle town and its highly structured hereditary feudal relationships were worlds apart from the egalitarian peasant mentality of China's Chu Yüan-chang and the meritocratic, bureaucratic system he set up as founding father of the Ming dynasty and as sponsor of the official Neo-Confucian orthodoxy. Nevertheless, Neo-Confucian ethical constants could provide a plausible rationale for order and authority in both cases. To the extent that they affirmed the universality and immutability of values attaching to human relationships and saw all life as governed by a rational structure of static, unchanging norms, Neo-Confucianism upheld a view which could be invoked in behalf of elements in almost any authority system—and equally, we might add, in behalf of challenges to the status quo for failing to meet these norms.

Hayashi Razan, however, as the intellectual leader and founder of the Bakufu orthodoxy, was a Neo-Confucian who largely followed Lo Ch'in-shun's Ming reformulation of Ch'eng-Chu philosophy, which paid primary allegiance not to static norms and principles but to the dynamic, psychophysical element of *ch'i (ki)* and to objective principles as found in a world of change and growth. At times he questioned the existence of a metaphysical "Supreme Norm" *(t'ai chi; taikyoku)*, and was puzzled over the prominent place given to it and to the dubious concept of an unconditioned ultimate reality *(wu-chi)* in Chu Hsi's *Reflections on Things at Hand (Chin-ssu lu)*; he showed a persistent skepticism in regard to the supposedly authoritative example of the ancient sages in China and the accounts of the Divine Emperors in Japan.[31]

The same factors must be borne in mind when one generalizes about the absoluteness of the moral and political imperatives of Chu Hsi orthodoxy in the early Tokugawa period. What gave Bakufu orthodoxy its absolute quality was, in fact, the unquestioned success, power, and authority of the regime in its early years. The official ideology received a sanction from the irresistible authority of the Tokugawa regime, more compelling than the inherent fitness of Chu Hsi's philosophy to the historical situation. Nor was the ideology likely to remain unquestioned if the critical inquiry and scholarly study represented by Razan were allowed any scope.

Indeed, Razan was no anomaly in this respect. The attitude of skeptical questioning and critical inquiry which came down to him from Chu Hsi and Lo Ch'in-shun (among others) was carried on by several of Razan's disciples, including Kaibara Ekken (1630–1714) and Yamaga Sokō (1622–1685). Similarly, with Razan's emphasis on the dynamic ether *(ki)* and on principle *(ri)* as an objective rather than a subjective reality—this attitude too became a vital current in Japanese Neo-Confucianism, and watered the seeds of independent thought in the next generation.[32] The view of some writers that Bakufu orthodoxy was exclusively concerned with upholding nor-

mative principles *(li)* does not take into account the ambiguities of the situation, as reflected, for example, in the matter-of-fact but unexpected observation of Professor Abe concerning Yamaga Sokō, that "since he was a disciple of Hayashi Razan, it is quite understandable that he denied Chu Hsi's *li* philosophy."[33] How, we ask, could Razan be spoken of as rejecting Chu Hsi's *li* philosophy? To answer this one must go beyond the usual view of Razan as simply an adherent of Chu Hsi or an upholder of principle, and recognize that what Abe actually refers to is the view of *li* as transcendent principle immanent in the mind, whereas Razan, by contrast, stressed the objective study of principles in things.

The point of these observations is not to deny that Neo-Confucian orthodoxy or Ch'eng-Chu philosophy could provide the Bakufu with normative concepts and hierarchical structures which might serve as a rationale for its own rule and give meaning to the life-experience of Japanese in a feudal social structure. It is rather to highlight the indubitable and indeed seminal role of attitudes of mind no less central than these to Neo-Confucian thought: the inclination to raise questions and attempt answers on an evidential basis, and the ability to challenge as well as to accept established authority, both intellectual and political. In this, Neo-Confucianism had a capacity for self-criticism which also gave it the power of continued growth.

Whatever one's view of the uses of ideology and the abuses of Confucian philosophy, it is clear that Seika and Razan functioned in two familiar Neo-Confucian roles: as critics of Buddhism, and as proponents of secular society and culture. It was an accident of history that Chu Yüan-chang, the founder of Ming orthodoxy, and these two Japanese leaders of the Neo-Confucian movement were alike in being ex-monks and tending to be anticlerical. But it was not accidental that the Tokugawa, seeking to build a new and more unified secular order, turned to a humanism which offered a positive attitude toward human society, an ethical system on which stable social relations could be built, and a body of learning which could help civilize the feudal, military class. Thus Ishida is certainly correct in considering the Bakufu's choice of Neo-Confucianism to be no accident of history.[34] This is shown by the parallel between early Sung

China and early Tokugawa Japan. In both periods there was a new emphasis on civil, as opposed to military, rule, and on a secular order as contrasted to the clerical dominance of Buddhism. And in both periods Neo-Confucianism responded to the trend.

Nevertheless, as Ishida says, the new humanism was not without an important religious or spiritual dimension. Instead, however, of being identified simply with reverence for external authority, it is most genuinely expressed in the type of spirituality found in the Neo-Confucian School(s) of the Mind, represented initially by Seika. What we have then are parallel strains of Neo-Confucian thought: one, emerging from Seika's spiritual cultivation, was centered on the experience of the unity of principle in active contemplation (or contemplative action), and the other, stemming from Razan, was more rational, scholarly, and intellectual and more given to the study of both human society and natural science.

Given these divergent strains of Neo-Confucian "orthodoxy," reflecting the range of human activity and experience comprehended in Chu Hsi's system, it becomes all the more important that we recognize the process of interaction among them. In what might be called the high tradition of Neo-Confucianism in Tokugawa Japan, significant contrasting examples are afforded by Yamazaki Ansai and Kaibara Ekken. These have been discussed more fully by Professor Okada Takehiko than I could undertake to do here, and the reader is referred to his essays in *Principle and Practicality*. On the more popular level the Learning of the Mind-and-Heart is represented by Ishida Baigan, featured in Robert Bellah's work on *Tokugawa Religion* [35] as a kind of Protestant ethic. Baigan's teaching was known in Japanese as *shingaku*, corresponding to the Chinese *hsin-hsüeh*. This actually owes little, if anything, to the so-called School of the Mind identified with Lu Hsiang-shan and Wang Yang-ming. Baigan's school is rather an independent outgrowth of the orthodox Ch'eng-Chu teaching. In this fact alone there is much significance. *Shingaku*, from this standpoint, is more Catholic than Protestant. There is even a sense, as we shall see, in which it is more Catholic than the Pope, i.e., more orthodox than Tokugawa orthodoxy.

Those familiar with Neo-Confucian spirituality in China will find in Baigan's teaching all its usual earmarks:

"The highest aim of *gakumon* [Confucian learning] is to exhaust one's heart and know one's nature. Knowing one's nature one knows Heaven." Knowing Heaven, at least for Baigan, means that one's own heart is united with the heart of Heaven and earth. However, being darkened by human desires, this heart is lost. Consequently when we speak of exhausting the heart and returning to the heart of Heaven and earth, we are saying to seek the lost heart. If one seeks and attains it, one becomes the heart of Heaven and earth. When one says, "becomes the heart of Heaven and earth," one says "without a heart *(mushin)*." The good person *(jinsha)* "makes his heart united with Heaven and earth and all things." There is nothing which can be said not to be himself. . . . The sage penetrates heaven and earth and all things with his own heart.[36]

Here, allowing for certain variations in the translation of key terms, is the doctrine of Ch'eng Hao concerning the "humanity which forms one body with Heaven and earth and all things."[37] Bellah translates the term *shin* (Ch. *hsin*) as "heart" rather than "mind," no doubt to emphasize the ethical and affective aspects of this very broad concept.[38] This is, nonetheless, the typical Neo-Confucian doctrine of the mind-and-heart which figures so prominently in the thought of the Sung and Ming. Alternatively, one can identify it as the Neo-Confucian doctrine of no-mind *(wu-hsin)*, meaning that the humane man has "no mind" of his own but sees and acts toward all things with the mind of Heaven-and-earth.[39] The psychological and religious phenomena associated with this experience, as described by Bellah for Baigan and his disciples, are likewise almost a stereotype of the mystical experience found especially in Ming thinkers.[40] "As in mysticism generally, what is indicated is some dissolution of the boundary between self and non-self. This union is accompanied by a feeling of great happiness and tranquility, but also a great feeling of power."[41]

What is noteworthy here, as I have put it above, is that this represents the typical Neo-Confucian "doctrine of the mind-and-heart." By this I mean to distinguish it from the so-called Lu-Wang School of the Mind, for, as I stated earlier, Baigan has no special connection with that, and his thinking reflects rather the teaching and cultivation of the mind as it is found in the "orthodox" Ch'eng-Chu school.

Though this latter school is usually identified as the "School of Principle," the conventional dichotomy which has developed between "principle" and "mind" in describing these two main lines of Neo-Confucian thought tends to obscure the most fundamental role of the mind-and-heart in this movement as a whole.[42] These conventional designations serve to differentiate these schools from one another but do not adequately express even more fundamental points of agreement. The School of Principle *(li-hsüeh),* as applied to the Ch'eng-Chu school, focuses attention on what is indeed a basic doctrine of this school: its belief in fixed moral principles and in the underlying rationality of all things. The significance of the term derives from this school's rejection of Buddhist "emptiness" as the ultimate reality and its insistence that there is a "principle in the midst of emptiness," as Chu Hsi put it.[43] But the principles Chu Hsi was talking about were as much principles of the mind as principles in things, and the importance of Mencius to this movement (as brought out in the quotations from Dr. Bellah) lies in the basis he provided for a Neo-Confucian philosophy of the mind as an alternative to the Buddhist.[44] Thus in Chu Hsi's system as it was conveyed to Baigan, there was already a heavy emphasis on cultivation of the mind. It drew upon earlier Sung thinkers like Chou Tun-i and the Ch'eng brothers, who, whether they be seen to reflect a strain of quietism in Sung thought or not, certainly showed the influence of Buddhism in their emphasis on the primacy of mind and the importance of mental cultivation in forms closely resembling those of Zen Buddhism.[45]

In *The Unfolding of Neo-Confucianism,* Araki Kengo has discussed these designations in the broader context of Sung thought, which includes the Buddhist School of the Mind. He suggests that use of the same term for the Lu-Wang school tends to identify it too exclusively with the mind and fails to bring out how strongly Wang Yang-ming adhered to the notion of principle, even though he did not conceive of it as fixed. Precisely the same can be said in reverse about the Ch'eng-Chu school. It is truly a school of the mind-and-heart as well as of principle.

Baigan's *shingaku,* then, is a school of the mind-and-heart in this sense. Though it has its own specific Japanese characteristics,

including some direct influence of Zen and a syncretism characteristic of the late seventeenth and eighteenth centuries in Tokugawa
Japan, in a most fundamental sense his teaching of the mind-and-
heart faithfully transmits to this new setting what is known as the
orthodox Ch'eng-Chu teaching and practice in this respect. If one
had conceived of its orthodoxy in terms of adherence above all to
"principle," one would be surprised perhaps to discover that its
fidelity to the Ch'eng-Chu school consisted for practical purposes in
its employment of the method of self-examination and contemplation which was as much a fixture in this tradition as examination of
conscience and confession have been to the Roman Catholic. It is in
this specific sense that I have spoken of *shingaku* as being more
Catholic than Protestant, though there are of course other resem-
blances in it to Protestantism.⁴⁶

Bellah alludes to this in his discussion of the formal practice
of meditation by Baigan as a means of "exhausting the heart" and
"knowing one's nature." "This exhausting the heart had with the
Sung Confucians already become a clearly defined technique. Baigan
calls it *kufū* or *seiza*. *Kufū* implies the expenditure of effort and *seiza*
simply means quiet-sitting. What is involved is a sort of concentration of the will. Words and all external things are as much as possible
abandoned. Baigan's technique of meditation was, in fact, strongly
influenced by the Zen sect of Buddhism."⁴⁷

The term *kufū*, above, corresponds to the Chinese *kung-fu*,
which was already an important term for religious practice in
Chinese Ch'an Buddhism before it came into similar use by the Neo-
Confucians. *Seiza* corresponds to the Chinese *ching-tso*, a type of
quiet-sitting influenced by Ch'an Buddhism but distinguishable
from Ch'an (Zen) "sitting in meditation" *(tso-ch'an,* Japanese *zazen).*
The significant, though often subtle, influences of Ch'an on the Neo-
Confucian practice of quiet-sitting in the Sung, as well as the equally
significant differences between the two, complicate the question of
a separate and direct Zen influence on Baigan; it is a matter requiring
some delicacy of treatment and, being secondary to our purpose
here, must be held over to a later time.

Enough has been seen so far to establish that the Neo-Confucianism we are dealing with here is less of a philosophical system

than it is a type and method of spirituality. Indeed, if there is any purpose in our giving attention to Japanese *shingaku*, which was not that important as an historical movement, it is to bring out the more religious aspect of orthodox Neo-Confucianism and suggest the need for a reinterpretation of the main line of development in Neo-Confucian thought.

Previously, the complexity of the developmental process has been underestimated, and misleading conclusions have been drawn from an oversimplified version of early Japanese Neo-Confucianism. Hence, one might well be wary of any generalizations on the subject. As guidelines for further inquiry, however, one may consider the following conclusions drawn from studies reported on here:

First, when the Japanese turned their main attention to Neo-Confucianism, they assimilated quickly not only the original Ch'eng-Chu teaching but also much that had subsequently emerged in the later, conflicted development of Neo-Confucian thought. Their value commitments were made with some awareness of the ambiguities attached and the issues in dispute.

Second, as a reflection of this receptivity and catholicity, Japanese Neo-Confucianism came to exhibit many of the same trends and characteristics seen in the thought and scholarship of the Ming period.[48] Beyond testifying to the remarkable replicative powers of the Japanese, these shared characteristics are suggestive of underlying continuities and a pattern of growth within the Neo-Confucian system which asserted themselves even in the very different historical circumstances of Tokugawa Japan. One can point to distinctive Japanese aspects in any such development, but their singularity can be seen and appreciated only against the background of the comparable Chinese experience.

Third, because Neo-Confucianism was less authoritarian and doctrinaire than has been commonly supposed, far more self-critical, and more productive of dynamic reactivity within the system, one must be conscious of the give-and-take and of the contending values that compete for attention within the system. Conflict and controversy cannot in themselves be taken as signs of disaffection or deviation from Neo-Confucianism as a whole.

Fourth, once we recognize the existence of alternatives within the tradition, as well as different phases in the development of its central values, we can appreciate how the spread of Neo-Confucianism to Japan presented opportunities for fuller growth in certain areas of thought and scholarship, which the Japanese took to more eagerly than the Chinese.

The examples which follow are illustrative. Lo Ch'in-shun is an example of a major Ch'eng-Chu thinker and a principal alternative to Wang Yang-ming in his time, whose influence blossomed out in Japan after he had been largely lost sight of in seventeenth-century China. Lo's brand of orthodoxy—a revisionist view sympathetic toward Chu Hsi, but constructively critical of him—contributed to the growth in Japan of a practical learning with strong empirical and naturalistic tendencies.

The "Sung" school of the early Ch'ing, which found Lo's critical rationalism uncomfortable, developed along lines more characteristic of the alternative orthodoxy represented in the early Ming by Hu Chü-jen (1434–1484). The Sung school in late seventeenth-century China has been characterized in one earlier study as marked by an extreme subjective idealism and psychological interiorization, and in another study by its "pragmatic" and "practical" quality.[49] At variance though these two interpretations might appear to be, they are probably not mutually exclusive; as noted in Seika's case, the psychological discipline *(hsin-fa)* of the Ch'eng-Chu school had been conceived as both a prelude to moral action and as a retrospection upon it. But the suggestion that this system in China is worlds apart from Tokugawa Confucianism, and that its peculiarly inverted or involuted quality is to be explained by the repressive character of Ch'ing absolutism in a highly centralized autocracy,[50] seems gratuitous when one recognizes the existence in Japan of a close parallel to this moral discipline and spiritual training in Seika himself, as well as in Yamazaki Ansai and Ishida Baigan. These schools exhibited both the introverted and extroverted forms of Ch'eng-Chu teaching. To this extent, they shared a common legacy with Chinese Neo-Confucians but in circumstances so different systemically from the Chinese case as to render the social and political setting of either country a negligible factor in accounting for the common methods of thought and self-cultivation.

Another significant parallel is to be found in the case of Yen Yüan (1635–1704), long known for his outright rejection of the Ch'eng-Chu system and his advocacy of a practical learning that stressed "pragmatic" action. Chung-ying Cheng attempts to show the affinities that exist between both Chu Hsi and Wang Yang-ming and the type of practical learning which ostensibly broke away from them.[51] Professor Cheng's line of argument, stressing the continuities amid the discontinuities of Neo-Confucian thought, is not without relevance to a parallel Japanese development in the so-called school of Ancient Learning *(Kogaku)*. In the latter case there is a comparable break with the Ch'eng-Chu system of self-cultivation, but the Ancient Learning carries forward, as Yen Yüan does not, the "broad-learning," empirical study, and critical rationality engendered by Neo-Confucianism as one aspect of its practical learning.

In both Yen Yüan and the *Kogaku,* we observe a fundamentalist reaction to Neo-Confucianism in the urge to return to the classical sources of Confucianism as found in both the original texts and the irreducible ethical teachings of the school. Chu Shun-shui (1600–1689), the Chinese expatriate and Ming loyalist who is usually considered the Neo-Confucian godfather of the Mito school in Japan, appears in Julia Ching's study[52] as combining these seemingly opposed attitudes; he was both a follower of the orthodox Ch'eng-Chu school and a fundamentalist whose Neo-Confucian sense of "reverence" or "seriousness" *(ching)* eschewed the metaphysical speculation of the Sung and devoted itself to the more practical forms of education. In thus pursuing only the practical side of Chu Hsi's teaching, Shun-shui was a typical product of the late Ming (as indeed was Yen Yüan himself) with its preference for concrete action over metaphysical speculation.

Interpretations of Japanese Confucianism have sometimes seen it as expressing a similar preference—spoken of as a "typical" Japanese penchant for action over abstraction and for the concrete over the universal. The case of Chu Shun-shui, however, warns us away from any such facile differentiations between Chinese and Japanese attitudes. There was nothing un-Chinese about Chu or the late Ming style of antimetaphysical thought which he brought to Japan. If it proved congenial to the Japanese, this in itself evidences a convergence of needs and interests, not a basic divergence in outlook.

The same Confucian virtues, it is true, may have become invested with different values according to the varying social and political circumstances of China and Japan. The loyalism, for example, which Chu, as a symbol of Ming resistance to the Manchus, imparted to the Japanese, no doubt developed differently in the hands of the Mito school than it could in any Ch'ing school under a foreign dynasty or in any society and culture which lacked the vital traditions of clan loyalty still prevailing in Tokugawa Japan. If, however, we are tempted to view this as evidence that the Japanese stressed loyalty to the ruler over filial piety, or that the Chinese, conversely, placed filial piety ahead of political loyalties, such simple contrasts are belied by the examples cited here. Chu Shun-shui, as a Ming loyalist, is not untypical of the Chinese scholars of his time. On the other hand, the Japanese Nakae Tōju, though perhaps not so exclusively motivated by filial devotion to his mother as pious legend would have it, did find in filial piety the primary basis for Confucian reverence, and in turn established the latter as the ground of moral action.

As Professor Yamashita Ryūji traces the development of Tōju's thought, it becomes apparent that Tōju, instead of simply reflecting the teaching of Wang Yang-ming with which he is usually identified, actually followed his own course of evolution out of the Ch'eng-Chu system, working up to Wang in his excursion from Chu Hsi at the same time that he worked back to Wang through study of his late Ming followers.[53] From either direction, Tōju sought a way out of the more rationalistic and rigid demands of the formalized Ch'eng-Chu system to the underlying sources of Neo-Confucian religiosity as a wellspring of moral action.

A circumstance in Japan which lent itself to this religious development was the lively presence of Shinto tradition. Tōju's own involvement with religion, however, arose from more than simply local circumstance or native tradition. In the Wang Yang-ming school there had continued to be a close relation between religious transcendence and ethical action, that is between "emptiness" (*hsü*) as a creative detachment or vital spirituality on the one hand, and realism or practicality *(shih)* as a commitment to positive action on the other. In this respect the theistic influences and moral activism which Tōju received from the late Ming were quite compatible with Shinto worship, and the two tended to be mutually reinforcing.

In his preface to *Studies in the Intellectual History of Tokugawa Japan,* Professor Masao Maruyama expressed doubts about his own earlier assumption that early Tokugawa Confucianism was as unadulterated as if it had just arrived from China, thus overlooking its genuinely Japanese characteristics:

It is, of course, true that Yamazaki Ansai and his school *claimed* a fierce orthodoxy in their exposition of Chu Hsi's doctrines. . . . But whether or not their own outlook, or their choice of texts or of emphasis, coincided *objectively* with those of Chu Hsi is an entirely different matter. For all their subjective intentions one might, ironically, see the Ansai school precisely as a characteristic illustration of the distance between Japanese Neo-Confucianism and that of China. . . . However, if one starts by bringing out much more clearly how much not only Ansai's Confucianism, but also that of Hayashi Razan who stands right at the very point of departure of Tokugawa Confucianism, rested on essentially revisionist interpretations, one would arrive at a version of Tokugawa intellectual history rather considerably different from the perspective of this book.[54]

Notwithstanding these concessions, it would be unfortunate if one were left here with only a choice of radically opposed Chinese and Japanese alternatives. Both Razan and Ansai represent plausible interpretations of Chu Hsi's philosophy and at the same time variant adaptations of it to the Japanese scene. Ansai's "fierce orthodoxy" has its counterpart in other Ch'eng-Chu schoolmen of China and Korea, and draws upon an authentic strain of idealistic, moralistic rationalism in Chu Hsi's teaching. At the same time, Ansai pays due tribute, as Professor Okada shows, to the need for textual evidence and a close familiarity with the relevant sources, which Chu Hsi too would have insisted upon.[55] None of this, however, prevented the Ansai school from developing its own brand of Japanese nationalism or from selectively emphasizing such doctrines of self-sacrificing loyalty as "the highest duty is to fulfill one's allotted function *(taigi meibun)*"—a doctrine which does not figure prominently, if at all, in the Neo-Confucian orthodoxies of China. One could argue from this that the *taigi meibun* theory is peculiarly Japanese. More reasonably, however, one could take it as a distinctive Japanese formulation of a religious/moral attitude which finds diverse expression both within and among the cultural traditions sharing the Neo-Confucian legacy.

Later this same religious and moral dynamism was to be a significant force in the thinking of the activists at the end of the Tokugawa period. Though it has not been within the scope of the present work to pursue this later development, the renewed vitality and influence of both the Chu Hsi *(Shushi)* and Wang Yang-ming *(Ōyōmei)* schools in nineteenth-century Japan suggest that the practical learning of Neo-Confucianism survived not only in the form of a protoscientific empirical rationalism but also as a radical moral activism which was no less significant a factor in Japan's modernization.

Against this background it is clear that the relation between a changing Neo-Confucianism and an evolving practical learning is not a simple one, but rather a matter of growing complexity over time. Initially almost a synonym for the Neo-Confucian Learning of the Mind-and-Heart, practical learning became increasingly identified with one or another of its component values or activities as each claimed a higher priority on men's attentions or a greater relevance to the needs of the age. One such prime value in practical learning was moral solidity. Another was social applicability. Still another was intellectual substantiality, as rational speculation was subject to confirmation by extensive inquiry, broad learning, and concrete evidence.

Separately and together these tendencies underwent development in the hands of successive thinkers and schools. Each new growth exhibits continuities with the past, as well as discontinuities from it, and since there is no fixed reference point or finished form which can serve as the basis for comparison, it becomes problematical indeed to determine what remains "Neo-Confucian" in the successive stages of this process.

If there is any criterion which may be usefully applied to such judgments, however, it must be the test of balance, integration, and wholeness. Reality for the Neo-Confucian was to be attained through an integrative process of self-realization based on a synthesis of humanistic (especially philosophical) studies, social action, and personal praxis. To find the unifying thread, the balancing mean, the underlying value, or the all-embracing conception remained the fundamental aim of Neo-Confucian teaching. Here the prime symbols are the sage, as microcosm, model of human integrity, and exemplar of self-fulfillment in action; and the Way, as macrocosm, overarching unity, and ultimate process. As the separate values in the Neo-Confucian synthesis underwent their own development in constantly changing and ever more complex historical and cultural circumstances, their meaning and validity were tested in relation to such unifying conceptions. Among these the Neo-Confucian view of the mind-and-heart remained central, as the creative pivot of the human enterprise in its fullest dimensions, deepest reflections, and most dynamic activity.

Notes

The following standard abbreviations are used:

SPPY	Ssu-pu pei-yao
SPTK	Ssu-pu ts'ung-k'an
SSGTK	Shushigaku taikei
SYHA	Sung-Yüan hsüeh-an
YS	Yüan shih
HYS	Hsin Yüan shih
KHCPTS	Kuo-hsüeh chi-pen ts'ung-shu
TSCC	Ts'ung-shu chi-ch'eng
NST	Nihon shisō taikei

Part I: THE RISE OF NEO-CONFUCIAN
ORTHODOXY IN YÜAN CHINA

I wish to acknowledge here many helpful comments and suggestions by Professors Yoshikawa Kōjirō, Shimada Kenji, and Hok-lam Chan in the preparation of this essay.

1. See James T. C. Liu, "How Did a Neo-Confucian School Become the State Orthodoxy? *Philosophy East and West* (1973), 23(4):484–505. The essential import of this study is to redefine the question posed in the title. Given the inadvertencies, arbitrariness, and hypocrisy of state actions for and against the School of the Way, the net result of its nominal sanctioning is characterized by Professor Liu as "little more than a political gesture" (p. 503), implying that Neo-Confucianism had not yet really become a state orthodoxy.

See also Conrad Schirokauer, "Neo-Confucianism Under Attack: The Condemnation of Wei-hsüeh," in *Crisis and Prosperity in Sung China*, ed. John W. Haeger (Tucson: University of Arizona Press, 1975), pp. 163–98.

2. Pi Yüan, *Hsü Tzu-chih t'ung-chien* (Chia-ch'ing 6 [1801] ed.), 167:23a, 170:8ab.

3. Chu's commentaries on the *Analects* and *Mencius* were sanctioned for official schools, but nothing was done for the Four Books as a whole in the fashion set later

by the Yüan system. In other words, the content and form of the Sung examinations remained essentially unchanged, and the two texts Chu had given unprecedented attention to were officially ignored.

4. See Lu Kuang-huan, "The Shu-yüan Institution Developed by Sung-Ming Neo-Confucian Philosophers," *Chinese Culture* (1968) 9(3):102–15.

5. Adapted from W. T. de Bary, et al., *Sources of Chinese Tradition*, (New York: Columbia University Press, 1960), pp. 431–34.

6. Ch'eng I, *I-ch'uan wen-chi*, 7:7b, in *Erh Ch'eng ch'üan-shu* (SPPY ed.; Taipei: Chung-hua Book Co., 1976). Hereafter cited as *Wen-chi*.

7. *Ibid.*, 7:6ab. Quoted also in Chu Hsi's *Chin-ssu lu*, *Chu Tzu i-shu* (I-wen ed.; Taipei reprint of K'ang-hsi ed.), 14:2b–4a; translation by Wing-tsit Chan in *Reflections on Things at Hand* (New York: Columbia University Press, 1967), pp. 299–301 (hereafter cited as *Reflections*).

8. As recounted in *Analects* 20:1.

9. *Book of History*, "Counsels of Great Yü," in James Legge, *The Chinese Classics*, (2d ed., rev.; rpt., Taipei, 1966), 3:61.

10. Chu Hsi, Preface to *Chung-yung chang-chü*, SSGTK (Tokyo: Meitoku Shuppansha, 1974), 8:451–52 (11–14). In references to this edition the Chinese text is cited first, the Japanese second. My translation has benefited from consulting, in addition to the Japanese translation of Tanaka Masaru and notes of Kurihara Keisuke, the draft translation by Wing-tsit Chan being prepared for the *Sources of Neo-Confucianism* project.

11. See Herrlee Creel, *Confucius: The Man and the Myth* (New York: John Day, 1949), pp. 7–11, 291–94.

12. My sense of the "heroic and the epic" in the Neo-Confucian contexts should be understood as rooted in a classical conception to which attention has been drawn by C. H. Wang in his discussion of the Chinese heroic ideal and the "epic perception of reality" as glorifying humble virtue, forbearance, and nonviolent courage. See his "Towards Defining a Chinese Heroism," *Journal of the American Oriental Society* (1975), 95(1):25–35.

13. Wing-tsit Chan, "Chu Hsi's Completion of Neo-Confucianism" in *Études Song—Sung Studies, In Memoriam Etienne Balazs*, ed. Françoise Aubin (Paris and The Hague: Mouton, 1973), pp. 55–90 (hereafter cited as "Completion").

14. See Chan, "Completion," p. 76 as just one example. Others will be given below.

15. Chu, Preface to *Chung-yung chang-chü*, in SSGTK, 8:449 (see errata for revised paging).

16. T'ang Chün-i, "The Spirit and Development of Neo-Confucianism," *Inquiry* (1971), 14:59–60.

17. *Hsi-shan wen-chi* (KHCPTS ed.) 26:449; "Nan-hsiung chou-hsüeh ssu hsien-sheng ssu-t'an chi."

18. Huang Kan, *Sheng-hsien tao-t'ung ch'uan-shou ts'ung-hsü shuo*, SSGTK, 10:432–33 (82–85).

19. *Ibid.*, p. 433 (84).

20. *Ibid.*

21. The Supreme Norm or Ultimate is incorporated in the initial cosmological setting drawn from the *Book of Changes*, while Chou Tun-i's teaching is cited for the attributes of the sage as set forth in the *T'ung shu*. Thus it is probable that Chou

influenced Huang's cosmological views, but in the matter of *tao-t'ung* other considerations of ethical cultivation took precedence in identifying Chou's contribution to the orthodox tradition.

22. See pp. 16–17 below: also Wu Ch'eng, "Tsun te-hsing tao wen-hsüeh chai chi, SSGTK, 10:183 (467); and Huang Tsung-hsi, *Ming-ju hsüeh-an* (Wan-yu wen-k'u ed.), 32:93, "Wang I-an hsien-sheng yü-lu."

23. See Wing-tsit Chan, "Chu Hsi and Yüan Neo-Confucianism" (paper delivered at the Conference on Yüan Thought sponsored by the American Council of Learned Societies, Issaquah, Washington, January 1978), pp. 8–10; W. T. de Bary, "Neo-Confucian Cultivation and Enlightenment," in *The Unfolding of Neo-Confucianism* (New York: Columbia University Press, 1975), p. 192 (hereafter cited as *Unfolding*); and Christian Murck, *Chu Yün-ming (1461–1527) and Cultural Commitment in Su Chou* (Ann Arbor: University Microfilms, 1978), p. 329.

24. Chan, "Chu Hsi and Yüan Neo-Confucianism," p. 19.

25. These categories are by no means exhaustive. A pietistic view may also be distinguished, expressing an almost blind, fundamentalist faith, undirected toward rational goals or scholarly learning.

26. See the following accounts in Su T'ien-chüeh, *Yüan wen-lei* (Chiang-su shu-chü ed. of Kuang-hsü 15) (hereafter cited as *Wen-lei*): Yü Chi, "Hao-shan shu-yüan chi," 30:8b–10b (esp. 9b); "Hsi-shan shu-yüan chi," *ibid.*, 29:9a–11b; "Chang-shih hsin-ying chi," *Ibid.*, 30:10ab; Ou-yang Hsüan, "Chao Chung-chien kung ssu-t'ang chi," *ibid.*, 31:13ab.

27. See W. T. de Bary, "Neo-Confucian Cultivation and Enlightenment," in *The Unfolding of Neo-Confucianism,* (New York: Columbia University Press, 1975), pp. 164–70.

28. See, for example, the touch of sarcasm in his interview with Tung Wen-chung and the defensiveness of Tung's reply, pp. 40–41 herein.

29. See Carsun Chang, *The Development of Neo-Confucian Thought* (New York: Bookman, 1957), pp. 210–11.

30. Morohashi Tetsuji, *Jukyō no mokuteki to Sōju no katsudō* (Tokyo: Taishūkan, 1926), pp. 22–23 (hereafter cited as *Mokuteki*) and Wing-tsit Chan, biographies of Ch'eng Hao and Ch'eng I in *Sung Biographies*, ed. H. Franke (Wiesbaden: Franz Steiner, 1976), pp. 171–72, 177–78.

31. See Morohashi, *Mokuteki*, pp. 678 ff., 728–60 for an extended discussion of the ideological issues in these factional struggles. See also Schirokauer, "Neo-Confucianism Under Attack."

32. See his *The Paranoid Style in American Politics* (New York: Knopf, 1965).

33. Liu, "How Did a Neo-Confucian School," pp. 498–501.

34. John Dardess, "Confucian Doctrine, Local Reform, and Centralization in Late Yüan Chekiang" (paper delivered at the Conference on Yüan Thought sponsored by the American Council of Learned Societies, Issaquah, Washington, January 1978), p. 33.

35. Cited in the official Ming anthology of Neo-Confucian orthodoxy, *Hsing-li ta-ch'üan* (Ssu-k'u chen-pen ed.), 36:10b.

36. *Sung shih* (I-wen yin-shu-kuan, reprint of Wu ying tien ed. of Ch'ien lung 4, *Erh-shih wu shih*), 437:5317; Wei Liao-weng, *Ho-shan hsien-sheng ta-ch'üan-chi*, SPTK, 69:21a.

37. Shimada Kenji, *Shushigaku to Yōmeigaku* (Tokyo: Iwanami, 1967), p. 96. For

another definition and more extreme manifestation of loyalty see Frederick W. Mote, "Confucian Eremitism in the Yüan Period," in *The Confucian Persuasion*, ed. A. F. Wright (Stanford: Stanford University Press, 1962), pp. 229–36.

38. Wang Tzu-ts'ai and Feng Yün-hao, *Sung-Yüan hsüeh-an pu-i* (Ssu-ming ts'ung-shu ed.), 49:197b, which identifies the text as Chu Hsi's commentary on the *Great Learning*, but does not embellish the account. Cited hereafter as SYHA Pu-i.

39. A similar phenomenon occurred at the end of the Yüan, when large numbers of Confucian officials sacrificed their lives for the Mongol dynasty. Miyazaki Ichisada, the social and institutional historian, concedes that this phenomenon transcends purely dynastic or ethnic considerations and can only be explained in religious terms. See *Miyazaki Ichisada Ajia shi ronkō* (Tokyo: Asahi, 1976) 3:122.

40. On social stratification in the Yüan, see Meng Ssu-ming, *Yüan-tai she-hui chieh-chi chih-tu* (Hong Kong: Lung-men shu-tien, 1967 rpt.). See also Ch'en Yüan, *Western and Central Asians in China under the Mongols*, tr. Ch'ien Hsing-hai and L. Carrington Goodrich, Monumenta Serica Monograph 15 (Los Angeles: University of California, 1966), pp. 290–91. (Hereafter cited as *Western and Central Asians*.)

41. See Yang Chün-li, "Yüan-tai k'o-chü chang-ch'i t'ing-fei ti yüan-yin chi ch'i shih-t'i chü-lei," *K'ao-cheng tzu-liao* (Taipei, 1963), 6(2):9–10 (hereafter cited as "Yüan-tai k'o-chü"); Kano Naoki, *Chūgoku tetsugaku-shi* (Tokyo: Iwanami, 1953), pp. 445–46.

42. YS, 81:972. On Yeh-lü Ch'u-ts'ai, see Igor de Rachewiltz, "Yeh-lü Ch'u-ts'ai (1189–1243) Buddhist Idealist and Confucian Statesman," in *Confucian Personalities*, ed. A. Wright and D. Twitchett (Stanford: Stanford University Press, 1962), pp. 189–216.

43. Yoshikawa Kōjirō, "Shushigaku hokuden zenshi" (hereinafter cited as "Hokuden") in *Uno Tetsuto Sensei Hakuju Shukuga Kinen Tōyō Ronsō* (Tokyo: Tōhō Gakkai, 1974), p. 1246. Ou-yang Hsiu was another Sung scholar much admired in the Chin. See Hsü Wen-yü, "Chin-Yüan ti wen-yü," in *Chung-kuo wen-hsüeh yen-chiu*, ed. Cheng Chen-to (Hong Kong: Li-sheng shu-tien, 1963 rpt.), pp. 677–714.

44. Sun K'o-k'uan, *Yüan-tai Han-wen-hua chih huo-tung*, (Taipei: Chung-hua Book Co., 1968), pp. 108–38 (hereafter cited as *Han-wen-hua*); Abe Takeo, *Gendaishi no kenkyū* (Tokyo: Sōbunsha, 1972), pp. 9–29 (hereafter cited as *Gendaishi*).

45. Yoshikawa, "Hokuden," p. 1246. The "iron curtain" existed only during hostilities between the Sung and Chin, but after the peace treaty in 1165 Sung books became more available in the North. See Liu Ming-shu, "Sung-tai ch'u-pan fa chi tui Liao Chin chih shu-chien," *Chung-kuo wen-hua yen-chiu-so hui-k'an*, Chengtu, 5 (Sept. 1945), pp. 95–114.

46. Max Weber, *Gesammelte Aufsätze zur Religions-sociologie* (Tübingen, 1922–33), 1:181; 2:360.

47. Sun, *Han-wen-hua*, pp. 163–67.

48. *Ibid.*, pp. 156–77. See also Hsiao Ch'i-ch'ing, "Hu-pi-lieh shih-tai ch'ien-ti chiu-lu' k'ao," *Ta-lu tsa-chih* (1962) 25(1,2,3):16–22, 57–60, 86–91.

49. An extensive and highly informative biography of Liu is given in Hok-lam Chan, "Liu Ping-chung (1216–74): A Buddhist-Taoist Statesman at the Court of Khubilai Khan," *T'oung Pao* (1967), 52(1–3):98–146 (hereafter cited as "Liu Ping-chung").

50. Conference draft, cited in note 23 above.

51. See Sun, *Han-wen-hua*, p. 168 and Hok-lam Chan, "Yao Shu," in *Papers on Far Eastern History* (Australian National University, Canberra), no. 22 (September 1980), pp. 17–50. (Hereafter cited as "Yao Shu.")

52. Yao Sui, "Hsü Chiang-han hsien-sheng ssu-sheng," in Su, *Wen-lei*, 34:2a–3a. *Hsin Yüan shih* (I-wen ed.), 234:2093, Biog. of Chao Fu (hereafter cited as HYS).

53. YS, 189:2068, Biog. of Chao Fu; HYS 234:2093; Sun, *Han-wen-hua*, p. 159; Abe, *Gendaishi*, p. 32.

54. Yamada Keiji, *Chūgoku no kagaku to kagakusha* (Kyōto: Kyoto daigaku jimbun kagaku kenkyūsho, 1978), p. 112 (hereafter cited as *Kagaku*). As background for this see also Yü Chi, "Chang shih hsin ying chi," in Su, *Wen-lei*, 30:11b.

55. Su T'ien-chüeh, *Yüan [Kuo]-ch'ao ming-ch'en shih-lüeh* (Peking: Chung-hua Book Co., 1962; rpt. of 1335 ed.), 8:3b–11b (hereafter cited as *Shih-lüeh*); YS, 158:1771–73; Hok-lam Chan, "Liu Ping-chung," pp. 41–43. See also Wing-tsit Chan, "Chu Hsi and Yüan Neo-Confucianism."

56. Su, *Shih-lüeh*, 8:1b.

57. *Ibid.*

58. *Ibid.*, 13:8a; YS, 164:1836a–37a; Sun, *Han-wen-hua*, p. 230.

59. Su, *Shih-lüeh*, 13:8a.

60. Huang Tsung-hsi and Ch'üan Tsu-wang, *Sung-Yüan hsüeh-an* (Kuo-hsüeh chi-pen ts'ung-shu ed.) (Taiwan: Commercial Press, 1968), 91:148; Frederick W. Mote, "Confucian Eremitism in the Yüan Period," in Wright, ed., *The Confucian Persuasion*, p. 212–13.

61. See Yüan Kuo-fan (i.e., Yüan Chi), *Yüan Hsü Lu-chai p'ing-shu* (Taipei: Commercial Press, 1972). See Part II for a fuller discussion of Hsü's contributions to Yüan Neo-Confucianism.

62. Su, *Shih-lüeh*, 8:13ab.

63. *Ibid.*, 8:13b.

64. *Ibid.*

65. *Ibid.*, 8:13b–14a.

66. Chu Hsi, *Lün-yü chi-chu* 2; SSGTK 8:403 (86).

67. Hsü Heng, *Yü-lu* A, in *Hsü Wen-cheng kung i-shu*, (T'ang shih ching-kuan ts'ung-shu ed.), 1:7b (hereafter cited as *I-shu*.)

68. Sun, *Han-wen-hua*, pp. 156–57, 166–76, 209–12, 234. This attitude was not confined to the Neo-Confucians but extended to the Ch'üan-chen Taoists. See Yao Tsung-wu, *Tung-pei shih lun-ts'ung* (Taipei: Commercial Press, 1972).

69. See *I-shu*, 2:24a.

70. Ch'eng I, *I-chüan* (Erh-Ch'eng ch'üan-shu ed.), 3:9a; *Chin-ssu lu*, 7:2a; Chan, *Reflections*, p. 186.

71. Sun, *Han-wen-hua*, p. 176; Yao Ts'ung-wu, "Yüan Shih-tsu ch'ung-hsing K'ung-hsüeh ch'eng-kung yü so tsao-yü ti k'un-nan" (hereafter cited as "K'ung-hsüeh"), *Shih-hsüeh hui-k'an* (1969) 2:5.

72. Su, *Wen-lei*, 14:1a–4a.

73. *Ibid.*; Sun, *Han-wen-hua*, pp. 169–71: Hok-Lam Chan, "Liu Ping-chung," p. 11.

74. Su, *Wen-lei*, 13:8a–9a; Sun, *Han-wen-hua*, pp. 180–81.

75. Hsü Heng, *Kuo-hsüeh shih-chi*, *I-shu*, *chüan mo*, 3b. Hsü's position aroused much later controversy from, among others, Wang Yang-ming, Liu Tsung-chou, and Satō Issai; see, e.g., Abe, *Gendaishi*, p. 48.

76. Su, *Shih-lüeh*, 8:12b; Sun, *Han-wen-hua*, pp. 167, 212; Abe, *Gendaishi*, p. 33.

77. Yamada, *Kagaku*, pp. 112–14, 143, 145, 150–51, 160, 183.

78. Su, *Shih-lüeh*, 8:3b–11b; YS, 158:1771; Sun, *Han-wen-hua*, p. 168. Hok-lam

Chan, "Yao Shu," pp. 22–23, offers a more extensive and detailed discussion of these recommendations.

79. Chan, "Liu Ping-chung," p. 131.

80. Herbert Franke, "Wang Yün, a Transmitter of Confucian Values" (paper delivered at the Conference on Yüan Thought sponsored by the American Council of Learned Societies, Issaquah, Washington, January 1978).

81. SYHA, 13:4, "Ming-tao hsüeh-an."

82. Most of section 7 of the Chin-ssu lu, dealing with serving and not serving in the government, treats issues of this kind, as discussed by Ch'eng I. See Chan, Reflections, pp. 183–201.

83. As quoted by Ch'eng I, I-chüan (Erh-Ch'eng ch'üan-shu ed.), 1:17a and in Chin-ssu lu, 7:1a; Chan, Reflections, p. 183. On this point see also Shimada Kenji, Shushigaku to Yōmeigaku, pp. 28, 38, 97–101; and Morohashi, Mokuteki, pp. 773–75. There is a long history of debate on this issue among Japanese Neo-Confucians from Yamazaki Ansai to Yoshida Shōin and Hattori Unokichi, who tended to be critical of the Ch'eng-Chu position on loyalty to the ruler as too relativistic and almost contumacious. Shimada agrees with their reading of Chu Hsi, though not with their criticism. For a contrasting view, see Mote, "Confucian Eremitism," pp. 209–12, 229–40. See also Conrad Schirokauer, "Chu Hsi's Political Thought," Journal of Chinese Philosophy, 5(2):141–43, which concludes: "The potential conflict of priorities between loyalty to virtue and to the ruler remained a theoretical problem although it was less troublesome in practice since loyalty did not imply complete obedience, and the truly loyal minister was one who admonished and reprimanded a wayward emperor."

84. Ch'eng I, I-chüan, 1:17a. Chin-ssu lu, 7:3b; Chan, Reflections, p. 190.

85. Chin-ssu lu, 7:4b; Chan, Reflections, p. 193 adapted.

86. On the institution of the lectures from the classics mat, which Robert Hartwell calls "imperial seminars," see his "Historical Analogism, Public Policy, and Social Science in Eleventh and Twelfth Century China," American Historical Review (1971), 76(3):690–727. On the institution in Korea there is no comparable study known to me, but see JaHyun Kim Haboush, "A Heritage of Kings: One Man's Monarchy in the Confucian World." (Ph.D. diss., Columbia University; Ann Arbor: University Microfilms, 1978), pp. 200–22.

87. See Wang Ying-lin, Yü-hai (Kuang-su 9 [1883] ed. of Che-chiang shu-chü), ch. 26, 27; Jüan Yüan, Ssu-k'u ch'üan-shu ts'ung-mu t'i-yao, wei-shou shu-mu t'i-yao, (Shanghai: Commercial Press, 1933), 91:17 (1889).

88. Chu Hsi, I-lo yüan-yüan lu (Cheng-i t'ang ed., 7:6ab; Ming-ch'en yen-hsing lu (SPTK ed.), 10:3a.

89. Jüan Yüan, Ssu-k'u t'i-yao, 91:17; a ten-chüan version is reported earlier by Ma Tuan-lin (Wen-hsien t'ung-k'ao, Commercial Press Shih-t'ung ed., 210:1727) but this is probably an error, as nothing seems missing from the extant eight-chüan versions.

90. Fan t'ai-shih chi (Ssu-k'u chen-pen ed., 1st ser.; Shanghai: Commercial Press, 1935), 14:11a, "Ch'üan-hsüeh cha-tzu."

91. Ch'en Chang-fang, Wei-shih chi (Ssu-k'u ch'üan-shu chen-pen, ed., 1st ser.; Shanghai: Commercial Press, 1935) 1:1a–3b, "Ti-hsüeh lun."

92. SYHA, 2:18b.

93. Ch'eng Hao, Ming-tao wen-chi, in Erh-Ch'eng ch'üan-shu, 2:1ab.

94. *I-lo yüan-yüan lu* (Cheng-i t'ang ed.) 4:2ab, 15b–16a; Ch'eng I, *I-shu*, 19:9b.

95. Following the interpretation of Utsunomiya Ton'an and Wing-tsit Chan. See Chan, *Reflections*, p. 204, n. 8.

96. Ch'eng I, *Wen-chi*, 1:3a.

97. Ch'eng I, *I-shu*, 19:9ab.

98. *Chin-ssu lu*, 7:6a; Chan, *Reflections*, pp. 196–97.

99. Chu Hsi, *Hui-an hsien-sheng Chu Wen-kung wen-chi* (SPTK) 15:1 ff. (hereafter cited as *Wen-chi*); *Chu Tzu yü-lei* (Taipei: Cheng-chung shu-chü, 1970, rpt. of 1473 ed.), 130:4978.

100. Chu, *Wen-chi*, 11:1a–11a, "Jen-wu ying-ch'ao feng-shih." See also Conrad Schirokauer, "Chu Hsi's Political Career" in *Confucian Personalities*, ed. A. Wright (Stanford: Stanford University Press, 1962).

101. Chu, *Wen-chi*, 11:3b. The same theme is repeated with almost identical wording in Chu's sealed memorial of 1188. See *Wen-chi*, 11:35b–36a.

102. *I-wei t'ung-kua-yen* (Kuang-ya reprint of Wu-ying tien ed.), pt. 2, 5b; *Li-chi, ching-chieh, Shih-san ching* (Commercial Press ed.), p. 184.

103. Chu, *Wen-chi*, 11:3b–4a.

104. *Ibid.*, 11:4b.

105. *Ibid.*, 11:9a–10a; see also 11:11b, 15b–16a.

106. *Ibid.*, 11:35b–36a.

107. On these points see Chu Hsi, *Wen-chi*, 15:1; Fan Tsu-yü, *Ti-hsüeh* (Seikado Bunko Ch'ing ed.), ch. 1, 2; Chen Te-hsiu, *Hsi-shan Chen Wen-chung kung wen-chi*, SPTK, 18:293–316, and *Ta-hsüeh yen-i*, ch. 2–4.

108. See Wang Ying-lin, *Yü hai* (Tao kuang 6 ed. of Chang pai chüeh Lo shih), ch. 26, 27, and especially for Fan Tsu-yü's connection 26:9.

109. This work and Chen's *Classic of the Mind-and-Heart* are dealt with further in Part II.

110. Sun, *Han-wen-hua*, pp. 181–83. See also John D. Langlois, Jr., "Yü Chi and his Mongol Sovereign: The Scholar as Apologist," *Journal of Asian Studies* (1978), 38(1):101 ff.

111. See John W. Dardess, *Conquerors and Confucians* (New York: Columbia University Press, 1973), pp. 76, 86.

112. YS, 115:1370–71; Yamada, *Kagaku*, pp. 106–7.

113. See Chan, "Liu Ping-chung," p. 139 and references cited in his n. 83.

114. Sun, *Han-wen-hua*, p. 183.

115. Su, *Shih-lüeh*, 8:1b.

116. Su, *Shih-lüeh*, 8:3b; YS, 158:1771.

117. Sun, *Han-wen-hua*, p. 183.

118. Yamada, *Kagaku*, pp. 106–7; Abe, *Gendaishi*, p. 38.

119. Su, *Wen-lei*, 13:1a; Hsü, *I-shu*, 7:1ab; YS, 158:1774.

120. Hsü, *I-shu*, 7:10b; Su, *Wen-lei*, 13:7a; YS, 158:1776–77.

121. On the importance of a public spirit or impartiality *(kung)* see also his memorial of 1266, Su, *Wen-lei*, 13:1b, 6b–7b; Hsü, *I-shu*, 7:1b, 2a; and SSGTK, 10:474 (205); on its Neo-Confucian antecedents, see *Erh-Ch'eng ch'üan-shu, Erh-Ch'eng i-shu*, 14:2a; *Ming-tao wen-chi*, 3:1a.

122. Hsü, *I-shu*, 3:5b–6b, 8b–9a, "Ta-hsüeh yao-lüeh."

123. *Ibid.*, 3:8b–9a.

124. *Ibid.*, 3:12a.

125. *Ibid.*, 3:12b.

126. For more on the Neo-Confucian basis of this view see *Chin-ssu lu*, 8:1b, 5b, 6b; Chan, *Reflections*, pp. 204, 212–13, 215–16. The useful appended translations of later commentary by Professor Chan confirm the continuing importance of this type of thinking in later tradition. See also his *Source Book in Chinese Philosophy* (Princeton: Princeton University Press, 1963), pp. 525–26, 542. See also Wu K'ang, "Wan Sung chi Yüan chih li-hsüeh," *Hsüeh-shu chi-k'an* (1956), 4(4):12–13.

127. Abe Takeo considered it a particular mark of this group that it stressed broad learning; *Gendaishi*, p. 49.

128. Hsü, *I-shu*, 7:16b–17b.

129. YS, 160:1794–95; HYS, 185:1728–29; Fujieda Akira, *Seifuku ōcho* (Osaka, 1948), pp. 121–28. On Wang O, see Hok-lam Chan, "Wang O (1190–1273)," *Papers on Far Eastern History* (Sept. 1975), 12:43–70.

130. YS, 81:973; Yang Shu-fan, "Yüan tai k'o-chü chih-tu," *Kuo-li cheng-chih ta-hsüeh hsüeh-pao*, (May 1968), 17:100, 119–20. (Hereafter cited as "K'o-chü.")

131. HYS, 141:1376–77, Biog. of Tung Wen-chung, gives an abridged version of this event. On Tung's forebears, see Yao Ts'ung-wu, "Hu-pi-lieh tui-yü Han-wen-hua t'ai-tu ti fen-hsi," (1955), 11(1):25.

132. Not an exact quotation, but parallel in sense to *Analects* 9:15, *Mencius* 1A:5, and the *Record of Rites*, shi-i.

133. Su, *Shih-lüeh*, 14:15a.

134. Chu, *Wen-chi*, 69:23a, 74:12a–13b; *Chin-ssu lu*, 7:7a (Chan, *Reflections*, p. 200).

135. Wang, SYHA Pu-i, 78:31b–32a, Biog. of T'u-tan Kung-lu. I am indebted to Professor Herbert Franke for the correct spelling of this Jurchen name.

136. See Su, *Wen-lei*, 9:2b–3a.

137. Su, *Shih-lüeh*, 14:15b–16a, citing the spirit way tablet by Yao Sui. Cf. also Su, *Wen-lei*, 61:5b–6a. The version given at HYS 141:1376 varies somewhat from this, and my rendering tries to make the best sense of both.

138. Chu, *Wen-chi*, 69:12a–13b.

139. Su, *Shih-lüeh*, 13:9a; YS, 164:1836; HYS, 171:1619.

140. Su, *Shih-lüeh*, 8:14a.

141. Hsü Heng, *Hsü Lu-chai hsien-sheng hsin-fa*, (preface of Han Shih-ch'i dated 1522), pp. 29b, 38a, 41a (Hereafter cited as *Hsin-fa*).

142. See "Ching-shih ta-tien hsü-lu," in Su, *Wen-lei*, 41:4b *Kung-chü*.

143. On Mongol and Central Asian fears of the Chinese gaining the upper hand through the examinations, see Hsiao Ch'i-ch'ing, *Hsi-yüeh jen yü Yüan-ch'u cheng-chih* (Taipei: Faculty of Letters, National Taiwan University, 1966); and for the problems facing Khubilai, see Yao, "K'ung-hsüeh," pp. 1–15.

144. Abe, *Gendaishi*, pp. 15–29; Sun, *Han-wen-hua*, pp. 108–38. Yüan Kuo-fan, "Tung-ping Yen-shih mu-fu jen-wu yü hsing-hsüeh ch'u-k'ao," *Ta-lu tsa-chih* (1961), 23(12) 11–14.

145. Sun, *Han-wen-hua*, pp. 169, 216.

146. Hao Ching, *Hao Wen-chung kung chi*, in *Ch'ien-k'un cheng-ch'i chi*, (1848 ed.) 7:8b–9a. Abe Takeo's classification of the opposing parties in this debate into the "Literary Party" and the "Moral Action" party is based on this passage from Hao Ching; see *Gendaishi*, p. 45.

147. See Sun, *Han-wen-hua*, p. 173.
148. See Lu Chih, "Han-lin shih-tu hsüeh-shih Hao kung shen-tao-pei," in Su, *Wen-lei*, 58:10b.
149. *Chin-ssu lu*, 7:6a–7a; Chan, *Reflections*, pp. 198–99.
150. Abe, *Gendaishi*, p. 52; Yang Shu-fan, "K'o-chü," p. 100.
151. *Sources of Chinese Tradition*, pp. 393 ff.
152. Abe, *Gendaishi*, p. 49; Chan, "Liu Ping-chung," p. 121.
153. *Sources of Chinese Tradition*, p. 87.
154. Hsü, *I-shu*, 3:4ab.
155. Hsü, *I-shu*, 7:11b–13a; "Nung-sang hsüeh-hsiao." On the measures to promote agriculture, which cannot be gone into here, see Sun, *Han-wen-hua*, pp. 180–81.
156. The language and style of argument here is reminiscent of Fan's memorial "Ch'üan-hsüeh cha-tzu." Cf. *Fan t'ai-shih chi* (Ssu-k'u chen-pen ed.), 14:10b–13b.
157. Hsü, *I-shu*, Yü-lü A, 1:8b; 4:1a, "Ta-hsüeh chih chieh."
158. Hsü, *I-shu*, 3:4b, "Ta-hsüeh yao-lüeh"; *Hsin-fa*, 8a, 36b.
159. *Ssu-k'u ch'uan-shu tsung-mu t'i-yao*, 166:3486.
160. Hsü, *Hsin-fa*, 36b.
161. Hsü, *I-shu*, *chüan-mo*, 1ab, 3a; Sun, Han-wen-hua, p. 215.
162. Ch'eng Chü-fu, "Lu-chai shu-yüan chi," in *Ch'u-kuo wen-hsien kung Yüeh-lou Ch'eng hsien-sheng wen-chi* (1913 photo reprint of Hung-wu ed.), 13:15a–16b; Sun, *Han-wen-hua*, p. 160. For the success of these efforts see Ch'en Yüan, *Western and Central Asians*, chap. 11; and Yao, "K'ung-hsüeh," p. 7.
163. Politically, of course, the problem was more complicated, as indicated in Yao, "K'ung-hsüeh," pp. 1–15.
164. YS, 81:978, 115:1370–71; Abe, *Gendaishi*, pp. 38, 41–42; Yamada, *Kagaku*, pp. 106–7. Jinggim also received Buddhist training from the monk Hai-yün.
165. Su, *Shih-lüeh*, 8:2b–3a; Sun, *Han-wen-hua*, pp. 158–60, 178–80, 215.
166. YS, 81:981; HYS, 64:701.
167. Though the Kuo-tzu-chien is commonly referred to as the National University, it had a relatively small staff of instruction and student body, and it is misleading to suggest that it was either "national" or a "university" in the modern sense. It was, however, clearly identified with imperial rule and had some of the characteristics of a medieval collegium. A similar college for the education of Mongols was set up in 1277, along with a Mongolian branch of the Hanlin Academy and the History Office. See YS 87:1055–56.
168. On these educational developments, see YS, 81:978–80 and HYS, 64:701–4; "Ch'ing-shih ta-tien hsü-lu," in Su, *Wen-lei*, 41:3b–4a; Hayashi Tomoharu, "Gen-Min jidai no shoin kyōiku" in his *Kinsei Chūgoku kyōikushi kenkyū* (Tokyo: Koku-dosha, 1958), pp. 3–7.
169. Wang Ch'i, *Hsü wen-hsien t'ung-k'ao*, 60:6a; Hayashi, "Gen-Min jidai no shoin kyōiku," p. 5.
170. Abe, *Gendaishi*, pp. 39–43; Sun, *Han-wen-hua*, pp. 189, 194, 223.
171. YS, 81:979; HYS, 64:702.
172. Abe, *Gendaishi*, pp. 41–42.
173. Wang, SYHA Pu-i, 90:31; Sun, *Han-wen-hua*, p. 215.
174. See Makino, Shūji, "Gendai no jugaku kyōiku," *Tōyōshi kenkyū* (1979) 37(4):67–71.

175. On the development of academies in Yüan times, see also Ho Yu-sen, "Yüan-tai shu-yüan chih ti-li fen-pu," *Hsin-ya hsüeh-pao* (1956), 2(1):361–408.

176. For a contemporary statement to this effect see Yü Chi, "Hao-shan shu-yüan chi," in Su, *Wen-lei*, 30:9a.

177. Hayashi, "Gen-Min jidai no shoin kyōiku," pp. 6–7.

178. Sun, *Han-wen-hua*, 202–7.

179. See Hayashi, "Gen-Min jidai no shoin kyōiku," n. 167; Ho Yu-sen, "Yüan-tai shu-yüan," n. 174; Ping-ti Ho, *The Ladder of Success in Imperial China* (New York: Columbia University Press, 1962), p. 197; and John William Chaffee, "Education and Examinations in Sung Society" (unpublished Ph.D. diss., University of Chicago, 1979), p. 167. The exact comparability of these figures is open to some question, both as to time period and as to thoroughness of coverage, but for our purposes here they suffice to demonstrate a vigorous growth in the Yüan.

180. Yoshikawa, "Hokuden," p. 1257.

181. See Sun, *Han-wen-hua*, pp. 163–67.

182. *Ibid.*, p. 201; Hok-lam Chan, "Liu Ping-chung," p. 140. The resemblance is of course limited, as shown by the eventual difference of outcomes. See also Hsiao Ch'i-ching, "Hsi-yüeh jen."

183. Wm. Theodore de Bary, "Some Common Tendencies in Neo-Confucianism," in *Confucianism in Action*, ed. Arthur F. Wright (Stanford: Stanford University Press, 1959), pp. 25–33; William G. Beasley, "Self-Strengthening and Restoration," *Acta Asiatica* (1974) no. 26, pp. 99–107; Abe Yoshio, "The Characteristics of Japanese Confucianism," *Acta Asiatica* (1973), no. 25, pp. 17–20.

184. [Ts'ao-lu] *Wu Wen-cheng kung ch'üan-chi*, (Ch'ung-jen Wan Huang chiao-k'an pen, 1756), *ts'e* 1, *chüan shou*, 34b *Nien-p'u*; David Gedalecia, "Wu Ch'eng: A Neo-Confucian of the Yüan," (Ph.D. diss., Harvard University; Ann Arbor: University Microfilms, 1971), pp. 40–43.

185. YS, 81:973; HYS, 64:707; Teng Ssu-yü, *Chung-kuo k'ao-shih chih-tu shih* (Taipei: Taiwan hsüeh-sheng shu-chü, 1966) (hereafter cited as *K'ao-shih*), pp. 186–87.

186. YS, 182:2008–10; HYS, 206:1890–91; SYHA Pu-i, 82:52: "Pei-shan ssu-hsien-sheng hsüeh-an."

187. Hsü, *I-shu, chüan mo*, 4a, "Shen tao pei"; Ou-yang Hsüan, *Kuei-chai wen-chi*, SPTK, 9:1a.

188. For a more favorable view of Khubilai in Yüan times, see Yao Tsung-wu, "K'ung-hsüeh," pp. 23–24.

189. Sun, *Han-wen-hua*, p. 223.

190. T'ao Tsung-i, *Cho keng lu* (TSCC ed.), 2:37; Hsu, *I-shu*, 6:6ab; Yukawa Takahiro, SSGTK, 10:28; Sun K'o-k'uan, *Han-wen-hua*, p. 222; Mote, "Confucian Eremetism," p. 224.

191. See Ch'iu Chün, *Chung-pien Ch'iung-t'ai hui-kao shih wen chi* (1879 ed.), ch. 2; 25 pp.; Okada Takehiko, "Practical Learning in the Chu Hsi School: Yamazaki Ansai and Kaibara Ekken," in *Principle and Practicality: Essays in Neo-Confucianism and Practical Learning*, ed. Wm. Theodore de Bary and Irene Bloom (New York: Columbia University Press, 1979).

192. Chao I, *Nien-erh shih cha-chi* (Kuang-ya shu-chü ed.), 30:1b–4a.

193. For a more balanced assessment, see Hok-lam Chan, "Liu Ping-chung," pp. 145–46.

194. YS, 81:973; HYS, 64:706–7.

195. An abbreviated draft of the document, covering these four points, is found in Ch'eng Chü-fu, *Ch'u-kuo Wen-hsien kung Yüeh-lou Ch'eng hsien-sheng wen-chi*, 1:2b.

196. YS, 81:973; HYS, 64:706–7.

197. HYS, 64:707.

198. The *tz'u* had replaced the *shih* in the Chin exams. See Teng, *K'ao-shih*, pp. 193–94, 215.

199. Hsü, *I-shu, chüan mo* 28ab; YS, 81:973; HYS, 64:707.

200. HYS, 189:1758, Biog. of Ch'eng Chü-fu. See also HYS, 64:707.

201. HYS, 189:1758; YS, 172:1921.

202. See Yoshikawa Kōjirō, "Gen no shotei no bungaku," *Yoshikawa Kōjirō zenshū* (Tokyo, 1969), 15:232–303.

203. YS, 24:311; see also commemorative inscription of Ch'eng Chü-fu in Su, *Wen-lei*, 19:1b.

204. YS, 24:299.

205. YS, 81:973; HYS, 64:707; Dardess, *Conquerors*, p. 36.

206. HS, 81:973–74; HYS, 64:706.

207. YS, 81:978; HYS, 64:702.

208. See Miyazaki, *Ajia shi ronkō*, 3:98–126.

209. *Chu Tzu yü-lei* (Kyoto: Chūbun shuppansha, 1979), 14:24b; SYHA 87(22): 62–63; cf. Makino, "Gendai no jugaku kyōiku," pp. 69–71.

210. YS 81:973–74; HYS 64:707; Teng, *K'ao-shih*, p. 196.

211. Makino, "Gendai no jugaku kyōiku," pp. 67–70.

212. Su, *Wen-lei*, ch. 46, 47; Yang Chün-li, "Yüan-tai k'o-chü," pp. 9–10.

213. Chu, *Wen-chi*, 69:24ab.

214. *Ibid.*, 69:24ab.

215. *Ibid.*, 69:23b.

216. *Ibid.*

217. *Ibid.*, 69:24a.

218. See de Bary, *Sources of Chinese Tradition*, pp. 384–85.

219. Wu, *Ch'üan-chi, chüan shou* 34b, supp. *ch.* 1:1a–8b; YS, 171:1918; Pi Yüan, *Hsü Tzu-chih t'ung-chien* 198:2b; Gedalecia, *Wu Ch'eng*, pp. 369, 382.

220. Pi-Yüan, *Hsü Tzu-chih t'ung-chien*, 198:2b.

221. Chu, *Wen-chi*, 69:21a.

222. *Ibid.*, 69:22a.

223. See Chan, *Reflections*, pp. 198–99.

224. On the difference in cultural tone between the Sung and Yüan, see the astute observations of the late Ming prime minister Chang Chü-cheng, who stressed that the Ming itself was heir to the simpler style of the Yüan and should not be thought of in the same terms as the more sophisticated Sung. See Robert Crawford, "Chang Chü-cheng's Confucian Legalism," in *Self and Society in Ming Thought*, ed. W. T. de Bary (New York: Columbia University Press, 1970), pp. 377 ff. See also Yoshikawa Kōjirō, *Gen Min shi gaisetsu* (Tokyo: Iwanami, 1977), pp. 125–29.

225. See, for instance, Huang Tsung-hsi, who was closer to Wang Yang-ming in philosophy but spoke approvingly of Chu Hsi's proposals in the *Ming-i tai-fang lu*. See W. T. de Bary, "Chinese Despotism and the Confucian Ideal," in *Chinese Thought and Institutions*, ed. J. K. Fairbank (Chicago: University of Chicago Press, 1957), pp. 181–82. See also Ku Yen-wu, *Jih-chih lu* (Sui-chu t'ang ed. of K'ang-hsi 34, 16:14b), *ch.* 16 passim.

226. See Yao Ts'ung-wu, "Liao Chin Yüan shih-ch'i t'ung-shih k'ao" in [Kuo-li Taiwan ta-hsüeh] *Wen-shih-chih hsüeh-pao* (1967) 16(10):207–21.

227. Dardess, *Conquerors*, p. 74.

228. See the cases cited by Dardess in his "Confucian Doctrine, Local Reform, and Centralization," namely the Mongol *chin-shih* Tai Buqa; the Tanguts Yü Chüeh (*chin-shih* 1333) and Mai-li-ku-su (Marcus?) (*chin-shih* 1334), and the Central Asian Chiu-chu. See also Ch'en Yüan, *Western and Central Asians*. Ch'en speaks of the large number of non-Chinese who studied under Hsü Heng and Wu Ch'en[g] (and some who studied Chu Hsi on their own), whose commitment to their principles was exemplary. See esp. pp. 34 ff, 61 ff.

229. See, e.g., Chao I, *Nien-erh shih cha-chi*, 30:24a–25a.

230. *Ming shih* (I-wen ed.), 70:725; Jung Chao-tsu; *Ming-tai ssu-hsiang shih*, (K'ai-m'ing reprint; Taipei 1962), pp. 1–2: Yoshikawa, *Gen Min shi gaisetsu*, pp. 125–26; de Bary, *Self and Society*, pp. 6–7; Ho, *Ladder of Success*, p. 216.

231. See Sano Kōji, "Mindai zenhanki no shisō kō," *Nihon Chūgoku gakkai hō* (1974), 26:112–13. The ready acceptance of the Four Books and especially the *Ta hsüeh* as basic texts in the system is reflected in Ku Yen-wu's treatment of developments in the Hung-wu period, though Ku himself was highly critical of the abuses to which so simplified a procedure was prone. See *Jih-chih lu* 16:11a, 12b.

232. Ku Ying-t'ai, *Ming-shih chi-shih pen-mo* (T'ung-chih 13 ed.), 14:31a; Teng, *K'ao-shih*, pp. 243–44; citing *Huang Ming chin-shih teng-k'o k'ao 1*. My synopsis is drawn from the slightly variant versions in these three different texts.

233. See MS 70:725; *Ming-shih chi-shih pen-mo*, 14:31a; Teng, *K'ao-shih*, 245–46.

234. *Hsing-li ta-ch'uan shu* (Ssu-k'u chen-pen ed.; 5th ser., Taipei, 1974) 55:29b–35b.

235. Ch'ien Ta-hsin, *Nien-erh shih k'ao-i* (Kuang-ya ed.), 90:7ab.

236. For the official Ch'ing view confirming the essence of this "orthodox" teaching as found in the doctrine of the mind formulated in the Learning of the Emperors and Kings and the Method of the Mind of the Emperors and Kings, see the imperial preface to the K'ang-hsi edition of the *Hsing-li ta-ch'uan shu*, 1:1a–2a.

237. Ch'eng Chü-fu, "Kuo-tzu-hsüeh hsien-shih miao-pei," in Su, *Wen-lei*, 19:1b.

238. Ch'eng, *Wen-chi*, 10:13b.

239. See Wing-tsit Chan, "Chu Hsi and Yüan Neo-Confucianism," pp. 35–36.

240. See Abe, *Gendaishi*, pp. 48–49; Sun, *Han-wen-hua*, p. 215.

241. See Hsiung Ho, "K'ao-ting shu-yüan chi," in Su, *Wen-lei*, 29:10ab.

Part II: THE NEO-CONFUCIAN LEARNING OF THE MIND-AND-HEART

1. Chu Hsi, *Chu Tzu yü-lei*, (rpt., Kyoto: Chūbun shuppansha, 1979), 12: esp. 334; Ch'ien Mu, *Chu tzu hsin hsüeh-an* (Taipei: San-min shu-chü, 1971), 2:301–2.

2. The edition of the *Hsin ching* cited here is the early Ming edition in the National Central Library, Taipei (*Kuo-li chung-yang t'u-shu-kuan shan-pen shu-mu, tseng-ting pen* 2, p. 439). This edition includes a postface by Yen Jo-yü dated 1234 and a preface of Wang Mai dated 1242. I have found no significant differences among

extant editions, and in any event this is unlikely, given the secondary nature of the text. The National Central Library also has the original Sung edition of Ch'un-yü 2(1242), but the print is less legible.

3. *Hsin ching*, 1a.

4. *Hsin ching*, 1a; Chu Hsi, *Chung-yung chang-chu, hsü* in SSGTK, 8:11–12.

5. *Hsin ching*, 2a–4a.

6. *Hsin ching*, 5b, 7a.

7. *Li chi* (I-wen reprint of *Shih san ching chu-su*, Sung, Wen-hsüan lou ed., Taipei, 1955), 50:849, "Ai-kung-wen."

8. *Hsin ching*, 3a; *I ching*, hexagram 2, Richard Wilhelm and Cary F. Baynes, *The I ching* (Princeton: Princeton University Press, 1950), pp. 393–94 (hereafter cited as Wilhelm-Baynes); Wing-tsit Chan, *A Source Book in Chinese Philosophy* (Princeton: Princeton University Press, 1963), p. 264 (hereafter cited as Chan, *Source Book*).

9. *Hsin ching*, 3ab; *Erh-Ch'eng ch'üan-shu* (Kinsei kanseki sōkan ed.; Kyoto: Chūbun shuppansha, 1972), 1st. ser., 16:36a.

10. *Hsin ching*, 4a; *I ching*, hexagram 24; Wilhelm-Baynes, pp. 98–99.

11. *I ching*, hexagram 24; Wilhelm-Baynes, p. 507.

12. *Hsin ching*, 5a; Chu, *Ssu-shu chi-chu* (Shushigaku taikei ed.; Tokyo: Meitoku Publishing Co., 1974); *Lun yü*, "Yen Yüan," SSGTK, 7:218, 421.

13. *Hsin ching*, 8a; *Ta hsüeh*, 7.

14. *Hsin ching*, 10a–18b.

15. *Hsin ching*, 10a.

16. *Hsin ching*, 19ab; Chou, *T'ung-shu* (Taipei: Commercial Press, 1978), 1:165. Also quoted in *Chin-ssu lu* 2; cf., Chan, *Source Book*, p. 473, and Wing-tsit Chan, *Reflections on Things at Hand* (New York: Columbia University Press, 1967), p. 36 (hereafter cited as Chan, *Reflections*).

17. *Hsin ching*, 19b and earlier citation at 4b; *Erh-Ch'eng ch'üan-shu*, 62:10a–11a; "Ssu chen."

18. "Ching chai chen," in *Chu Tzu ta ch'üan* (SPPY ed.; Taipei: Taiwan Chung-hua shu chü, 1970), 85:5b–6a; *ibid.*, 85:3b; "Ch'iu-fang-hsin chai ming"; *ibid.*, 85:3a; "Tsun-te-hsing chai ming."

19. "Nan-hsiung chou-hsüeh ssu hsien-sheng ssu-t'ang chi," in *Chen Hsi-shan wen-chi* (KHCPTS ed.), 26:448–49; SSGTK, 10:96–97, 437 (hereafter abbreviated as *Hsi-shan wen-chi*).

20. *Hsi-shan wen-chi*, 31:547–48; "Wen kang yü yü"; SSGTK, 10:109–10, 442.

21. *Hsi-shan wen-chi*, 33:583–84; "Chih-tao tzu shuo"; SSGTK:113, 444.

22. Cf., for instance, the treatment of this subject in Chan, *Source Book*, pp. 630–32, and his "Neo-Confucian Solution to the Problem of Evil," in *Studies Presented to Hu Shih on His 65th Birthday (Bulletin of the Institute of History and Philology)* (Taiwan: Academia Sinica, 1957), pp. 773–91.

23. See, for instance, the criticisms of the Ch'eng-Chu school in Chung-ying Cheng, "Reason, Substance, and Human Desires in Seventeenth Century Neo-Confucianism," *The Unfolding of Neo-Confucianism*, ed. W. T. de Bary, (New York: Columbia University Press, 1975), pp. 469–507.

24. See Ch'ien Mu, *Chu Tzu hsin hsüeh-an* (Taipei: San-min shu-chü, 1971), 1:406; Fung Yu-lan, *A History of Chinese Philosophy* (Princeton: Princeton University Press, 1953), 2:656–57, 668.

25. Preface of Yen Jo-yü dated 1234, 10 month, in Ming edition in the National

Central Library; also *Ssu-k'u ch'üan-shu tsung-mu t'i-yao* (Shanghai: Commercial Press, 1933), 92:1913–14 (Hereafter cited as *Ssu-k'u t'i-yao*).

26. *Wen-hsien t'ung-k'ao* (Shih t'ung ed.; Shanghai: Commercial Press, 1936), 210:1728. Ma lists the work as *Hsin-ching fa-yü*, which, according to the Ssu-k'u editors, appears to be the singular instance. See *Ssu-k'u t'i-yao*, 92:1913.

27. See JaHyun Kim Haboush, "A Heritage of Kings," (Ph.D. diss., Columbia University, Ann Arbor: University Microfilms, 1978), p. 92.

28. See Abe Yoshio, *Nihon Shushigaku to Chōsen* (Tokyo, 1967), pp. 174, 244–46, 254–45, 424, 510.

29. *Naikaku bunko kanseki bunrui mokuroku* (Tokyo, 1971), p. 433; *Seikado bunko kanseki bunrui mokuroku* (Tokyo, 1930), p. 172; *Hōsa bunko kanseki bunrui mokuroku* (Nagoya, 1965), p. 53.

30. Unless otherwise indicated, this brief biography is based on Wei Liao-weng's inscription for Chen's spirit-way tablet *(shen-tao-pei)* in *Ho-shan hsien-sheng ta-ch'üan chi*, (SPTK ed.), 69:11b–22a (hereafter cited as Wei, *Shen-tao-pei*); Liu K'o-chuang's "Hsi-shan Chen Wen-chung kung hsing-chuang" in *Hou-ts'un hsien-sheng ta-ch'üan chi* (SPTK ed.), 168:1a–40b; Chen's official biography in *Sung shih* (Peking: Chung-hua shu-chü, 1977), 437:12957–64; the account in Huang Tsung-hsi, et al., *Sung-Yüan hsüeh-an* (Taipei: Ho-lo t'u-shu ch'ü-pan she ed., 1975), 81:117; and the chronological biography *(Nien-p'u)* appearing in Chen's Complete Works, *Chen Wen-chung kung ch'üan-chi*, Wan-li 26 (1598) ed. For other references, see biography by Julia Ching in *Sung Biographies*, ed. Herbert Franke (Wiesbaden: Franz Steiner 1976), pp. 88–90; and Ch'ang Pi-te, et al., *Sung-jen chuan-chi tzu-liao so-yin* (hereafter abbreviated *Sung-jen so-yin*, pp. 1818–20).

31. Chan, *Reflections*, p. xxxviii.

32. Chan T'i-jen, T. Yüan-shan, *chin-shih* 1163; *Sung shih*, 393:12019–22; *Sung-Yüan hsüeh-an*, 69:30; *Sung-jen so-yin*, p. 3280.

33. Wei, *Shen-tao-pei*, 69:14a; *Sung shih*, 437:12958–59.

34. Pi Yüan, *Hsü Tzu-chih t'ung chien* (Ming Chia-ching 6[1527] ed.), 167:23a, Tuan-p'ing 1 (1234).

35. *Sung shih*, 414:12415; *Sung-jen so-yin*, p. 492. Shih Mi-yüan's policies at this time, Chen's critique of the government's inadequate measures vis-à-vis the Jurchen and Mongols, and Chen's proposals for strengthening border defenses in the Huai River area, receive extensive treatment and incisive comment in Charles A. Peterson's "First Sung Evaluations of the Mongol Invasion of the North 1211–1217," in *Crisis and Prosperity in Sung China*, ed. John Haeger (Tucson: University of Arizona Press, 1975), pp. 215–51.

36. See Kusumoto Masatsugu, *Chūgoku tetsugaku kenkyū* (Tokyo: Kokushikan daigaku toshokan, 1975), pp. 327–44, 390 ff. (Hereafter cited as *Chūgoku tetsugaku*).

37. See Chen's *Yü su wen* (TSCC reprint of Hsüeh hai lei-pien ed.).

38. *Sung shih*, 393:12021; SYHA, 81:117.

39. *Hsi-shan cheng-hsün* (TSCC reprint of Pao yen t'ang ed.), pp. 1–4; *Sung shih*, 437:12961.

40. Wei, *Shen-tao-pei*, 69:18ab; *Sung shih*, 437:12961.

41. Wei, *Shen-tao-pei*, 69:19a.

42. Chen, *Wen-chi*, 18:293–317; Chu Hsi, *Hui-an hsien-sheng Chu Wen-kung wen-chi*, in *Chu Tzu ta-ch'üan* (SPPY ed.), 15:1a–19a.

43. Japanese woodblock edition preserved in Sonkeikaku Collection; see *Son-keikaku bunko kanseki bunrui mokuroku* (Tokyo, 1934–35), p. 95.

44. *Sung shih*, 437:12963.

45. Wang Ying-lin, *Yü-hai* (Che-chiang shu-chü ed. of Kuang-su 9 [1883]), 39:30ab; *Sung shih*, 41:803, 437:12963.

46. *Nien-p'u*, 9ab.

47. See Mano Senryū, *Mindai bunkashi kenkyū* (Kyoto: Dōhōsha, 1979), p. 143 (hereafter cited as *Mindai bunkashi*)

48. *Sung shih*, 42:807.

49. *Nien-p'u*, 12a.

50. Wei, *Shen-tao-pei*, 21ab.

51. *Sung shih*, 437:12964.

52. *Hsi-shan hsien-sheng Chen Wen-chung kung wen-chi*, 51 *ch*. The edition used here is the reprint of the Ming Cheng-te 15 (1520) edition in the KHCPTS series, 2 vols., also contained in SPTK. See the comment of M. Yamauchi in *A Sung Bibliography*, ed. Y. Hervouet (Hong Kong: Chinese University Press, 1978), p. 494 (hereafter cited as *Sung Bibliography*).

53. *Ssu-shu chi-pien*, completed by his student Liu Ch'eng, who compiled the notes on the *Analects* and *Mencius*. See *Ssu-k'u t'i-yao*, 35:727–28; Hervouet, *Sung Bibliography*, p. 46.

54. *Wen-chang cheng-tsung*, 30 *ch*., and *Hsü pien*, 12 *ch*., in *Chen Wen-chung kung Hsi-shan hsien-sheng ch'üan-chi*, preface dated Wan-li 26 (1598): cf. also Korean movable type ed. in *Hōsa bunko kanseki bunrui mokuroku* (Nagoya, 1965), p. 131.

55. *Hsi-shan hsien-sheng Chen Wen-kung tu-shu chi*, 40 *ch*.; Hervouet, *Sung Bibliography*, pp. 226, 494; *Ssu-k'u t'i yao*, 92:1913.

56. *Cheng ching*, 1 *ch*. Ming reprint of Sung 1242 ed. in National Central Library, Taipei. See *Chung-yang t'u-shu-kuan shan-pen shu-mu* (Taipei, 1967), p. 439; Hervouet, *Sung Bibliography*, p. 172.

57. *Ssu-k'u t'i-yao*, 92:1914.

58. *Ibid.*

59. *Cheng ching*, 25b.

60. *Nien-p'u*, 7 ab.

61. The edition cited here is the 40-*chüan* version of 1739 included in the *Hsi-shan hsien-sheng Chen Wen-chung kung ch'üan-chi* of T'ung-chih 3 (1865). For the history of this text see *Ssu-k'u t'i-yao*, 92:1913, which concludes that the extant edition, together with the *Ta-hsüeh yen-i*, probably represents all that Chen was able to complete of the four series spoken of in early bibliographical notices. Copies of the Sung K'ai-ch'ing 1 (1259) 61-*chüan* edition are to be found in the Peking Library (*Pei-ching t'u-shu-kuan shan-pen shu-mu*, [Peking, 1959], 4:13a); in the Shanghai Library (*Shanghai t'u-shu-kuan shan pen shu-mu* [Shanghai, 1957]); in the National Central Library, Taipei (*Kuo-li chung-yang t'u-shu-kua shan-pen shu-mu* [Taipei, 1967], 2:437); in the Seikadō Library, Tokyo (*Seikadō bunko kanseki bunrui mokuroku* [Tokyo, 1930], p. 433). Twenty-two *chüan* of the second section of this edition are combined in *ch*. 33 of the 40-*chüan* edition more commonly available. Comparison of the above has revealed no significant difference in the text. See Hervouet, *Sung Bibliography*, p. 226.

62. *Ssu-k'u t'i-yao*, 92:1913.

63. See Fumoto Yasutaka, *Kinsei jugaku hensen-shiron* (Tokyo: Kokusho kankōkai, 1976), pp. 22–43 (hereafter cited as *Kinsei jugaku*). See also Mano Senryū, *Shushi to Ō Yōmei* (Tokyo: Shimizu shoin, 1979), pp. 136–45.

64. Fumoto, *Kinsei jugaku*, p. 23.

65. Ch'en I-chi, *Shih-shan t'ang ts'ang-shu-lu*, in *Chih-pu-tsu chai tsung-shu* (Ch'ien-lung-Tao-kuang ed.), *chüan-shang* 13a. See also Fumoto, *Kinsei jugaku*, p. 25.

66. *Yü-shan chiang-i*, in *Chu Tzu ta-ch'üan*, 74:18a–19b.

67. *Ta-hsüeh huo-wen* (Kinsei kanseki sōkan ed; Kyoto: Chūbun shuppansha, 1972), p. 2, 18–19; *Chu Tzu yü-lei* (Kyoto: Chūbun shuppansha, 1979), 14:397; Fumoto, *Kinsei jugaku*, p. 32.

68. Chu Hsi, *Hui-an hsien-sheng Chu Wen-kung wen-chi* (hereafter cited as Chu, *Wen-chi*) SPTK, 11:3b; see also pp. 33–35 above.

69. *Ti-hsüeh*, 8 ch. The edition used here is the Ch'ing edition in the Seikadō bunko, Tokyo (*Seikadō bunko kanseki bunrui mokuroku*, p. 426). Recently this text as preserved in the National Central Library, Taipei, has been reprinted in the series Chung-kuo tzu-hsüeh ming-chu chi-ch'eng, no. 031 (Taipei, 1978). The relative inaccessibility of the rare manuscript editions of the *Ti-hsüeh* probably explains the lack of any reference to it in Robert Hartwell's important study, "Historical Analogism, Public Policy, and Social Science in Eleventh and Twelfth Century China," *American Historical Review* (1971), 76(3): 690–727. The reprint only became available after my own use of the manuscript versions in the Seikadō, National Central Library, and the Ssu-k'u ch'üan-shu ed. in the Palace Museum.

70. Fan Tsu-yü, T. Shun-fu, *Sung-shih*, 337:10794–10800; SYHA, 21:56–58; Hartwell, "Historical Analogism," p. 698.

71. Chu Hsi, *I Lo yüan-yüan lu* (Cheng-i t'ang ed.), 7:6ab; *Ming-ch'en yen-hsing lu* (SPTK ed.), 10:3a; Chan, *Reflections*, p. 119.

72. In addition to the versions cited above, there is one in the private colleciton of Professor Fumoto Yasutaka and discussed by him in *Kinsei jugaku*, p. 772. With the wider availability of Fan's work, it is time for a fuller study of both him and Chen Te-hsiu as contributors to the major trends of thought and scholarship linking what Hartwell calls the "historical analogism" of the Northern Sung with the new form of "classicism" in the Ch'eng-Chu school, centering on the *Great Learning*, which tended to supersede the Wang An-shih–Ts'ai Ching form. Fan anticipates Chen Te-hsiu's combination of "historical analogism" and "moral didacticism." See Hartwell, "Historical Analogism," pp. 712–17.

73. The *Wen-hsien t'ung-k'ao*, 210:1727 lists the *Ti-hsüeh* in 10 *chüan*, but there is no reason to believe that the 8-*chüan* version is incomplete. Chiao Hung in the late Ming, however, also lists the *Ti-hsüeh* in 10 *chüan* in his *Kuo-shih ching-chi chih* (Yüeh-ya t'ang ed.), 44:5a.

74. Wang Ying-lin, *Yü-hai* (Che-chiang shu-chü ed. of 1883), *ch.* 26, 27; for Fan's contribution, esp. 26:9b.

75. *Ssu-k'u t'i-yao*, 91:1889.

76. Ch'eng I, *I-ch'uan wen-chi*, 7:7b in *Erh Ch'eng ch'üan-shu* (SPPY ed.; Taipei: Chung-hua Book Co., 1976) (hereafter cited as *Wen-chi*).

77. SYHA, 13:4, *Ming-tao hsüeh-an*.

78. Huang Kan, T. Chih-ch'ing, H. Mien-chai, *Sung shih*, 430:12777; SYHA, 63:5; SSGTK 10:1–3, 35–90.

79. Ch'en Ch'un, T. An-ching, H. Pei-hsi, *Sung shih*, 430:12788; SYHA, 68:1.

80. See the first essay, pp. 00–00 above.

81. Chen, *Wen-chi*, 26:448–9; SSGTK, 10:96–98, 437–38; "Nan-hsiung chou-hsüeh ssu hsien-sheng ssu-t'ang chi." Kusumoto, *Chūgoku tetsugaku*, pp. 203–4, 371–72, 374, 383.

82. Chen, *Wen-chi,* 24:409–10; SSGTK, 10:91–94, 436–37; "Ming-tao hsien-sheng shu-t'ang chi." The final quotation approximates *Wai-shu* 12:4a in *Erh-Ch'eng ch'üan-shu* (SPPY ed.); *Shang-ts'ai yü-lu* (Chūbun ed.), A:6a.

83. Chen, *Wen-chi,* 24:410; SSGTK, 10:94, 437.

84. Chen, *Wen-chi,* 26:449; SSGTK, 10:97, 438.

85. Chen, *Wen-chi,* 30:533–34; SSGTK, 10:104–5, 440–41.

86. Chen, *Wen-chi,* 33:583–84; SSGTK, 10:111–13, 443–44; "Chih-tao tzu shuo."

87. Chen, *Wen-chi,* 25:425; "Ch'ien-shan hsien hsiu-hsüeh chi."

88. *Cheng ching,* 1a.

89. *Li chi,* "Shih-san-ching chu-su," 1:5a; *Tien shang* 1.

90. *Chuang tzu, ch.* 2, "Ch'i wu lun" (Harvard-Yenching Concordance to Chuang tzu, p. 3); B. Watson, *Complete Works of Chuang Tzu* (New York: Columbia University Press, 1968), p. 3.

91. *Wen-chi,* 25:426; SSGTK, 10:94–95, 437; "Ching-ssu chai chi."

92. See Chan, *Source Book,* p. 267.

93. *Erh-Ch'eng ch'üan-shu* (SPPY ed.) *I-shu,* 1:3a; Chan, *Source Book,* p. 527.

94. *Wen-chi,* 30:528; SSGTK, 10:103, 440; "Wen ta-hsüeh chih shuo ko wu . . ."

95. Bradford Langley in Franke, *Sung Biographies,* p. 1175.

96. The edition used here is the Ming official woodblock edition of Chia-ching 6 (1556), 43 *chüan,* in the National Central Library, Taipei (*Shan-pen mu-lu,* p. 438), which also has a copy of the Sung K'ai-ch'ing 1 ed. (1259). Numerous other editions exist, but I have found no significant differences among those preserved in major libraries and special collections in China and Japan. Of some interest to the history of Neo-Confucianism in Japan is the Ming Ch'ung-chen edition preserved in the Nai-kaku bunko, Tokyo, with the handwritten annotations and punctuation of Hayashi Gahō (1618–1680), successor to Hayashi Razan as head of the official Tokugawa school at Edo. A Korean movable-type edition preserved in the Hōsa bunko, Nagoya bears the seal of Tokugawa Ieyasu and was given to his son enfeoffed in the Owari domain. *Hōsa bunko kanseki bunrui mokuroku,* p. 54; see also Hervouet, *Sung Bibliography,* pp. 215–16.

97. *Yen-i* in Morohashi Tetsuji, *Daikanwa jiten* (Tokyo: Taishūkan, 1955), no. 34033–8.

98. Chen, *Wen-chi,* 18:293, "Chin tu *Ta-hsüeh* chüan tzu."

99. *Hsi-shan ch'üan chi* ed. of *Ta-hsüeh yen-i;* "Piao-p'ing cha tzu," 7b–8a.

100. See Chan, *Source Book,* pp. 450–59.

101. On Chu Hsi's exposition of the *Great Learning* at court, see the first essay, pp. 33–35.

102. *Ta-hsüeh yen-i hsü,* Wen-chi, 29:516–17; SSGTK, 10:100–3, 439–40.

103. *Ssu-k'u t'i-yao,* 92:1912–13.

104. *Ibid.*

105. Chu, *Wen-chi,* 74:16b–17a.

106. Ch'iu Chün, *Ta-hsüeh yen-i pu,* Imperial reprint of Chia-ching 38 (1559) (National Central Library, Taipei, *Shan-pen mu-lu,* p. 443). Preface of Ch'iu Chün, and Memorial of Presentation dated Ch'eng-hua 23 (1487). The NCL also has the Hung-chih 1 (1488) ed.

107. James Legge, *The Chinese Classics* (2d ed., rev.; Taipei, 1966), *Shoo king,* 3:15–17.

108. *Ta-hsüeh yen-i*, 1:3ab.
109. Legge, *Chinese Classics*, 3:68–69.
110. *Ta-hsüeh yen-i*, 1:4a.
111. Tung Chung-shu, *Tung Tzu wen-chi* (Chi-fu ts'ung-shu ed.), 1:5b.
112. *Ta-hsüeh yen-i*, 1:20b–21a.
113. Yang Hsiung, *Yang tzu fa-yen* (Chu-tzu chi-ch'eng ed.) (Peking: Chung-hua Book Co., 1957), 13:42.
114. *Ta-hsüeh yen-i*, 1:21b.
115. *Ibid.*, 2:2b–3b.
116. *Ibid.*, 2:9b.
117. *Ibid.*, 2:10a.
118. *Shu ching*, "Li cheng"; Legge, *Chinese Classics* 3:508bb.
119. *Ta-hsüeh yen-i*, 2:10b–11a.
120. *Ibid.*, 3:3a, 4a.
121. *Ibid.*, 4:1b–2a.
122. *Ibid.*, 4:11b–12a.
123. *Ibid.*, 5:1b–2a.
124. *Ibid.*, 5:33a–34a.
125. *Ibid.*, 6:1a.
126. *Ibid.*, 6:7a.
127. *Ibid.*, 9:4a–10b.
128. *Ibid.*, 9:28ab.
129. *Ibid.*, 10:1ab.
130. *Ibid.*, 10:4ab.
131. *Ibid.*, 11:10a.
132. *Ibid.*, 10:11b. For Ch'eng I as quoted by Chu Hsi, see p. 129.
133. *Ibid.*, 11:11b.
134. *Ibid.*, ch. 13, 14.
135. *Ibid.*, 20:20ab.
136. *Ibid.*, 27:25a.
137. *Ibid.*, 28:1b.
138. *Ibid.*, 28:4a.
139. *Ibid.*, ch. 30, esp. 11ab.
140. *Ibid.*, ch. 31–34.
141. *Ibid.*, ch. 36–43.
142. See Hervouet, *Sung Bibliography*, p. 216.
143. YS, 159:3747; *SYHA Pu-i*, 81:66a.
144. YS, 24:536.
145. YS, 24:557.
146. Yü Chi, *Tao-yüan hsüeh-ku lu*, SPTK, 7:1a–2a; "Hsi-shan shu-yüan chi"; Su T'ien-chüeh, *Yüan wen-lei* (Chiang-su shu-chü ed. of Kuang-su 15 [1889]), 30:7b–8a.
147. YS, 26:586.
148. YS, 27:608.
149. YS, 29:644. Mano Senryū, *Mindai Bunkaishi*, pp. 144–45, gives further details on the great attention drawn to the work in these years.
150. See my "Neo-Confucian Cultivation and Enlightenment," in de Bary, *Unfolding*, pp. 153–62.

151. Morohashi, *Daikanwa jiten*, no. 10295–359.

152. Morohashi, *ibid*; Oda Tokunō, *Bukkyō daijiten* (rev. ed.; Tokyo: Ōkura shoten, 1930), p. 883. An example of the original Buddhist use of the term *hsin-fa* as it appears in Chu Yün-ming's (1461–1527) critique of Neo-Confucian *hsin-hsüeh* (or *hsin-fa*) may be found in Christian Murck, *Chu Yün-ming and Cultural Commitment in Su Chou* (Ann Arbor: University Microfilms International, 1978), p. 506.

153. On the Neo-Confucian-Buddhist dialogue concerning the mind, see Miriam Levering, "Neo-Confucianism and Buddhism in the Sung as movements within a single *shih-tai-fu* culture: Buddhist interpretations of Confucian discourse" (paper presented to the University Seminar on Neo-Confucianism, Columbia University, March 2, 1979).

154. See *Huang-chi ching-shih shu* (SPPY ed.), 7A–14G. I am grateful to Wing-tsit Chan for bringing this reference to my attention.

155. Ch'en Chang-fang, *Wei shih chi* (Ssu-k'u ch'üan-shu chen-pen ed.) (Shanghai: Commercial Press, 1935), 1:1a–3b; "Ti-hsüeh lun."

156. SSGTK, 8:15, 450 (rpt. of SPPY ed).

157. See *Erh-Ch'eng i-shu*, 15:14a, 15:8b; *Wai-shu*, 11:1a; and *I-shu*, 14:1a. See also Ōtsuki Nobuo, *Shushi shisho shuju tenkyo kō* (Kyoto: Chūbun shuppansha, 1976), p. 609.

158. *Erh Ch'eng wai-shu*, 11:1a.

159. SSGTK, 8:11, 449.

160. Hsü, *Lu-chai chi* (TSCC ed.), 5:77; "Pa Tao-t'ung-lu."

161. Unless otherwise noted, biographical information on Hsü is based on the spirit-way tablet inscription by Ou-yang Hsüan in *Kuei-chai wen-chi*, SPTK, 9:1a ff (also contained in *Hsü Wen-cheng kung i-shu* (T'ang shih ching kuan ts'ung-shu ed.), *chüan mo*, 4a ff (hereafter cited as *I-shu*); the biographical materials in Su T'ien-chüeh, *Yüan ch'ao ming-ch'en shih-lüeh* (Peking: Chung-hua Book Co., 1962; reprint of 1335 ed.) (hereafter referred to as *Shih-lüeh*); or his biography in YS, 158:3716–29. I have also benefited from seeing an unpublished paper on Hsü Heng by Professor Julia Ching prepared for the Conference on Yüan Thought sponsored by the American Council of Learned Societies, Issaquah, Washington, January 1978.

162. Su, *Shih-lüeh*, 8:12ab.

163. *Ibid.*, 8:13ab.

164. Su, *Shih-lüeh*, 8:12b: Sun K'o-k'uan, *Yüan-tai han-wen-hua chih huo-tung* (Taipei: Chung-hua Book Co., 1968), pp. 209–12 (hereafter cited as *Han-wen-hua*); Abe Takeo, *Gendaishi no kenkyū* (Tokyo: Sōbunsha, 1972), p. 33 (hereafter cited as *Gendaishi*).

165. Hok-lam Chan, "Liu Ping-chung (1216–1274): A Buddhist-Taoist Statesman at the Court of Khubilai Khan," *T'oung Pao* (1967) 52(1–3):131 ff.

166. Su T'ien-chüeh, *Yüan wen-lei*, 13:1a–4a.

167. *Ibid.*, 13:13ab.

168. Su, *Yüan wen-lei*, 13:1a; Hsü, *I-shu*, 7:1ab.

169. See the first essay, p. 44.

170. Su, *Shih-lüeh*, 8:14a.

171. See pp. 38–44 above.

172. Sun, *Han-wen-hua*, p. 183.

173. YS, 115:2889; and as summarized in Yamada Keiji, *Chūgoku no kagaku to kagakusha* (Kyoto: Daigaku jimbun kagaku kenkyūsho, 1978), pp. 106–7.

174. Su, *Shih-lüeh*, 8:2a–3b; YS, 81:2029; Sun, *Han-wen-hua*, pp. 158–60, 178–80.

175. Yeh-lu Yu-shang, "Kuo-hsüeh shih chi," in Hsü, *I-shu, chüan mo* 1b; YS, 158:3729.

176. Yeh-lu Yu-shang, "Kuo-hsüeh shih chi," 2a.

177. *Ibid.*, 1a–3a.

178. Sun, *Han-wen-hua*, pp. 160–61.

179. Ch'en Yüan, *Western and Central Asians in China*, by Ch'ien Hsing-hai and L. Carrington Goodrich, Monumenta Serica Monograph 15 (Los Angeles: University of California, 1966), p. 66.

180. Su, *Shih-lüeh*, 8:13ab.

181. *Lu-chai ch'üan-shu* (Kinsei kanseki sōkan ed.), 5:15ab; SSGTK, 10:217, 478, "Yü tzu Shih-k'o."

182. Letter to Yeh-lu Wei-chung, *Lu-chai ch'üan shu*, 5:24a; SSGTK 10:215, 478.

183. See *I-shu, ch.* 3, 4, 5.

184. See Yao Tsung-wu, "Liao Chin Yüan shih-ch'i t'ung-shih k'ao," *Wen shih chih hsüeh-pao* (1967) 16:218–19; Herbert Franke, "Could Mongol Emperors Read and Write Chinese?" *Asia Major* (1953), 3:28–29.

185. "Chung-yung chih-chieh," in *I-shu*, 5:1a.

186. The edition cited here is the Ming edition of 1522 collated by Han Shih-ch'i (*chin-shih*, 1502) who says in his preface that he had had the work printed from a handwritten copy in order to make up for its omission from the *Lu-chai ch'üan-shu*. This assertion is questioned by the editors of the *Ssu-k'u t'i-yao* (95:1963), who point out that its contents are all from the *Yü-lu* included in the *Ch'üan-shu*. Original copies of the Ming edition are kept in the Kyoto University Research Institute of Humanistic Sciences and in the Hōsa bunko, Nagoya. Korean and Japanese (Genroku 4 [1691]) editions, based on Han Shih-ch'i's, are preserved in the Naikaku bunko, Tokyo (see Abe, *Nihon Shushigaku to Chōsen*, p. 181–83). The Genroku edition has been reprinted in *Kinsei kanseki sokan*, shisō zokuhen, vol. 5, Chūbun shuppansha, Kyoto.

Ch'ien Ta-hsin, in his supplement to the bibliographical treatise of the *Yüan History* (*Pu Yüan-shih i-wen-chih*, 3:1a), lists this as a Yüan work, the compiler of which is unknown. There is obviously no question as to the authencity of the contents themselves.

The so-called "original preface" contained in *Hsü Wen-cheng kung i-shu* is Han Shih-ch'i's. In one sense his assertion with regard to the unavailability of the *Hsin-fa* itself is confirmed by Chiao Hung's failure to mention it among the extant works of Hsü in the sixteenth century. See his *Kuo-shih ching-chi chih* (1590); Yüeh-ya t'ang ed., 4:6a. Its absence from the latter was also noted by Itō Jinsai (1627–1705); see Abe, *Gendaishi*, p. 182.

187. Hsü, *I-shu*, 3:1a–3a; "Hsiao-hsüeh ta-i"; SSGTK, 10:210–11, 475–77.

188. Hsü, *I-shu*, 3:1ab; cf. also 3:15ab, "Tsung-lun ta-hsüeh hsiao-hsüeh."

189. Cf. Chu Hsi, *Hsiao-hsüeh*, as edited by Uno Seiichi in *Shōgaku shin-shaku kambun taikei* (Tokyo: Meiji shoin, 1965).

190. *Li chi chu-su* (Shih san ching: I-wen reprint, Taipei, 1955), 50:10b (849). "Ai kung wen."

191. Cf. *Shōgaku*, p. 39, and commentary by Uno Seiichi.

192. Hsü, *I-shu*, 3:2a–3a; SSGTK, 10:210–11, 476.

193. Uno, *Shōgaku*, pp. 139–40.

194. Hsü, *I-shu*, 4:1a; "*Ta-hsüeh* chih-chieh."

195. Hsü, *I-shu*, 3:14b; "Lun ming-ming-te."

196. Hsü, *I-shu*, 4:1a.

197. *I-shu*, 3:6ab; "*Ta-hsüeh* yao-lüeh."

198. *I-shu*, 4:4a; "*Ta-hsüeh* chih-chieh."

199. *I-shu*, 3:7a; "*Ta-hsüeh* yao-lüeh."

200. *Ibid.*, 3:9b.

201. *Ibid.*, 3:12a.

202. *I-shu*, 4:14b–15a; "*Ta-hsüeh* chih-chieh."

203. *I-shu*, 5:1a–2a; "*Chung-yung* chih-chieh."

204. *Lu-chai hsin-fa*, 1a, 2a.

205. *Ibid.*, 1b.

206. *I-shu*, 5:2ab, 6b; "*Chung-yung* chih-chieh."

207. *Ibid.*, 5:4a.

208. *Ibid.*, 5:4b.

209. *Ibid.*, 5:50b.

210. *Ibid.*, 3:4b, 13ab; 4:1a, 6ab, 15a.

211. *Ibid.*, 5:9a, 19a, 60a–61a; Lu-chai *Hsin-fa*, 4a.

212. *I-shu, chüan-mo*, 8b–9a.

213. Kusumoto, *Chūgoku tetsugaku*, pp. 360 ff.

214. Sun, *Han-wen-hua*, pp. 122–38.

215. *Yoshikawa Kōjirō zenshū* (Tokyo: Chikuma shobō, 1974), 14:129 ff, 369 ff.

216. YS 81:2030.

217. Su, *Yüan wen-lei*, 19:1a–2a, "Kuo-tzu-hsüeh hsien-shih miao-pei."

218. Ou-yang Hsüan, *Kuei chai wen-chi*, SPTK, 9:1a; Hsü, *I-shu, chüan mo* 4a; "Shen-tao-pei."

219. Ch'eng Chu-fu, *Ch'u-kuo Wen-hsien kung Hsüeh-lou Ch'eng hsien-sheng wen-chi* (1913 rpt. of Ming Hung-wu ed.), 10:13b–14a.

220. See the first essay, pp. 59–60.

221. See the extensive studies of Kusumoto in *Chūgoku tetsugaku*, pp. 353–92.

222. Wu Ch'eng, *Wu Wen-cheng chi* (Ssu-k'u chen-pen ed.) 48:13b; "Hsien ch'eng pen-hsin lou chi."

223. See the discussion of Itō Tomoatsu in SSGTK, 10:6.

224. Hsiung Ho (1247–1312), H. Wu-hsien, SYHA, 64:40, 46–57; *Pu-i*, 64:47b, 81:53b.

225. Hsiung Ho, *K'ao-ting shu-yüan chi* in Su, *Yüan wen-lei*, 29:9ab.

226. *Ibid.*, 29:10a.

227. Tu Pen, T. Po-yüan, H. Ch'ing-pi, YS, 199;˙4477–79; SYHA, 92:29a; *Pu-i*, 92:65b.

228. Yü Chi, "Ssu-hsüeh-chai chi," in Su, *Yüan wen-lei*, 30:3a.

229. Shan-ssu (1278–1351), T. Te-chieh, YS, 190:4351–53; Ch'en Yüan, *Western and Central Asians*, pp. 60–62.

230. YS, 190:4351.

231. Ch'en Yüan, *Western and Central Asians*, p. 62.

232. See Jung Chao-tsu, *Ming-tai ssu-hsiang shih* (Kaiming reprint; Taipei, 1962), p. 4; Sano Kōji, "Mindai zempanki no shisōkō," in *Nihon Chūgoku gakkai hō* (1974), 26:112 ff.

233. Cf. YS, 89:4318–20; SYHA *Pu-i*, 82:227b–228a.

234. L. Carrington Goodrich and Chaoying Fang, eds., *Dictionary of Ming Biography* (New York: Columbia University Press, 1976), p. 90, Biog. by Romeyn Taylor (hereafter cited as DMB); John Dardess, "Confucian Doctrine, Local Reform, and Centralization in Late Yüan Chekiang" (paper delivered at the Conference on Yüan Thought, Issaquah, Washington, January 1978), pp. 31–32.

235. Chu Lien, T. Po-ch'ing, *Ming-shih* (hereafter MS) (Chung-hua shu-chü ed., Peking, 1974), 285:7318–20; SYHA *Pu-i*, 70:118b, 138b, 140a.

236. See DMB, p. 1225, Biog. by F. W. Mote; Araki Kengo, *Mindai shisō kenkyū* (Tokyo: Sōbunsha, 1972), pp. 3–22; Wing-tsit Chan, "The Ch'eng-Chu School in the Early Ming," in *Self and Society in Ming Thought*, ed. W. T. de Bary (New York, Columbia University Press, 1970), p. 44.

237. See DMB, p. 1445, Biog. by A. R. Davis; Jung, *Ming-tai ssu-hsiang shih*, p. 9.

238. See DMB, p. 932, Biog. by Hok-lam Chan.

239. MS, 70:1693; Jung Chao-tsu, "Liu Chi ti che-hsüeh ssu-hsiang chi ch'i she-hui kuan-tien," *Che-hsüeh yen-chiu* (1961), no. 3, p. 41. Jung questions the *Ming shih* assertion of Liu Chi's involvement, since he finds no other supporting evidence, and in general he would disassociate Liu from what he views as Ming T'ai-tsu's betrayal of the peasant revolution and reestablishment of dynastic rule. On the other hand, there being no evidence of opposition to reestablishment of the civil service examinations in this form, we have no reason to believe that Liu would have resisted it.

240. See Sakai Tadao, *Chūgoku zensho no kenkyū* (Tokyo: Kōbundō, 1960), pp. 226–33 (hereafter cited as Zensho): Araki, *Mindai shisō kenkyū*, p. 9.

241. Sung Lien, *Sung hsüeh-shih wen-chi* (Wan-yu wen-k'u ed.), 51:877–78; 58:965–66.

242. Araki, *Mindai shisō kenkyū*, p. 5.

243. *Ibid.*

244. *Ibid. Hsiang-shan hsien-sheng ch'üan-chi* (SPTK) 36:5a; 22:8b.

245. *Ibid.*, p. 6. The limitations of Sung Lien's type of genial, accommodative syncretism are discussed in Murck, *Chu Yün-ming*, pp. 536–38.

246. Quoted by P'eng Shao-sheng in *Chü-shih chuan* (Dainihon Zokuzōkyō ed.), 37:464a.

247. *Hua-ch'uan chih-tz'u* (Chin-hua ts'ung-shu ed.), p. 2a.

248. *Wang Chung-wen kung chi* (TSCC ed.) 3:61–62; "Sung Lo Chung-pen hsü."

249. *Ibid.*, 1:4; "Liu ching lun."

250. See Jung, *Ming-tai ssu-hsiang shih*, p. 13.

251. Araki, *Mindai shisō kenkyū*, pp. 11–13.

252. MS, 128:3786.

253. Mano, *Mindai bunka shi*, p. 147.

254. See Sakai Tadao, *Zensho*, pp. 8–34.

255. See Mano, *Mindai bunkashi*, p. 148; Sakai, *Zensho*, pp. 9–16. Charles Hucker, *The Ming Dynasty: Its Origins and Evolving Institutions* (Ann Arbor: University of Michigan Center for Chinese Studies, 1978), pp. 53–54.

256. See Romeyn Taylor, *Basic Annals of Ming T'ai-tsu* (San Francisco: Chinese Materials and Research Aids Center, 1975), p. 86; Hucker, *Ming Dynasty*, pp. 44–45, 66–73.

257. See Mo Po-chi, *Wu shih wan ch'üan lou ts'ang-shu mu-lu ch'u-pien* (1931

ed.), 3:160b, "Meng Tzu chieh-wen"; L. C. Goodrich, "A Study of Literary Persecution during the Ming," *Harvard Journal of Asiatic Studies* (1939), 3:299–301; Hucker, *Ming Dynasty*, p. 98.

258. See *Ming T'ai-tsung shih-lu* (Chung-yang yen-chiu yüan ed.), 88:116, Yung lo 7 (1409), 2d month, *Chia hsü*; and Sakai, *Zensho*, p. 19.

259. Sakai, *Zensho*, p. 20.

260. An original copy of the *Sheng-hsüeh hsin-fa* is contained in the National Central Library, Taipei, and identical reprints in the Naikaku bunko, Tokyo, and Hōsa bunko, Nagoya. The edition used here was the 1559 reprint of the Yung-lo 7 (1409) edition, 4 *ch.* in the Naikaku bunko, but page references here correspond to the NCL edition as recently reprinted in the Chung-kuo tzu-hsüeh ming-chu chi-ch'eng ed., no. 038. Chiao Hung in *Kuo shih ching-chi chih* (Yüeh-ya t'ang ed.), 1:1b, lists it as *Ch'eng-tsu huang-ti sheng-hsüeh hsin-fa*; 5 ch.

261. *Sheng-hsüeh hsin-fa*, 1:55 a–56b.

262. *Ibid.*, 2:36b–37b; "Hsin-hsüeh."

263. *Ibid.*, 2:39ab; "Hsin hsüeh."

264. *Ibid.*, 2:47a–48b; "Hsin hsüeh."

265. *Ibid.*, 2:52a; "Hsin hsüeh."

266. *Ibid.*, 2:78ab; "Hsin hsüeh."

267. *Ibid.*, 3:41a.

268. *Ibid.*, 4:9a; "Hsin hsüeh."

269. *Ibid.*, 4:59b; "Hsin hsüeh."

270. *Ibid.*, 4:62b, 65b; "Hsin hsüeh."

271. *Ssu-k'u t'i-yao*, p. 1964.

272. *Ibid.*

273. *Ming T'ai-tsung shih-lu*, 158:2a, Yung-lo 12, 11th month; 168:2b, Yung-lo 13, 9th month, *chi-yu*.

274. Although originally identified in the *Veritable Records* as the *Compendia on the Five Classics, Four Books, and Human Nature and Principle*, the *Compendia* could be listed separately or together, in varying order according to the source and catalogue. In relation to the examinations, for which they were the standard texts, priority was given to the Four Books. Thus the *Ming shih* treatise on the examinations refers to the *Compendia on the Four Books and Five Classics* (70:1694). Ku Yen-wu does the same in his discussion of the *Compendia* (*Jih-chih lu* 18[6]:103): the *Ssu-k'u t'i-yao* lists them separately but explains how the *Compendium on the Four Books* came to have priority over the others by virtue of its importance in the examination system (36:742, *Ssu-shu ta-ch'üan*).

275. MS, 70:1693; Taylor, *Basic Annals of Ming T'ai-tsu*, pp. 66, 70, 89, 92, 95.

276. *Ssu-shu ta-ch'üan*, manuscript edition in National Central Library, Taipei.

277. *Ssu-k'u t'i-yao*, 36:742.

278. *Chu tzu yü-lei*, 14:397. The organization of Chu Hsi's comments on the classics in the *Classified Conversations (Yü-lei)* also follows this order.

279. *Ssu-k'u t'i-yao*, 93:1925.

280. *Ming T'ai-tsung shih-lu*, 158:2a, Yung-lo 12, 11th month, *chia-yin*.

281. *Ibid.*, 186:1b, Yung-lo 15, 3d month, *i-wei*.

282. Preface to the original 1415 edition of the *Hsing-li ta-ch'üan* preserved in the National Palace Museum and National Central Library, Taipei; also in the *Ming T'ai-tsung shih-lu*, 168:2b–4a, Yung-lo 12, 9th month, *chi-yu*.

283. *Ming T'ai-tsung shih-lu*, 186:1b, Yung lo 15, 3d month, *i-wei*.

284. *Ssu-k'u t'i-yao*, 36:742.

285. *Ming Hsüan-tsung shih-lu*, 22:4b, Hsüan-te 1, 10th month, *hsin-wei*.

286. See Wing-tsit Chan, "The *Hsing-li ching-i* and the Ch'eng-Chu School of the Seventeenth Century," in de Bary, *Unfolding*, pp. 544 ff.

287. *Hsing-li ta-ch'üan* (Ssu-k'u ch'üan-shu chen-pen ed., 5th ser.; Taipei: Commercial Press, 1974), ia–iia; Kang-hsi 12 (1673) ed.

288. Ku Yen-wu, *Jih-chih lu*, 18:104; "Ssu-shu wu-ching ta-ch'üan."

289. *Ibid.*

290. Mano Senryū, *Shushi to Ō Yōmei* (Tokyo: Shimizu shoin, 1974), p. 158.

291. *Ibid.*

292. See Jung Chao-tsu, *Ming-tai ssu-hsiang shih*, p. 3; DMB, pp. 431–32, Biog. of Fang Hsiao-ju by F. W. Mote.

293. Ku, *Jih-chih lu*, 18:104.

294. See his "Inquiry on the Great Learning" *(Ta-hsüeh wen)* in Wing-tsit Chan, tr., *Instructions for Practical Living* (New York: Columbia University Press, 1963), pp. 269–80.

295. See Irene Bloom, "On the Abstraction of Ming Thought: Some Concrete Evidence from the Philosophy of Lo Ch'in-shun," in *Principle and Practicality*, ed. de Bary and Bloom (New York: Columbia University Press, 1979), pp. 106–10.

296. Tsai Shen (1167–1230), T. Chung-mo, H. Chiu-feng, *Shang-shu chi-chuan (Sung Bibloigraphy*, pp. 22–23), Shu t'ang ed. 1:32a.

297. Ku, *Jih-chih lu*, 18:107–109.

298. de Bary, *Unfolding*, p. 192.

299. See Huang Ssu-ai, *Nan-lei hsüeh-an* (Nanking, 1936), p. 7; Koh Byong-ik, "Huang Tsung-hsi's Expectation of the New Era," *Journal of Social Sciences and Humanities* (Seoul, 1969), pp. 61–62.

300. See Jung, *Ming-tai ssu-hsiang shih*, pp. 13–33; Wing-tsit Chan, "The Ch'eng-Chu School in the Early Ming," in de Bary, *Self and Society in Ming Thought*, pp. 29–30, and Sano, "Mindai zempanki no shisōkō," pp. 113–16.

301. See earlier reference in n. 186. It is true that *Lu-chai hsin-fa* had almost ceased to exist as a separate text and is missing from the listing of Hsü Heng's works in Chiao Hung's Ming bibliography (*Kuo-ch'ao ching-chi chih*, Yüeh-ya-t'ang ed., 4A:6a). Han's reprint was in turn reprinted in Korea and from there found its way to Japan, where it was studied by Hayashi Razan, among others, and was reprinted in Genroku 4 (1691). See Abe, *Nihon Shushigaku to Chōsen*, pp. 174, 181–83.

302. Hsü, *Lu-chai hsin-fa*, 1ab. Preface of Han Shih-ch'i.

303. Wang Ming, T. Shih-chen (*chin-shih* 1511), native of Chin-hsi in Kiangsi and one-time education officer of Chekiang. Also the author of other works on the *hsin-hsüeh*. See Chiao Hung, *Kuo-ch'ao hsien-cheng lu* (Taipei: Hsüeh-sheng shu-chü) 84:183a–185a. Funerary inscription of Wang Shao-yüan.

304. *Chu Tzu hsin-hsüeh lu, 7 ch.* Japanese reprint of Meiwa 6 (1769) of the Ming Chia-ching 21 (1542) ed., with preface by Wang Ming dated 1534, preserved in the Naikaku bunko, Tokyo. See *Naikaku bunko kanseki mokuroku*, p. 171.

305. Ch'eng Min-cheng, T. K'o-chin (*chin-shih* 1466). See Chiao Hung, *Kuo-ch'ao hsien-cheng lu*, 35, 43; MS, 286:7343; Okada Takehiko, *Sō-Min tetsugaku josetsu* (Tokyo: Bungensha, 1977), pp. 280–83; DMB, pp. 552, 890, 941, 1095.

306. The edition of the *Hsin-ching fu-chu* used here is the 4-*chüan* Japanese edition of 1649 reprinted in the Kinsei Kanseki sōkan, shisō sampen (Kyoto: Chūbun

shuppansha, 1976). Also consulted was the Korean edition of Yi T'oegye, preserved in the Naikaku bunko, Tokyo (*Naikaku bunko kanseki mokuroku*, p. 172). Cf. also the catalog of the Chinese Collection in the Gyujanggag, Seoul University Library, 1972, p. 346, for copy of Yi T'oegye.

307. See *Hsin-ching fu-chu*, preface, p. 1a.

308. *Hsin-ching fu-chu*, pp. 265–66.

309. Kusumoto, *Chūgoku tetsugaku*, p. 369.

310. *Hsin ching fu-chu* (4 ch., Kinsei kanseki sōkan ed.), pp. 271–82; the Korean edition in the Naikaku bunko also has Hayashi Razan's handwritten transcription of this epilogue.

311. See Abe Yoshio, *Nihon Shushigaku to Chōsen*, p. 167, 174, 178, 192–93.

312. See Kusumoto, *Sō Min jidai jugaku shisō no kenkyū* (Kashiwa-shi: Hiroike gakuen, 1962), p. 391.

313. See DMB, pp. 912–15, Biog. by Lien-che Tu Fang.

314. See Part III, pp. 189, 199–202.

315. *Wang Chung-wen kung chi* (TSCC ed.), 3:65; "Ching yen lu hou hsü."

316. See the imperial preface of the Chia-ching emperor, dated 1527, which recites the previous honors paid to it in the Ming. The preface may be found in the Ming edition of the *Ta-hsüeh yen-i* cited in n. 96.

317. See the edition included in *Hsi-shan hsien-sheng Chen Wen-cheng kung ch'üan-chi*, 1865 ed. (*Sung Bibliography*, p. 494).

318. Copies preserved in Naikaku bunko, National Central Library, Taipei, and Columbia University East Asian Library; see *Naikaku bunko kanseki bunrui mokuroku*, p. 171.

319. See Haboush, "A Heritage of Kings," p. 92 and passim.

320. Cf. the Ming edition of 1632 preserved in the Naikaku bunko with handwritten annotations of Hayashi Gahō, as listed in *Naikaku bunko kanseki bunrui mokuroku*, p. 171.

321. On this point see the discussion of Shimada Kenji in his *Shushigaku to Yōmeigaku* (Tokyo: Iwanami, 1967), p. 101.

322. For these and numerous other examples see Kusumoto, *Chūgoku tetsugaku*, pp. 375–79.

323. DMB, pp. 249–52, Biog. by Wu Chi-hua and Ray Huang.

324. See his preface to the *Ta-hsüeh yen-i pu*, 160-chüan Chia-ching 38 (1559) reprint of Hung chih 1 (1488) edition as preserved in the National Central Library, Taipei, p. 7b.

325. *Ta-hsüeh yen-i pu*, Preface of Ch'iu Chün, p. 2b.

326. DMB, pp. 250–51.

327. *Ta-hsüeh yen-i pu*, Preface, p. 2b.

328. *Ibid.*, pp. 4b–5a.

329. *Ibid.*, p. 7ab.

330. *Ibid.*, pp. 1a, 2b.

331. *Ibid.*, pp. 3ab, 4b, 7ab.

332. *Ibid.*, pp. 1a–3a.

333. Ch'iu Chün, *Ch'ung-pien Ch'iung-t'ai hui-k'ao shih wen-chi* (1879 ed.) 2:26b.

334. Satō Naokata, *Unzōroku zoku shūi* in *Satō Naokata zenshū* (Kawasaki: Nihon koten gakkai, 1941), 1:610; Araki Kengo, Introduction to *Hsin ching fu-chu*, *Kinsei kanseki sōkan, shisō*, 3d ser. vol. 12.

335. See de Bary, *Principle and Practicality*, pp. 150–51, 164–65.

336. SSGTK, 10:103, 440.
337. See de Bary, *Self and Society in Ming Thought*, p. 7; *Unfolding*, pp. 27–29; Sano, "Mindai zempanki no shisōkō," pp. 112–24; Araki, *Mindai shisō*, pp. 23–50.
338. DMB, p. 416.

Part III: NEO-CONFUCIAN ORTHODOXIES AND THE LEARNING OF THE MIND-AND-HEART IN EARLY TOKUGAWA JAPAN

This part has been adapted from previous writings, rearranged here to make a coherent, sequential presentation of the topic; see *Principle and Practicality* (CUP, 1979), pp. 15–22, 25–33, 130–39, and *The Unfolding of Neo-Confucianism* (CUP, 1975), pp. 148–53.

1. Masao Maruyama, *Studies in the Intellectual History of Tokugawa Japan* (Princeton: Princeton University Press, 1975).
2. See W. T. de Bary, ed., *The Unfolding of Neo-Confucianism* (New York: Columbia University Press, 1975), pp. 19–23, 28.
3. See Judith Berling, *The Syncretic Religion of Lin Chao-en* (New York: Columbia University Press, 1980), pp. 74, 103–8, 143, 203.
4. Abe Yoshio, *Nihon Shushigaku to Chōsen* (Tokyo: Tokyo University Press, 1965), part 1; Ishida Ichirō and Kanaya Osamu, *Fujiwara Seika, Hayashi Razan* (Nihon shisō taikei ed.; Tokyo, 1975), 28:411–89.
5. See Albert Craig's reformulation of the Maruyama thesis in "Science and Confucianism in Tokugawa Japan," in *Changing Japanese Attitudes Toward Modernization*, ed. Marius B. Jansen (Princeton: Princeton University Press, 1965), pp. 155–56.
6. See Maruyama, *Intellectual History*, p. 33. By failing to take into account the intervening formulations of Lo Ch'in-shun, Yi T'oegye, Lin Chao-en, and others who influenced Seika and Razan, Maruyama interprets as pure Chu Hsi thought what has actually undergone considerable development in other hands, and the real issues at stake are sometimes missed. Maruyama concludes that "Razan did no more than present simple explanations of Chu Hsi philosophy" (p. 35), but some of the passages he cites from Seika and Razan as reflecting "the distinctive features of the Chu Hsi school" are virtual quotations from Lin Chao-en of the late Ming. When Ishida cites the same passages as evidence of the influence on Seika of the Wang Yang-ming school, the confusion is apparent. Actually Lin's *hsin-fa* represents the kind of *hsin-hsüeh* which he synthesized as the common ground between Chu and Wang, so that both Maruyama and Ishida can be both right and wrong! Cf. Ishida and Kanaya *Fujiwara Seika, Hayashi Razan*, 28:420, 440–41.
7. Maruyama, *Intellectual History*, p. 33.
8. Wajima Yoshio, *Nihon Sōgakushi no kenkyū* (Tokyo: Yoshikawa kōbunkan, 1962), p. 296.
9. Fujiwara Seika, "Kokon i-anjo," *Seika sensei bunshū* (NST ed.), 28:82.
10. *Fujiwara Seika shū* (Tokyo: Kokumin seishin bunka kenkyū-jo, 1938–1939), 2:395; Hayashi Razan, *Hayashi Razan bunshū* (Tokyo: Kōbun-sha, 1930), p. 349.

11. Wajima Yoshio, *Nihon Sōgakushi no kenkyū* (Tokyo: Yoshikawa kōbunkan, 1962), p. 294.

12. Okada Takehiko, "Shushi no chichi to shi," part 2, *Seinan gakuin daigaku bunri ronshū*, 14(2):72–77; Abe, *Shushigaku to Chōsen*, pp. 105–6.

13. Cf. Chu Hsi, *Yen-p'ing ta-wen* (Chu Tzu i-shu ed., I-wen yin-shu-kuan reprint of K'ang-hsi ed.), 1:23a–24b, 26b–28a. Okada, "Shushi no shi," pp. 82–86; Abe, *Shushigaku to Chōsen*, pp. 97, 106; Tomoeda Ryūtarō, *Shushi no shisō keisei* (Tokyo: Shunjū-sha, 1969), pp. 51–60.

14. Chu Hsi, *Yen-p'ing ta-wen* 1:17a; *Ta-hsüeh chang-chü*, commentary on *ko-wu*, *Shushigaku taikei*, 7:359 (444).

15. Tomoeda Ryūtarō, *Shushi no shisō keisei* (Tokyo: Shunjūsha, 1969), pp. 57–59; Wajima Yoshio, Nihon *Sōgakushi no kenkyū*, (Tokyo: Yoshikawa kōbunkan, 1962), p. 296; Kanaya, *Fujiwara Seika, Hayashi Razan*, pp. 465–68.

16. Kanaya, *Fujiwara Seika, Hayashi Razan*. I did not appreciate this fully when I prepared the material on Seika some years ago for Ryusaku Tsunoda, W. T. de Bary, and Donald Keene, eds., *Sources of Japanese Tradition* (New York: Columbia University Press, 1958), chap. 16.

17. See Abe, *Shushigaku to Chōsen*, p. 104.

18. See Kanaya Osamu, "On the Confucianism of Fujiwara Seika" (paper delivered to the Regional Seminar in Neo-Confucian Studies, Columbia University, March 28, 1975).

19. See Tomoeda, *Shushi no shisō*, p. 56.

20. See the background essays of Professor Ishida Ichirō and Kanaya Osamu in the above cited *Fujiwara Seika, Hayashi Razan*, esp. pp. 437–48, 461–63.

21. See de Bary, "Neo-Confucian Cultivation and the Seventeenth-Century 'Enlightenment,' " in de Bary, *Unfolding*, pp. 201–2, 205.

22. T'ang Chün-i, "Liu Tsung-chou's Doctrine of Moral Mind and Practice and His Critique of Wang Yang-ming," in de Bary, *Unfolding*, p. 323.

23. See Wajima, *Sōgakushi*, pp. 301, 305–6.

24. Abe, *Shushigaku to Chōsen*, pp. 520–28.

25. See Ishida, *Fujiwara Seika, Hayashi Razan*, pp. 419–25, 440–44, 476–79.

26. Ishida Ichirō, "Tokugawa hōken shakai to Shushigakuha no shisō," *Tōhoku daigaku bungakubu kenkyū nempō* (1963), 13B:72–138, English preface, p. 4; also "Tokugawa Feudal Society and Neo-Confucian Thought," *Philosophical Studies of Japan* (1964), 5:17–24.

27. *Ibid.*, p. 17.

28. *Ibid.*, p. 32.

29. *Ibid.*, p. 31.

30. *Ibid.*, p. 31

31. *Hayashi Razan bunshū*, 34:384–99.

32. Abe, *Shushigaku to Chōsen*, pp. 520–23.

33. "The influence of Lo Ch'in-shun's *K'un chih chi* in the early Edo period," (paper delivered at the Conference on Practical Learning, Honolulu, June 1974), p. 5. Professor Ishida, on the other hand, has been at some pains to establish that in his later years, after Seika's death, Razan had turned toward a view of principle closer to Chu Hsi's. It is a matter of some complexity; for our purposes here it may suffice to say that Razan's view of the objective reality of principle was consistent with a philosophy of principle and ether as opposed to (1) a dualism or (2) a monism of either

principle or ether. He neither denied principle in favor of a monism of ether nor abandoned his view of the objective reality of principle.

34. Cf. Ishida, *Fujiwara Seika, Hayashi Razan*, pp. 419–25, 442–45; Ishida, "Tokugawa Feudal Society," p. 3. The point is reemphasized in his more recent essay on "The Ideology of the Early Bakuhan System and the Thought of the Chu Hsi School," in *Fujiwara Seika, Hayashi Razan*, pp. 411 ff.

35. Robert Bellah, *Tokugawa Religion: The Values of Pre-Industrial Japan* (Glencoe, Ill.: Free Press, 1957).

36. *Ibid.*, pp. 150–51.

37. Cf. Wing-tsit Chan, *A Source Book in Chinese Philosophy* (Princeton: Princeton University Press, 1963), p. 523; and W. T. de Bary, *Self and Society in Ming Thought* (New York: Columbia University Press, 1970), pp. 14, 26–27 (n. 26–27).

38. de Bary, *Self and Society*, p. 20.

39. See W. T. de Bary, ed., *Sources of Chinese Tradition* (New York: Columbia University Press, 1960), p. 561; Chan, *Source Book*, p. 525; de Bary, *Self and Society*, p. 200.

40. de Bary, *Self and Society*, p. 14.

41. Cf. Bellah, *Tokugawa Religion*, p. 150; de Bary, *Self and Society*, p. 12. See also de Bary, *Unfolding*, p. 165; W. T. Chan, "The Ch'eng-Chu School in the Early Ming," in *Self and Society*, pp. 29 ff.

42. Araki Kengo in *Unfolding*, pp. 39–66.

43. *Ibid.*, pp. 39–40.

44. Fung Yu-lan, *History of Chinese Philosophy* (Princeton: Princeton University Press, 1953), 2:551–58, 566–71; J. P. Bruce, *Chu Hsi and His Masters* (London, 1923), pp. 245–60.

45. See de Bary, *Self and Society*, pp. 15–16.

46. In its tendency toward popularization, use of the vernacular, adaptation to middle-class values, "this-worldly asceticism," nationalism, and so on.

47. Bellah, *Tokugawa Religion*, p. 151.

48. See *Principle and Practicality*, pp. 22–23.

49. Jansen, *Changing Japanese Attitudes*, pp. 278–79; Wing-tsit Chan, "The *Hsing-li ching-i* and the Ch'eng-Chu School of the Seventeenth Century," in de Bary, *Unfolding*, pp. 543–72.

50. See Jansen, *Changing Japanese Attitudes*, pp. 278–79.

51. See *Principle and Practicality*, pp. 38–43.

52. *Ibid.*, pp. 189–230.

53. *Ibid.*, pp. 307–36.

54. Maruyama, *Intellectual History*, pp. xxxv–xxxvi.

55. See *Principle and Practicality*, pp. 233–34.

Glossaries

Glossary of Names, Terms, and Titles Cited in the Text

Abe Yoshio 阿部吉雄

ai 愛

bakufu 幕府

Chan T'i-jen 詹體仁

Chang I 章溢

Chang Shih 張栻

Chao Fu 趙復

Chao I 趙翼

Chao Pi 趙璧

ch'ao wen tao, hsi ssu k'o i 朝聞道，夕死可矣

chen 箴

Chen-kuan cheng-yao 貞觀政要

Chen Te-hsiu, Ching-yüan, Hsi-shan 眞德秀，景元，西山

Ch'en Ch'ang-fang 陳長方

Ch'en Ch'un 陳淳

Ch'en Hsien-chang, Pai-sha 陳獻章，白沙

Ch'en Yüan 陳垣

Cheng ching 政經

Ch'eng Chü-fu 程鉅夫

Ch'eng Hao, Ming-tao, Po-ch'un 程顥，明道，伯淳

Ch'eng [-wang] 成王

Ch'eng I, I-ch'uan, Cheng-shu 程頤，伊川，正叔

Ch'eng Min-cheng, K'o-chin 程敏政，克勤

Che-tsung (Sung) 哲宗

chi-wei 己未

chi-yu 己酉

ch'i (Jap. ki) ether, material force 氣

ch'i (implements, concrete things) 器

ch'i-chih 氣質

ch'i ch'ing 七情

chia-jen 家人

chia-yin 甲寅

Ch'ien Ta-hsin 錢大昕

chih-hsin chih shu 治心之術

chih tao (dedicated to the Way) 志道

chih tao (way of governance) 治道

chin-hsin p'ing-hsin.... 盡心平心而已，盡心而無愧，平心而無偏

Chin-lien ch'uan 金蓮川

Chin-ssu lu 近思錄

ch'in-min 親民

ching 敬

ching i chih nei, i i fang wai 敬以直內，義以方外

ching-i ju-shen 精義入神

ching-shih chih-yung 經世致用

ching-tso (Jap. seiza) 靜坐

ching-yen 經筵

Ching-yen chiang-i (Jap. Kei'en kōgi) 經筵講義

ch'ing hsin 清心

Ch'iu Chün 邱濬

chiu-shih 救世

ch'iung-li (Jap. kyūri) 窮理

Chou Tun-i, Lien-hsi, Mao-shu 周敦頤，
　濂溪，茂叔

Chu Chih-yü, Shun-shui 朱之瑜，舜水

chu-ching 主靜

chu i 主一

Chu Lien, Po-ch'ing 朱濂，伯清

Chu Tzu hsin-hsüeh lu 朱子心學錄

Chu Yüan-chang 朱元璋

ch'uan 傳

Ch'uan-hsin yao-lüeh 傳心要略

chü-ching (Jap. kyokei) 居敬

chü-ching ch'iung-li (Jap. kyokei kyūri)
　居敬窮理

Ch'üan-chou 泉州

ch'üan-t'i ta-yung 全體大用

chün-tzu 君子

chün-tzu shen ch'i tu 君子慎其獨

chün-tzu wu pu ching 君子無不敬

chung-shu sheng 中書省

Chung-yung chih chieh 中庸直解

fa-tsu 法祖

Fan Ch'un-jen 范純仁

Fan Chung-yen 范仲淹

Fan Tsu-yü 范祖禹

Fang Hsiao-ju 方孝孺

fu 賦

Fujiwara Seika 藤原惺窩

Gyujanggag 奎章閣

Haein-sa 海印寺

Han Shih-ch'i 韓士奇

Han T'o-chou 韓侂冑

Han Yü 韓愈

Hao Ching 郝經

Hayashi Gahō 林鵝峯

Hayashi Razan 林羅山

Ho Chi 何基

Hori Kyōan 堀杏庵

Hsiao hsüeh 小學

Hsiao-hsüeh ta-i 小學大義

hsien-t'ien chih hsüeh, hsin-fa yeh
　先天之學，心法也

hsin 心

Hsin cheng 新鄭

Hsin ching 心經

Hsin ching fu-chu 心經附註

hsin-fa 心法

hsin-hsüeh 心學

hsing 性

hsing-li 性理

Hsing-li ta-ch'üan 性理大全

hsiu-shen chih-jen 修身治人

hsiu-shen chih-kuo 修身治國

hsiu-shen tsai cheng ch'i hsin
　修身在正其心

Hsiung Ho, Wu-hsüan 熊禾，勿軒

Hsü Ch'ien 許謙

Hsü Heng, Chung-p'ing, Lu-chai 許衡，
　仲平，魯齋

Hsü Yüan 許元

Hsüan-tsung (Ming) 宣宗

Hsüeh Hsüan 薛瑄

Hu An-kuo 胡安國

Hu Chü-jen 胡居仁

Hu Kuang 胡廣

Hu Yüan 胡瑗

Huang Kan, Chih-ch'ing, Mien-chai
　黃榦，直卿，勉齋

Huang Tsung-hsi 黃宗義

hun-jan i-t'i 渾然一體

huo-jan kuan-t'ung 豁然貫通

I 義

I-hsün 伊訓

Ishida Baigan 石田梅岩

Ishida Ichirō 石田一郎

i tao-hsüeh tzu-jen 以道學自任

Itō Jinsai 伊藤仁齋

Itō Tomoatsu 伊東倫厚

jen 仁

jen-che (Jap. jinsha) 仁者
jen-chu hsin-fa 人主心法
jen-hsin wei i 人心惟危
jen tao 任道
Jen-tsung (Sung, Yüan) 仁宗
Jih chih lu (Ku Yen-wu) 日知錄
jikkō no gaku 実行の学
Kaibara Ekken 貝原益軒
Kanaya Osamu 金谷治
K'ao-ting shu-yüan 考定書院
Kao-tsung 高宗
Kao-yao mo 皐陶謨
ken-pei 艮背
Kimon gaku 崎門学
k'o-chi 克己
kogaku 古学
Ku Yen-wu 顧炎武
kua-yü 寡欲
Kuang-wu ti (Han) 光武帝
Kumazawa Banzan 熊澤蕃山
K'un chih chi 困知記
kung 公
kung-fu (Jap. kufū) 工夫
k'ung (Jap. kū) 空
Kuo-tzu-chien 國子監
li (Jap. ri) 理
Li Ch'un-fu 李純甫
li-fa 立法
li-hsüeh 理學
li-i fen-shu (Jap. ri'ichi bunshu)
　理一分殊
Li-tsung 理宗
Li T'ung, Yen-p'ing 李侗, 延平
Lin Chao-en 林兆恩
Liu Ch'eng 劉承
Liu Chi 劉基
Liu Ping-chung 劉秉忠
Liu Tsung-chou 劉宗周
Liu Yin 劉因
Lo Ch'in-shun 羅欽順

Lu-chai hsien-sheng hsin-fa 魯齋先生心法
Lu Chih 陸贄
lu chi i lien.... 律己以廉, 撫民以仁,
　存心以公, 蒞事以勤
Lu Hsiu-fu 陸秀夫
Lü Tsu-ch'ien 呂祖謙
Lung-ch'üan 龍泉
Lung-hsing 隆興
Ma Tuan-lin 馬端臨
ming 銘
Ming-hsin pao-chien 明心寶鑑
ming-ming-te 明明德
ming-te 明德
mu-fu 幕府
Nakae Tōju 中江藤樹
Nan-ch'ang 南昌
"Nan-hsiung chou-hsüeh ssu hsien-
　sheng tz'u-t'ang chi" (Chen Te-hsiu)
　南雄州學四先生祠堂記
Ning-tsung 寧宗 (Sung)
Ou-yang Hsüan, Yüan-kung, Kuei-chai
　歐陽玄, 原功, 圭齋
pa-t'iao-mu 八條目
Po Chü-i 白居易
po-hsüeh hung-tz'u 博學宏詞
po-shih 博士
P'u-ch'eng 浦城
P'u-ch'eng po 浦城伯
pu-jen 不忍
sa-lo (Jap. sharaku) 洒落
San-chiao i-chih 三教一致
Satō Naokata 佐藤直方
Sekimon 石門
Shan-ssu 瞻思
Shao Po-wen 邵伯溫
shen-tao-pei 神道碑
"Sheng-hsien tao-t'ung ch'uan-shou
　ts'ung-hsü shuo" (Huang Kan)
　聖賢道統傳授總敍說
Sheng-hsüeh hsin-fa 聖學心法

sheng-tao 聖道

Shen-tsung 神宗 (Sung)

shih 詩

shih-hsien 實現

shih-hsüeh (J. jitsugaku) 實學

Shih Mi-yüan 史彌遠

shih-wu wu shih 時務五事

shih-yen 實驗

Shou-shih li 授時歷

shu-yüan 書院

ssu 私

Ssu-hsüeh chai 思學齋

ssu-li chien 司禮監

Ssu-ma Kuang 司馬光

Ssu-shu chi-pien 四書集編

Ssu-shu ta-ch'üan 四書大全

ssu-tuan ch'i-ch'ing 四端七情

Sun K'o-k'uan 孫克寬

Sung Lien 宋濂

ta-chang-fu 大丈夫

Ta-hsüeh chang-chü 大學章句

Ta-hsüeh chih chieh 大學直解

Ta-hsüeh huo-wen 大學或問

Ta-hsüeh yao-lüeh 大學要略

Ta-hsüeh yen-i 大學衍義

Ta-hsüeh yen-i pu 大學衍義補

T'ai-chi shu-yüan 太極書院

taigi meibun 大義名分

t'ai-shih 太師

T'ai-ting 泰定

t'ai-tzu shao-shih 太子少師

T'an-chou 潭州

T'ang chien 唐鑑

T'ang Hsüan-tsung, Ming-huang 唐玄宗, 明皇

T'ang T'ai-tsung 唐太宗

tao-hsin wei wei 道心惟微

tao-hsüeh 道學

tao-t'ung 道統

tao wen-hsüeh 道問學

Te-an 德安

te-hsing 德性

te-hsing 德行

Te-tsung (T'ang) 德宗

Ti fan 帝範

ti-hsüeh 帝學

"Ti-hsüeh lun" 帝學論

ti-wang chih hsüeh 帝王之學

ti-wang chih hsüeh-wen 帝王之學問

ti-wang hsin-fa 帝王心法

t'i-jen (Jap. tainin) 體認

t'i yung wen 體用文

Tosan sŏwŏn 陶山書院

Tou Mo 竇默

Ts'ai Shen, Chung-mo, Chiu-feng 蔡沈, 仲默, 九峯

tsan 讚

ts'an-chih-cheng-shih 參治政事

Ts'ao Tuan 曹端

tso-ch'an (Jap. zazen) 坐禪

tsun-te-hsing 尊德性

ts'un-ch'eng 存誠

Tu Pen, Po-yüan, Ch'ing-pi 杜本, 伯原, 清碧

Tu-shu chi 讀書記

T'u-tan Kung-lu 徒單公履

Tuan-p'ing 端平

Tung Chung-shu 董仲舒

Tung-p'ing 東平

Tung Wen-chung 董文忠

T'ung-chien kang-mu 通鑑綱目

Tzu-chih t'ung-chien 資治通鑑

tzu-jen ssu-wen 自任斯文

tzu-jen yü tao 自任於道

tzu-te 自得

tz'u 詞

Wang An-shih 王安石

Wang Hsün 王恂

Wang I 王毅

Wang Mai 王邁

Wang Mang 王莽

Wang Ming, Shih-chen, Chin-hsi
王蕘, 時楨, 金谿

Wang O 王鶚

Wang Po 王柏

Wang Shao-yüan 王紹元

Wang Ta-shen 王大紳

Wang Wei 王褘

Wang Wen-t'ung 王文統

Wang Yang-ming 王陽明

Wang Ying-lin 王應麟

Wang Yün 王惲

Wei Cheng 魏徵

wei-ching wei-i 惟精惟一

wei-hsüeh 偽學

wei-hsüeh chih hsü.... 爲學之序,
修身之要, 處事之要, 接物之要

Wei Liao-weng, Hua-fu, Ho-shan
魏了翁, 華父, 鶴山

wen 文

Wen-chang cheng-tsung 文章正宗

Wen-hsien t'ung-k'ao 文獻通考

wu (Jap. butsu) 物

Wu Ch'eng, Yu-ch'ing, Tsao-lu
吳澄, 幼清, 草廬

wu-chi 無極

wu-chi erh t'ai-chi 無極而太極

Wu-ching ssu-shu hsing-li ta-ch'üan
五經四書性理大全

Wu hou 武后

wu-hsin (Jap. mushin) 無心

Wu-tsung 武宗

wu-wei 無爲

wu-yü (desire for things) 物欲

wu-yü (without desires) 無欲

Wu Yü-pi 吳與弼

Yamada Keiji 山田慶兒

Yamaga Sokō 山鹿素行

Yamazaki Ansai 山崎闇齋

Yang Hsiung 揚雄

Yang Kung-i 楊恭懿

Yao Shu 姚樞

Yao Sui 姚燧

Yao tien 堯典

Yao Ts'ung-wu 姚從吾

Yeh-lü Ch'u-ts'ai 耶律楚材

Yeh-lü Wei-chung 耶律惟重

Yeh-lü Yu-shang 耶律有尚

Yen Jo-yü 顏若愚

Yen Yüan 顏元

Yi T'oegye 李退溪

Ying-tsung (Sung, Yüan, Ming) 英宗

Yüan Hao-wen 元好問

Yüan tao 源道

Yüeh chi 樂記

Yü Chi 虞集

Yü hai 玉海

Yukawa Takahiro 湯川敬弘

yü-lei 語類

Yü-lu 語錄

yün-chih chüeh-chung 允執厥中

Glossary of Chinese and Japanese Works Cited in the Notes

Abe Takeo 安部健夫, *Gendaishi no kenkyū* 元代史の研究, Sōbunsha 創文社
Abe Yoshio 阿部吉雄, *Nihon Shushigaku to Chōsen* 日本朱子学と朝鮮, Tokyo
    University Press 東京大学出版会
Araki Kengo 荒木見悟, *Mindai shisō kenkyū* 明代思想研究, Sōbunsha 創文社
Chao I 趙翼, *Nien-erh shih cha-chi* 廿二史箚記, Kuang-ya shu-chü 廣雅書局
Chen Te-hsiu 眞德秀, *Cheng ching* 政經
—— *Chen Wen-chung kung ch'üan-chi* 眞文忠公全集
—— *Hsin ching* 心經
—— *Hsi-shan cheng-hsün* 西山政訓, Pao-yen t'ang 寶顏堂
—— *Hsi-shan hsien-sheng Chen Wen-chung kung ch'üan-chi* 西山先生眞文忠公全集
—— *Hsi-shan hsien-sheng Chen Wen-chung kung tu-shu chi* 西山先生眞文忠公讀書記
—— *Hsi-shan wen chi* 西山文集
—— *Hsi-shan hsien-sheng Chen Wen-chung kung wen-chi* 西山先生眞文忠公文集
Ch'en Chang-fang 陳長方, *Wei-shih-chi* 唯室集, Ssu-k'u chen-pen 四庫珍本, "Ti-
    hsüeh lun" 帝學論
Ch'en I-ch'i 陳一齊, *Shih-shan t'ang ts'ang-shu-lu* 世善堂藏書錄, in *Chih-pu-tsu chai
    ts'ung-shu* 知不足齋叢書
Ch'eng Chü-fu 程鉅夫, "Kuo-tzu-hsüeh hsien-shih miao-pei," 國子學先師廟碑 in
    Su, *Yüan wen-lei* 元文類
—— *Ch'u-kuo Wen-hsien kung Hsüeh-lou Ch'eng hsien-sheng wen-chi* 楚國文獻公
    雪樓程先生文集
Ch'eng Hao 程顥, *Ming-tao wen-chi* 明道文集, *Erh-Ch'eng ch'üan-shu* 二程全書
Ch'eng Hao 程顥, and Ch'eng I 程頤, *Erh-Ch'eng ch'üan-shu* 二程全書 SPPY (Part
    I), *Kinsei kanseki sōkan* 近世漢籍叢刊, Chūbun shuppansha 中文出版社 (Part II)
Ch'eng I 程頤, *I-chüan* 易傳, in *Erh-Ch'eng ch'üan-shu* 二程全書
—— *I-ch'uan wen chi* 伊川文集, in *Erh Ch'eng ch'üan-shu* 二程全書
Ch'eng Min-cheng 程敏政, *Hsin-ching fu-chu* 心經附註, *Kinsei kanseki sōkan, shisō
    sampen* 近世漢籍叢刊, 思想三編, Chūbun shuppansha 中文出版社
Ch'eng-tsu huang-ti sheng-hsüeh hsin-fa 成祖皇帝聖學心法

Chiao Hung 焦竑, *Kuo-ch'ao hsien-cheng lu* 國朝獻徵錄, Hsüeh-sheng shu-chü 學生書局

—— *Kuo-shih ching-chi chih* 國史經籍志

—— *Yüeh-ya t'ang* 粵雅堂

Ch'ien Mu 錢穆, *Chu Tzu hsin hsüeh-an* 朱子新學案, San-min shu-chü 三民書局

"Ch'ien-shan hsien hsiu-hsüeh chi" 鉛山縣修學記 (Chen Te-hsiu)

Ch'ien Ta-hsin 錢大昕, *Nien-erh shih k'ao-i* 廿二史考異, Kuang-ya ed. 廣雅

—— *Pu Yüan-shih i-wen-chih* 補元史藝文志

"Chih-tao tzu shuo" 志道子說 (Chen Te-hsiu)

"Chin tu Ta-hsüeh chüan tzu" 進讀大學卷子 (Chu Hsi)

"Ching-chai chen" 敬齋箴 (Chu Hsi)

"Ching-shih ta-tien hsü-lu" (Su T'ien-chüeh) 經世大典序錄

"Ching-ssu chai chi" 敬思齋記 (Chen Te-hsiu)

Ch'iu Chün 邱濬, *Chung-pien ch'iung-t'ai hui-k'ao shih-wen chi* 重編瓊臺會稿詩文集

—— *Ta-hsüeh yen-i pu* 大學衍義補

Chou Tun-i 周敦頤, *T'ung-shu* 通書

Chu Hsi 朱熹, *Chin-ssu lu* 近思錄, in *Chu Tzu i-shu* 朱子遺書

—— *Chu Tzi i-shu* 朱子遺書, I-wen yin-shu kuan 藝文印書館

—— *Chu Tzu ta-ch'üan* 朱子大全, Taiwan Chung-hua shu-chü 台灣中華書局

—— *Chu Tzu yü-lei* 朱子語類, Cheng-chung shu-chü 正中書局 (Part I); Chūbun shuppansha 中文出版社 (Part II)

—— *Chung-yung chang-chü* 中庸章句, Meitoku Shuppansha 明德出版社

—— *Hsiao hsüeh* 小學

—— *Hui-an hsien-sheng Chu Wen-kung wen-chi* 晦菴先生朱文公文集

—— *I-lo yüan-yüan lu* 伊洛淵源錄, Cheng-i t'ang ed. 正誼堂

—— *Lun-yü chi-chu* 論語集注

—— *Ming-ch'en yen-hsing lu* 名臣言行錄

—— *Ssu-shu chi-chu* 四書集註, Shushigaku taikei ed. 朱子學大系, Meitoku Shuppansha 明德出版社

—— *Ta-hsüeh chang-chü* 大學章句

—— *Ta-hsüeh huo-wen* 大學或問, in *Kinsei kanseki sōkan* 近世漢籍叢刊, Chūbun shuppansha 中文出版社

—— *Yen-p'ing ta-wen* 延平答問, in *Chu Tzu i-shu* 朱子遺書

Chu Tzu hsin-hsüeh lu 朱子心學錄

Chung-yang t'u-shu-kuan shan-pen shu-mu 中央圖書館善本書目

"Chung-yung chih-chieh" 中庸直解 (Hsü Heng)

Erh-Ch'eng ch'üan-shu 二程全書 (Ch'eng Hao, Ch'eng I)

Erh-Ch'eng i-shu 二程遺書 (Ch'eng Hao, Ch'eng I)

Fan Tsu-yü 范祖禹, *Fan t'ai-shih chi* 范太史集, Ssu-k'u chen-pen ed. 四庫珍本, "Ch'üan-hsüeh cha-tzu" 勸學劄子

—— *Ti-hsüeh* 希學, Seikadō bunko 靜嘉堂文庫, *Chung-kuo tzu-hsüeh ming-chu chi-ch'eng* 中國子學名著集成

Fujieda Akira 藤枝晃, *Seifuku ōchō* 征服王朝

Fujiwara Seika 藤原惺窩, "Kokon i-anjo" 古今醫案序

—— *Seika sensei bunshū* 惺窩先生文集

—— *Fujiwara Seika shū* 藤原惺窩集

Fumoto Yasutaka 麓保孝, *Kinsei jugaku hensen shiron* 近世儒學變遷史論, Kokusho kankōkai 國書刊行會

Hao Ching 郝經, *Hao Wen-chung kung chi* 郝文忠公集, in *Ch'ien-k'un cheng-ch'i chi* 乾坤正氣集

Hayashi Razan bunshū 林羅山文集

Hayashi Tomoharu 林友春, "Gen-Min jidai no shoin kyōiku" 元明時代の書院教育, in *Kinsei Chūgoku kyōikushi kenkyū* 近世中国教育史研究, Kokudosha 国土社

Ho Yu-sen 何佑森, "Yüan-tai shu-yüan chih ti-li fen-pu," 元代書院之地理分佈, *Hsin-ya hsüeh-pao* 新亞學報

Hōsa bunko kanseki bunrui mokuroku 蓬左文庫漢籍分類目錄

Hsi-shan hsien-sheng Chen Wen-chung kung ch'üan-chi 西山先生眞文忠公全集 (Chen Te-hsiu)

Hsi-shan hsien-sheng Chen Wen-chung kung tu-shu chi 西山先生眞文忠公讀書記 (Chen Te-hsiu)

Hsi-shan hsien-sheng Chen Wen-chung kung wen-chi 西山先生眞文忠公文集 (Chen Te-hsiu)

Hsi-shan wen-chi 西山文集 (Chen Te-hsiu)

Hsiao Ch'i-ch'ing 蕭啓慶, *Hsi-yü jen yü Yüan-ch'u cheng-chih* 西域人與元初政治

—— "Hu-pi-lieh shih-tai 'ch'ien-ti chiu-lu' k'ao" 忽必烈時代「晉邸舊侶」考, *Ta-lu tsa-chih* 大陸雜誌

Hsin-ching fa-yü 心經法語

"Hsiao-hsüeh ta-i" 小學大義 (Hsü Heng)

Hsieh Liang-tso 謝良佐, *Shang-ts'ai yü-lu* 上蔡語錄 *Kinsei kanseki sōkan* 近世漢籍叢刊 Chūbun shuppansha 中文出版社

Hsing-li ta-ch'üan 性理大全 (Hu Kuang)

Hsiung Ho 熊禾, *K'ao-t'ing shu-yüan chi* 考亭書院記

Hsü Heng 許衡, *Hsü Lu-chai hsien-sheng hsin-fa* 許魯齋先生心法

—— *Hsü Wen-cheng kung i-shu* 許文正公遺書, *T'ang-shih ching-kuan ts'ung-shu* 唐氏經館叢書

—— *Lu-chai chi* 魯齋集

—— *Lu-chai ch'üan-shu* 魯齋全書, *Kinsei kanseki sōkan* 近世漢籍叢刊

—— *Yü-lu* 語錄, in *Hsü Wen-cheng kung i-shu* 許文正公遺書

Hsü Wen-yü 許文玉, "Chin-yüan ti wen-yu" 金源的文圍, in *Chung-kuo wen-hsüeh* yen-chiu 中國文學研究; Cheng Chen-to ed. 鄭辰鐸, Li-sheng shu-tien 立生書店

Hu Kuang 胡廣, *Hsing-li ta-ch'üan* 性理大全, *Ssu-k'u chen-pen* 四庫珍本

—— *Ssu shu ta-ch'üan* 四書大全

Huang Ming chin-shih teng-k'o k'ao 皇明進士登科考

Huang Ssu-ai 黃嗣艾, *Nan-lei hsüeh-an* 南雷學案

Huang Tsung-hsi 黃宗羲, *Ming-i tai-fang lu* 明夷待訪錄 Huang Tsung-hsi 黃宗羲,
　Ming-ju hsüeh-an 明儒學案, Wan-yu wen-k'u ed. 萬有文庫

Huang Tsung-hsi and Ch'üan Tsu-wang 黃宗羲, 全祖望, *Sung-yüan hsüeh-an*
　宋元學案, *Kuo-hsüeh chi-pen ts'ung-shu* ed. 國學基本叢書 (Pt. 1) Ho-lo t'u-shu
　ch'u-pan she 河洛圖書出版社 (Pt. 2)

Ishida Ichirō 石田一郎, "Tokugawa hōken seido to Shushigaku no shisō" 德川
　封建制度と朱子学の思想, *Tōhoku daigaku bungakubu kenkyū nempō*
　東北大学文学部研究年報

Ishida Ichirō 石田一良, and Kanaya Osamu 金谷治, *Fujiwara Seika Hayashi Razan*
　藤原惺窩林羅山, *Nihon shisō taikei* 日本思想大系, Kōbunsha 弘文社

I-wei t'ung-kua-yen 易緯通卦驗, Kuang-ya 廣雅, Wu-ying-tien 武英殿

"Jen-wu ying-ch'ao feng-shih" 壬午應詔封事 (Chu Hsi)

Jüan Yüan 阮元, *Ssu-k'u ch'üan-shu tsung-mu t'i-yao, wei-shou shu-mu t'i-yao*
　四庫全書總目提要, 未收書目提要

Jung Chao-tsu 容肇祖, "Liu Chi ti che-hsüeh ssu-hsiang chi ch'i she-hui kuan-tien"
　劉基的哲學思想及其社會觀點, *Che-hsüeh yen-chiu* 哲學研究

—— *Ming-tai ssu-hsiang shih* 明代思想史, K'ai-ming 開明

Kano Naoki 狩野直喜, *Chūgoku tetsugaku-shi* 中国哲学史 Iwanami 岩波

Ku Yen-wu 顧炎武, *Jih chih lu* 日知錄

Ku Ying-t'ai 谷應泰, *Ming-shih chi-shih pen-mo* 明史紀事本末

"Kuo-hsüeh shih-chi" 國學事跡 (Yeh-lü Yu-shang)

Kuo-li chung-yang t'u-shu-kuan shan-pen shu-mu, tseng-ting pen 國立中央圖書館
　善本書目, 增訂本

Kusumoto Masatsugu 楠本正継, *Chūgoku tetsugaku kenkyū* 中国哲学研究,
　Kokushikan daigaku toshokan 国士館大学圖書館

—— *Sō Min jidai jugaku shisō no kenkyū* 宋明時代儒学思想の研究, Kashiwa shi
　柏市, Hiroike gakuen 廣池学園

Li-chi 禮記, *ching-chieh* 經解, *Shih-san ching* 十三經

Li-chi chu-su 禮記注疏, I-wen 藝文, reprint of *Shih-san-ching chu-su*, Sung ed.
　宋本十三經注疏

Liu K'o-chuang 劉克莊, "Hsi-shan Chen Wen-chung kung hsing-chuang" 西山
　眞文忠公行狀, in *Hou-ts'un hsien-sheng ta-ch'üan-chi* 後村先生大全集

Liu Ming-shu 劉銘恕, "Sung-tai ch'u-pan fa chi tui Liao Chin chih shu-chin"
　宋代出版法及對遼金之書禁, Chung-kuo wen-hua yen-chiu-so hui-k'an
　中國文化研究所彙刊

Lu-chai ch'üan-shu 魯齋全書 (Hsü Heng)

"Lu-chai shu-yüan chi" 魯齋書院記 (Ch'eng Chu-fu)

Lu Chih 盧贄, "Han-lin shih-tu hsüeh-shih Hao kung shen-tao-pei" 翰林侍讀學士
郝公神道碑

Makino Shūji 牧野修次, "Gendai no jugaku kyōiku" 元代の儒学教育, *Tōyōshi
kenkyū* 東洋史研究

Mano Senryū 間野潛龍, *Mindai bunkashi kenkyū* 明代文化史研究, Dōhōsha
同朋舍

—— *Shushi to Ō Yōmei* 朱子と王陽明, Shimizu shoin 清水書院

Ma Tuan-lin 馬端臨, *Wen-hsien t'ung k'ao* 文獻通考, Shih t'ung ed. 十通

Meng Ssu-ming 蒙思明, *Yüan-tai she-hui chieh-chi chih-tu* 元代社會階級制度,
Lung-men shu-tien 龍門書店

Ming Hsüan-tsung shih lu 明宣宗實錄, Chung-yang yen-chiu yüan 中央研究院

Ming T'ai-tsung shih-lu 明太宗實錄, Chung-yang yen-chiu yüan 中央研究院

"*Ming-tao hsüeh-an*" 明道學案 (Huang Tsung-hsi)

Miyazaki Ichisada 宮崎一定 *Ajia shi ronkō* アジア史論考, Asahi 朝日

Mo Po-chi 莫伯驥, *Wu-shih-wan-chüan lou ts'ang-shu mu-lu ch'u-pien* 五十萬卷
樓藏書目錄, 初編, "Meng Tzu chieh-wen" 孟子節文

Morohashi Tetsuji 諸橋轍次, *Daikanwa jiten* 大漢和辞典, Taishūkan 大修館

—— *Jukyō no mokuteki to Sōju no katsudō* 儒教の目的と宋儒の活動, Taishūkan
大修館

—— *Shushigaku taikei* 朱子学大系, Meitoku shuppansha 明德出版社

Naikaku bunko kanseki bunrui mokuroku 內閣文庫漢籍分類目錄

"Nan-hsiung chou-hsüeh ssu hsien-sheng tz'u-t'ang chi" 南雄州学四先生詞堂記
(Chen Te-hsiu)

"Nung-sang hsüeh-hsiao" 農桑學校 (Hsü Heng)

Oda Tokunō 織田得能, *Bukkyō daijiten* 佛教大辞典, Ōkura shoten 大倉書店

Okada Takehiko, ed. 岡田武彦 *Kinsei kanseki sōkan* 近世漢籍叢刊 *shisō hen* 思想編,
shisō zokuhen 思想續編, *shisō sampen* 思想三編, Chūbun shuppansha 中文出版社

—— "Shushi no chichi to shi" 朱子の父と師, Seinan gakuin daigaku bunri ronshū
西南学院大学文理論集

—— *Sō-Min tetsugaku josetsu* 宋明哲学序説, Bungensha 文言社

Ōtsuki Nobuo 大槻信良, *Shushi shisho shūju tenkyo kō* 朱子四書集註典拠考,
Chūbun shuppansha 中文出版社

Ou-yang Hsüan 歐陽玄, "Chao Chung-chien kung ssu-t'ang chi" 趙忠簡公司堂記

—— *Kuei-chai wen-chi* 圭齋文集

"Pa Tao-t'ung lu" 跋道統錄 (Hsü Heng)

Pei-ching t'u-shu-kuan shan-pen shu-mu 北京圖書館善本書目

"Pei-shan ssu-hsien-sheng hsüeh-an" 北山四先生學案

P'eng Shao-sheng 彭紹升, *Chü-shih chuan* 居士傳, Dainihon Zokuzōkyō ed.
大日本續藏經

Pi Yüan 畢沅, *Hsü Tzu-chih t'ung-chien* 續資治通鑑

"Piao-p'ing cha tzu" 表丼答子 (Chen Te-hsiu)

Sakai Tadao 酒井忠夫, *Chūgoku zensho no kenkyū* 中国善書の研究, Kōbundō
弘文堂

Sano Kōji 佐野公治, "Mindai zempanki no shisōkō" 明代前半期の思想向, *Nihon
Chūgoku gakkai hō* 日本中国学会報

Satō Naokata 佐藤直方, *Unzōroku zoku shui* 韞藏録, 続拾遺, *Satō Naokata zenshū*
佐藤直方全集, Nihon koten gakkai 日本古典学会

Seikadō bunko kanseki bunrui mokuroku 静嘉堂文庫漢籍分類目録

Shanghai t'u-shu-kuan shan-pen shu-mu 上海圖書館善本書目

Shimada Kenji 島田虔次, *Shushigaku to Yōmeigaku* 朱子学と陽明学, Iwanami 岩波

Shushigaku taikei 朱子学太系 (Morohashi)

Ssu-k'u ch'üan-shu tsung-mu t'i-yao 四庫全書總目提要

Ssu-shu chi-pien 四書集編 (Chen Te-hsiu)

Shu ching 書經, Li cheng 立政

Su T'ien-chüeh 蘇天爵, *Yüan [Kuo]-ch'ao ming-ch'en shih lüeh* 元[國]朝名臣事略,
Chung-hua Book Co. 中華書局

—— *Yüan wen-lei* [國朝] 元文類, Chiang-su shu-chü ed. 江蘇書局

Sun K'o-k'uan 孫克寬, *Yüan-tai Han-wen-hua chih huo-tung* 元代漢文化之活動,
Chung-hua Book Co. 中華書局

Sung Lien 宋濂, *Sung hsüeh-shih wen-chi* 宋學士文集, Wan-yu wen-k'u ed.
萬有文庫

Sung shih 宋史, I-wen yin-shu-kuan, 藝文印書館, Wu ying tien ed. 武英殿, *Erh-
shih wu shih* 二十五史 (Part I), Chung-hua Book Co. 中華書局 (Part II)

"Ta-hsüeh chih-chieh" 大學直解 (Hsü Heng)

Ta-hsüeh wen 大學問 (Wang Yang-ming)

"Ta-hsüeh yao-lüeh" 大學要略 (Hsü Heng)

Ta-hsüeh yen-i hsü 大學衍義序 (Chen Te-hsiu)

T'ao Tsung-i 陶宗儀, *Cho keng lu* 輟耕録

Teng Ssu-yü 鄧嗣禹, *Chung-kuo k'ao shih chih-tu shih* 中國考式制度史, Taiwan
hsüeh-sheng shu-chü 台灣學生書局

Tomoeda Ryūtarō 友枝龍太郎, *Shushi no shisō keisei* 朱子の思想形成, Shunjūsha
春秋社

Ts'ai Shen 蔡沈, *Shang-shu chi-chuan* 尚書集傳 Shu t'ang ed. 恕堂

"Tsun-te-hsing tao-wen-hsüeh chai chi" 尊德性道問學齋記 (Wu Ch'eng)

"Tsung-lun ta-hsüeh hsiao-hsüeh" 總論大學小學 (Hsü Heng)

Tung Chung-shu 董仲舒, *Tung Tzu wen-chi* 董子文集, Chi-fu ts'ung-shu ed.
畿輔叢書

T'ung shu 通書 (Chou Tun-i)

Uno Seiichi 宇野正一, *Shōgaku* 小学, Shin-shaku kambun taikei 新釈漢文大系,
Meiji shoin 明治書院

Wajima Yoshio 和島芳男, *Nihon Sōgakushi no kenkyū* 日本宋学史の研究, Yoshikawa kōbunkan 吉川弘文館

Wang Ch'i 王圻, *Hsü wen-hsien t'ung-kao* 續文獻通考

Wang Tzu-ts'ai 王梓材 and Feng Yün-hao 馮雲濠, *Sung-Yüan hsüeh-an pu-i* 宋元學案補遺, *Ssu-ming ts'ung-shu* 四明叢書

Wang Wei 王褘, *Hua-ch'uan chih tz'u* 華川厄辭, *Chin-hua ts'ung-shu* 金華叢書

Wang Wei 王褘, *Wang Chung-wen kung chi* 王忠文公集; "Sung Lo Chung-pen hsü" 送樂仲本序, "Liu-ching lun" 六經論, "Ching-yen lu hou hsü" 經筵錄後序

Wang Ying-lin 王應麟, *Yü-hai* 玉海, Che-chiang shu-chü ed. 浙江書局

Wei Liao-weng 魏了翁, *Ho-shan hsien-sheng ta-ch'üan-chi* 鶴山先生大全集

Wen-chang cheng-tsung 文章正宗 and *Hsü pien* 續編, *Chen Wen-chung kung hsi-shan hsien-sheng ch'üan-chi* 眞文忠公西山先生全集

"Wen kang yü yü" 問剛與慾 (Chen Te-hsiu)

"Wen Ta-hsüeh chih shuo ko-wu . . ." 問大學只說格物 (Chen Te-hsiu)

Wu Ch'eng 吳澄, "Ts'un te-hsing tao wen-hsüeh chai chi" 尊德性道問學齋記

—— *Wu Wen-cheng chi* 吳文正集, "Hsien-ch'eng pen-hsin lou chi" 仙城本心樓記

—— [Tsao-lu] *Wu Wen-cheng kung ch'üan-chi* 草廬吳文正公全集, Ch'ung-jen Wan Huang chiao-k'an pen 崇仁萬潢校刊本

Wu K'ang 吳康, "Wan Sung chi Yüan chih li-hsüeh" 晚宋及元之理學, *Hsüeh-shu chi-k'an* 學術季刊

Yamada Keiji 山田慶次, *Chūgoku no kagaku to kagakusha* 中国の科学と科学者, Kyoto daigaku jimbun kagaku kenkyūsho 京都大学人文科学研究所

Yang Chün-mai 楊君勱, "Yüan-tai k'o-chü chang-ch'i t'ing-fei ti yüan-yin chi ch'i shih-t'i chü-lei" 元代科舉長期停廢的原因及其式題舉例, *K'ao-cheng tzu-liao* 考政資料

Yang Hsiung 揚雄, *Yang tzu fa-yen* 楊子法言, Chu-tzu chi-ch'eng ed. 諸子集成

Yang Shu-fan 楊樹藩, "Yüan tai k'o-chü chih-tu" 元代科舉制度, *Kuo-li cheng-chih ta-hsüeh hsüeh-pao* 國立政治大學學報

Yao Sui 姚燧, "Hsü Chiang-han hsien-sheng ssu-sheng" 序江漢先生死生

Yao Ts'ung-wu 姚從吾, "Hu-pi-lieh tui-yü han-wen-hua t'ai-tu ti fen-hsi" 忽必烈對於漢文化態度的分析, *Ta-lu tsa-chih* 大陸雜誌

—— "Liao Chin Yüan shih-ch'i t'ung-shih k'ao" 遼金元時期通事考, in [Kuo-li Taiwan ta-hsüeh] *Wen-shih-chih hsüeh-pao* 國立台灣大學文史哲學報

—— "Yüan Shih-tsu ch'ung-hsing K'ung-hsüeh ti ch'eng-kung yü so tsao-yü ti k'un-nan" 元世祖崇行孔學的成功與所遭遇的困難, *Shih-hsüeh hui-k'an* 史學彙刊

Yeh-lü Yu-shang 耶律有尚, "Kuo-hsüeh shih-chi" 國學事跡, in Hsü Heng 許衡, *I-shu* 遺書

Yoshikawa Kōjirō 吉川幸次郎, *Gen Min shi gaisetsu* 元明詩概説, Iwanami 岩波

—— "Gen no shotei no bungaku," 元の諸帝の文学, in *Yoshikawa Kōjirō zenshū* 吉川幸次郎全集

—— "Shushigaku hokuden zenshi" 朱子学北伝前史, in *Uno Tetsuto Sensei* ...
   Kinen Tōyō Ronsō 宇野哲人先生...記念東洋論叢, Tokyo: Tōhō Gakkai, 1974.

Yoshikawa Kōjirō zenshū 吉川幸次郎全集 Chikuma shobō 筑摩書房

Yü Chi 虞集, "Ssu-hsüeh-chai chi" 思學齋記

—— *Tao-yüan hsüeh-ku lu* 道元學古錄

"*Yü-shan chiang-i*" 玉山講義 (Chu Hsi)

Yü su wen 諭俗文 (Chen Te-hsiu)

Yüan Kuo-fan 袁國藩, "Tung-p'ing Yen shih mu-fu jen-wu yü hsing-hsüeh ch'u-
   k'ao" 東平嚴實幕府人物與興學初考, *Ta-lu tsa-chih* 大陸雜誌

—— *Yüan Hsü Lu-chai p'ing-shu* 元許魯齋平述

Yüan shih 元史, I-wen yin-shu kuan 藝文印書館 reprint of Wu-ying tien ed. of *Erh
   shih wu shih* 二十五史 (Part I), Chung-hua Book Co. 中華書局 (Part II)

Index

Abe Yoshio, 192, 205
"Abiding in reverence" (chü-ching), 12, 14, 180, 192
"Abiding in reverence and fathoming principle" (chü-ching ch'iung-li), 198
Academies, local, 49, 50
Academy of the Supreme Ultimate (T'ai-chi shu-yüan)
Action, 103, 104, 122, 151
Ancient Learning (Kogaku), 212
Art (or Practice) of Governing the Mind, 69
"Articles of the Academy of the White Deer Grotto," 112
Ayurbarwada, see Jen-tsung (Yüan)

Bakufu orthodoxy, 50, 190, 204
Bellah, Robert, 206
Book of Changes (I ching), 33, 75, 76, 104, 132
Book of Documents or History, 8, 172
Buddha-nature, universal, 47
Buddhism, 3, 19, 51, 68, 77, 126–31, 155, 174, 208

"Canon of Yao" (Yao tien), 108
Case Studies of Ming Confucians, see Ming-ju hsüeh-an
Catalogue of the Imperial Manuscript Library (Ssu-k'u ch'üan-shu tsung-mu t'i-yao), 89, 90, 94, 163, 167
Central Asians, 18, 56, 59, 62, 134, 152
Chan T'i-jen (1143–1206), 83, 85
Chan, Wing-tsit, 7, 21, 65
Ch'an Buddhism, 40, 126, 129, 172

Chang I (1314–1369), 153
Chang Tsai (1020–1077), 80
Changes, see Book of Changes
Chao Fu (c. 1206–c. 1299), 13, 21, 132
Chao I (1727–1814), 53
Chao Pi (1220–1276), 124–25
Che-tsung (Sung, r. 1086–1093), 29, 93
Chen Te-hsiu (1178–1235), 13, 16, 35, 55, 67, 73–91, 98–126, 158–59, 161, 162, 171, 176, 177, 180, 183, 200
Ch'en Ch'ang-fang (1108–1148), 30, 129
Ch'en Ch'un (1153–1217), 150
Ch'en Hsien-chang (1428–1500), 180, 184
Cheng-te period (Ming, 1506–1522), 179
Ch'eng-Chu school, xvi, 68, 98, 150, 156, 169–71, 196, 199, 207, 213
Ch'eng Chü-fu (1249–1318), 55, 59, 65, 148, 149
Ch'eng Hao (1032–1085), 3, 4, 95, 99, 100, 104, 207
Ch'eng I (1033–1107), 3, 4, 7, 27, 32, 56, 76, 77, 129
Ch'eng Min-cheng (1445–1499+), 176
Ch'eng-tsu (Ming, r. 1402–1424), 158, 160–66, 178, 179
Chia-ching period (Ming, 1522–1567), 179
Ch'ien-lung Emperor, 179
Ch'ien Ta-hsin (1728–1804), 64
Chin dynasty, 25, 39, 41
Chin-lien ch'uan, 20, 51
Ching (reverence or seriousness), 14–17, 75, 76, 126–28
Ching-shih chih-yung, 24, 133
Ch'iu Chün (1420–1495), 53, 113, 180
Chou Tun-i (1017–1073), 12, 78, 99, 129

Chu Hsi (1130–1200), xi, 1, 43, 55–57, 60, 64, 68, 74, 77, 92, 108, 156, 177–78, 212, 215; Chu Hsi "orthodoxy," 169, 190, 193; Chu Hsi's commentaries on Four Books, 62, 69, 168; sealed memorial of 1162, 33; "Personal Proposals on Schools and Examinations," 59; *Commentary on the Great Learning*, 44; *Commentary on the Mean*, 44

Chu Lien, 153

Chu Shun-shui (1600–1689), 212, 213

Chu Yüan-chang, *see* Ming T'ai-tsu

Ch'üan (transmission), 99

Ch'üan-chou, 84, 86

Chuang Tzu, 58, 104

Chung-yung chih-chieh (Hsü Heng), 137

Civil service examinations, xii, 18, 39, 53, 125–26, 133, 148, 190; curriculum, xv, 12, 47, 48, 57, 62, 71, 146; discussion of system, 38–44, 42, 51, 54, 56, 152

"Clarifying Moral Relations" (Hsü Heng), 138, 139

Clarifying or illumining virtuous nature, 43, 46, 106, 114, 117, 141

Clarifying the mind-and-heart, 148, 149

Classic of the Mind-and-Heart (Hsin ching) (Chen Te-hsiu), 67–69, 73–83, 160, 177–180

Classic of the Mind-and-Heart, Supplemented and Annotated (Hsin-ching fu-chu) by Ch'eng Min-cheng, 176, 178

Classic on Government (Cheng ching) by Hsü Heng, 88, 89, 177, 181

Classics mat *(ching-yen)*, 29, 32, 35–37, 43, 86, 97, 134, 179

Collected Commentaries on the Four Books (Ssu-chu chi-pien) by Chen Te-hsiu, 88

Compendium on the Four Books (Ssu-shu ta-ch'üan), 63, 164, 168

Concentrating on oneness *(chu-i)*, 80

Concentrating on quiescence *(chu-ching)*, 79

Conquer the self and return to decorum *(k'o-chi fu-li)*, 81, 119, 120, 140, 147

Conversions, 132

Counsels of Kao *(Kao-yao mo)*, 108

Cultivation of the person, 118, 140, 142, 157

Desire for things *(wu-yü)*, 80, 119, 139

Desires, 78, 80, 109, 122, 123

Dialogues with Yen-p'ing (Yen-p'ing ta-wen), 198

Eight steps *(pa-t'iao-mu)*, xx, 107, 181

Elementary Learning (Hsiao-hsüeh), 22, 45, 48, 49, 57, 59, 82, 136, 138, 145, 146, 190

"Emperors' and kings' system of the mind-and-heart" *(Ti-wang hsin-fa)*, 130, 152

Empirical learning, 91, 98, 104, 173

Empress Wu (T'ang, r. 691–704), 118

"Essay on the Learning of the Emperors" *(Ti-hsüeh lun)*, 30

Essence of Government in the Chen-kuan Era (Chen-kuan cheng-yao), 125

Essentials of the Great Learning (Ta-hsüeh yao-lüeh) by Hsü Heng, 44–45

Essentials of the Transmission of the Mind-and-Heart (Ch'uan-hsin yao-lüeh), 159

Evidential inquiry, 200

Examination debate, 38–44; *see also* Civil service examinations

Extended Meaning of the Great Learning (Ta-hsüeh yen-i), 35, 55, 87, 91, 97, 105, 106–26, 133, 157, 158–60, 180–81

"False learning" *(wei-hsüeh)*, 15, 83

Fan Ch'un-jen (1027–1101), 31, 86, 92

Fan Chung-yen (989–1052), 31, 92, 173

Fan Tsu-yü (1041–1098), 29, 32, 86, 92, 93–98, 105, 159, 161, 162

Fang Hsiao-ju (1357–1402), 169, 173

"Fathoming principle," 12, 104, 166, 180, 192

Filial piety, 119, 213

"Finding the Way for oneself," *see* Tzu-te

Five Classics, 42, 57, 63, 64

Five Point Memorial (Hsü Heng), 36, 133, 134

Five Human Relationships, 134

Four Books, 22, 35, 41, 42, 44, 48, 52, 55–57, 62–64, 72, 92, 136, 141, 146, 156, 177
Four Noble Truths, 74
Franke, Herbert, 27
Fu poetry, 40, 41, 54
Fujiwara Seika, 178, 194
Function *(yung)*, 69, 107, 178

General Mirror for Aid in Government (Tzu-chih t'ung-chien) (Ssu-ma Kuang), 36, 93, 125
"General Significance of the *Elementary Learning*" *(Hsiao-hsüeh ta-i)*, 138
General welfare, *see kung*
Goodness of human nature, 81, 119, 127–28, 140, 199–200
Governing men through self-discipline *(hsiu-shen chih-jen)*, 37, 46, 195
Great Compendia on the Five Classics, Four Books, and Human Nature and Principle (Wu ching, Ssu-shu, Hsing-li ta-ch'üan), 63–64, 164
Great Compendium on Human Nature and Principle (Hsing-li ta-ch'üan), 165, 166, 190
"Great functioning," 127, 160, 184
Great Learning, 17, 30, 31, 33–38, 43, 45, 55, 56, 60, 69, 77, 86, 91–93, 97, 105, 107, 111, 133, 134, 141, 142, 156, 180
"Great man" *(ta-chang-fu)*, 6
Ground of the mind-and-heart, 68

Hae-in sa, 67
Han Fei Tzu, 58
Hanlin Academy, 48
Han Shih-ch'i (c.s. 1502), 175, 176
Han T'o-chou (1151–1202), 84
Hao Ching (1223–1275), 43, 44
Han Yü (768–824), 101, 108
Having no desires *(wu-yü)*, 78
Hayashi Razan (1583–1657), 50–51, 178, 195, 200, 201–2, 204
Hearing the Way, 17
Heart Classic, see Classic of the Mind-and-Heart
Heart Sutra (Hsin ching), 67
Heaven's principle, 99–100, 103

Ho Chi (1188–1268), 150
Holding fast the Mean, 33, 93, 161
Holding to reverence *(ch'ih-ching)*, 141, 144
Honoring the moral nature, 79, 156, 177
Hsiao-hsüeh ta-i, 137
Hsin ching, see Classic of the Mind-and-Heart; Heart Sutra
Hsin-fa (System of the Mind-and-Heart), 129, 189, 211
Hsiung Ho (1253–1312), 13, 66, 150
Hsü Ch'ien (1270–1337), 13, 153
Hsü Heng (1209–1281), 22–24, 36–38, 41–42, 44–47, 54, 131–48, 155–56
Hsü Lu-chai hsien-sheng hsin-fa (Hsü Heng), 137, 144–45
Hsü Yüan, 153
Hsüan-tsung (Ming, r. 1425–1435), 167
Hsüeh Hsüan (1389–1464), 175, 180
Hsün Tzu, 58
Hu Chü-jen (1434–1484), 175, 180, 211
Hu Kuang (1370–1418), 163, 165
Hu Yüan (993–1059), 59
Huang Kan (1152–1221), 10–12, 150, 177
Huang Tsung-hsi (1610–1695), 173, 174, 189
Human desires, 81, 128, 207
Humaneness *(jen)*, 77, 101, 102, 106, 119, 127

I-tao tzu-jen (take responsibility for the Way), 32
Imperial College *(Kuo-tzu-chien)*, 48, 52, 84, 147
Imperial Pattern (Ti-fan), 125
"Instructions of I Yin" *(I-hsün)*, 108
Investigation of principle to the utmost *(ch'iung-li)*, 65, 200
"Investigation of things," 104, 107, 119
Ishida Baigan (1685–1744), 193, 206
Ishida Ichirō, 202

Jen-tsung (Sung, r. 1023–1064), 96
Jen-tsung (Yüan, r. 1312–1320), 35, 54, 55, 125
Jurchen, 19

Kaibara Ekken (1630–1714), 82, 204, 206
Kanaya Osamu, 199
K'ao-t'ing Academy, 150
Kei'en kōgi (Lectures from the Classics
    Mat), 86
Khubilai, 26, 27, 36–38, 40, 42, 44, 48,
    50, 52, 62, 124, 132, 135, 137, 146, 148,
    155, 157
Kimon school, 82
Ku Yen-wu (1613–1682), 168, 170, 173
Kuang-wu (r. 25–57 A.D.), 118
Kufū, 198, 209
K'un-chih chi (Lo Ch'in-shun), 200
Kung (the public interest, common
    good), 34, 37, 38
Kung-fu, 198

Lao Tzu, 58
Laws, 133
Learning of the Emperors, 27–31, 33–37,
    57, 69, 93–95, 107, 116–17, 123, 124,
    130, 157, 159
Learning of the Emperors (Fan Tsu-yü),
    see Ti-hsüeh
Learning of principle, xv
"Learning of sagehood," xvi
"Learning of the sages," xv
Learning of the Mind-and-Heart (*hsin-
    hsüeh*), xiii, xiv, 68, 69, 70, 72, 85, 86,
    116, 123, 151, 153–55, 160, 162, 171,
    172, 206
"Learning of the Way" (*tao-hsüeh*), xv, 2,
    44, 47, 60
Lectures to the court, *see* Classics mat
Li, see Principle; Unity of principle
Li Ao, 108
Li Ch'un-fu (1185–1231), 19
Li-tsung (Sung, r. 1225–1265), 82, 85, 124
Li T'ung (1093–1163), 144, 151, 176, 198,
    199
Lin Chao-en (1517–1598), 178, 189, 197
Literary expression (*wen*), 69
Liu Chi (1311–1375), 154, 174
Liu Ping-chung (1216–1274), 20, 44, 51
Liu Tsung-chou (1578–1645), 189
Liu Yin (1249–1293), 52–3
Lo Ch'in-shun (1465–1547), 197, 200,
    201, 204

Local academies (*shu-yüan*), 49, 50
Loving the people (*ch'in-min*), 141–42
Lowest common denominator, 38, 57
Loyalism, 213
Lu Chih (754–805), 118
Lu Hsiang-shan (1139–1193), 155–56,
    177, 206
Lu Hsiu-fu (1238–1279), 17
Lu-Wang School of the Mind, 196, 207
Luminous virtue, 106
Lung-hsing prefecture (Hunan), 84

Ma Tuan-lin (1254–1324/5), 94
Mahayana Buddhism, 14
Mandarin orthodoxy, 50, 60, 62, 190
Maruyama Masao, 187
"Material force" (*ch'i*), xvi
Mean, the, 5, 30, 69, 99; holding fast the
    Mean, 33, 93, 161
Memorial of 1188 (Chu Hsi), 34
Memorial of 1266 (Hsü Heng), 44
Mencius, 3–5, 77, 92, 158
"Mind of man" (*jen-hsin*), 116, 167
Mind of the Way (*tao hsin*), 116, 167
Mind-rectification, 70, 156
Ming-hsin pao-chien, 200
Ming-ju hsüeh-an (Case Studies of Ming
    Confucians), xiv
Ming T'ai-tsu (Chu Yüan-chang; r. 1368–
    1399), 62, 153, 154, 157, 178, 179, 203,
    205; proclamation of 1370, 63
Minister, relation with ruler, 28, 57; *see
    also* Learning of the Emperors
Mirror of the T'ang (T'ang chien), 93, 159
Mito school, 212
Mongols, 18, 19, 42, 59, 62, 125, 134, 152
Moral mind or Mind of the Way (*tao-
    hsin*), 8
Moral nature, 46, 65, 77, 80
Moral relations, 151, 152
Moral seriousness, 126
Mu-fu (military government), 50, 51

Nakae Tōju (1608–1648), 194, 213
Neo-Confucian orthodoxy, 50, 70, 124;
    see also Orthodoxy; "Orthodox
    tradition"
Neo-orthodoxy of Tung-lin school, 189

New orthodoxy of Chu Hsi, 61, 72; *see also* Orthodoxy
Ning-tsung (Sung, r. 1195–1224), 108
"Noble man" *(chün-tzu),* 139
No-mind, 207
No-thought, 104
North China, 19, 24, 27

Odes, 75
Ögödei (r. 1229–1241), 18, 39
"Ordering the state through self-cultivation" *(hsiu-shen chih-kuo),* 125
"Orthodox tradition" *(tao-t'ung),* xv, 2–13, 28–29, 31, 42, 52, 57, 60, 66, 79, 98, 130, 156, 169
Orthodoxy, x, 2, 50–56, 61, 70, 72, 120, 124, 154, 157, 167, 170, 188–89, 191
Ou-yang Hsiu (1007–1072), 92
Ou-yang Hsüan (1283–1357), 13, 52, 145, 148

"Paranoid style," 16
Pariah orthodoxy, 20
Person *(shen),* 141, 147
Personal responsibility *(tzu-jen),* 32
Philosophical orthodoxy, 189, 191
"Philosophy of *ch'i,*" xvi
Physical nature of man *(ch'i-chih chih hsing),* 199, 200
Potter's Mountain Academy (Tosan Sŏwŏn), 67
Practical learning *(shih-hsüeh),* 14, 105, 171, 173
Preface to the *Mean (Chung-yung),* 73
Principle *(li),* xii, 7, 99–100
Private academies, 2
Proclamation of 1261, 48
"Prophetic" revelation, 9, 11, 13, 100
P'u-ch'eng (Fukien), 83, 87
Public granary system, 85
Public interest *(kung),* 39
Public philosophy, 71
Puritanism, 81
Pursuit of scholarship *(tao wen-hsüeh),* 156

Questions on the Great Learning (Ta-hsüeh huo-wen), 92, 108

Quiescence *(ching),* 79, 103, 104, 122, 144, 151
Quiet-sitting *(ching-tso),* 198, 199
Quota system, civil service, 55

Reading Notes (Tu-shu chi) (Chen Te-hsiu), 88, 90, 159, 177
Record of Chu Hsi's Learning of the Mind-and-Heart (Chu tzu hsin-hsüeh lu), 176
Record of Music (Yüeh-chi), 99
Record of Rites (Li chi), 33, 92, 140
Record of Daily Knowledge (Jih-chih lu) (Ku Yen-wu), 168, 172–73
Recovering the lost mind, 79
Rectification of the mind-and-heart *(cheng-hsin),* 34, 35, 38, 43, 65, 69, 77, 115, 118, 122, 142, 158, 160
Reducing the desires *(kua-yü),* 78
Refinement, 33, 74, 92, 93, 99, 116, 120, 161
Refining moral principles and entering into their spiritual essence *(ching-i ju-shen),* 145
Reflections on Things at Hand (Chin-ssu lu), 22, 28, 32, 60, 82, 177, 190, 204
Renewing the people *(hsin min),* 142
"Repossession of the Way" *(tao-t'ung),* 2, 13; *see also* Orthodox tradition
"Rescue the times" *(chiu-shih),* 133
Restraining of desires, 109, 122
Reverence or seriousness *(ching),* 13, 75–79, 98, 103, 109, 122, 126–28, 160, 163, 195, 212
"Reverencing the person" *(ching-shen),* 138–40
Righteousness or duty *(i),* 3, 13
Rigorism, 78, 81, 124, 193, 199
Rituals, 26
Ruler-minister relationship, 28, 57; *see also* Learning of the Emperors

Sagehood, 78, 151
Sams, 152
Satō Naokata (1650–1719), 183
School of Principle *(li-hsüeh),* 208
School of the Way *(tao-hsüeh),* 11, 16, 17, 19, 27, 41, 61, 65
"Scholastic" transmission, 9

Schools, local, under Khubilai, 47–48, 54
Sea of Jade (Yü-hai) (Wang Ying-lin), 35, 94
Sealed memorial of 1188 (Chu Hsi), 34
Self-cultivation for the governance of men *(hsiu-shen chih-jen)*, 54–55, 125
Self-discipline *(hsiu-shen)*, 195
Selfish desires, 77, 78, 81, 114, 121, 127, 160
Selfish interests *(ssu)*, 15
Self-watchfulness, 77
Seriousness *(ching)*, see Reverence
"Seven emotions," 199
Shao Po-wen (1057–1134), 129
Shao Yung (1011–1077), 129
Shen-tsung (Sung, r. 1068–1085), 28, 95
Shih poetry, 40, 41, 54
Shih-hsüeh (real or practical learning), 41, 42
Shih Mi-yüan (1164–1233), 84, 86
Shimada Kenji, 17
Shingaku, 193, 208
Shinto, 213
Shou-shih calendar of 1280, 26
Singleness of mind *(wei-i)*, 33, 74, 78, 92–3, 99, 116, 117, 120, 122, 144, 161
Six Classics, 166
"Sprinkling and sweeping," 136, 138, 145, 146
Ssu (selfishness), 15, 34, 37
Ssu-ma Kuang (1019–1086), 16, 86
State orthodoxy, 1, 189; *see also* Orthodoxy
"Stilling in the back" *(ken-pei)*, 202
"Study [or learning] of human nature and principle" *(hsing-li hsüeh)*, xv
Su Tung-p'o (Su Shih) (1036–1101), 16, 43, 58
Substance *(t'i)*, 69, 99, 107, 178
Substance and function *(t'i yung)*, 10, 102–3, 106, 182, 185
Substance of the mind *(hsin-t'i)*, 144
"Sudden and total penetration of the pervading unity" *(huo-jan kuan-t'ung)*, 142, 198
Sun K'o-k'uan, 24–25, 36, 134
Sung Lien (1310–1381), 153–54, 157–58, 169, 174, 179

Sung school, 211
Supplement to the Extended Meaning of the Great Learning (Ta-hsüeh yen-i pu) (Ch'iu Chün), 180
Supreme Norm or Ultimate *(t'ai chi)*, 11, 155, 204
Sweeping up and responding to questions, 45
System of the Mind-and-Heart *(hsin-fa)*, 69, 70, 79, 117, 120, 128, 129, 143–44, 151, 160, 167–68, 173, 175, 178
System of the Mind-and-Heart in the Learning of the Sage (Sheng-hsüeh hsin-fa), 159, 163, 166

Ta-hsüeh chih-chieh (Hsü Heng), 137
Ta-hsüeh yao-lüeh (Hsü Heng), 137
T'ai-ting (Yesun Temur) (r. 1324–1327), 125
Taigi meibun, 214
"Taking personal responsibility for the Way" *(tzu-jen yü tao)*, 8, 23
T'an-chou, 84
T'ang Hsüan-tsung (or Ming-huang, r. 712–756), 118
Tao-t'ung, see Orthodox tradition; Repossession of the Way
Taoism, 3, 19, 77
Temple of Confucius, 1
Three Teachings are One, 154, 168
Ti-hsüeh (Learning of the Emperors) by Fan Tsu-yü, 29, 30, 93–98
"To be ever reverent" *(wu pu ching)*, 103
Tokugawa Ieyasu, 50, 201
Tokugawa Religion (Robert Bellah), 206
Total realization of oneness *(hun-jan i-t'i)*, 198
Tou Mo (1196–1280), 21, 23, 36, 41, 44, 47, 48, 132, 134
Ts'ai Shen (1167–1230), 172
Ts'ao Tuan (1376–1434), 175
Tu Pen (1276–1350), 151
T'u-tan Kung-lu, 40, 43
Tuan-p'ing period (Sung), 87
Tung Chung-shu (c. 179–c. 104), 16, 115, 118
Tung-lin school, 189
Tung-p'ing region, 19, 27

Tung Wen-chung (d. 1281), 40
Tzu-jen (taking personal responsibility),
    8, 23
Tzu-te (finding the Way for oneself), 8,
    23, 33, 99, 117

Unity of principle and diversity of its
    particularizations *(li-i fen-shu)*, 14, 144,
    197, 198
Universal education, 45, 133
"Untrammeled spontaneity" *(sa-lo)*, 198

Virtuous conduct *(te-hsing)*, 43, 54
Virtuous nature *(te-hsing)*, 38, 80, 106

Wang An-shih (1021–1086), 16
Wang Hsün (1235–1281), 26, 47–48
Wang I (1303–1354), 16
Wang Mang (29 B.C.–23 A.D.), 118
Wang Ming (c.s. 1511), 176
Wang O (1190–1273), 39, 43
Wang Po (1197–1274), 13
Wang Ta-shen (n.d., Ch'ing period), 155
Wang Wei (1323–1374), 153, 155–56, 176
Wang Yang-ming (1472–1529), xvi, 13,
    73, 178, 194, 201, 206, 212, 215; *see also*
    Lu-Wang School of the Mind
Wang Ying-lin (1223–1296), 35, 94, 105
Wang Yün (1227–1304), 27
"Way of the sage-kings," xvi
Way of Yao and Shun, 45
Wei Cheng (589–643), 118
Wei Liao-weng (1178–1237), 17, 87, 150,
    156
Wen (Culture, Literary Expression), 99
Wen-chang cheng-tsung (Chen Te-hsiu),
    88

Whole substance (of the mind-and-
    heart), 127, 145, 160, 184
Whole substance and great functioning
    (ch'üan-t'i ta-yung), 69, 98, 101, 105,
    143, 150, 177, 182, 183
*Words and Phrases in the Great Learning
    (Ta-hsüeh chang-chü)* (Chu Hsi), 108,
    142
Wu Ch'eng (1249–1333), 13, 51, 53, 59,
    60, 149–50, 154, 156, 177
Wu Yü-pi (1392–1469), 175, 184, 189
Wu-tsung (Yüan, r. 1308–1312), 125

Yamaga Sokō, 205
Yamazaki Ansai (1618–1682), 53, 82, 193,
    206, 214
Yang Hsiung (53 B.C.–A.D. 18), 58, 115
Yang Kung-i (d. 1294), 26, 41
Yang Wei-chung (1206–1260), 49
Yao Shu (1203–1280), 20–21, 26, 41, 44,
    47–49, 132, 134
Yao Sui (1238–1313), 49
Yao Ts'ung-wu, 25
Yeh-lü Ch'u-ts'ai (1190–1244), 18
Yeh-lü Yu-shang (1236–1320), 135
Yen Yüan (1635–1704), 212
Yesun Temur, 125
Yi dynasty, 29
Yi T'oegye (1501–1570), 67, 82, 197
Ying-tsung, 87
Yoshikawa Kōjirō, 19, 50
Yuan Hao-wen (1190–1257), 25, 152
Yu Chi (1272–1348), 13
Yüeh chi, 100
Yung (function), 99

Zen, 195, 202

Neo-Confucian Studies

*Instructions for Practical Living and Other Neo-Confucian Writings by
Wang Yang-ming*, tr. Wing-tsit Chan.   1963
Reflections on Things at Hand: The Neo-Confucian Anthology, comp.
Chu Hsi and Lü Tsu-ch'ien, tr. Wing-tsit Chan   1967
Self and Society in Ming Thought, by Wm. Theodore de Bary and the
Conference on Ming Thought. Also in paperback ed.   1970
The Unfolding of Neo-Confucianism, by Wm. Theodore de Bary and
the Conference on Seventeenth-Century Chinese Thought. Also
in paperback ed.   1975
*Principle and Practicality: Essays in Neo-Confucianism and Practical
Learning*, ed. Wm. Theodore de Bary and Irene Bloom. Also in
paperback ed.   1979
The Syncretic Religion of Lin Chao-en, by Judith A. Berling   1980
*The Renewal of Buddhism in China: Chu-hung and the Late Ming
Synthesis*, by Chün-fang Yü   1981
Neo-Confucian Orthodoxy and the Learning of the Mind-and-Heart, by
Wm. Theodore de Bary   1981

Modern Asian Literature Series

Modern Japanese Drama: An Anthology, ed. and tr. Ted T. Takaya.
Also in paperback ed.   1979
Mask and Sword: Two Plays for the Contemporary Japanese Theater,
Yamazaki Masakazu, tr. J. Thomas Rimer   1980
Yokomitsu Riichi, Modernist, by Dennis Keene   1980
Nepali Visions, Nepali Dreams: The Poetry of Laxmiprasad Devokota,
tr. David Rubin   1980
Literature of the Hundred Flowers, Vol. I: *Criticism and Polemics*, ed.
Hualing Nieh   1981
Literature of the Hundred Flowers, Vol. II: *Poetry and Fiction*, ed.
Hualing Nieh   1981
Modern Chinese Stories and Novellas, 1919–1949, ed. Joseph S. M.
Lau, C. T. Hsia, and Leo Ou-fan Lee. Also in paperback ed.   1981

Translations from the Oriental Classics

Major Plays of Chikamatsu, tr. Donald Keene	1961
Records of the Grand Historian of China, translated from the Shih chi of Ssu-ma Ch'ien, tr. Burton Watson, 2 vols.	1961
Instructions for Practical Living and Other Neo-Confucian Writings by Wang Yang-ming, tr. Wing-tsit Chan	1963
Chuang Tzu: Basic Writings, tr. Burton Watson, paperback ed. only	1964
The Mahābhārata, tr. Chakravarthi V. Narasimhan	1965
The Manyōshū, Nippon Gakujutsu Shinkōkai edition	1965
Su Tung-p'o: Selections from a Sung Dynasty Poet, tr. Burton Watson	1965
Bhartrihari: Poems, tr. Barbara Stoler Miller. Also in paperback ed.	1967
Basic Writings of Mo Tzu, Hsün Tzu, and Han Fei Tzu, tr. Burton Watson. Also in separate paperback eds.	1967
The Awakening of Faith, attributed to Aśvaghosha, tr. Yoshito S. Hakeda	1967
Reflections on Things at Hand: The Neo-Confucian Anthology, comp. Chu Hsi and Lü Tsu-ch'ien, tr. Wing-tsit Chan	1967
The Platform Sutra of the Sixth Patriarch, tr. Philip B. Yampolsky	1967
Essays in Idleness: The Tsurezuregusa of Kenkō, tr. Donald Keene	1967
The Pillow Book of Sei Shōnagon, tr. Ivan Morris, 2 vols.	1967
Two Plays of Ancient India: The Little Clay Cart and the Minister's Seal, tr. J. A. B. van Buitenen	1968
The Complete Works of Chuang Tzu, tr. Burton Watson	1968
The Romance of the Western Chamber (Hsi Hsiang chi), tr. S. I. Hsiung	1968
The Manyōshū, Nippon Gakujutsu Shinkōkai edition. Paperback text edition.	1969
Records of the Historian: Chapters from the Shih chi of Ssu-ma Ch'ien. Paperback text edition, tr. Burton Watson	1969
Cold Mountain: 100 Poems by the T'ang Poet Han-shan, tr. Burton Watson. Also in paperback ed.	1970
Twenty Plays of the Nō Theatre, ed. Donald Keene. Also in paperback ed.	1970
Chūshingura: The Treasury of Loyal Retainers, tr. Donald Keene	1971
The Zen Master Hakuin: Selected Writings, tr. Philip B. Yampolsky	1971
Chinese Rhyme-Prose, tr. Burton Watson	1971
Kūkai: Major Works, tr. Yoshito S. Hakeda	1972
The Old Man Who Does as He Pleases: Selections from the Poetry and Prose of Lu Yu, tr. Burton Watson	1973
The Lion's Roar of Queen Śrīmālā, tr. Alex & Hideko Wayman	1974
Courtier and Commoner in Ancient China: Selections from the History of The Former Han by Pan Ku, tr. Burton Watson	1974

Japanese Literature in Chinese, Vol. I: *Poetry and Prose in Chinese by Japanese Writers of the Early Period*, tr. Burton Watson   1975

Japanese Literature in Chinese. Vol. II: Poetry and Prose in Chinese by Japanese Writers of the Later Period, tr. Burton Watson   1976

Scripture of the Lotus Blossom of the Fine Dharma, tr. Leon Hurvitz. Also in paperback ed.   1976

Love Song of the Dark Lord: Jayadeva's Gītagovinda, tr. Barbara Stoler Miller. Also in paperback ed. Cloth ed. includes critical text of the Sanskrit.   1977

Ryōkan: Zen Monk-Poet of Japan, tr. Burton Watson   1977

Calming the Mind and Discerning the Real: From the Lam rim chen mo of Tson-kha-pa, tr. Alex Wayman   1978

The Hermit and the Love-Thief: Sanskrit Poems of Bhartrihari and Bilhana, tr. Barbara Stoler Miller   1978

The Lute: Kao Ming's P'i-p'a chi, tr. Jean Mulligan. Also in paperback ed.   1980

A Chronicle of Gods and Sovereigns: Jinnō Shōtōki of Kitabatake Chikafusa, tr. H. Paul Varley   1980

Studies in Oriental Culture

1. *The Ōnin War: History of Its Origins and Background, with a Selective Translation of the Chronicle of Ōnin*, by Paul Varley   1967
2. *Chinese Government in Ming Times: Seven Studies*, ed. Charles O. Hucker   1969
3. *The Actors' Analects (Yakusha Rongo)*, ed. and tr. by Charles J. Dunn and Bunzō Torigoe   1969
4. *Self and Society in Ming Thought*, by Wm. Theodore de Bary and the Conference on Ming Thought   1970
5. *A History of Islamic Philosophy*, by Majid Fakhry   1970
6. *Phantasies of a Love Thief: The Caurapañcāśikā Attributed to Bilhana*, by Barbara S. Miller   1971
7. *Iqbal: Poet-Philosopher of Pakistan*, ed. Hafeez Malik   1971
8. *The Golden Tradition: An Anthology of Urdu Poetry*, by Ahmed Ali   1973
9. *Conquerors and Confucians: Aspects of Political Change in the Late Yüan China*, by John W. Dardess   1973
10. *The Unfolding of Neo-Confucianism*, by Wm. Theodore de Bary and the Conference on Seventeenth-Century Chinese Thought   1975
11. *To Acquire Wisdom: The Way of Wang Yang-ming*, by Julia Ching.   1976
12. *Gods, Priests, and Warriors: The Bhrgus of the Mahābhārata*, by Robert P. Goldman   1977
13. *Mei Yao-ch'en and the Development of Early Sung Poetry*, by Jonathan Chaves   1976

14. *The Legend of Seminaru, Blind Musician of Japan,* by Susan
    Matisoff   1977
15. *Sir Sayyid Ahmad Khan and Muslim Modernization in India and
    Pakistan,* by Hafeez Malik   1980
16. *The Khilafat Movement: Religious Symbolism and Political
    Mobilization in India,* by Gail Minault   1981

Companions to Asian Studies

Approaches to the Oriental Classics, ed. Wm. Theodore de Bary   1959
Early Chinese Literature, by Burton Watson   1962
Approaches to Asian Civilizations, ed. Wm. Theodore de Bary and
    Ainslie T. Embree   1964
The Classic Chinese Novel: A Critical Introduction, by C. T. Hsia 1968
Chinese Lyricism: Shih Poetry from the Second to the Twelfth Century,
    tr. Burton Watson   1971
A Syllabus of Indian Civilization,, by Leonard A. Gordon and Barbara
    Stoler Miller   1971
Twentieth-Century Chinese Stories, ed. C. T. Hsia and Joseph S. M.
    Lau   1971
A Syllabus of Chinese Civilization, by J. Mason Gentzler, 2d ed.   1972
A Syllabus of Japanese Civilization, by Paul Varley, 2d ed.   1972
An Introduction to Chinese Civilization, ed. John Meskill, with the
    assistance of J. Mason Gentzler   1973
An Introduction to Japanese Civilization, ed. Arthur E., Tiedemann 1974
A Guide to Oriental Classics, ed. Wm. Theodore de Bary and Ainslie
    T. Embree, 2d ed.   1975

Introduction to Oriental Civilizations

Wm. Theodore de Bary, Editor

Sources of Japanese Tradition   1958   Paperback ed., 2 vols. 1964
Sources of Indian Tradition   1958   Paperback ed., 2 vols. 1964
Sources of Chinese Tradition   1960   Paperback ed., 2 vols. 1964